International Negotiation

Negotiation has always been an important alternative to the use of force in managing international disputes. This textbook provides students with the insight and knowledge needed to evaluate how negotiation can produce effective conflict settlement, political change and international policy-making. Students are guided through the processes by which actors make decisions, communicate, develop bargaining strategies and explore compatibilities between different positions, while attempting to maximize their own interests. In examining the basic ingredients of negotiation, the book draws together major strands of negotiation theory and illustrates their relevance to particular negotiation contexts. Examples of well-known international conflicts and illustrations of everyday situations lead students to understand how theory is utilized to resolve real-world problems, and how negotiation is applied to diverse world events. The textbook is accompanied by a rich suite of online resources, including lecture notes, case studies, discussion questions and suggestions for further reading.

Ho-Won Jeong is Professor of Conflict Analysis and Resolution at George Mason University. Professor Jeong is a founding editor of the journals *Peace and Conflict Studies* and *International Journal of Peace Studies*. His previous books include *Understanding Conflict and Conflict Analysis* (2008), *Conflict Management and Resolution* (2009) and *Peacebuilding in Postconflict Societies* (2005).

International Negotiation

Process and Strategies

Ho-Won Jeong

CAMBRIDGE
UNIVERSITY PRESS

University Printing House, Cambridge CB2 8BS, United Kingdom

One Liberty Plaza, 20th Floor, New York, NY 10006, USA

477 Williamstown Road, Port Melbourne, VIC 3207, Australia

314-321, 3rd Floor, Plot 3, Splendor Forum, Jasola District Centre, New Delhi - 110025, India

79 Anson Road, #06-04/06, Singapore 079906

Cambridge University Press is part of the University of Cambridge.

It furthers the University's mission by disseminating knowledge in the pursuit of education, learning and research at the highest international levels of excellence.

www.cambridge.org
Information on this title: www.cambridge.org/9781107651487

© Ho-Won Jeong 2016

This publication is in copyright. Subject to statutory exception and to the provisions of relevant collective licensing agreements, no reproduction of any part may take place without the written permission of Cambridge University Press.

First published 2016

A catalogue record for this publication is available from the British Library

Library of Congress Cataloging in Publication data
Jeong, Ho-Won.
International negotiation : process and strategies / Ho-Won Jeong.
   pages   cm
Includes bibliographical references and index.
ISBN 978-1-107-02640-7 (hardback)
1. Diplomatic negotiations in international disputes.   2. Negotiation.
3. Conflict management.   4. Negotiation in business.   I. Title.
JZ6045.J46   2015
327.2 – dc23   2015014537

ISBN 978-1-107-02640-7 Hardback
ISBN 978-1-107-65148-7 Paperback

Additional resources for this publication at www.cambridge.org/jeong

Cambridge University Press has no responsibility for the persistence or accuracy of URLs for external or third-party internet websites referred to in this publication, and does not guarantee that any content on such websites is, or will remain, accurate or appropriate.

For my brother Ukdon, who always puts other people's interests, needs and feelings before his own

Contents

List of figures   *page* ix
List of tables   x
Preface   xi

Introduction

1   Negotiation: an overall framework   3

Part I   Strategic analysis

2   Game theory: basics and perspectives   21

3   Strategies for conflict and cooperation   43

4   Sequential games and strategic moves   68

5   Bargaining games   89

Part II   Negotiation process, behavior and context

6   Negotiation dynamics   107

7   Negotiation process and activities   126

8   Bargaining behavior   152

9   Psychological and institutional context   172

Part III Extensions and variants

10 Mediation   199

11 Multilateral negotiation   219

12 Reflection and synthesis   238

References   260
Index   279

Figures

4.1   Prisoner's Dilemma in an extensive form   *page* 69
4.2   Troop mobilization   71
4.3   Game of Chicken   72
4.4   Battle of the Sexes   72
4.5   Colonial Struggle   73
4.6   Colonial Struggle in a repeated game   74
4.7   Defense of an ally   76
4.8   Negotiation with terrorists   78
4.9   Credibility of the US threat in a trade dispute   82
4.10 US threat with unknown North Korean types   85
5.1   An Ultimatum game: a choice between bargaining and fighting   95
8.1   A unidimensional contract zone   155
8.2   Geometric representation of bargaining space   157
8.3   A fair solution on a Pareto optimal frontier   159
8.4   Concession rates and patterns: exponential decay model   164
8.5   Self- and other-directed forces   167

Tables

2.1	Prisoner's Dilemma in its original form	page 29
2.2	Prisoner's Dilemma with ordinal payoffs	29
2.3	Prisoner's Dilemma in a generic form	31
2.4	Prisoner's Dilemma with letter payoffs	31
2.5	Minimax: the Battle of the Bismarck Sea	36
2.6	Minimax in a mixed equilibrium	40
3.1a	Move from defection to cooperation in Prisoner's Dilemma	44
3.1b	Move from cooperation to defection in Prisoner's Dilemma	45
3.2	The game of Chicken	46
3.3	The game of Chicken with letter payoffs	46
3.4	Game of Chicken: Cuban Missile Crisis	48
3.5	The Battle of the Sexes	49
3.6	The Battle of the Sexes with letter payoffs	50
3.7	Stag Hunt	51
3.8	Deadlock game	53
3.9	Deadlock game with letter payoffs	54
3.10	Battle of the Sexes with side payments	55
3.11	Battle of the Sexes with threats	56
3.12	The game of Bully	59
3.13	The Tragedy of the Commons	62
4.1	Troop mobilization	71
4.2	Colonial Struggle	72
4.3	United States–China trade	81
5.1	Subgame-perfect equilibrium of infinite-horizon games	101

Preface

In providing an introduction to international negotiation and bargaining, this book presents essential concepts and approaches. Its ultimate goal is to serve as a guide for readers to cultivate an ability to analyze negotiation problems and circumstances. Thus the book is oriented toward helping students, diplomats or other practitioners develop an overarching knowledge base with a look at pertinent social science theories relevant to examining and tackling real-world issues.

Understanding international negotiation and analysis will be an important task in considering the costs of ignoring many problems faced by humanity. There is no shortage of disputes, involving territorial claims, trade imbalance, security dilemma, pollution and so forth. It would be ideal to achieve results that are beneficial to all parties concerned. However, that may often not be the case due to competitive settings inherent in international politics. Thus it becomes more important, in a negotiation analysis, to uncover the characteristics of interdependent interests embedded in a structural relationship. This book approaches negotiation from the perspectives of strategic interaction where one actor's situation is fully dependent on another actor's action. Bargaining strategies can be considered in the context of cooperation and conflict embedded in negotiating relationships.

An interactive process in various settings can be succinctly illustrated by game theories that provide basic tools in understanding the structure of bargaining relationships. Reflecting on this theme, the first part of this book is devoted to game theories, laying a foundation for more complex analysis. For those who are not familiar with game theories, the core concepts are introduced in a step-by-step manner. In so doing, game theory chapters start with basic assumptions and eventually move on to illustrate the theory's relevance to diverse settings such as global warming and North Korean denuclearization.

In the real world, we should not hold an illusion that a single theory provides all-encompassing answers, predicting the outcomes of our interactions with others. Guided by diverse research traditions in international negotiation, multidisciplinary contributions are quite evident in this book. Behavioral, psychological, political and institutional aspects of decision-making are brought to understanding a negotiation process in the remainder of the book. Thus different theories have been pulled together to provide both sufficient depth and breadth in developing a coherent picture of a complex phenomenon of international negotiation.

Part of the underlying tenet of this book is represented by such questions as how we define rationality and power in a negotiation context and how they actually translate into specific strategies and outcomes. In addition, when, why and how do negotiators deviate from rational behavior to their own disadvantage? This book should be able to offer some answers to why negotiations are stalled in a failed attempt to settle many ethnic and territorial conflicts as well as controlling climate change and other global issues. Could we draw lessons from past successful experiences, including but not limited to multilateral negotiations on ozone layer protection, the preservation of Antarctica and the law of the sea as well as peaceful settlements in Northern Ireland, South Africa, El Salvador, Guatemala, Bosnia-Herzegovina and other intractable conflicts. These cases are relevant in discussion about whether the course of negotiation is predetermined, what shapes the ability of actors to reach agreements, and ways in which negotiators can overcome impediments to narrowing differences.

This book aims to help students develop an integral picture or framework in examining the mechanics of negotiation. It regards students as critical thinkers rather than as passive learners in advancing their own learning and knowledge-seeking process. Sustainable solutions necessitate coordinated actions in a multifaceted world, full of discord and contention. The capacity to properly diagnose problems is part of a core negotiating skill. This textbook will assist students in enhancing their own thinking about what negotiators should consider before taking any action.

We are far from living in a peaceful world. As seen in the China–Tibet case and others, unfortunately negotiation is often not equipped to bring about justice. Normative concerns are not the main tenet of this book, and answering this kind of question would require a different kind of analysis as illustrated in Cecilia Albin (2001), Madan Pillutla and Keith Murnighan (2003) and Tom Tyler *et al.* (2004). More future research may perhaps be required to properly assess what can and cannot be ultimately achieved when the power differentials are externally imposed. It may also need to raise questions about whether negotiations can be left to the primary participants of a totally asymmetric conflict.

A vast array of individual cases have been examined in developing this book, but the number of examples mentioned had to be reduced due to limited space. In the main text, these examples have been put in the context of explaining specific negotiation theories and concepts. For those who are particularly interested, for instance, in more detailed negotiation episodes on US–Soviet arms-control talks, the 1994 framework agreement between the United States and North Korea on the latter's denuclearization, the 1978 Camp David Peace Accord, and ozone diplomacy, there are well-written books by former diplomat-scholars representing their firsthand observations. These include books by Gerard Smith (1985), George Bunn (1992), Joel Wit *et al.* (2004), William Quandt (1986) and Richard Elliot Benedick (1991). Also greatly beneficial are comparative case studies, ranging from territorial disputes to trade negotiations, both bilateral and multilateral, theoretically interpreted by John W. Odell (2000), Thomas Princen (1992) and William M. Habeeb (1988).

Various aspects of conceptual thinking in this book were aided by gaining insight from much of the existing literature accumulated over the past several decades. The main task has been integrating a diverse spectrum of negotiation research traditions ranging from bargaining theory to political coalition-building to social psychology. While there are many important academic works that have formed my thoughts, below are some of the examples for chapters on strategic analysis and sociopsychological approaches to negotiation. In developing chapters on strategic analysis and bargaining theories, particularly helpful were Barry O'Neill (1999), Robert Powell (1999, 2002), Abhinay Muthoo (1999), Thomas Schelling (1960), Anatol Rapoport (1974), Rudolf Avenhaus (2008), William Poundstone (1992), Ariel Rubinstein (1982) and John Sutton (1986). In organizing sections on psychological aspects of negotiation behavior in Chapter 8, I greatly benefited from Laurie Weingart and Mara Olekalns (2004), Max Bazerman and Margaret Neale (1991), Daniel Druckman (2013) and Wendi Adair and Jeanne Brett (2005) as well as classic works such as Amos Tversky and Daniel Kahneman (1974). In reflectively synthesizing diverse research streams, particularly helpful were John Odell (2000), Terrence Hopmann (1996), Thomas Princen (1992), Howard Raiffa (2002) and James Sebenius (2009).

In referring to two-actor negotiations or games, for consistency purposes, the first person is often referred to him; the second one is denoted as her throughout the text. In identifying a single person in a sentence, I used either "him" or "her" interchangeably. For the nonmathematical audience, ignoring math equations (necessitated as logical proof) would not really hamper the understanding of the basic bargaining theory concepts in Chapter 5. This book can be compatibly used with existing simulation exercises on competitive or collaborative decision-making and role play as well as a collection of case studies.

I would like to thank editors John Haslam and Carrie Parkinson at Cambridge University Press for patiently managing the review process and bringing this book project to a successful end. While the opinions of several reviewers on this book's initial proposal were interesting, particularly the two anonymous reviewers provided an invaluable suggestion that this manuscript should be more tilted toward strategic aspects of negotiation informed by game and other formal theories. They have also offered very thorough point-by-point comments on the detailed features of the book's structure that are reflected in this eventual product. I am also very grateful for kind and supportive words and comments from John Odell, Barry O'Neill, Thomas Princen, Robert Powell and Abhinay Muthoo. However, any shortcomings or oversights are solely the fault of this author.

Much debt is owed to US Army Colonel Guy Jones who has carefully read each sentence in the majority of chapters from a practitioner's perspective. Whereas I have profited from some of his insightful editorial comments, these represent his own personal scholarly interest and are not connected to any part of his service for the US government. I would also like to express many thanks to my research assistants Francesca Watson, Charles Davidson, Caitlin Turner, Kwaw G. de Graft-Johnson and Caroline Saskia, who managed to organize the vast amount of bibliographic information and supported editorial work. My university librarian Philip Glidewell's assistance was invaluable in identifying and obtaining many books needed in the completion of this project. Finally, I appreciate the support of Mary and Nimmy in my endeavor to complete this book's typescript.

Introduction

1 Negotiation: an overall framework

NEGOTIATION is involved, either at personal, group or international levels, in managing almost every arena of human affairs. In particular, joint solutions are required in many public spheres, both domestic and international, sometimes with grave consequences to the welfare of larger collective communities. Many international actors argue over the terms of settling territorial boundaries, arms control, termination of long-term hostilities, reduced pollution, protection of endangered species, free trade, monetary systems or other shared problems. When more than one solution exists, actors may have different preferences for types of mutually desirable agreements. This produces dilemmas for negotiation.

Negotiation is a unique set of social interactions in which negotiators differ but have complementary needs or desires. Facing one of the largest threats to the future of humanity, for instance, every reasonable person would accept the necessity for collective action to reduce greenhouse gas emissions responsible for the irrevocable damage to the global atmosphere, but it has proven difficult for governments to agree to measures to be taken to obtain the objective. Though it has now become part of history (from the 1950s to the early 1990s), the United States and the Soviet Union kept increasing their stockpiles of nuclear weapons the use of which would have left neither side with any chance of survival. Although both sides realized the need to control the arms race through negotiation, they still competed to gain military superiority. It took more than two decades and cost approximately one million lives to end the civil war between the Sudanese government and the south's 'liberation forces' prior to the conclusion of a peaceful settlement in 2005. In all these incidents, any one actor's security and welfare cannot be achieved alone, requiring mutually agreed actions.

In entering negotiation, each party has certain expectations, but one's objectives cannot be realized without joint solutions to the shared problems. In negotiation settings, a mutually acceptable solution is sought by two or more parties, who have differing preferences over feasible outcomes. Even if the attainment of one party's goals is in fundamental conflict with those of the other parties, negotiation still takes place due to converging interests as well as opposing ones. Incompatible preferences can be resolved through the recognition of the interdependence in which cooperation becomes an inevitable part. Trading concessions for getting something desired is, in part, the heart of a negotiation. The process can be less competitive if the interests are complementary, not overlapping.

In a classic academic definition, "negotiation is a process in which explicit proposals are put forward ostensibly for the purpose of reaching agreement on an exchange or on the realization of common interest where conflicting interests are present" (Iklé 1964, 3–4). The present book conceptualizes, to a great extent, international negotiation as a strategic interaction between and among various types of actors who are engaged in establishing conditions for improving mutual welfare in many arenas of world affairs. The main attention is paid to negotiator strategies to influence each other's behavior as well as their interactive patterns which are composed of competition and cooperation. The complexity of negotiation increases with the involvement of more actors, their perceptional and cognitive differences, institutional and group decision-making requirements, the necessity of coalition-building, and the impact of external events on bargaining dynamics.

Negotiators may want to promote cooperation for mutual welfare as opposed to competition that might be very costly, as exemplified by managing an arms race, trade wars, a deadly ethnic conflict, overexploitation of an ecological system, etc. In all of these cases, it would be difficult to develop strategies for coordinated actions in the absence of the identification of shared interests. Negotiators can deploy a diverse set of strategies either to influence the other's motives and calculations or to minimize the negative effects of an opposing party's actions. In this process, different patterns of conflict and cooperative relationships emerge as an underlying negotiation structure. Prior to reaching a landmark agreement with Iran on July 14, 2015, the United States and other major powers were engaged in a decade-long struggle to put substantial restrictions on Tehran's nuclear capabilities. In defiance of economic sanctions cripping its economy, Iran continued to expand a uranium-enrichment program with bomb-making potential. Despite the vast differences initially perceived to be too wide to be narrowed, a compromise for a contained nuclear program was eventually struck with the realization that the alternative was a far more costly confrontation heading toward a military strike and smoldering war.

International negotiation is a divergent phenomenon, given that multiple factors – actor-specific or idiosyncratic as well as system-oriented – all have an impact on the negotiator's understanding of one's own interests, the other's motives and the surrounding environment for their interactions. Various characteristics of each negotiation differ by decision-making systems of actors, issue characteristics (e.g., the environment, trade and security, which have different prospects for coordinative actions) as well as the dynamics of mutual interactions. Each party may face variant external-system constraints as well as dissimilar abilities to cope with a spectrum of challenges to meeting their own objectives. As an overview of the entire book, this introductory chapter presents an overall picture of negotiating problems and conceptual analysis as well as a negotiation process that will be explained in a more in-depth manner in the following chapters.

Essence of negotiation

When two or more actors strive for specific outcomes to be jointly determined, they often agree that a solution is possible but may still disagree over which solution is best, either individually or collectively. In spite of the desirability of making an agreement, both parties may not be exactly sure of what form it ought to take. In fact, the outcome may favor one party more than the other, but should still be considered better than a lack of a jointly agreed-upon action. In negotiation settings, each party maneuvers to attain the best deal possible within a range of available options. In general, a bargaining problem is understood in the context of how two or more agents should cooperate when noncooperation leads to an inefficient suboptimal outcome. A simple example below can illustrate the point.

Two children are given an orange and have to divide it. They each have a self-interest in dividing an orange as favorably as possible for them individually. Is it the best strategy for each child to attempt to have as much of the orange as possible? What would be an optimal outcome to this bargaining problem? Should it be a compromise of 50/50 split or disproportionate division? If the latter is the case, on what basis? And how could parents convince the children to accept it?

It all hinges on what purpose each child wants to have an orange for. The utility of the orange differs or is the same, depending on what they want to do with the orange (e.g., cooking or eating). Differences in utilities can explain whether equal or differential division of the orange is a solution to this game. If one child needs just juice for making a cake, she would be happy with only a small portion of the orange. Then it should not matter whether the other child has a larger portion for eating. As in this example of dividing the orange, a solution does not need to arise from each child's sense of fairness or benevolent acts but from self-interest.

A negotiation situation can more often be characterized by different mixtures of not only conflicting priorities and competition but also shared interests. Many solutions to shared problems entail different degrees of desirable and undesirable outcomes for individual actors, inducing them to bargain hard for their favorite settlement. Most importantly, what is desirable could be considered in terms of subjective utility functions.

Whereas two countries may compete for more tonnage in the allocation of water in a shared river, the quantity could be adjusted to each side's seasonal needs that reflect their different strengths in industrial and agricultural production.

The effects of each actor's decisions in an interdependent world will not be fully assessed if we lack an understanding of their interactive nature. As completely opposed interests are not typical, many bargaining situations can be characterized by a potential for either mutual gain or mutual harm. As often happens in industrial disputes, for example, the business owner and workers may have opposing interests in wages and compensation, but they will be mutually better off if a factory shutdown is prevented. All could be winners or losers at the end of the dispute, as illustrated by comparison between an improved working environment and increased productivity vs. the company's decreased market share and job loss following a strike. The prosperity of the company is not an incompatible goal with the improvement in workers' wellbeing.

In many international negotiations, similarly, prosperity and security are goals to be achieved reciprocally. For instance, Israeli security might ultimately be enhanced with Palestinian cooperation that derives from the return of the West Bank and other parts of land occupied during the 1967 War. The power-sharing arrangements between Catholics and Protestants in Northern Ireland, made through the 1997 Belfast Agreement, have largely ended sectarian violence (including terrorist bombing campaigns by the Irish Republican Army), paving the way for mutual prosperity.

The strategic aspects of negotiation have been studied in the context of cooperation and competition. The outcome of interactive decision-making reflects the degree of goal divergence or convergence. In reaching a successful peace accord to end an ethnic conflict, once they realize the painful effects of war of attrition, each adversarial party must put a higher value on a shared interest in peace than on the desire for domination over the other. Then their strategies may involve coordination of divergent interests and exploration of a formula to resolve differences.

Negotiation structure: basic analysis

The number of parties and issues has various implications for a set of feasible courses of action that determine negotiation dynamics. At the simplest structural level, two monolithic parties are engaged in a bilateral encounter over a single issue with the sole possible result of a win–lose outcome. In competitive bargains, parties value limited resources equally with almost strictly opposing interests (Raiffa 1982). In conflicts over territorial sovereignty of a small Southeast Asian island, for instance, between China and Japan, one gains and the other loses. A lack of mutually agreeable standards of fairness leads to few potential points of agreement.

In many instances, even a simple division can be transformed by adding new or hidden issues. A territorial dispute, with seemingly no obvious single solution, can be resolved by the consideration of multiple dimensions of the issue that allow tradeoffs. In the division of land, discussion does not need to be limited to the proportion of its ownership but also its quality and usage. A distributive situation in a territorial conflict between two countries can be transformed with a focus, for example, on sharing oil revenue instead of a precise division of the available land. Multiple issues allow creative exchanges among their differently valued interests. In addition, joint gains can be made possible by expanding the zone of possible agreement with the involvement of ancillary issues.

Interactions are influenced by alterations in the number of parties as well as number of issues. A bilateral negotiation turns into a three-way interaction with the addition of another party. While two sets of interests and one interaction exist for two parties, the network of three parties produces "three sets of individual interests, three possible interactions between any two players, and one interaction of all three" (Bazerman and Neale 1992, 128). Thus the increase in the number of actors brings about changes to bargaining interactions and options available to each party and payoff structures. At the beginning stage of the 1995 Dayton negotiation over the terms of settlement in Bosnia-Herzegovina, Serbian president Slobodan Milosevic and Croatian president Franjo Tudjman shared many ideas about territorial divisions. This apparent rapprochement between the Serbs and Croats prompted growing concerns for the Bosnian delegation, because the deal between the former two could have meant carving up the territory in favor of their own political entities. This fear created an early priority to seek "an agreement between Bosnia's Muslims and Croats on a firmer and sounder basis for the Federation" in an effort to prevent its being annexed to either Serbia or Croatia (Bildt 1998, 127).

The presence of several parties opens the possibility of grouping on the basis of affinities to the point of relegating the negotiations to bilateral encounters. Through European Union negotiation in the early 1970s, Germany, Belgium and the Netherlands jointly faced the bloc of countries composed of France, Italy and Spain in determining not only tariff concessions but also subsidies for the modernization of fishing fleets. The two different issues within the common fisheries policy were linked together in order to reach an agreement acceptable to all involved parties (da Conceição-Heldt 2008). If a reversion to bilateralism is not possible, negotiators can form a series of crosscutting coalitions that piece together agreements out of a number of issues, as happed to producing multilateral trade pacts (e.g., the Uruguay Round of multilateral trade negotiations that involved the participation of 123 countries, spanning the period 1986–94). The complexity of negotiating many issues among multiple parties can be tamed by issue coalitions, bringing in parties behind a package of tradeoffs.

Strategies: integrative vs. distributive bargaining

A negotiation situation generally fits in a spectrum ranging from a distributive, zero-sum structure to an integrative "win–win" one. At the zero-sum end, whatever one party gains becomes another's loss with the division of a fixed "pie." At the opposite end, negotiators have either shared or complementary interests, allowing them to be engaged in integrative problem-solving that increases value for all. Between the purely distributive and integrative ends lies a wide range of "mixed-motive" situations that contain both common and conflicting interests (Walton and McKersie 1965). These two elements are normally manifested simultaneously in many real-world negotiations. Whereas the absence of common interests leaves nothing to negotiate for, negotiators have nothing to settle on without any conflicting interests (Iklé 1964).

In win–lose zero-sum distributive bargaining situations, one actor gains at the other's expense. In basic distributive conflict, the more one gets, the less is available to the other party, as commonly seen in an everyday example of haggling over a car price. In general, strictly opposed interests generate more competitive behavior to obtain relative advantage in the division of fixed resources. A distributive strategy involves a value-claiming process. Each side wants to have distributive gains in its favor by winning the biggest possible share of whatever value is to be divided. Making excessive demands as well as refusing concessions are part of maneuvers for claiming as much value as possible. It is vividly illustrated by Iceland's recurring demands for additional fishing territories and quotas in the North Atlantic through a series of confrontations with Britain during the two decades of "the Cod Wars" between 1958 and 1976.

The Icelandic objective was the preservation of as much of the surrounding fish stock as possible for their own fishermen. In 1958, they started from a unilateral extension of the fisheries limit to 12 miles without anything in exchange. Once their goal was met through a series of harassment tactics against British trawlers in 1961, the Icelandic government announced the extension of the country's fisheries to 50 miles with an outright demand for acceptance by the British. With much confidence gained by the previous success in unilateral extension, Iceland even used gunboats to fire on British trawlers to intimidate their fishermen in pursuing maximalist positions. Not long after the second "Cod War" ended in November 1973 with the British concession, Iceland, in 1975, initiated another confrontation with the unilateral extension of its fisheries limit to 200 miles in much the same way as the earlier two. This time, Iceland raised the stakes in the outcome by threatening to withdraw from NATO and making an overture to its Cold War opponent, the Soviet Union, beyond a series of trawler wire cuttings (Habeeb 1988). As the conflict wore down the British, Iceland eventually got its way in the negotiations. Whereas this case may illustrate the success of strictly adversarial tactics by the Icelandic government, this type of approach often invites a costly war of attrition, without any gain to the aggressive party, if the other party adopts the same strategy.

An integrative approach seeks joint gains by enlarging the benefits available to all negotiating parties (e.g., increased company profit to be shared with labor after a growth in productivity). Cooperative strategies are essential to integrative bargaining which has to create a larger amount of value to be shared (Walton and McKersie 1965). The difference between the status quo and status quo ante for each party becomes a more important concern than how well each fares relative to the other. A mutually satisfactory solution can be found by value creation that contributes to absolute gains to all (Odell 2002). When complementary interests form the basis for a mutually beneficial exchange, the benefit stems from tradeoffs between different priorities.

In a quest for one's own goals, most importantly, both value creation and claiming have to be put in a broader context of a competitive–cooperative realm. Value creation does not necessarily eliminate a competitive aspect of negotiation. Even after the creation of a larger pie (through an integrative process), negotiators still have to work on how to divide it. The parties may turn to competition by demanding a larger share through distributive bargaining. As integrative and distributive strategies become interdependent components within a single negotiation, there is a latent tension between value-claiming and value creation within a process of conflict and cooperation. At different stages of a negotiation, one of these strategic approaches is likely to be predominant. In the end, some negotiations tend to be tilted toward the distributive side of the spectrum while others are slanted toward the integrative pole (Odell 2000).

Bargaining range

For each negotiator, possible settlements are found within a range of outcomes from an upper to a lower boundary. The upper boundary is referred to as a negotiator's aspiration point, and the lower one is identified as a reservation (i.e., walk-away) point. While the former represents an ideal outcome from the negotiation, the latter constitutes a minimum outcome. Negotiators are likely to set their ultimate goals within this range of acceptable solutions between the minimum and maximum values. At a reservation point, a party prefers exercising "outside options" as an alternative to negotiation because an agreement is no longer advantageous. Indeed, a rational actor would not be willing to take less than the value they can get by acting unilaterally (Hopmann, 1996; Odell 2000; Princen 1992). Therefore, a bargaining range is a set of settlement points that each side prefers over their nonagreement outcome.

If a bargaining space permits only a more or less linear division, negotiators reach agreement through concession-making until the positions of the parties converge somewhere in the middle. If there is no such bargaining space, either one or more parties may misperceive that there is such a space, or there may be a real conflict of interest. In bilateral negotiation, outcomes do generally fall within the rough bargaining space that exists between the opposite ends of two reservation levels. If a seller's reservation price (i.e., the lowest acceptable price) is $200,000 in the example of a house sale, a buyer's reservation price (i.e., the highest price he is prepared to pay) should be larger than the seller's. If a buyer's reservation point is $250,000, a deal can be struck somewhere between the two reservation values.

Theoretically speaking, any settlement in the possible agreement zone brings at least some gain to both sides (in the case above, between $200,000 and $250,000), being considered better than reverting to no agreement. At the same time, multiple settlement points along the continuum have varied values for each side. When concessions are made in a linear bargaining range between the two opposing reservation levels, settling on one point is essentially distributive, benefiting one side more than the other. In order to maximize an individual gain of a particular kind, each party desires to settle near the other's reservation value. In fact, concessions can be offered up to a point where a stalemate is preferred over continuing negotiation (Princen 1992). In this indeterminate situation, a negotiation's fate depends on what the other side does, but neither is likely to know the other's intentions and reservation value clearly, often producing a costly delay.

A process of bargaining is comprised of concessions and convergence toward producing an agreement. Its key aspects are illuminated by (1) initial offers presented by each party to the other, (2) an initial adjustment to each other's positions, (3) commitments to a particular value with an effort to stand firm, (4) concessions required to move closer to one another and (5) resistance against the pressures of diversion in an endeavor to converge upon agreement (Hopmann 1995). Bargaining's competitive nature is highlighted by a struggle to advance one's own interests relative to the other.

The distribution of costs and benefits can follow once an end point is discovered, with convergence of opposing positions onto a joint one. In converging through a series of concessions, each party attempts to move the other closer to its own position. While not revealing or even manipulating information about one's own genuine objectives and priorities (e.g., a seller's faking the existence of a competitive bidder), negotiators may even exaggerate their reservation points for an advantage. The negotiator's bargaining behavior tends to be shaped by initial expectations and modified by the perceptions of the other party's concession behavior. In this reactive process, the concession patterns of one party can be adjusted to the other side's shifting bargaining behavior (from tough to soft or vice versa).

In high-stakes negotiations, each side wants to test the other's limits before it is ready to close. The amount of ultimate concessions might be attributed, for example, to internal time pressures (e.g., urgent need to buy or sell) or external circumstances (e.g., a tax exemption deadline) that increase the cost of haggling. Thus a haggling process will determine who is willing to concede more, but it is not costless in terms of both time and opportunity cost. In the end, the question becomes who has more patience and who has a strong desire or need to settle quickly.

While the above case shows a struggle over a simple price issue, in many negotiations multiple and complex issues are linked in such a way that they cannot readily be negotiated one by one. Instead of dividing up a gain or loss on each issue, a whole settlement package can be produced to realize all parties' priorities simultaneously by trading off concessions on different issues with complementary interests. In breaking the impasse during the 1982 Law of the Sea negotiation relating to minerals on the seabed beyond national jurisdiction, the bargaining space was carved up by disaggregating single issues (such as fees and taxation on seabed mining) into multiple subissues along different dimensions (including the collection and distribution of the seabed mining royalties as well as the establishment of an International Seabed Authority for the authorization of seabed exploration and mining). In the end, different levels of payments were tied to the amount of profits projected by multinational corporations' proposals for deep sea mining (Sebenius 1984).

Relative bargaining power

Bargaining power is generally understood to mean having an alternative superior to the status quo. If negotiation with a third party offers the possibility of using alternative options to get a better deal, it improves one's bargaining power. In its 1971 negotiation with the British over renewing naval base rights, Malta solicited the Soviet Union's interest as part of a strategy to strengthen its position by playing off one great power against another. During the Cold War period, the worst nightmare for Britain and its NATO allies was the Soviet naval presence in the Mediterranean Sea. This strategic importance gave Malta lucrative financial packages and other benefits (Lax and Sebenius 1991). Unilateral steps can be taken to increase the cost of a breakdown to the other side, thus worsening their alternative to an agreement. In fact, one side may threaten to initiate action detrimental to others in the absence of their capitulation to its demands (e.g., economic sanctions against Iran in nuclear negotiations). The threats have to be credible, not just cheap talk, if they are to be believable.

Relative bargaining power can be improved with moves intended to manipulate an opponent's subjective beliefs about the distribution of an outcome. The Panama Canal negotiations between the US government and the French company the Compagnie Nouvelle, concluded in the early twentieth century, illustrate each side's actions intended to affect the perceptions of the other side's possible agreement zone. The

French company began its work on a canal in 1881 but went bankrupt eight years later. In the American acquisition of French holdings in Panama, the main concern was the amount of money to be paid. As a strategy to yield a favorable outcome, the US government announced a plan to construct a canal in Nicaragua to drive down the French holdings' price even if the US plan could have been more costly. The French company had also concocted their own ploy by hinting at Russian and British financing of the continued construction of the canal. In the end, it was the French who became agitated by a "leaked" US commission's report to recommend the Nicaraguan path, facing intense pressure from stockholders to sell at any price (Raiffa 1982).

The negotiation process

A negotiation process can be conceptualized as the way negotiators sequence their activities, as illustrated by making initial offers and a commitment to a position prior to narrowing differences through concession-making. The life span of negotiation, broadly defined, could be described as different phases involving informal prenegotiation discussion, the process of reaching an agreement and its implementation. Prenegotiation is generally characterized by unofficial contact that sets the conditions for talks and decisions on timing for formal negotiation. Activities in a formal negotiation process feature a sequence of actions such as agenda-setting and discussion, proposal making and exchanges, bargaining or problem-solving, and decisions on implementation details.

The central elements of a negotiation process are the actions of negotiators, but this needs to be put in an interactive context. The process shapes mutual decision-making dynamics along with the identification of each other's interests and exchanges of concessions as well as a search for common steps toward a goal of reaching an agreement (Adair and Loewenstein 2013). Building a mutually acceptable package may emerge from conceptual ideas about ways to meet each other's key interests or demands simultaneously or methods to resolve differences such as a 50/50 split. The gaps in opposing interests can be narrowed by the linkage of issues with different degrees of priority to each party. In the end, tradeoffs may have to involve transforming, enlarging or excluding issues. In the example of the house sale mentioned earlier, the scope of the deal can be restructured by involving such issues as a payment for closing costs by a seller on behalf of a buyer, removal of contingencies by a buyer and a cash offer, etc.

A negotiation process is also characterized by a cluster of similar activities (e.g., information sharing vs. influence) and strategies (e.g., integrative vs. distributive) at varying phases of negotiation (e.g., beginning, closing, etc.). The movement toward reaching agreement is not always linear, as each party does not easily accept the other's initial offer and subsequent proposals. As to communication patterns, information sharing (e.g., facts related to an offer) and influence activities (e.g., presenting a logic behind a position) prevail at different stages of negotiation even though they may show some recurring sequences and overlaps. Some experimental studies show that negotiators are more inclined to utilize persuasion and other influential activities in the second half of negotiation, while information sharing plays a more prominent role in the first half. These activities may not necessarily be linear and tend to alternate or be mixed throughout the negotiation.

Negotiation processes generally have a sequential mixture of integrative (i.e., in favor of value creation) and distributive (i.e., associated with value-claiming) tactics. In some analysis, "cooperative and competitive behaviors wax and wane across four stages: relational positioning, identifying the problem, generating solutions, and reaching agreement" (Adair and Brett 2005, 33). Negotiators tend to rely on integrative strategies more frequently than distributive ones with progression toward settlement. In the middle of negotiation, the prevalence of conflicting interests may encourage a stronger party to resort to unilateral measures such as coercive force or sanctions. Whereas dependence on heavy-handed tactics is designed to draw unilateral concessions, competitive bargaining has a propensity to produce stalemate. In a successful negotiation, parties are willing to make concessions after weighing each other's demands and counterdemands so that various interests will be satisfied in crafting a mutually acceptable outcome.

A micro-level analysis of a negotiation framework focuses on the immediate circumstances surrounding negotiator interactions (Taylor and Thomas 2008). In seeking to understand what happens at the negotiation table, a communication perspective examines a medium for exchanging both verbal and nonverbal messages (e.g., statements on actors' intentions). Most importantly, issue interpretation and argumentation are part of a communication process in tandem with information disclosures and exchanges (Putnam 2010). As a circular process, communication connects actors' messages and signals to a contextual environment that produces feedback effects (Dupont and Faure 2002). The order of messages and information can be organized to alter the other negotiator's stance. In addition, psychological tactics are involved in developing messages designed to influence the opponent's perceptions and attitudes.

In negotiating across the table, complex interactions take place within each side. External negotiations have to be synchronized with resolving internal differences (Odell 2000; Putnam 1988). As negotiation is not taking place in a social vacuum, negotiating positions might be bound by public opinion as well as powerful interest groups. Negotiators not only dance with the other party's representatives but also face internal constraints such as political or constituent pressure. As a focal person, a negotiator not only holds her own expectations about the negotiation vis-à-vis the other side, but she also has to communicate those expectations to her superiors and to others who have diverse stakes. Thus a "boundary role conflict" is created by a demand not only from across the table but also from her own organization (Walton and McKersie 1965). Internal conflict and external negotiation are so closely interlocked that representatives are often engaged in playing a mix of roles. In the end, negotiators have to manage conflict between the sides as well as advancing their partisan interests.

Abundant examples illustrate multiple rounds of negotiations with the interference of a long period of entrapment and stalemate. Plural or multilateral interactions can be created by links to other negotiations via parties and issues. For instance, the United States brought bilateral trade pressure to key developing countries which resisted its priority agenda on intellectual property and services during the Uruguay Round of multilateral trade negotiations that were completed in 1994. The limitation of options might stem from new constraints imposed by the changing nature of external events. A more macro-level analysis looks at dynamics beyond the control of individual actors or actions taken at the negotiation table.

Overall approaches

Before a serious application of behavioral social science approaches in the early 1960s, studies of international negotiation were treated as a part of diplomatic history that largely focused on a set of ad hoc case studies that interpreted each event as unique. Over the past several decades, research on actor motives and behaviors and the structure of bargaining relationships has been propelled by such foundational work as *The Strategy of Conflict* by Thomas Schelling (1960) and *Two-Person Game Theory* by Anatol Rapoport (1966). Reflecting on the tradition of formal game theories, these works recognized the coexistence of both common and conflicting interests in many negotiating settings. This orientation was also illustrated by various examples of international diplomacy in Fred Charles Iklé's *How Nations Negotiate* (1964), which is more aligned with traditional international relations theory. Later, more integrative work utilized the application of game and decision-making theories not only to bilateral bargaining but also to multiparty negotiation situations (Raiffa 1982).

In yet another research tradition, Richard Walton and Robert McKersie acknowledged the inseparability of intra-organizational negotiation from bargaining with an outside group (1965). By utilizing the cases of negotiation between labor and management, their work also distinguishes integrative (i.e., win–win) vs. distributive (i.e., win–lose) strategies. Sociopsychological approaches have drawn attention to bias, distortion and other cognitive limitations in communication and negotiator decision-making (Bazerman 1983; Tversky and Kahneman 1974). In understanding a conversion process (for narrowing differences in bargaining positions), a substantial amount of work was focused on the patterns of concession-making behavior in various experimental studies (Bartos 1974). Beyond the analysis of the parties' interests and no-deal options, the realm of strategic and tactical choices is embedded in a communication sequence and negotiation process. More complex understanding treats negotiation as not only a strategic game but also a political and social process reflecting on institutional and system constraints (Putnam 1988).

As reflected in the discussion above, studies on international negotiation represent progress in a multidisciplinary endeavor: bargaining and strategic games; nonrational bargaining behavior by experimental economics; activities at different phases of a negotiation process (communication); cognitive and emotional influences (psychology); intergroup interactions and culture (sociology and anthropology); and an institutional process and coalition politics (political science).

Overview

There are different levels of complexity from a two-person bargaining game to a collective decision on multiple issues (e.g., multilateral trade or environmental negotiations). These differ in payoff structures, negotiation processes and bargaining dynamics (involving coalition-building and mobilization of internal support). In a simple bargaining model, two actors may be concerned only with utility maximization along with the identification of strategic choices available to each actor whose decision-making process is made easy by transparency of information. Analytical and communication skills as well as personal orientations (e.g., patience with decision-making) have little significance in determining a negotiation outcome, so long as each player is motivated to pursue their best interests with complete information about their options and payoffs. In complex models, negotiators face many more difficulties in developing coherent strategies owing not only to limited information about the other party's goals and strategies but also to constraints arising from competing priorities and division within their own party, as well as the need for adjustment to the changing internal and external environment of negotiation. In explaining a diverse set of negotiations, this book reflects recent advancement in theory development and research in the wider disciplinary field of negotiation.

This introductory chapter has so far presented an overall sketch of bargaining situations and the negotiation process, which will be explained in more depth in the following chapters. The remainder of this book starts with the most simplistic strategic model where two parties are engaged in an interactive decision-making setting with no anticipated repetitions. The process becomes more complex with the addition of more parties and issues as well as strategies. At the same time, the psychological and behavioral processes are involved in not only intraparty decision-making but also interparty interactions. Thus negotiation strategies may reflect on the negotiator's perception of parameters imposed by internal divisions as well as an external environment (limiting choices of action).

The book has three main parts. The first part explores various game theories to be applied to an interactive decision-making context, including negotiation. The second part features a negotiation process, bargaining dynamics and psychological, political and institutional factors involved in shaping negotiation behavior and outcomes. In the third part, chapters on mediation and multilateral negotiation illuminate variations in the interactions during more complex negotiations.

A strategic aspect of negotiation focuses on decision-making in an interactive setting, where the other's decisions are crucial to the determination of the outcome of one's own choices and have to be part of the calculation. Chapter 2 describes the main concepts of game theory that help us understand the nature of strategic interactions and the elements that determine each party's choices and payoffs. With a rationality assumption, individual players attempt to maximize their expected value.

In Chapter 3, different situations of cooperation and competition are explained using the concept of the Nash equilibrium, which suggests the best strategic choice of each player against the other's given strategy. It provides an insight into an optimal solution to negotiation problems based on each party's attempt at the maximization of their own payoff. This concept is also applied to collective action situations where the uncoordinated pursuit of an individual actors' self-interest produces undesirable consequences.

In understanding behavior and motives, basic concepts and approaches of game-theoretic models have been extended to how each decision made by individual players interacts in a series of sequential moves that produce an outcome. Sequential models in Chapter 4 illustrate the ultimate results of strategic choices made at any given point during a negotiation. Imperfect or incomplete information games provide insight into a negotiation setting plagued by limited information. If the outcome is not certain, uncertainty can be taken into account by selecting strategies based on the probability of different outcomes.

In Chapter 5, formal theory of bargaining games elucidates a process that covers several iterations of offers and counteroffers as well as "ultimatums" ("take-it-or-leave-it"). The models of alternating offers analyze the set of outcomes affected by continuing bargaining. The division of gains is ultimately derived from each party's bargaining power, which is, in turn, determined by the existence of a better outside option, patience, time and other costs involved in bargaining.

While these bargaining theories shed light on an efficient solution to negotiation problems based on each party's bargaining power, many international negotiations often entail a nongame-theoretic process. Chapter 6 illuminates a sequence of negotiation process such as information sharing and proposal exchanges in an evolutionary context, largely understood as a communication process. However, an agreement is not likely to be produced by a linear, orderly procession. A mixture of strategies (e.g., competitive and cooperative) can be observed across phases. In Chapter 7, the main characteristics of different negotiation stages are described in the context of how the process moves along prior to reaching an agreement. Negotiation activities involve proposal making, issue redefinition and conceptualization, bargaining and a search for implementing details.

Reflecting that a bargaining problem persists with competition for relative gains in real-world negotiations, concession-making behavior has been an integral part of negotiation research. Utilizing action-reaction models, complemented by chaos and complexity theories, Chapter 8 examines the patterns of concession-making toward agreement through sequential bargaining moves of each party. To a great extent, a negotiation outcome evolves from a series of movements characterized by opening offers and the rate, magnitude and frequency of concessions prior to final offers. As seen in negotiation on water allocation between upstream and downstream states (e.g., India and Bangladesh), the convergence process can be very slow and painful even after parties agree to such conceptual principles as needs and equity.

Chapter 9 covers contextual factors involved in a negotiation outcome as well as those influencing bargaining behavior. A cognitive and other "nonrational" psychological process interferes in information processing, constraining decision-making capabilities. Psychological bias leads to misperceiving others' intentions and the rejection of new information that does not coincide with established beliefs. For instance, individual psychological orientations differ in the levels of tolerance of risk-taking and acceptance of ambiguities. Beyond an individual decision-making process, negotiators not only have to deal with internal political processes but also face external, structural constraints.

Bilateral interaction can be altered by the intervention of an intermediary whose role ranges from mere support for a communication process, to the facilitation of discussion, to the formulation of proposals and even to the manipulation of bargaining outcomes. These styles have different impacts on the strategic bargaining environment. In examining mediation functions, Chapter 10 sheds light on mediators as an extra-game actor in transforming bargaining dynamics based on bilateral negotiating relationships.

Through multilateral negotiation, self-interested actors are supposed to collaborate to create a public good that cannot emerge from bilateral negotiation (e.g., control of climate change). Complications are inevitable in considering challenges from the participation of many international actors (often more than 100 states) with disparate interests. Chapter 11 focuses on issue linkages and tradeoffs among multiple issues, as well as effective group representation and coalition-building (based ideally on the optimal aggregation of subgroup interests). In contrast to bilateral negotiations, issue linkages are made by the mechanisms of coalition-building that enable similar perspectives and the interests of multiple actors to coalesce through group representation.

The relatively short final chapter revisits some of the main topics as a way to bring together integral views about the most important themes and overall discussion in the previous chapters. The extent of generalizability of negotiation theories is discussed in the specific context of their application to various settings, involving different types of problems and actors. The last chapter also suggests future directions for negotiation research.

PART I

Strategic analysis

2 Game theory: basics and perspectives

> If you must be selfish, then be wise and not narrow-minded in your selfishness.
>
> Dalai Lama, 2002

NEGOTIATION is often characterized as interdependent actions involving a set of two or more decision-making units which have different preferences over the possible outcomes. By considering a negotiation process as a strategic interaction, we can shed light on interactive decision-making among actors who have a set of actions to choose from. In an interactive process, the actual or likely decisions by one agent have an impact on the other's choice of actions. Viewing this decision-making process within the structure of a game helps us explore different possibilities for solutions to conflicting preferences. In fact, game-theoretic analysis assists in uncovering order in seemingly chaotic interactions among negotiators. This chapter introduces a game-theoretic perspective in building a foundation for understanding structural conditions embedded in many conflict settings. It starts with theoretical assumptions about interactive decision-making and moves on to basic concepts involving the Prisoner's Dilemma and minimax. By introducing these and other concepts such as a dominant strategy and an equilibrium, the chapter lays the groundwork for further discussion about the dynamics of cooperation and conflict that will come later.

Strategic interaction in negotiation

In strategic situations where the outcome for each participant relies on mutual decisions, an individual's success depends on the choices of others. For instance, when one country concedes part of a disputed territory, they would want to have measures taken to ensure the territory is prevented from being used to attack. Not only one's own choices but also those of other actors drive the allocation of values. In other words, an ability to realize one's own desires hinges on what the other does (Schelling 1960). Thus the outcome derives from *mutual* influence of each other's actions and strategies, reflecting the decisions of all the concerned parties who have different interests.

In general, negotiation has long been defined such that "choices of the actors will determine the allocation of some values," and "the outcome for each participant is a function of the behavior of the other" (O. Young 1975, 5). More specifically, bargaining takes place because each actor's welfare is affected by the other's decisions. In this context, human interaction is either implicitly or explicitly driven by a series of strategically motivated decisions (even though all the actors may not have the same degree of sophistication or level of ability to identify good or bad choices).

A focus on strategic interaction places negotiation beyond the context of a general theory of individual choice. Each party must assess how to maximize his or her own gain in the context of potential interference from others. The strategic aspects of decision-making may shed light on forward thinking about consequences (i.e., thinking ahead of a likely future event) and backward induction of the most optimal choices (considering the current action in the context of future consequences). It differs from pure intuition or arbitrary choices of action based on personal impulses or idiosyncrasies.

Strategic behavior basically differs from decisions made in a neutral environment that does not demand direct interaction among people. One's best strategy derives from taking into account what the other player(s) choose to do or not to do. One player's strategy needs to be devised by bearing an opponent's ongoing decisions in mind.

Therefore, the best action in an interactive setting is based on the anticipation of the other's moves since the outcome for everyone relies on the choices of all. As is the case with a series of the United States–European Union (EU) sanctions on Russia over the latter's support for Ukraine rebels in 2014, the success in economic sanctions depends on what the target country is (or is not) able to do. Any other actions such as military threats should be considered in the context of the other party's reactions. Agents observe and interpret each other's actions, aware of their behavior being monitored by the other. Each tries to create new expectations or reshape existing expectations of the opponents based on their actions.

When a competitive setting arises, negotiation is more likely to be full of strategic moves such as commitments and threats to take certain actions that are unfavorable to an opponent. In a deadlock, such strategic moves as threatening sanctions or military strikes against an adversary aim to create an edge over competitors. A strategic move is designed to improve an outcome that is not obtainable without it. Of course, whether it will be taken seriously by the other actor or whether it will produce the desired effects is a totally different matter. All the strategic moves and responses have different effects, creating a new context for future actions (further escalation or forcing an adversary to back down). Even though physical strength, financial resources and other conventional measures of power may matter, they bear weight on the outcome only to the extent that they have an impact on the strategic choices available to the other actor.

Certain features of strategic interactive decision-making can be significantly different, depending on the number of actors involved. Interactions among more than two parties allow the formation of coalitions, which transforms a game. For instance, two can join to win against the third when what is good for one party may be bad for the second one but good for the third, opening the possibility of forming an alliance (Poundstone 1992). Such coalitions can be formed even on a larger scale, when subordinate groups gang up against strong ones. During the 1960s and 1970s, Third World countries organized nonalignment movements, independent of both American and Soviet influence, and even played off great powers against each other through coalitional strategies. In addition, alliances can be built between weak parties and a strong one as seen in such cases as NATO. Many stable potential coalitions, for instance, in multilateral trade negotiations, can be built differently, depending on who is likely to form them and on what basis.

Strategic models illustrate how individual preferences and their interactions map into outcomes beyond the context of a general theory of individual decision-making. Strategic actors must have an ability to assess good or bad decisions in a given situation. More effective negotiation models should enable decision-makers to identify and ultimately navigate dangerous or other complex situations with great care, serving as a compass needed to set a ship's course in the uncharted waters of a vast ocean often beset by sudden storms.

Elements of game theory

In general, "games are interactions in which the outcome is determined by the combination of each person's action" (Heap and Varoufakis 2004, 44). In their deliberations, agents have to bear in mind the reactions of their partners, who consider the former's decisions before their actions. In fact, game theory would not have much appeal if independent decisions were made irrespective of the other's actions. What matters most in a game theory is a set of strategies for each of the players, and the specification of explicit rules for their ordering. Players' strategies have to be consistent with the information they have and the way they rate the desirability of resulting outcomes (Camerer and Fehr 2004). In a game theory, a set of rules describes how agents act in interdependent decision situations, most consistent with their conflicting interests on the basis of full understanding of their choices and effects.

The best-known academic definition of game theory is thus the study of strategic interaction among rational decision-makers who attempt to determine the optimal actions in a given setting (or who seek the best possible outcome in a given situation).

This approach enables all types of negotiation to be "conceptualized as different kind of games" (Brams 1990, 90). In bargaining, for instance, strategies have to be adapted to an interactive process of exchanging offers and counteroffers. Negotiation has indeed long been considered "a process closely related to the problems associated with the classical theory of games" of division (Bartos 1974, 3). Most critically, game theory illuminates "the underlying structure of a negotiation and how players take advantage of their position within that structure" (Neale and Bazerman 1991, 9). It presents all the sets of payoff combinations associated with various possible agreements, serving to reduc the number of credible outcomes.

By using a formal methodology, game theories attempt to construct a model that cultivates the potential to present a clearer view of many aspects of human conflict situations in an interdisciplinary approach. Through deductive reasoning, a powerful set of game-theoretic tools offers the generalization of the structure of a game in mathematical logic. Themes in social and behavioral sciences have been utilized in the examination of many interactions, including market competition, war, trade and other international relations (Fearon 1995; O'Neill 1999; Powell 1999, 2002; Austen-Smith 2009; Morrow 1994; Slantchev 2003).

Game theory offers a "toolbox," from which the right choices should be selected with a formal description of a strategic situation. Its primary concern lies in identifying the characteristics of permissible solutions along with the outcomes of predictable choices. In modeling a game situation, we need to explicitly enumerate three important components: players (i.e., decision-makers), strategies (indicated by available options or moves) and payoffs (based on the consideration of preferences and reactions in outcomes). In the analysis of game situations, decision-makers involved in strategic interactions are referred to as players, each of whom has available a set of actions from which to pick. A discrete set of decisions facing players may comprise, for instance, how to respond to a huge trade deficit with another country, whether to negotiate or continue to fight in a civil war and so on. Strategies encompass a complete plan of all the possible actions under every contingency that might arise. In general, each player has to be able to anticipate what payoff they will receive after all the players choose their strategies. Being strategic, players are concerned with the ultimate distribution of payoffs and should be able to figure out how to maximize gains with an inference from the other's actions.

Possible outcomes are assigned different values representing players' preferences. Payoffs display a set of more or less desirable outcomes after each play of the game (i.e., produced by the interaction of each player's separate choices). In the evaluations of consequences, payoffs carry a numerical value that reflects the desirability of an outcome (de Bruin 2010). In general, payoffs are "defined in terms of units of value called utilities" that provide a method of measuring actual preferences for specific outcomes with notional quantitative values (Hopmann 1996, 39). Thus they manifest how much a player prefers particular outcomes. Higher payoff numbers are attached to better outcomes in a player's rating system. The desired outcome may include national pride, legitimate rights for group survival and so forth.

Numerical relationships between choices can be described either by the order of preference of outcomes or by the strength of their desirability. In simple ordinal preferences among outcomes, the order from least to greatest is more important than the exact amounts; the actual cardinality of the utilities does not matter. Most payoffs do not need to be compared according to interval scales. For instance, order is good enough, in ordinary situations, to make a decision on choices as to whether to study, exercise or go to a party. In comparison with ordinal utility function, the numbers featured in a cardinal utility function actually measure strength of preferences; the gap between payoffs can be measurable in cardinal payoff.

Each person has different utility functions when they have dissimilar scales of measurement of satisfaction with preferred outcomes (Heap and Varoufakis 2004). In that sense, payoffs of two different players cannot be directly compared; for instance, suicide bombers' payoff for blowing themselves up in a crowd would be totally different from ordinary people's. Different payoff characterization reflects what people care about. Personal preferences (directly reflected in the payoff values) often do not represent logic but differences in sense of fairness, values, morals, and risk profiles associated with how individuals see the world. The decisions may well be affected by an emotional modifier such as anger derived from unfairness, for instance, in lopsided division of money or a low-ball offer in negotiation.

In a game-theoretic sense, the meanings attached to negotiated outcomes are represented by the preference functions that in turn reflect the subjective nature of desired outcomes. In a nutshell, the nature of a payoff for each individual can differ significantly precisely because it is grounded in subjective aspects of welfare for the player (i.e., it is not determined from the outside). Since interpersonal comparisons have no place in standard game theory, people do not need to agree with each other's values or personal orientations behind their preferences (O'Neill 1999). However, payoffs for different situations (i.e., surrender vs. fighting to the death) by the same player need to be compared.

In game-theoretical models of negotiation, "[e]ach player is assumed to be able to evaluate, on a numerical scale, the attractiveness of every conceivable outcome, including the possibility of no agreement" according to their subjective payoff or utility for the outcome. More specifically, the value assigned to an outcome (by a negotiator) needs to be assessed by "the set of all payoff combinations from the various possible agreements" (H. P. Young 1991a, 3). The choice of strategies by decision-makers is derived from the subjective expected utilities of each action. Decision-makers do not have uniform ways to calculate utilities (as seen in support for diverse options, ranging from air strikes to blockade, within a small US decision-making circle during the Cuban Missile Crisis).

It is often quite difficult to precisely measure utilities of international actors. For instance, Iran and North Korea might have different values attached to international isolation vs. denuclearization. It is especially the case that we do not know much about their key decision-makers' preferences and risk profiles, which are associated with utility functions. This in turn creates difficulties in knowing which strategy is better in negotiations with the leadership in Tehran or Pyongyang, or how they would respond to the threat of an air strike or severe economic sanctions.

Rationality and common knowledge

The choices of strategies (or moves) made by a player are "evaluated in terms of their rationality, based on the rules of play and the rationality rules" (Brams 2011, 65). The basis of a player's preferences itself does not define being rational or irrational. For instance, a player's preferences can be founded on emotions as much as material motivations. The main determination for rationality is the player's consistent maximization of the expected value, given the knowledge of the game and expected payoffs (Heap and Varoufakis 2004). That means choosing a strategy that yields the most-preferred outcome with the consideration of the actions of all other players. Being rational does not mean that the player's payoffs make sense to an observer. A higher payoff for a terrorist is irrational from conventional viewpoints, but rational from their own utility calculation if causing maximum damage to public facilities is a higher goal for them. Whether actions are derived from either altruistic or selfish motives, they have to be reflected in the payoffs. Selecting actions from sets of alternatives involves the instrumental rationality of evaluating individual actions (rather than making moral judgment about the end result). Overall, game theory represents abstract problems of maximization of payoffs expressed by numerical values. It has nothing to do with individual characteristics.

In interactive decision-making, the outcome for each participant is deduced from the anticipated actions of all. The choice sets for the players have to be sufficiently known to each other so that they could form correct expectations about the impact of their actions on another. A player is rational only to the extent that she has anticipation of what others will do and acts accordingly. All players know that the others know their strategies, and vice versa. It is generally assumed in game theory that the rationality of all players as well as the rules of the game are common knowledge (possessed by everyone). The knowledge about rationality is necessary when players have to think about each other's response (Aumann 1995; Bicchieri 1993; O'Neill 1999). If players are supposed to be aware of opponents' preferences, they should put themselves in the opponents' shoes without imposing their own reasoning. It is elegantly elaborated by John

Harsanyi's famous declaration: "when two rational individuals have the same information, they must draw the same inferences and come, independently, to the same conclusion" (Heap and Varoufakis 2004, 28). A fact becomes common knowledge once all players know it, and this information is known by each. In a nutshell, a player needs to be entirely confident that the others have the information, and that they know that we know it, and so forth (Perea 2012).

If the US invasion of Iraq (in 2003) had been solely provoked by concerns about the possession of weapons of mass destruction (WMD) by Saddam Hussein, it could have revolved around common-knowledge questions. Saddam Hussein would have had common-knowledge level I that if he were to possess WMD, he would be attacked by the United States. At the same time, the United States should have had common-knowledge level II that Hussein knew the rules of the game. Hussein then needed to be assured, at common-knowledge level III, that the United States had common knowledge level II. Hussein was desperate to prove that he did not possess WMD and attempted to do that by permitting a very penetrative international inspection not previously seen in other similar situations.

Even in the era of intelligence satellites that spots even a small movement on the ground, meeting the standard for common knowledge is often challenging. This is true, in particular, with the avoidance of direct negotiation or other forms of communication with adversaries. Imperfect information is not uncommon in many bargaining settings. Difficulties often faced by the US government in international negotiation often arise from a lack of information about their opponents' intentions, motives, goals and uncertainty about their payoffs and strategies.

Application

Rational behavior, information, choice under uncertainty and other theoretical concepts have proven relevant in the analysis of real-world situations. Being predicated on common knowledge and beliefs, players are supposed to reason their way toward resolution. In negotiation, we should be able to identify the set of diverse payoff combinations from all the possible agreed outcomes as well as ranking issues according to their importance. In addition, no rational party is expected to accept an agreement leaving her worse off than no agreement. This requires, at a minimum, a player's ability to assign her subjective payoff or utility to every conceivable outcome and determine its attractiveness on a numerical scale.

Game theory offers insights of practical importance for decision-makers as well as scholars in all branches of social sciences (Baird *et al.* 1994; O'Neill 2007; Gintis 2009). Game theory has been applied to brokering a treaty and to international conflict resolution as well as to politics, business, and various areas of social life. It has a lot of utility in the analysis of international crises and bargaining such as the Cuban Missile Crisis, trade disputes between the United States and China, and difficulties in terminating internal violence and civil wars as well as responses to many current types of environmental degradation, for example, global warming and the extinction of species on the planet. Game theory provides a logic and ways to approach these problems in an interactive decision-making context.

Prisoner's Dilemma

As the most studied matrix game of all time since its presentation by mathematician Albert Tucker in the early 1950s, Prisoner's Dilemma has been retold in many different contexts. Its simplicity and parsimony allow it to serve as an analytical tool and guide in examining strategic situations where an individual attempt at selfish gain and mistrust of others produce overall less desirable outcomes than does mutual cooperation.

In the conventional tradition of presenting game theory, narrative stories are presented first and then put in a numerical payoff matrix (Grüne-Yanoff and Schweinzer 2008). Here the narrative (episode) is secondary, designed to illuminate a structure that can be applied to a similar strategic game. The classical story behind the name Prisoner's Dilemma is as follows (Luce and Raiffa 1957). Two suspects are arrested and held for a robbery. There is not sufficient judicial evidence for a conviction. The police separate both suspects and make the same offer to each of them simultaneously. If one admits to the crime, he will be rewarded for the confession and be exempt from prosecution. In this event, the silent accomplice ends up serving the full twenty-year sentence while the confessor enjoys freedom. This deal is valid only under the condition that the other suspect does not testify against the confessor. If both confess the crime, their punishment will be a ten-year prison for each of them. On the other hand, if both reject the police offer and stay quiet, they will be imprisoned only for a year on the minor charge of possessing concealed weapons.

All this can be compactly expressed in a rectangular matrix array that has become fairly standard in game theory. The matrix reveals the totality of strategic sets and outcomes. It lists each player's strategies in a simultaneous move game, and the outcomes that are produced by each possible combination of choices. The interactive nature of a decision-making structure indicates that the other's decisions are crucial to the determination of the utility of choices available to each player.

The matrix table provides a logical computational structure. In Table 2.1, rows represent the strategies of player 1 with columns for those of player 2. In the matrix, each prisoner has two options, namely staying quiet or confessing. The combination of their strategies produces the payoffs to both players in each cell of the matrix (shown in the intersection of row and column). By convention, the first figures in each cell represent

Table 2.1 Prisoner's Dilemma in its original form

		Player 2	
		Confess	Stay silent
Player 1	Confess	10yrs, 10yrs	0yr, 20yrs
	Stay silent	20yrs, 0yr	1yr, 1yr

Table 2.2 Prisoner's Dilemma with ordinal payoffs

		Player 2	
		Confess	Stay silent
Player 1	Confess	1, 1	3, 0
	Stay silent	0, 3	2, 2

the row player's payoffs, while the second one is the column player's payoffs, reflecting the evaluation of strategic outcomes.

Each player reasons that, depending on what their counterpart does, one of two consequences will follow. For the sake of more tidy explanation, this book will assign a male identity to player 1, and a female identity to player 2 hereafter. Suppose player 2 confesses, player 1 will have to spend twenty years in jail if he doesn't confess; he will serve ten years if he also confesses. So it is better for him to confess. The refusal of player 2 to confess also has two different consequences for player 1, depending on what he does. If he does not either, he will get a year-long prison term. However, his confession allows him to go free, as long as she stays quiet. Even when she does not confess, it is still better for him to confess.

Since each player has identical choices and resulting outcomes, it is a symmetric game. As player 2 has the same reasoning process, both players choose to confess and end up having a ten-year jail term each. On second thoughts, each of them could have been better off with one year in jail with both keeping quiet. Thus mutual confession is much worse than if both remain silent.

A different version of the payoff matrix for this game is presented in Table 2.2, which captures the interaction of each player's separate choices in a similar manner. The only difference from Table 2.1 is the representation of the payoffs with a number that measures how much the player prefers the outcome. Here prison terms are converted into utility functions. It allows the representation of preference order in a mathematical relationship through a rank order of outcomes in Table 2.1. Ordinal payoffs 3,2,1,0 are assigned to going free > one year's imprisonment > ten years > twenty years respectively. These numerical payoffs are arbitrarily set, ranking nothing more than ordering preferences (Heap and Varoufakis 2004). These utility numbers do not convey the strength or intensity of the preference as is done by interval scale – the magnitudes of the numbers are irrelevant. Whichever actual number is used does not really matter in ordinal payoffs as long as the structure of Prisoner's Dilemma is kept intact; a shorter prison term should have a higher payoff number than a longer one. In defining "rational behavior" on the basis of the mathematically complete principles, strategies are determined by payoff differences; the highest available payoffs are pursued for utility maximization purposes.

Dominant strategy and equilibrium

Theoretically speaking, a dominant strategy exists if the best choice remains constant, being indifferent to others' actions. One person's best choice is the same regardless of another player's action. In the above matrix, confession earns a player a larger payoff than silence irrespective of the strategy chosen by the other player. In Prisoner's Dilemma, the dominant strategy is always confession.

When each player retains a dominant strategy, then this combination of strategies generates an equilibrium. In turn, an equilibrium creates endogenously stable states where players always choose the same action. It is a self-regulating agreement that holds up in the absence of external enforcement; self-interests motivate the agents to stick to it. An equilibrium in a one-time-only Prisoners' Dilemma is formed by mutual confession (Kuhn 2007). All the causal forces internal to the system keep the balance intact as long as no exogenous force (i.e., change in the rules of a game or payoff structures) disrupts the stable state.

In a game-theoretical language discussed so far, confession reflects the rational pursuit of one's own interests. But it produces a collectively self-defeating outcome, as both of the suspects make the same decision based on self-interest. It is collectively better to remain silent, lessening the penalty for both of them from ten years to one year. Below is a general game structure of the Prisoner's Dilemma applicable to many real-world examples. The players' strategies are now interpreted as "cooperation" and "defection" which are labeled as C and D in Table 2.3. Here "cooperation" is the equivalent of silence and "defection" corresponds to confession.

Table 2.3 is identical to Table 2.2 except that now the strategy set has been converted into cooperation and defection. A dominant strategy equilibrium is that everyone always defects even though both players will be better off if they cooperate.

Table 2.3 Prisoner's Dilemma in a generic form

		Player 2	
		C	D
Player 1	C	2, 2	0, 3
	D	3, 0	1, 1

Table 2.4 Prisoner's Dilemma with letter payoffs

		Player 2	
		C_2	D_2
Player 1	C_1	R_1, R_2	S_1, T_2
	D_1	T_1, S_2	P_1, P_2

Table 2.4 represents the payoffs in alphabet letters T, S, R, and P instead of numerical numbers. However, the preference order (T>R>P>S) remains the same. Here T stands for "temptation"; S represents "sucker"; R is a payoff for "reward"; and P represents "punishment." The subscript numbers 1 and 2 attached to these payoff letters indicate player 1 and player 2. As indicated in Table 2.4, defection (D_1) produces "temptation" (T_1) for player 1 when the other player cooperates (C_2). Cooperation (C_1) earns a "sucker" (S_1) if player 2 defects (D_2). Player 2 has a symmetric payoff structure, as C_1D_2 yields S_1T_2. These strategy sets and payoff relationships are listed simultaneously in each cell of the table (e.g., S_1T_2 produced by C_1D_2). Reward (R_1R_2) is provided for both cooperators (C_1, C_2), and punishment (P_1P_2) for both defectors (D_1, D_2).

Overall, DC>CC>DD>CD produces the corresponding payoff order described as TS>RR>PP>ST. By double-crossing the other player who sticks with cooperation, the defector can have the payoff of temptation. However, the other player will also defect to avoid being a "sucker." Given the assumption that both players are rational, D_1C_2 and C_1D_2 are not likely to happen. Paradoxically, however, both players could have received higher payoffs if both had cooperated. Each other's cooperation is needed to move from punishment (P_1P_2) to reward (R_1R_2).

The disturbing conclusion is that a rational thing to do in a one-shot Prisoner's Dilemma is to defect (Neill 2003). Defection is rational, for it always gives each player a higher payoff (for a given strategy set by the other player). Altering one's choice does not have any causal effect on the other player's; forgoing the gains of defection would not affect the other player's actions.

As represented by the above two-person (or -player) game structure, each person's privately best choice does not necessarily produce a collectively optimal result. In fact, individually self-interested rationality produces a poor outcome. Social dilemma arises in various social contexts where each person's independent maximization of self-utility yields an inefficient outcome. Its main property is that a dominant strategy equilibrium produces a disincentive to a cooperative solution. In a social dilemma, cooperation gets harder with the involvement of more than two parties.

In the example of the Prisoner's Dilemma, the two suspects fail to coordinate their strategies despite mutual preference to do so (Edgar 2001). What prevents them from cooperating in the first place is the fact that both defecting is a stable equilibrium. Even if they agree to cooperate, each player knows the other player has an incentive to cheat. Cooperation is not sustainable in equilibrium where both are inclined to defect. The equilibrium condition serves as a mutually constraining force, creating an entrapment situation. However, a dominant strategy equilibrium is not an optimal solution in Prisoner's Dilemma. Each player's dominant strategy driven by self-interest is a self-defeating choice.

Pareto optimality

The above outcome is aptly explained by a measure of efficiency called Pareto optimality. A move from one value distribution to another is considered superior if that makes at least one player strictly better off without causing reduction in welfare for everyone else (Osborne 2004). When an increase in one player's payoff occurs without a decrease in the other player's payoff, it brings about Pareto optimality. By moving to a Pareto optimal solution, some parties can become better off, but not making another worse off. It is not Pareto optimal (also sometimes called efficient) if an outcome has room for improvement in either individual or joint gains. The equilibrium in Prisoner's Dilemma is not Pareto optimal. By moving from DD to CC, both players can improve their welfare. In fact, this move allows both players to be better off.

Efficiency in games and morality

The mathematical notions of game strategies can be applied to the analysis of typical sociopolitical behavior. Social dilemma situations have been identified in many international contexts as well as interpersonal or interorganizational ones (e.g., litigation instead of settlement or a price war). Typical international examples include arms races, environmental pollution and depletion of natural resources. Inefficiency in competitive individual action revealed in game-theoretical analysis can help justify a case for treaties and laws, which either incentivize or enforce cooperation.

The elements of cooperation and defection are simultaneously present in battling the joint dilemma (Bergstrom 2002; Murnighan 1991). Both players are well aware that they will be rewarded if they cooperate. Yet they are punished by both defecting. This raises a question: "Do you trust and expect them to act in an enlightened manner?" In an example of competition among convenience stores observable in many towns, for instance, store owners may ask themselves: "Shall I cut prices to protect my profit?" Competitors would think in the same way for their own individual benefit. Is it still sensible to seek a joint outcome while knowing that the other player has every incentive to double-cross?

Below is a more serious entrapment example that entails an ethical dilemma behind the logic for building the atomic bomb. Many involved in the project later professed that they wished that the bomb had not successfully exploded despite the amount of effort put into it. The world would be much better off and safer without the bomb. "But we have to try to build it because our enemy will... It is better for us to have than just an enemy." It is still better that "both sides have the bomb than just our enemy." If everyone has an atomic bomb, the world is better without it (Poundstone 1992, 220–21). This logic is relevant to the development of each new potent arsenal (whose use has a devastating impact on all) since World War II.

In explaining human behavior, does immorality have anything to do with playing a game? In Prisoner's Dilemma, both prisoners are totally selfish with their goal of minimizing their own jail terms. The players are not ashamed of deceiving and taking advantage of their friends. A game becomes an instance of Prisoner's Dilemma only because of its payoff structure. It is a utility function that each player is supposed to care about, representing everything about the player (Lipman 1986). However, if we consider the issues of defection as a matter of psychology, it is fear of the other person's defection that influences the eventual decision. As uncertainties remain a main factor in arms competition during the Cold War period, according to one of the key arms-control negotiators in the early 1970s, "[n]either side could be sure what the other's capabilities and intentions would be in the future. Both sides felt some *necessity to assume the worst*" (Smith 1985, 87 [emphasis added]).

Cooperation will never occur if all players depend on their expectations of what their opponents will do and what they care about. Could we embrace a conscious policy of cooperating in Prisoner's Dilemmas because of our knowledge about trouble brought in by our individual rationality? As a matter of fact, we certainly would not have Prisoner's Dilemma in a world of perfect communication and complete honesty (Poundstone 1992). The Prisoner's Dilemma could perhaps be minimized by communicating our intentions and resolve to cooperate every time we face it, and confer beforehand to come to an enforceable agreement.[1] Indeed, strategic barriers to cooperation such as a lack of trust and fear of being cheated can be overcome by making future gains contingent upon meeting current obligations as well as the ability to verify compliance. When an agreement is built on flimsy trust, its implementation proceeds in an incremental and mutually verifiable step (e.g., gradually easing sanctions in reciprocation for Tehran's upholding its own end of the bargain by keeping uranium enrichment at a very small level as stipulated in the July 2015 Iran nuclear agreement).

Where a choice is not faithfully maximizing individual gain in tangible winnings, the analogy of Prisoner's Dilemma falters (Worden and Levin 2007). We do not have anything really left to decide for someone with an iron-clad rule about cooperation (e.g., the Dalai Lama in his negotiation with the Chinese government, seeking self-determination for his own people). For them, it is a matter of faith. It is not a dilemma at all, irrespective of the payoff table. Here we find a parallel between matrices of numbers and human passions (Poundstone 1992). Perhaps, the payoffs in the tables may not always be the entire story in understanding human behavior and negotiation.

Minimax

In a zero-sum game where players compete for a fixed set of available payoffs, one player's potential gain exactly the inverse of the other's. Since the amounts won or lost are equal, the sum is zero for each set of strategies selected in a game; players attempt to garner as much of this fixed quantity of rewards as possible. It is contrasted with nonzero-sum, where one's gain is not the other's loss.

The everyday folk tale below elucidates a highly regarded strategy for a zero-sum game. Two equally hungry children have to split a fruit pie that their mother has just baked. This pie problem is a conflict of interest: a larger piece for one means a smaller piece for the other. Each child desires as much pie as possible. The mother knows that if she cuts the pie, the children would each feel slighted with a smaller piece no matter how fairly she divides it. The solution is to let one child cut the pie and the other chooses the piece. The first child would not complain that he received the smaller portion of the pie because he carved up the pie himself. The second child should not object since it is she who has chosen her piece. The eventual share reflects the way one child splits the pie and which piece the other picks. The cutter will divide the pie in a way that the chooser's slice is as small as possible. The chooser in turn wants to leave the cutter with the smallest piece possible.

There are numerous ways to cut the pie. It is imperative, however, that the first child anticipates what the second will do before he acts. If the pie is cut disproportionately, the cutter will end up with the smaller piece, permitting the chooser to get a bigger portion. The cutter will only be able to have what is left after the chooser has decided which piece she wants; so it is in his best interest to slice the pie as evenly as possible, knowing that the chooser is to take a larger portion if the two pieces are unequal. The cutter's piece is tied to the chooser's because her gain is what he has to give up. The even division is therefore the ultimate solution to this game. In this pie division, fairness is assured by greed (Poundstone 1992).

The solution concept for zero-sum games, proposed by John von Neumann and Oskar Morgenstern in 1944, is called minimax. Each player has the following thinking: the limited amount of reward means that when more is available to my opponent, less is left for me. Thus, his advantage becomes my disadvantage. As the opponent always attempts to grab as much as possible, my gain hinges upon how I can maximize what is obtainable in each situation (Grüne-Yanoff 2008; Heap and Varoufakis 2004).

In a strictly competitive zero-sum setting, each player always attempts to minimize his or her own losses. In any conflict situation or competition, by taking a pessimistic view, strategies designed to minimize the risk of maximum loss (known as minimax) work best when an opponent selects maximum among their minimum gains (called maximin). This situation is applicable, in particular, to any outcome in a constant-sum game where the two payoffs add up to the same in the way that one player's gain equals the other's loss. The smallest of possible gains by an opponent coincides with the smallest of possible losses for oneself and vice versa (Hopmann 1996). A constant-sum (also called zero-sum) game is thus characterized by mirror images of each other's payoffs where highly ranked outcomes for one player translate into low-ranked ones for the other (as interests are diametrically opposed). Thus my opponent's maximum gain is the worst loss for me. The real-world examples are illustrated by minimization of the risk of terrorist infiltration inside national borders and a favorable division of goods or other objects with a limited supply.

A minimax procedure serves as the concept of a solution for two-person zero-sum games where one player's utility can be improved only by making the other player worse off. A minimax solution methodology is characterized by maximization of the worst-case payoff that can occur. The minimax value is obtained by striving to minimize one's maximum losses in anticipation of the worst scenario. The best strategy to be prepared for the worst possible consequences is to "choose the action that leads to the least bad outcomes" (Dixit and Skeath 2004, 100). A minimax strategy produces as favorable a minimum outcome as possible, no matter what the other might do.

The opposite strategy to minimax is to maximize one's own minimum payoff; this maximin procedure counters an opponent's strategy of "minimax." In a two-person constant-sum game with perfect information, the maximin and minimax values of the players are equal (Binmore 2007; Hopmann 1996). Once an adversary adopts minimax strategies, we cannot do any better by adopting other than a strategy of maximizing our minimum. They are a unique combination of strategies that equalizes all the players' payoffs.

Table 2.5 Minimax: the Battle of the Bismarck Sea

		Japan	
		North	South
Allies	North	2	2
	South	1	3

In Table 2.5, a strategy of maximizing minimum damage to an adversary is the corresponding response to their attempt to minimize the maximum loss. It comes from the real-life version of minimax played out in the Battle of the Bismarck Sea in the South Pacific in March 1943 (Carmichael 2005). The Japanese navy was convoying reinforcement troops across the Bismarck Sea from an island called New Britain to a city in nearby New Guinea; the Allies planned to bomb them. The Japanese navy had to choose either a northern or southern route. The Allies needed to decide where to send reconnaissance planes to search for the Japanese vessels. If the planes were initially sent along the wrong route, they would have to be dispatched to the other. This decreased bombing days, with consequently less damage to the Japanese forces. The Japanese navy convoy can be bombed for longer along the southern path than the northern, which is shorter.

The payoffs in Table 2.5 indicate the number of bombing days. The payoff matrix is different from the one we saw earlier in Prisoner's Dilemma. It is a convention that only the row player's payoffs are entered in zero-sum games. Those of the column player are the same numbers with the opposite sign attached. Assuming that both adopt strategy "South" simultaneously, the row player's payoff is 3 while the column gets −3: choosing the longer, southern route exposes the Japanese to three days of bombing. In the zero-sum payoff matrix, the row player wants to have an outcome that is as the highest number possible. The column wants the outcome to be as low a number as possible.

The minimax value for the column player is found by looking for the maximum damage in each column and choosing the minimum. Japan's worst-case scenario payoff from North is 2 days of bombing; its worst from South is exposed to 3 days. The minimum of the column maxima is 2, which allows Japan to limit its loss to 2 days of bombing; this is Japan's minimax.

The maximin solution for a row player recommends that the United States chooses a strategy to seek the highest minimum. It can be obtained by comparing the minimum payoff in each row and then choosing the largest. The United States identifies the worst payoff (minimum) number in each row: 2 is the lowest from North; 1 from South. Selecting the largest of the row minima ensures the US maximin payoff 2.

The maximin (which is the largest row minimum) and minimax (the smallest column maximum) values are discovered in the same cell of the same table. It confirms that the US maximin strategy is its best response to Japan's minimax and vice versa. If Japan sails north, they cannot be bombed more than two days regardless of US decisions; thus it guarantees the best payoff no matter what their enemy does.

The other party cannot do better in a zero-sum game setting than by adopting a strategy other than maximization of minimum gain and minimization of maximum loss. It is each player's optimal strategy to be selected regardless of the other's choice. Nothing can go wrong by adopting minimax/maximin in a zero-sum game. When minimax and maximin values are in the same cell, this pair of strategies creates a unique solution as well as an equilibrium. As the payoff is ensured without consideration of what an opponent does, it is called a security point. Two rational players in constant-sum games receive payoffs that exactly match their security point level. Since each knows what the other player wants, they develop a strategy that guarantees the minimum over all possible payoffs for the other agent.

This outcome, based on the assumption of the worst-case expected utility, ensures a guaranteed minimum that cannot be made worse by whichever choice is taken by the other. The two players' equilibrium payoffs sum to zero when a maximin value equals a minimax. Neither player ends up having less than their security level unless they depend on the minimax criterion. In fact, one does even better if the other does not use the same criterion.

What induces a player to do something irrational? Greed! An attempt to obtain more than maximin will reduce the payoff, because it is a zero-sum game. In Table 2.5, could the United States have done better by choosing south, seeking three days of bombing? It is obviously the best outcome for the United States. Then would the Japanese allow that to happen? Only if the Japanese do not play their minimax strategy, leaving a door open for the US military commanders to take advantage of their decision. The only way that the Japanese could be bombed less than the maximum three days is going north. If the United States had gone south, they could have had one bombing day while the Japanese were in the north. It is worse than a security value for the United States.

Deviation from an equilibrium benefits only the opponent with the effect of harming one's own welfare. No other solution can prove better or fairer than minimax, and it is the only solution in a two-person zero-sum setting. Responding to the best you can is equivalent to simultaneously doing the same thing. If one player thinks that the other player is rational, he has a sufficient reason to believe that her objective is to minimize his maximum utility. It is a response based on a belief in what one's opponents will do (Dixit and Skeath 2004). Most importantly, caution is required: the minimax method does not work for nonzero-sum games where an opponent's best outcome is not our worst (i.e., interests between two opposing parties are not mutually incompatible).

The best payoff strategy in a zero-sum case for each player is independent of the other's. The minimax theorem is applicable to either opponent; the other agent may not have to be even rational. In fact, the theorem guarantees at least a minimum expected value irrespective of the other's strategy.

Could it have made any difference if American or Japanese commanders had announced their strategies in advance? Neither party would have been able to gain from this knowledge. A minimax solution in a zero-sum game is relegated to a totally unilateral affair with no requirement for communication; details apart from the mathematical structure of the payoff are eliminated from the game (Schelling 1960). By the nature of the game that does not require coordination, a minimax strategy is anti-communicative. Information about the opponent's action (except their preference order) is not essential to developing minimax strategy. In a zero-sum game, perhaps, negotiation might become a procedure to determine each party's payoff according to a minimax principle.

Minimax in mixed strategies

Another example from World War II below unfolded very differently from the Battle of the Bismarck Sea. The Allies were planning a major invasion across the English Channel. Pas-de-Calais (at the narrowest point between Britain and France) was more attractive than Normandy. Should the Allies have selected Pas-de-Calais? However, the Germans were preparing an invasion along France's northern coast by the end of 1943. The Allied leadership knew what the Germans were thinking of. Then, German commanders should have realized their thinking was known to the Allies, unleashing an endless chain of second guessing about a possible candidate for a landing (Easley and Kleinberg 2010). When one is faced with imperfect information as seen above, a random mix of strategies averts the exposure of patterns which could be exploited by an adversary. It lessens vulnerability against the worst possible loss by keeping one's own actions open against an adversary's strategy.

In a pursuit-evasion game, one player opts to have the same choice as the other, but the other maneuvers to avoid this. The absence of a shared security value opens a door to infinite reasoning of "you think" and "I think." A pursuit-evasion game is a typical example of infinite guessing, not knowing each other's moves. Games of imperfect information are common in international conflict; players do not know exactly what their adversary will do until they all act. Even if each player may move sequentially, as seen in the above landing case, it produces a simultaneous outcome. This type of game fails to find a solution in the set of pure strategies specified without any ambiguity in each contingency, by which one knows in advance the other player's choice irrespective of one's own strategy.

When we have two or more possible outcomes, we need to randomize our strategies, for any particular one does not appear to be best (Hopmann 1996; Thomas 2011). Mixed strategies are adopted as an innate mechanism for constant-sum games with imperfect information. A player randomly selects one of the equally plausible strategies according to the likelihood of a particular set of events. Specific probabilities measure chances for which each pure strategy might be played. Thus randomization within the set of pure strategies, with given probabilities, determines the player's decision.

The random selection among the available actions is guided by a probability distribution over pure strategies. The necessity for randomized moves is especially acute when one player prefers a coincidence of actions while his rival prefers to avoid it (Dixit and Skeath, 2004). As seen in a game of rock, paper and scissors, any pure strategy selected by an opponent generates a strong motivation to deviate (Osborne, 2004). If one player can predict the other's behavior, then the first player has more chance of winning. Randomness is inevitable to prevent predictable patterns of one's decision-making choices being exposed to others; choosing one strategy consistently invites exploitation by an adversary. Players therefore have an incentive to mix up their pure strategies. Randomizing one's own actions diminishes one's vulnerability against the worst loss.

The equilibrium concept loses much of its appeal without the benefit of selecting one strategy over the other. A predictable system of behavior does not exist in the absence of a shared security value (Dixit and Skeath, 2004). Randomized moves are beneficial and necessary to resolve the problem of a nonexistent pure-strategy equilibrium. When a player mixes strategies, there may be an equilibrium. The minimax method requires mixed strategy equlibria if no single pure strategy always maximizes the player's minimum payoff against all the other's possible choices.

Mechanics for calculating mixed-strategy payoffs

The example below illustrates how we can find a mixed-strategy equilibrium in a zero-sum game. A humanitarian aid group wants to protect food, medicine and other daily necessities for refugee camps. The international aid agency wants to protect as much aid as possible from being robbed by a militia group. The agency has two storage houses (coded as L_1 and L_2), but does not have a sufficient number of security guards to protect them and have to keep its guards at only one location each night. L_1 keeps $20,000 worth of supply material while the material kept at L_2 is worth $200,000. The question is which place is more likely to be targeted by the the armed bandits and which place should be protected more by the aid group.

Table 2.6 Minimax in a mixed equilibrium

		Aid agency guard		
		L_1 with p	L_2 with 1–p	p-mix
Local bandits	L_1	$0	$20,000	$20,000 × (1–p)
	L_2	$200,000	$0	$200,000p

In the above situation, players cannot deterministically choose one of their strategies, owing to the expectation of a random outcome. Thus, pure strategies have to be mixed up with certain probabilities. More precisely, a different payoff for each of these strategies is weighted with its probabilities. In other words, the calculation of expected utility has to reflect the probability of achieving a goal with a given strategy (Morrow 1994; O'Neill 1999; Powell 1999). What matters most in discovering a mixed-strategy equilibrium is, in a nutshell, the expected-utility value that comes from the averaged payoffs obtained by pure strategies. The payoffs of mixed strategy have to be measured by cardinal information, with a numerical measure of intensity of preference, in computing the outcomes.

Now back to our business of calculating the utility of each of the possible contingent payoffs for the above case. First we have to consider the probability that each payoff occurs and then weight it in order to come up with the overall average. The probability of the guard protecting location L_1 is p; then the probability for the guard to be at the second location L_2 is 1–p. As the bandit does not know for sure which place might be protected, he wants to choose a strategy that assures him the same payoff regardless of the other's decision.

The bandit's payoff for robbing L_1 depends on the probability for the guard to be at L_2 (1–p), leaving L_1 available to rob. Thus the probability of getting $20,000 at L_1 is 1–p, while probability of getting $0 is p. Thus the average gain by robbing L_1 is $20,000 × (1–p).

The expected payoff for robbing L_2 depends on the probability of the guards protecting L_1. The expected payoff for robbing L_2 is thus $200,000 with probability p; and $0 with probability 1–p. The expected payoff for the thieves going to L_2 is an average gain of $200,000p. These calculations are represented in Table 2.6.

No matter which location the bandit decides to storm, the protector's payoff should remain the same when $200,000p becomes equal to $20,000(1–p). The equation of the two values produces p = 1/11. Thus the aid agency guards L_1 one time out of eleven, while remaining at L_2 ten times out of eleven. The stolen amount each time should not be any larger than about $18,182 regardless of the robber's choice. The same kind of analysis is applied to the local bandits attempting to maximize their minimum payoff.

By adopting the above probability, they are guaranteed a minimum of $18,182 on average by raiding L_1 with probability 10/11 and L_2 with probability 1/11.

A random selection of strategy based on the designated probabilities creates a solution in this game. In a mixed equilibrium, thus, the payoffs depend on the probabilities. Nothing will be lost by declaring how many times each of them will be at a particular location. No better payoff is earned by the above ratio of mixing strategies as long as no predictable patterns are exhibited (Brams 2014).

Decisions under uncertainty

In a situation where players are unsure about what others will do, uncertainty becomes an important factor in playing a game (Gintis 2009). Questions arise about which strategy to choose when the absence of a dominant strategy produces uncertainty about the other player's action. Negotiators need to pursue "maximum benefit at minimum risk" (Borch and Mérida 2013, 102). A pure strategy is inferior in settings where the choices by other players are not known in advance and where thinking about the other's choice is fraught with uncertainty. As illuminated above, a rational way of dealing with payoff uncertainty is randomization.

In an international conflict, experienced negotiators do not depend on one strategy exclusively by randomizing their actions. The presence of uncertainty requires utility optimization by randomly picking from among available *pure* strategies. Players act somewhat unsystematically by selecting a different strategy some of the time. Randomization adds an element of surprise and helps deter costly action by an adversary. It is designed to hedge against a risk of being engaged in any determinate behavior such as always conceding, thus being taken advantage of.

Conclusion

There is a varying range of situations from pure conflict of interest at one end to pure harmony at the other. Negotiation is not necessary or important when everyone agrees to everything with the existence of completely identical interests or values (e.g., religious communities living in total harmony). Mimimax can be adopted as the best strategy in a total conflict of interests (such as a division of an international market share) where one party's gain always becomes another's loss. The absence of any mutually shared goals with totally incompatible interests eliminates the necessity for joint solutions. If a unilateral solution to the problem is more attractive than mutually coordinated actions, an opponent's decision does not matter much in the consideration of one's strategies.

In the game theory perspective reviewed in this chapter, the essence of negotiation can be interpreted from the general principles of rationality, common knowledge of payoff structures, available strategies, Pareto optimality and other concepts that explain the outcome of human interaction. Most of all, strategic action is aimed at realizing one's own goals while considering the other player's payoffs that in turn affect their strategies. As seen in the Prisoner's Dilemma, a mutual defection does not serve one's best self-interest when a better payoff is available through joint cooperative actions. Reaping reward through mutual cooperation is a tall order in many politically competitive relations that often lead actors to adopt a strategy of defection.

Note

1 In many international negotiations, a particular payoff is deduced not just from one primary interaction but a rather lengthy series of interactions. States are more likely to be engaged in cooperation when discrete moves are accompanied by payoffs and then by another set of moves and so on – "the shadow of the future" is long (Bearce *et al.* 2009; Fearon 1998). This is because repeated interaction is different from an anonymous one-time interaction (where payoffs are produced by each round of play in the absence of any anticipated future encounter). In the repeated games, short-term gains from defection sabotage future gains obtained by continuing cooperation (Axelrod 1984). In the absence of knowledge about the end of the interaction, repeated plays provide a self-correcting mechanism for cooperation through the punishment of present defection in the next move. According to the folk theorem based on a stage game played an indefinite number of times, strategies are "conditioned on the patterns of behavior, usually interpreted as cooperation and defection, in previous periods" (Bowles and Gintis 2009, 59).

3 Strategies for conflict and cooperation

> When I consider the lack of cooperation in human society, I can only conclude that it stems from ignorance of our interdependent nature.
>
> Dalai Lama, 2001

NEGOTIATION structures often entail different types of cooperation and conflict relationships that are complicated by uncertainty about the other actor's moves. During the Cuban Missile Crisis, each superpower's competitive strategies could have resulted in the outbreak of a nuclear war if the Soviets had not backed down. Despite the warnings of many scientists and the need for regulation, the competitive overfishing around the globe continues, which will eventually cause the collapse of the marine ecological system. As will be seen in this chapter, these and other settings can be explained by game-theoretical concepts and models. Even though they may not be able to present all the obvious solutions to various problems, the games of Chicken, Battle of the Sexes, Stag Hunt and their hybrids can at least tell us about types of obstacles to developing a cooperative arrangement that enhances everyone's welfare.

In competitive situations, commitments to a negotiated settlement might not be adhered to if cooperation has to be self-enforced with the involvement of costs. When individual incentives play a prominent role, this creates a situation where decision-makers have to act independently without being sure of the other's abiding by the contract. This chapter examines how different game-theoretical models explain the dynamics of cooperation and conflict under uncertainty in action. In some two-player games, as illuminated by a nuclear arms race, seeking to gain a competitive advantage does indeed impede cooperation. In other games such as Stag Hunt, maximum gains are attainable only through coordinated action, but there is no guarantee for actors to take such action. As is noticeable in this chapter, the Nash equilibrium serves as a key concept for explaining the stability or instability of strategic relationships. The chapter will also examine qualitative changes in the dynamics of relationships and payoffs with the extension of two-player games to multiparty interactions.

The Nash equilibrium

In a game where outcomes are derived from mutual interactions, deliberating one's best response stems from the consideration of what other players do. The Nash equilibrium (NE), the best-known solution concept, is actually based on a simple notion that every game has a set of strategies, each of which is the best response to the other player's corresponding one (Heap and Varoufakis 2004). However, the concept has made significant contributions to discovering diverse types of game structures. It is, in particular, salient for all noncooperative games where every player takes her action independently (Dixit and Skeath 2004, 139).

Table 3.1a Move from defection to cooperation in Prisoner's Dilemma

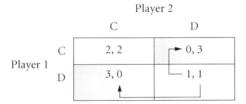

To reach a Nash equilibrium, each player has to adopt a strategy that cannot be improved in the absence of change in the other player's strategy. At an equilibrium point, thus, neither player has a reason to unilaterally change strategy. Once NE is reached, neither player can get a bigger payoff by switching to other strategies, provided the other player sticks to the same one (Grüne-Yanoff 2008, 139). A change in strategy by any one of them at an equilibrium would lead to that player earning less than if she had remained with her current strategy. Thus, the Nash equilibrium is construed as a self-enforcing arrangement (O'Neill 1999). It is not a Nash equilibrium if one player benefits by unilaterally altering strategy when all the other players adhere to the same action.

The Nash solution concept is applied to both zero-sum and nonzero-sum games. Minimax is an NE in a zero-sum game (where one player's winnings equal the other player's losses) since no one benefits from moving away from an equilibrium. No strategy is better than minimizing the maximum gain of an opponent when there is a limited amount of prize to be divided. In Prisoner's Dilemma (PD), defection is an NE strategy. No player benefits by switching their strategy from defection to cooperation as long as the other player's defection strategy stays unchanged. For instance, a sucker payoff is virtually guaranteed by moving unilaterally from the bottom right-hand corner cell NE to either the upper right one for player 1 or lower left one for player 2 (see Table 3.1a). On

Table 3.1b Move from cooperation to defection in Prisoner's Dilemma

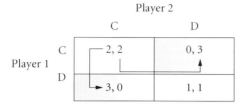

the other hand, cooperation is not a strategy to produce a Nash equilibrium (as shown in Table 3.1b). Even if each player decides to cooperate for a Pareto optimal solution (i.e., the upper left-hand corner payoff), there are strong incentives to defect owing to the fact that a temptation payoff (DC) is greater than a reward payoff (CC). While its application to Prisoner's Dilemma is simple, a Nash equilibrium in other nonzero-sum games often does not provide a clear prediction, as will be examined in the remaining sections.

The game of Chicken

In contrast with Prisoner's Dilemma (the outcome of which is all but certain), the game of Chicken, also known for a car racing episode, entails a lot of uncertainties due to the existence of two equilibria in pure strategies (O'Neill 1999). The structure of the game is determined by the following narrative originating from the 1950s competitive practice among gang members in California. The main part of the game involves two cars driving toward each other at uncontrollable speeds, with several people cheering on the side. Two cars are driving very fast down the center of the road from opposite directions. Head-on collision is apparent as the two drivers continue to head toward each other. If either driver swerves out of the way, he will be humiliated and called "chicken," becoming a loser. Meanwhile the winner is determined to be the one who keeps going straight. If both players swerve, however, both come out alive without much damage to their reputation; survival is much preferred to instant death from a head-on collision.

The strategic thinking in this game goes like this: each player has two choices, namely, swerving to avoid the collision (i.e., cooperating) or keeping straight (defecting). If your opponent swerves, your best possible outcome is straight ahead – looking brave and earning prestige among the group without risking your life. It is better to swerve to save your life if your opponent is driving straight. Suffering the stigma of being known as a

Table 3.2 The game of Chicken

	Player 2 Swerve (C)	Player 2 Straight (D)
Player 1 S (C)	2, 2	1, 3
Player 1 S (D)	3, 1	0, 0

Table 3.3 The game of Chicken with letter payoffs

	Player 2 C	Player 2 D
Player 1 C	R_1, R_2	S_1, T_2
Player 1 D	T_1, S_2	P_1, P_2

chicken is the next-to-worst outcome, but still better to be a chicken than dead (Oye 1985).

Swerving (C) is the best reply to an opponent's strategy "heading straight" (D); if the other swerves (C), though, the reverse is better (D). Two pure-strategy equilibria in the game of Chicken are swerve/straight (CD) and straight/swerve (DC). These strategy profiles are everyone's best response to the other's given strategy.

Discussion about the best strategy in a game of Chicken is condensed in the matrices in Tables 3.2 and 3.3. Two Nash equilibria are found in the lower left and upper right cells of Table 3.2. Defection along with the other's cooperation (DC) earns temptation payoff 3. A sucker (CD) payoff 1 is better off for the second player than punishment payoff 0 when the first player defects. Mutual cooperation (CC) awards reward payoff 2 for each.

In Table 3.3 corresponding to the numeric matrix 3.2, the payoff order is temptation (T)>reward (R)>sucker (S)>punishment (P). Each of the two NE (T_1, S_2 and S_1, T_2) favors a different player. Under Nash's theory, either of these two equilibria is an equally "rational" outcome. The loss from swerving (C, D) is minor compared to the crash (D, D) that occurs if everyone decides "straight ahead"; the reasonable strategy would be to swerve before a collision. The fear that the other driver may not swerve diminishes the allure of staying on a crash course. If players think that by playing D, both sides have too much to lose, mutual fear and uncertainty determine the outcome. If both players are sensible, fear of arriving at the worst possible outcome may encourage players to cooperate.

Knowing this, still, if one believes one's opponent is to be reasonable and he will turn around, one may well decide not to swerve at all; then each will continue down the center of the road, in the belief that his rival will be reasonable and eventually decide to swerve, leaving him the winner. It is consistent with a rational, Nash equilibrium solution – but unfortunately the result may well not be an equilibrium point at all. If both players think the same way, neither will back down, and then will all "rationally" crash. As each player avoids becoming a chicken, there is a real danger of DD (punishment)<CD (sucker). If both are tempted to win big, defection will bring about grievous suffering.

Sources of instability

The game is unstable due to a lack of a dominant-strategy solution; sometimes it is better to swerve, but at other times driving straight is better. In a game of Chicken, if an opponent's strategy remains unfixed, the players think that they may not be able to make a decision until they have to act. A curious aspect of a game of Chicken is that both players want to make the move that the other prefers to avoid, but they do not actually know what their rival will do.

The source of instability in Chicken therefore comes from the fact that there is more than one NE, and they can move back and forth each time when the game is played. The payoff structure of a game of Chicken (characterized by two unstable NE) illustrates differences in solutions and feasible strategies under different circumstances. The divergence of preferences challenges us with difficulties in making a strategic choice; what is a better strategy (either C or D) always depends on the other's choice. Chicken is essentially a guessing game about what the other player is going to do (O'Neill 1999).

In considering that the benefit of winning is substantial in the real life situation, an actual game becomes how to attain a preferred NE by inducing the other to play C (Dixit and Skeath, 2004); each has an incentive to threaten to choose D so that the other has no choice but C. In order to sway the outcome, one's rival needs to be convinced that one will not be a chicken. If one looks acquiescent, the other has every reason to force their way. Players have a strong motive to act aggressively for their own advantage. An attempt to intimidate rivals can be made by making an irreversible commitment to going straight; at the same time both have to make sure that the bad crash is prevented if all possible.

In many conflict settings, Chicken is comparable to escalation and brinkmanship (Kahn and Schelling 2009; O'Neill 1999; Powell 1990). The United States and the Soviet Union played a game of Chicken with nuclear weapons during the Cuban Missile

Table 3.4 Game of Chicken: Cuban Missile Crisis

		USA	
		Hold ground	Capitulate
Soviet Union	Hold ground	War, War	Soviet victory, US defeat
	Capitulate	Soviet defeat, US victory	Compromise, compromise

Crisis in 1961. Table 3.4 is a descriptive version of their payoff matrix where the Soviets are a row player, and the United States is a column player. In this game, two Nash equilibria (upper right, bottom left cells in Table 3.4) are mutually incompatible, creating a situation that each wants to hold ground before the other backs down. To win, the United States demanded the Soviet withdrawal of its missiles being installed in Cuba (i.e., the Soviets back down); Soviet victory (in the upper right cell) could be achieved by the continuing presence of Soviet missiles and the acceptance of the new status quo (i.e., the United States backs down). If neither side had backed down (the upper left cell), the confrontation would have gone down the path of nuclear exchange with devastating effects on both sides (Avenhaus 2008). The best strategy against the other's given strategy was not known until Soviet leader Nikita Khrushchev eventually blinked (with the acceptance of a sucker payoff in the bottom left cell). While the game ended with US victory, each superpower threatened the other to back down by flirting with a nuclear war.

What is most disturbing is that being irrational provides an upper hand in the Chicken dilemma. The "advantage" held by an irrational player comes from his recklessness and willingness to adopt a fatal strategy that takes everyone to the edge of a cliff. If a player is driving blindfolded and drunk, what is his opponent to do? While this does not command an answer for who won, what if the other driver was not watching or did not know the state of mind of his rival? If there are many passengers in the cars, the problem would become far more serious than a game played by a crazy gambler. When a madman theory is played out in international politics, it can confuse already complex matters further, especially with the involvement of nuclear weapons (Powell 1990).

Battle of the Sexes

Battle of the Sexes (BOS) presents yet another challenge to NE as a solution concept. A BOS game poses a coordination problem with conflicting interests. The preferred choices of the two players do not coincide with each other despite the need for an

Table 3.5 The Battle of the Sexes

		Husband Boxing	Husband Ballet
Wife	Boxing	2, 3	0, 0
	Ballet	1, 1	3, 2

agreement on one of the two NEs. Table 3.5 is a narrative for BOS. A couple wants to go out for an evening but insist on different venues (Luce and Raiffa 1957). Both prefer to be at the same place but have to agree on which of two events to attend. The man wants to go to the boxing match, but he would rather watch a ballet with his wife than going to a boxing match alone. Similarly, the wife would rather attend the boxing event with her husband than seeing the ballet alone. However, of course, it is far better if she can convince her husband to enjoy the ballet performance together. In a nutshell, the couple wants to go to either the ballet or boxing together even if their favorite choices differ.

The payoffs above represent the above preference order. The choice of their favored event with their spouse (3) > attending the other's favorite event together (2) > going to one's own event alone (1) > going to the other spouse's event alone (0). These payoff numbers are entered in the matrix above. It represents a nonzero-sum, nonstrictly competitive conflict. Higher payoffs are obtained when both have the preference of going together rather than going alone to their favored event separately.

In Table 3.5, it becomes evident that there are two pure-strategy equilibria. If the husband wants to go to boxing, then the wife has a higher payoff by going together instead of attending the ballet alone. Regarding the ballet, a similar choice has to be made by the husband to get a higher payoff. These pure NEs reflect the situation that both want to coordinate but each prefers a different outcome.

The conflict between the preferences demands deeper interpretations of "defection" and "cooperation" in BOS. Given their different preferences, cooperation means willingness to go to the other partner's event; defection denotes insisting on one's own choice that the other spouse dislikes. As boxing is not her own preferred type of entertainment, cooperation by the wife is going to boxing; likewise the choice of the ballet is cooperation by the husband; defection by the husband is to choose boxing.

Table 3.6 on the next page shows that BOS has two pure-strategy Nash equilibria, at (T_1, S_2) and (S_1, T_2), with Player 1 (i.e., the wife) preferring the former and Player 2 (i.e., the husband) hoping for the latter. The payoff values satisfy the relationship: $T(3) > S(2) > P(1) > R(0)$. A higher payoff is ensured by the order of $T > S$ and $P > R$ that stems from persistence on one's favorite choice (i.e., ballet for the wife, boxing for

Table 3.6 The Battle of the Sexes with letter payoffs

		Husband Cooperate	Husband Defect
Wife	Cooperate	R_1 (0), R_2 (0)	S_1 (2), T_2 (3)
	Defection	T_1 (3), S_2 (2)	P_1 (1), P_2 (1)

the husband). The inequality (T and S) > (P and R) means a higher payoff for both players being together than being separated at different events (Oye 1985; Rapoport and Chammah 1965).

Difficulties in making a strategic choice in Battle of the Sexes arise from a lack of stable, dominant strategy. When communication is permitted in a negotiating setting, both parties might adopt substantive or procedural decision-making rules (e.g., alternating choices or deference to an outside party). In international negotiation, the game applies to any situation where the favored outcomes of both parties are mutually exclusive, but agreement is much more desirable. In a protracted civil war in Angola and other divided countries, for instance, ending violence is mutually beneficial, but different preferences for political settlement have often become a source of contention.

Stag Hunt

In a situation imagined originally by the Enlightenment philosopher Jean-Jacques Rousseau, villagers have choices either to hunt and share a stag together or individually each catch a hare. It is far more desirable to go out for hunting a stag that offers a rather big meal. However, a stag cannot be caught without mutual cooperation; all the hunters have to stay alert when seeking a stag. While hunters lose a sense of certainty about the arrival of a stag along with the passage of more time, a hare occasionally bounces along the path within reach. The choices for the hunters are to keep their posts (i.e., cooperate) or to divert to catch a hare (i.e., defect), letting the trap laid for the stag be abandoned. Even though a hare is smaller and worth less than a stag, a hare is guaranteed since one person alone can catch it; on the other hand, a stag carries a big payoff if all the hunters cooperate; communal action (hunting) yields a higher return, assuming that all the players combine their skills.

In the game matrix in Table 3.7, each hunter's preference ordering is RR (3)>TS(2)>PP(1)>ST(0), respectively achieved by strategy sets CC>DC >DD>CD. A payoff of a stag to be shared (RR) ranks the highest; it is preferred to a hare easily

Table 3.7 Stag Hunt

	Player 2 Stag (C)	Player 2 Hare (D)
Player 1 Stag (C)	3 (R_1), 3 (R_2)	0 (S_1), 2 (T_2)
Player 1 Hare (D)	2 (T_1), 0 (S_2)	1 (P_1), 1 (P_2)

accessible to a single hunter. If one player goes out for a stag, it is better for the other to join in and hunt together than getting a hare. The "stag, stag" outcome is each other's best response. If others choose a hare, staying with a stag strategy leaves the player empty-handed. If the other player pursues a hare, then a stag is not good any more (CD), thus prompting a shift in strategy to pursue a hare (DD). Hunting a hare (when others do the same) is NE, but not the combination of hare and stag.

In Stag Hunt, mutual cooperation (RR) is the most desirable outcome. If one player chooses to cooperate, the other is better off cooperating, but lone cooperation is worse than unilateral defection (DC>CD). In fact, defecting is always a better response to the other player's defection. The two pure strategy equilibria are R_1, R_2 and P_1, P_2. Both cooperating is the only Pareto optimal NE, the most efficient solution. The main reasons for a strategy set of DD is a lack of assurance. Stag Hunt is best known as a coordination game (Gintis 2009); attaining the "stag, stag" equilibrium is preferred to "hare, hare," but it is not guaranteed. The main question remains as to how we induce the players to work on a common strategy for a bigger payoff.

Risk and payoff dominance

One equilibrium (cooperation, cooperation) is payoff-dominant, while the other (defection, defection) is risk-dominant. The payoffs are higher for both players to play the same strategy pair (CC) than the other pure-strategy set (DD). Mutual cooperation produces a higher payoff, but is an unstable equilibrium, demanding a measure of trust. The pursuit of an individually achievable goal does not carry such a risk. It does not depend on the other's cooperation but forgoes a higher payoff (Skyrms 2004). If uncertainty exists about the other player's action, unilateral action turns out better. In fact, a hare in the hand (DC) is better, as a sure thing, than a stag in the bush (CD) (Lepard 2010).

Stag Hunt describes a conflict between a bigger benefit that is socially shared and smaller individual security. DD risk dominates CC since the former has a guaranteed payoff, not carrying a risk of CD. The trick is to convince all the players to coordinate on a common task, not letting them be distracted by an easy individual gain.

The above explanation is applicable to the "separate peace" observed in trench warfare during World War I. Troops dug in only a few hundred feet away from each other's trenches. As the war became intractable, an unspoken understanding evolved between the trenches. A sniper killing by one side met an equal retaliation from the other side. If no one was killed for a time, conversely, this was recognized by the enemy side, sustaining a "truce." In this example, a truce is a fruit of CC that is payoff dominant.

In Stag Hunt, rationality depends on what one believes the other will do (O'Neill 1999; Skyrms 2004). In the absence of explicit communication, as in the above case, the soldiers on each side might have defected if they had believed that their counterpart would not abide by the truce; each side knew that this thinking was going in their adversary's mind. In fact, cooperation will be guaranteed only by everyone believing that all others would cooperate, forming positive self-fulfilling prophecies (or developing a positive reinforcement feedback). Without such beliefs, players would rather choose risk dominance. In a single-play Stag Hunt, a temptation to defect to guard against uncertainty about the other's action is countered by a universal desire for cooperation over a common good (Lewis 2003; Oye 1985). In preferring the same equilibrium, players should have shared interests, combined with a great vision for the common good. Whereas seeking stags is the most beneficial for both an individual and society, trust dilemma features challenges in a coordination game.

Brief comments on the Nash equilibrium

The concept of NE is not unambiguous nor does it always suggest an effective solution. The limitations of the Nash equilibrium as a solution concept are illustrated by the fact that NE does not often provide a decisive optimal solution. None of the above games has a unique (dominant) equilibrium, with an exception of Prisoner's Dilemma. A Nash equilibrium does not satisfactorily guide us to solve bargaining dilemmas, falling short of a clear prediction about the likely outcome, but reveals a reasoning process about how people choose an action.

The strategic structure of decision-making

The previous section covered modeling the process of players making choices out of their own interest. The game-theoretic analysis focuses on payoff maximization that in turn determines each player's strategies. Self-enforcing agreement emerges when no player can improve their payoffs by moving from an equilibrium point. The concept of a Nash equilibrium bestows a crucial insight into why cooperation can often be hard to come by.

The analysis of strategic choices becomes even more important in noncooperative games where an agreement cannot be enforced. If an agreement advances the interests of only some, it is mostly likely violated by those who are harmed. In deepening our understanding of this issue, a significant question to ask is "can cooperation emerge spontaneously from the interactions of rational egoists?" (McCain 2010, 19).

One game can be transformed into another by changing properties. As examined in the previous chapter, the four values have to gratify the relations: Temptation (T)>Reward (R)>Punishment (P)>Sucker (S) to stand for two-player PD games. Presuming the relative values of T, S, R, P are reordered, a new matrix features another game (McAdams 2008). PD can be converted to either Deadlock or Stag Hunt with different implications for cooperation and competition. When reward (CC) and temptation (DC) are switched in PD, it becomes Stag Hunt (Skyrms 2004). When reward and punishment payoffs of PD are interchanged, that becomes a Deadlock game.

Deadlock

As seen in Table 3.8, a Deadlock game is ordered T (DC)>P (DD)>R (CC)>S (CD). In this game, mutual cooperation yields a lesser payoff than mutual defection (DD>CC). No matter what happens, D is always better than C. Indeed, cooperation does not yield any positive payoff in this game, as D is always an optimal strategy. Oddly enough, a punishment payoff (DD) is Pareto optimal – mutual defections are efficient strategies, either individually or collectively. In a Deadlock game, each party is not concerned about the other player's moves as they have a dominant strategy D; it is the simplest game we have seen so far.

Table 3.8 Deadlock game

		Player 2 C	Player 2 D
Player 1	C	1, 1	0, 3
Player 1	D	3, 0	2, 2

Mutual stalemate in many international negotiations can be better explained by a Deadlock game. When entrenched positions are developed, a PD game turns into a Deadlock, leaving no bargaining space. In the absence of structural changes, Deadlock continues because it is NE. In a deadlocked negotiation, each side believes that the costs of reaching an agreement outweigh the status quo.

Table 3.9 Deadlock game with letter payoffs

		Player 2	
		C	D
Player 1	C	R, R	S, T
	D	T, S	P, P

Building cooperation in Stag Hunt

In general, both players prefer the same equilibrium which Pareto dominates the other. However, the players may fail to recognize that it is in their best interests to cooperate. They might, for example, arrange their strategies as if they were playing Prisoner's Dilemma. Despite the need to coordinate on the same strategy, players are unable to realize the disadvantage of unilateral defection. The proper coordination of expectations is essential to the selection of an equilibrium point with greater payoffs for all players.

If the United States and Soviet Union viewed the world similarly, arms-control negotiation could have turned into Stag Hunt. During the Cold War, each side pursued a risk-dominant (Cold War, hare, hare) payoff instead of a payoff-dominant outcome. However, it is certainly irrational to increase the number of weapons of mass destruction, which should not be used if everyone wants to survive. By using money for better purposes (peace and economy) and obtaining common security, both the United States and the Soviet Union have reward payoffs. Owing to a lack of assurance and uncertainty, however, both sides were concerned about an undesirable sucker payoff.

In the Cold War endgame, however, both sides acknowledged that they knew it was a wasteful use of their talent and resources to produce the most destructive weapons. This realization played a key role in the transformation of the game. In an interview, the last Soviet leader Mikhail Gorbachev explained: "Models made by Russian and American scientists showed that a nuclear war would result in a nuclear winter that would be extremely destructive to all life on Earth; the knowledge of that was a great stimulus to us, to people of honor and morality, to act in that situation" (*Salon*, September 7, 2000).

The trust dilemma of a coordination game lies in obtaining assurance; communication plays a large role in a coordination strategy in the selection of a payoff-dominant NE. Indeed, communication becomes an important matter for convergence of expectations, but unfortunately communication may not be always possible or not seriously pursued. Not only Stag Hunt but also other games may well be played simultaneously by the same two players. In a complex human world, everything is connected to everything else. The coordination in Stag Hunt may well be easily affected by an overarching mistrust and competitive relationships. During the height of the Cold War, in fact, citizen diplomacy actively conducted by conscious scientists, physicians and other professionals played a pivotal role in filling the hole left by the government communication channels.

Coordination of different preferences: Battle of the Sexes

Coordination challenges in Battle of the Sexes arise from different preferences in outcomes which induce conflict despite the need for coordination. It is not uncommon in negotiation settings that agreement is better but each of the options favors different parties (Princen 1992). What if two players have completely opposed payoffs without any possibility of division – for example, two roommates have to decide who will have the bigger and who the smaller room in an apartment? When the room size cannot be equalized, the two roommates might negotiate over how the acceptance of the small room can be compensated for by the person who will have bigger space. In international negotiation, it is difficult to have an agreement evenly favored by both sides, but agreement is often considered better than no agreement. This discrepancy is often settled by either bargaining with side payments or such a strategic move as threats.

Side payments

A side payment is a quid pro quo arrangement that makes everyone more contented. The compensation for taking a sucker payoff (CD) reduces the risk of competition (DD) that stems from insisting on one's own preference. Pareto optimality can be enhanced by incorporating side payments (McCain 2010). The solution can be made easier through issue linkages. The strategies of issue linkage effectively alter payoff structures by conjoining dissimilar games. Now the players have to bargain over how large the bribes are.

Table 3.10 Battle of the Sexes with side payments

		North Korea	
		Cooperate	Defect
United States	Cooperate	(2, 2)	(3, 4)
	Defect	(4 − c, 3 + v)	(1, 1)

Table 3.10 shows the Battle of the Sexes matrix including side payments. We can apply this modified matrix to the negotiated settlement between the United States and North Korea in October 1994. At that time, North Korea agreed to the dismantling

of its nuclear programs in return for the construction of light water reactors. In the matrix 3.10, c stands for the cost for the side payment to be paid by the United States, and v its value for North Korea. Now the payoffs have been altered. The new arrangement (4 − c, 3 + v) is also an equilibrium solution. A unique Pareto optimal solution can be achieved if c is smaller than 1 while v is larger than 1. Even though the upper right-hand cell payoff (3, 4) is given up by North Korea, the new payoff with side payments (3 + v) is an improvement on the original lower left-hand cell payoffs (4, 3). 4 − c is also a satisfactory solution to the US government especially if c gets closer to 0. As a matter of fact, both South Korea and Japan agreed to absorb the entire costs for building the light water reactors at no cost to US taxpayers. There is no better outcome than someone else being willing to pay for your costs.

Strategic moves: threats

A threat, like a side payment, is an extraneous element that, in effect, modifies the payoffs for a game. It diminishes the payoff for an opponent who does not cooperate. In this sense, a threat's function is dissimilar to a side payment which improves an opponent's payoff to induce cooperation. Prior to the October 1994 settlement mentioned above, the US government escalated the conflict to put pressure on North Korea to concede. In June 1994, the Clinton administration threatened air strikes on North Korean nuclear facilities. The North Korean leadership vowed to retaliate if that happened. The threat was employed as a payoff-modifying form of communication. However, it was estimated that a full-blown war would kill at least two million civilians as well as causing complete destruction in the Korean peninsula.

Table 3.11 Battle of the Sexes with threats

		North Korea Cooperate	North Korea Defect
United States	Cooperate	(2, 2)	(3, 4 − c_2)
United States	Defect	(4 − c_1, 3)	(1, 1)

Table 3.11 is a modified version of BOS payoff matrix incorporating a threat payoff. In general, threats inflict costs on both sides. North Korea stands to lose c_2 if it resists the American threat. Its payoff is displayed in the upper right cell as 4−c_2 if it sticks with its favorite option. The United States also stands to absorb a significant loss to force the North's cooperation; c_1 is designated as this loss in the matrix's lower left cell. In this new game, the cost is deducted from the temptation payoff 4. If c_1 is less than 1, the payoff with the deduction of the threat cost is still higher than a sucker payoff 3. The reverse

is true for the United States if c_1 is higher than 1. For North Korea, when c_2 appears to be greater than 1, then it would be better to take a sucker payoff 3. A unique Pareto optimal solution could be obtained by the US threat under the condition that c_1 is less than 1 and c_2 is greater than 1. This solution is also an equilibrium. Given the North Korean leadership's unpredictable reaction, however, c_1 was too great to actually carry out the threat. Fortunately former president Jimmy Carter successfully intervened, as a mediator, and brought both parties back to the negotiation table, eventually producing a settlement with the side payment noted above.

Management of escalated conflict in an anti-coordination game

As discussed in the previous section, preferences for incompatible outcomes on the part of each player create instability in games of Chicken. Mutual restraints could derive from the recognition of focal points, such as nonuse of nuclear, weapons, which are more easily acceptable than other alternatives. A real danger of a punishment payoff can be avoided in international conflict by back-channel negotiation, pregame communication or alternating cooperation and defection.

Back-channel negotiation

By the end of the 1950s, Western jurisdiction over West Berlin, despite its location deep inside East German territory, became an increasing liability for the Soviet Union, highlighting a sharp contrast between the capitalist and socialist systems, with a consequence of a mass exodus from the eastern side. In his November 1958 speech, Soviet premier Nikita Khrushchev demanded the departure of Western powers from West Berlin, sparking a three-year crisis which culminated in the construction of the Berlin Wall in August 1961. The Wall's erection was followed by an immediate stand-off between the United States and Soviet troops surrounding the checkpoints, creating one of the Cold War's tensest moments. The US tanks pointed toward the East German troops, being confronted by Soviet tanks beyond the wall. A conventional skirmish could have escalated into a war, along with any mistaken move such as knocking down the Wall. The crisis was eventually diffused by President John F. Kennedy's proposal made through a back-channel negotiation. The arrangement led Khrushchev to remove his tanks in return for US reciprocation.

Pregame communication

In strategic signaling, each side is well aware that their own statements and behavior are being watched and interpreted by an adversary. This in turn motivates each to act with a consciousness of the expectations they generate. Signaling one's intentions clearly, especially in a crisis situation, lessens the element of surprise and generates some predictability in a game (Fearon 1997). By making its planned action known prior to the match, a player gives the other party an opportunity to be prepared to develop a comparable strategy to avoid an outcome desired by no one. It is a good strategy to constrain one's own options so that an adversary has room to maneuver to achieve a way out of the crisis. In the example below, one party unilaterally declares their intentions, and the opponent adjusts their action accordingly.

Another game played by the United States and North Korea in their long history of animosity shows how both parties have occasionally played a game of Chicken with great restraints. The Obama administration successfully passed a UN Security Council Resolution which permitted searching of North Korean ships in an open sea as part of the punishment for the country's nuclear testing in 2008. North Korea challenged the resolution with a vow to fight any search. Immediately after the passage of the resolution, out of rage, the North Korean leadership sent a cargo ship in the East China Sea. However, it was in no one's interests to further escalate the confrontation.

The US government announced its policy not to stop North Korean ships in the sea, but persuaded its southeast Asian allies to search North Korean ships if they stopped by their harbors for fuel or other supplies. Given that North Korean behavior is generally known to be unpredictable, this episode generated great international attention. No one knew where the North Korean ship was heading. In the end, it turned out that the North Korean cargo ship was moving around in different international waters, as a show of defiance, and returned home without stopping anywhere. While the US government made it known to North Korea that its naval vessels were watching their every move closely, they never got close enough to provoke any unpredictable incident. The United States declared what it would do before the match, making its planned action common knowledge; North Korea acted within the boundaries. No one lost face.

Alternating as a tacit form of cooperation

The best interests of each player in a game of Chicken lie in selecting different choices, not the same due to the fact that each Nash equilibrium favors a different party. It generates the possibility that players may alternate in choosing C or D rather than moving simultaneously (Colman and Browning 2009; Neill 2003; Sugden 2001). Payoff maximization can be accomplished by alternating strategies for S and T payoffs under the condition that both players are willing to play their part.

This form of coordinated turn-taking is the only way to enable both players to maximize their payoffs if the combined S+T payoff exceeds R+R (i.e., S+T>2R). In ethnic conflict resolution, each party may alternate between tough and soft positions.

Occasionally allowing a moderate opponent to take a tough position strengthens their capacity to sway the hawkish opinion of their constituents. In their four years of negotiations, both President P. W. Botha and Nelson Mendela alternately adopted compromise and intransigence in a larger metagame of ending white minority rule in South Africa.

Hybrid game

Conflict and cooperation in a complex world would be modeled better by hybrid or blended games, in which one player has, for instance, the payoffs of Prisoner's Dilemma but the other's preferences are informed by a game of Chicken or Stag Hunt or something totally different. In hybrid games, thus, players' preferences are not symmetric (i.e., a particular strategy does not produce an identical payoff for each player). This is due to the fact that a mixture of incongruent game structures produces mismatching preferences, as seen in the game of Bully.

Game of Bully

A blend between Chicken and Deadlock features a game of Bully. One player has Chicken preferences which favor temptation but reflect fear of mutual defection. For the Deadlock player, defection is always preferred no matter what. These two sets of preferences are integrated in a Bully game matrix in Table 3.12.

Table 3.12 The game of Bully

		Deadlock player (China) C	D
Chicken player (Japan)	C	1, 0	0, 2
	D	2, −1	−1, 1

In the matrix, the row player's Chicken payoffs are combined with column Deadlock payoffs. For the column Deadlock player, defection is always a dominant strategy (with a guaranteed payoff 2). The row Chicken player is powerless to prevent this and ends up with payoff 0. Bully is a model for hostile confrontations featuring one actor moving aggressively, and the other wanting to avoid the fight at any cost. The game's outcome thus encourages the belligerent party to insist on its own way, resulting in the exploitation of the conciliatory one (Poundstone 1992).

The above model can be applied to settling an occasional confrontation between China and Japan over their disputed East China Sea islands. As Japan views protracted confrontation with China as a catastrophe, the row Chicken player (Japan) needs to resolve the conflict more quickly than the Deadlock column player (China). Japan tends to initially take a Chicken strategy, hoping for a quick resolution. As China does not budge (with a protracted conflict spilling over into trade and other areas of their relationship), Japan thinks that is not in their interests. As pressure builds on them, Japan generally acquiesces to Chinese demand. One of these incidents included Japanese capitulation to Chinese demands for the unconditional release of a Chinese fishing boat's crew who had been arrested for entering disputed territorial waters between China and Japan, in early 2011, after the Chinese ban on the export of a rare mineral critically needed for the Japanese car industry.

A Nash equilibrium in a Bully game is capitulation by the Chicken player (the upper right-hand cell). As is clear in Table 3.12, only a Deadlock player has a dominant strategy, constituting an asymmetric game in which the other has to adjust their strategy accordingly. When only one player has a dominant strategy, he does not need to consider the choices by the other player; thus the reasoning of one player becomes more important. It is contrasted with games which are symmetric with respect to the ordinal structure of the payoffs. In a symmetric game, each party's choices are equally important. In all the games presented earlier in this book (except Bully), each player is given the same payoff once they choose the same course of action; consequently, each party has no advantage or disadvantage in their payoffs after adopting the same strategy. In a symmetric game, each player faces the same strategic choice; and the exact payoffs are quantitatively symmetric.

Collective action game

Collective action games shed light on the decisions a rational individual should make in a collective environment. Examples include but are not limited to many contemporary international issues, ranging from control of pollution to preservation of the rainforests to selection of common technological standards, etc. By adopting a representative agent model, the analysis of two-person PD, Chicken and coordination games can be extended to choices in collective action. Even though players are assumed to be identical, they do not necessarily end up in the same situation (e.g., improvement in their welfare or its lack). As it does not always produce an intended outcome, making a choice of solution to a particular set of problems in a collective environment is full of paradoxes and dilemmas. As we shall see, many of the two-person game properties fall into a gray area of logic.

Handling a large number of players demands some simplifying assumptions (Earnest 2008). All of the participants are assumed to be representative agents who "have the same strategy options." Agents sharing many traits confront the same choice in the same manner; you are the kind of person who either defects or cooperates (McCain 2010).

The response collectively glides toward an instantaneous equilibrium. Most importantly, an individually best decision in a two-person game does not necessarily deduce the best payoff in a collective game where a community of players evolves over time through repeated exposure to a similar situation.

Tragedy of the commons

Prisoners' Dilemma in a two-person game can be expanded to many-person interactions. A multiplayer PD structure is manifested in the Tragedy of the Commons, made familiar by ecologist Garret Hardin's work published in the journal *Science* in 1968. Using an analogy of a group of herders grazing cattle on common land, it explains why collective resources are overexploited. Each farmer prefers to bring in more cattle to graze on the shared land but the grassland will soon be rendered unfit if it is overused. Driven by economic self-interest, each farmer has incentives to continue to add another animal to the commons, sacrificing everyone's welfare. As a consequence, the commons are inevitably degenerated to the point that the pasture is completely destroyed, no longer supporting the villagers' cattle. Forgoing sustainable use of the resource for each individual's selfish gain eventually leads to a "tragedy." Hardin employs this episode as a metaphor to display that individual self-interest fails to bring about benefit for the entire society.

The Tragedy of the Commons has grave consequences for the future of humanity. Overfishing in the East China Sea, the North Sea, the Grand Banks in North America and other international waters has ravaged fish stocks, thereby undercutting the economic wellbeing of those who depend on them. Other contemporary examples of the Tragedy of the Commons range from logging and deforestation to destruction of animal habitats and overhunting. The common element in all these examples is that individuals act independently, following their own self-interest. The resulting undesirable consequences contradict the main claims of neoclassical economics that independent pursuit of self-interests yields economically efficient outcomes. In many social dilemma situations, indeed, Adam Smith's "invisible hand" produces a very bad result for the society.

It is a Nash equilibrium in the Tragedy of the Commons for individuals to exploit the grass as much and fast as they can. The result that will be inferior for all participants arises from blindly carrying out individual actions, striving for a selfish end, as if in isolation (Szilagyi 2003). Given its undesirable outcomes, we would all be better off cooperating with each other, not playing a Nash equilibrium.

A matrix of a multiple player Prisoner's Dilemma is shown in Table 3.13 where N represents the number of players. The matrix presents a situation concerning how the individual's contribution should be made in a collective situation and how that choice

Table 3.13 The Tragedy of the Commons

		More than N work	N or fewer work
Individual Player	Work (C)	B – C	C
	Shirk (D)	B	0

can be rationally decided. This analysis has relevance to making social choices for group efforts to attain some common goal (Kuhn 2007). The examples may include pollution control, reduction in the use of fossil fuels, preservation of scarce resources and the protection of natural habitats.

In the payoff matrix in Table 3.13, B indicates social benefit. Assuming that it is created (in the left column of the matrix below), B is available to both shirkers and workers as a public good, irrespective of their efforts. C is a cost some members of the community voluntarily pay to produce B. In the matrix, the payoffs are ordered Benefit>(Benefit–Cost)>0>Cost. The most significant fact in this collective-game matrix is that the payoffs differ according to the threshold number of people who work (Pacheco *et al.* 2011).

In order to enjoy B, a sufficient number of people have to make a contribution to the creation or preservation of the social good. As seen in the bottom left-hand corner cell, shirkers earn benefit without cost when more than some threshold number N of people work. If there are more than N workers, each of them obtains reward payoff B–C. Here workers pay the cost for their benefit.

In the right-hand column where N or fewer people choose to work, no one gets anything (simply because benefit cannot be created by fewer people than required). In the event that not enough people choose to work, each worker bears only a negative cost payoff (a sucker payoff) while shirkers have a punishment payoff 0. The worker's cost is not compensated for in the absence of benefit.

What we see above is that the payoff sizes are dependent upon the number of cooperators in the game. The question does not arise if a sufficiently large number of people choose to take part in producing B. In general, workers are much better off being in a larger company of other workers or cooperators. For shirkers, their equilibrium strategy is not working up to a point where more than N people exist to produce B. As "free riders," they do not make any contribution, but are not excluded from access to B. On the tipping point of "N working," their choice makes a huge difference in not only their payoffs but also those of others. By switching to "work" (i.e., cooperate), a shirker improves his/her own payoff from punishment payoff 0 to a reward payoff (B–C) in the upper left-hand corner cell. This also means that the worker's payoff now moves from the right column sucker payoff C to the left column reward payoff B–C.

It looks apparent at first glance that, as in a two-person PD game, defection is a dominant strategy over cooperation (Kuhn 2007). So rational players choose to defect, and their payoffs are either 0 or B at no cost. However, their temptation payoff is achievable only when more than N choose to cooperate. It entails rather unique features, compared with the two-person PD in which each player's moves are made irrespective of the others; a move to shirking (i.e., defection) does not dominate working (equivalent of cooperation) at an N threshold point. In the event that precisely N others adopt C at the threshold, an individual player is better off cooperating. However, it is a different story if there is not a sufficient number of workers who can collectively produce B. Prior to the N threshold, it is "rational" to contribute nothing regardless of whatever anyone else does.

Volunteer's Dilemma

A multiperson version of the Chicken game is known as Volunteer's Dilemma where "volunteering" is akin to swerving for the common good (Poundstone 1992). Few volunteers need to take on an action or make a sacrifice that will benefit everyone in a group, but each member has a better payoff if others volunteer. As long as enough people elect to volunteer, the rest enjoy the positive effects by not doing so. The worst possible outcome for everyone comes from a lack of volunteers. In fostering the public good, a fixed number of cooperators is required to have the desired impact (Archetti and Scheuring 2011).

In the situation that someone has to jump off an overloaded lifeboat, N equilibria exist in an N-player Volunteer's Dilemma game. When one person volunteers in each equilibrium, it is the worst outcome to the individual. By sacrificing for the group, a player receives no benefit. If no one volunteers, however, all lose. Therefore, each player favors a pure-strategy equilibrium where someone else volunteers (a free-riding payoff). In the absence of any volunteer, a nonvolunteering payoff is the same as the payoff for voluntary sacrifice without benefit.

The Volunteer's Dilemma, like the Tragedy of the Commons, often produces an unsatisfactory outcome for the whole society. The more people are available to volunteer, the less likely it is that someone actually volunteers. An increase in the number of players diminishes the likelihood of individual volunteering, called the "bystander effect" by social psychologists. In this dilemma, ironically, the probability of the benefit for the group declines contrary to its size. The larger the group is, the more likely the bystander effect is to be observed (Archetti 2011). The diffusion of responsibility weighs deeply in Volunteer's Dilemma.

The "catastrophe" payoff (evident in the absence of any volunteers) is the worst form of Volunteer's Dilemma (Poundstone 1992). This payoff is virtually identical with the sacrifice payoff from volunteering. Imagine a lifeboat situation where all are in trouble if no person is willing to jump into the sea. One person needs to be sacrificed to spare all others. The most desirable outcome is, certainly, one's own survival.

It is the most disturbing, though, that everyone thinks that he or she ought to be salvaged, waiting each other out. The one who concedes becomes a loser. Even though water is coming up now to threaten everyone, no one wants to make the ultimate decision. Is there any way to determine who should go down and exactly when this moment might be? In this simultaneous-move game, players cannot act after observing a move made by someone else. Worst of all, reciprocation does not play any role in this decision-making.

In the case of the *Titanic* a century ago, when we compare the survival rates of women and men travelling in second class, women had a favorable 86 percent chance of surviving. The chances for the men were completely the opposite, a mere 14 percent. The rest perished in the freezing Atlantic Ocean. In this tragic incident, it did not take long for everyone to simultaneously conclude who ought to be sacrificed – the "[n]otions of male chivalry toward the weaker sex was a moral code with a force stronger than law in the Edwardian era" (*New York Times*, April 9, 2012).

If there exist expectations or even implicit commitments about what people should do, particular equilibria are naturally taken as more salient, or even accepted as a fair solution (O'Neill 1999). However, these focal points do not always stay constant regardless of time. Back to the moral code question, by the way, "it is no longer de rigueur for a man to yield his seat on a bus, or a lifeboat, to someone of the opposite sex" (*New York Times*, April 9, 2012). This was clearly exhibited by many young men pushing away pregnant or old women to get out first after the wrecking of an Italian cruise ship in spring 2012.

N-coordination game

Coordination is necessary when the outcomes preferred by both players are obtained by doing the same thing. In a pure coordination game, each player's utility is maximized by making the same choice. In a game of pure coordination, each person's interests perfectly coincide – driving on the left-hand or right-hand side of the road; the use of the same language or other symbols of communication. All that matters is coordinating on the same action; correspondence is more crucial than which action it is. The choice of action does not have an impact on the overall payoff, but every player has to act in the same manner. Even if groups may have different methods of selecting an equilibrium, having an identical outcome creates a situation of winning or losing together

(Binmore 2007). In a pure coordination game, therefore, the choice of the same strategy Pareto dominates discordant strategies.

In the driving example, the solution lies in selecting one of the two pure Nash equilibria – either the left side or the right. It really does not matter which side players pick, as long as the same choice is made by all. What is crucial is to agree to one of the equilibria. Both solutions (all driving on the left or all on right) are Pareto efficient. Neither is any more efficient than the other. The danger of a mutually inferior outcome derives from failure to have at least one shared equilibrium.

In a coordination equilibrium, no one would be better off if anyone played differently (Easley and Kleinberg 2010). We would be worse off if half of us drive on the left side of the road and the other half on the right. Here randomizing between them is not an answer either, causing gridlook. The coordinated action has to be persistent. The convention to choose either left or right is no less powerful in a country where the solution is all driving left than where the opposite is accepted.

The successful selection of an equilibrium point hinges on identifying beliefs or expectations about each other's actions. In pure coordination, the simple solution can be more practical than a sophisticated theoretical construct, not entailing more selective equilibrium criteria. The observation of public random variables may suffice to make an equilibrium decision. Sometimes a commitment to a given course of action can be made by a public institution as is illustrated by the Swedish parliamentary decision to switch from driving on the left to the right in 1968.

Collective Battle of the Sexes game

The payoffs in N-person BOS games depends on (1) the number of players with the same choices and (2) whether a player's decision is based on her favorite choice. A player gets a higher payoff when the individual collective is what the player prefers to one of those that diverge from her liking. An increase in the number of players in a group also improves the payoff of group members.

In the collective BOS game, different ways of coordinating create different outcomes, determining the effectiveness of collective decisions. This is the case for a language conflict in multiethnic societies. The origin of civil war in Sri Lanka (waged over several decades) was attributed to the exclusion of the Tamil language from public use in 1956 and subsequent discrimination in education and employment opportunities. In language coordination, groups often do not concede to a competing language strategy due to (perceived or real) political disadvantage or for sociocultural reasons. It is not Pareto optimal for an entire population to learn multiple languages spoken by major ethnic groups in the country. Yet when competition is involved in coordination with a potential for a destructive conflict, each option can be made mutually acceptable through a negotiated solution (e.g., the legitimization of a bilingual system in Canada or delegation of the decision-making authority to provinces in India).

The common knowledge of rationality and the structure of the game are not always sufficient to guarantee successful coordination in collective BOS games. When the selection of an optimal strategy may favor one group over another, it becomes politicized. It explains time-consuming efforts to search for convergence to a mutually acceptable equilibrium. For instance, intrabloc coalition-building in multinational negotiations frequently involves bargaining for complicated side payments and tradeoffs.

Challenges to multilateral cooperation

In collective action games, an equilibrium is not fixed, shifting according to the number of people who take the same action. In a collective BOS game, the increase in the size of the group adopting the same strategy increases individual bargaining power through coalition-building. In the multiplayer version of PD, one player's action (e.g., polluting the air) imposes a harmful externality on innocent parties, eventually hurting everyone's interests through collective effects. Owing to a harmful externality, the Nash equilibrium does not produce the best result. This situation is contrasted with positive network externalities of a pure coordination game, in which the benefit is reaped from being in the same collectivity with other agents.

As examined earlier, paradoxes and dilemmas of choice in the Tragedy of the Commons are ascribed to the existence of two equilibria. At an equilibrium point of universal defection (where everyone pollutes), any player unilaterally departing from this outcome is actually moving to negative payoff C from payoff 0. If a single person shifts from a tipping point equilibrium (attained by N+1), everyone's payoff suddenly becomes worse. This process can be quickly gravitated toward the universal defection equilibrium. This might suggest, as described below by a scientist at the US National Center for Atmospheric Research, that we have different problems from what a dinosaur faced many millions years ago: "Dinosaurs didn't have any technology to know something was coming, so they just woke up one day and found out that the planet was destroyed. But if we can know about it 30 years before that happens, and do something to cope with it, we can still mitigate the impact on human beings" (*Washington Post*, May 29, 2012).

In the Tragedy of the Commons, a nonequilibrium strategy is a solution to an inevitable and eternal conflict between the quest for one's own good and striving for the good of the group. The entire structure of a game can be transformed by creating asymmetric payoffs in the way cooperation becomes a reasonable choice, making defection unprofitable. Multilateral treaties on the protection of endangered species and the protection of the ozone layer reward cooperators with the transfer of technology and aid as well as transferrable individual quotas while excluding noncooperators from the benefit. This process develops positive externalities that encourage more countries to take cooperative action.

Conclusion

As examined in this chapter, game-theoretical structures can be applicable to many different negotiation circumstances. As seen in the case of the superpower rivalry, Prisoner's Dilemma becomes Stag Hunt, depending on how actors perceive their relationships. In an interactive decision-making environment, each party pursues the strategy most appropriate to achieve their goals. Depending on the features of games, different types of coordination are involved in crafting competitive and cooperative strategies.[1] In Battle of the Sexes and the game of Chicken, mutual defection can lead to disastrous outcomes. When these games can be repeated, each player can coordinate their actions either explicitly or implicitly by alternating their cooperation and defection strategies (Neill 2003).

The application of a Nash equilibrium can be reconfigured in many different ways by moving from two-player games to multiplayer interactions. Despite the selection of different strategies, in collective games, the agents can end up with the same equilibrium payoff, depending on how all individual actions add up. The number of players required to adopt cooperative strategies is directly linked to the payoffs of every player. In preserving rainforests, resembling Volunteer's Dilemma, for example, some countries have to be willing to sacrifice their economic interests. Multilateral negotiations have focused on the types and levels of compensation for the volunteers. In a climate control negotiation, the main concern lies in the creation of incentive structures to move a sufficient number of "shirkers" to "workers."

Note

1 Iteration increases the prospects for cooperation in Prisoners' Dilemma and Stag Hunt. The repeated plays of the game generate an incentive for cooperation among rational egoists over time. When a player's moves are based on an opponent's previous move, strategies such as tit-for-tat (TFT) allow a player to punish defectors. Through defection against an uncooperative opponent's move, all players soon learn non-cooperative behavior's poor payoffs for all. In TFT, the greatest rewards over time are obtained by mutual cooperation (Axelrod 1984).

4 Sequential games and strategic moves

Life can only be understood backwards, but it must be lived forwards.

Søren Kierkegaard, 1843

IN MANY interactive situations, the main concern is for each player to figure out how others will respond to one's own moves and anticipate where their decisions will eventually lead. The games introduced so far have not been adequate at elucidating how a series of moves by each player produces an outcome, as players move at the same time. In a game where players make their decisions simultaneously without knowing the other player's decision, it is interactive only with their current thinking about the other's present move and vice versa. If actions are arranged in a determined temporal order, the sequence of play can be represented in an extensive form displaying a choice at every decision point. It is an important departure from simultaneous games represented in the form of a payoff matrix. In general, a strategy in an extensive form game is constituted by a sequence of actions referred to as moves.

In this chapter our main focus is on sequential games that allow the players to move one after another. In tacit bargaining, nonverbal cooperation on a particular solution can arise from a process based on a move and a countermove. The choices of later players are contingent upon the moves made earlier by the other player. This time difference in actions has a strategic effect, as illustrated in the extensive form of a game of Chicken and Battle of the Sexes. At the same time, a player may devise a move outside the defined actions of a given game to gain a strategic advantage. As revealed in the chapter's last section, a chance element needs to be incorporated in the event that players are not able to see all the prior moves made by other players.

Sequential games

In a sequential-move game, each player sees what their opponent has done before choosing their next action. Having the knowledge of the other players' previous move

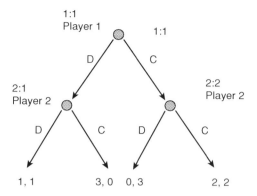

Figure 4.1 Prisoner's Dilemma in an extensive form

makes all the difference in a strategic interaction. The order of moves is encapsulated in a decision tree which represents how a game is to be played out over the course of a particular event (O'Neill 1999). A game tree reveals who moves when, and which sequences of actions result in what kind of outcomes.

Above is a game tree converted from a PD matrix (Table 2.3). All that has been changed from the original matrix is a sequential order. In a "tree" diagram, each move is specified at a branch point called a node; only one player makes a move at every node. The first move of the game begins from the root of the tree. The branches display the players' successive choices in a tree diagram. Each set of the two players' payoffs is shown at a terminal node descending from node 2.1 and 2.2 in Figure 4.1. The players need to foresee where an initial decision descends and eventually ends in reckoning their current best choice.

A set of connected nodes (for example, 1, 2.1 and 2.2) and branches constitutes, on its own, a subgame in an entire sequence of the play. The path selection between ordered nodes in the game tree shows the way in which the game progresses between different states. The complete plan of action embodies every contingency of the game even though some of them may never arise.

How could we solve the PD game in an extensive form? What would be the reasoning process for player 1, who moves first? If player 1 chooses C at node 1, the subgame descends to node 2.2 upon which player 2 has a choice between payoffs 3 and 2. She will choose a higher payoff 3, since every rational player will maximize her utility. That leaves player 1 with sucker payoff 0. The only way player 1 prohibits player 2 from suckering him is to play D at the initial node 1. As he goes down to node 2.1, player 2 also has to choose D to earn payoff 1 instead of 0. In Figure 4.1, not all paths are feasible to player 1, for the other player also takes part in selecting paths too, and she would not take an action that brings about a less-preferred outcome for her.

In the linear chain of reasoning for sequential games, players have to work out their opponent's response to their current move, and then formulate how they will respond in turn, and so forth. In making a decision at node 1, in Figure 4.1, player 1 needs to know what player 2 will do in the second node. Therefore, player 1 must put himself in her shoes and think as she would. In his evaluation of the game tree, he should not impose his own (wishful) thinking on her.

When a series of events progresses step by step, one move at a time, the principle behind determining each player's best strategy is to look ahead to all the feasible outcomes, then reason back to know what action to choose now (Heap and Varoufakis 2004). Each player has to compare the payoffs written at the terminal nodes, then look for a set of strategies that describe paths leading to one's favorite outcome. The task can be performed by imagining that the play starts at the end of the tree, then working backward.

Backward (or rollback) induction

A sequence of optimal actions at multiple nodes is determined by an iterative process which works from the end of the game back to the root. This procedure, called "backward induction," traces the sequence of plays. First, it considers the optimal strategy of a player who moves last in the game. Next, the optimal decision of the player moving second-to-last is identified, taking the last player's action as given. This process continues backwards in time all the way until all players' best actions are determined at every node on the decision-making path. By carrying out a backward induction process, players discard inferior choices, effectively deleting dominated strategies (Aumann 1995). More precisely, every abandoned strategy is dominated by a strategy selected at the node in question. Thus, backward induction in a finite game with a terminating end is employed to discover strategies for the player's maximum values.

Once a rollback induction is completed (using an iterative process), the optimal action for each node is specified, forming a Nash equilibrium for the original game (McCarty and Meirowitz 2007; Powell 1999). Actions on the equilibrium path maximize a player's payoff for the entire game. Each of these actions for optimization constitutes a Nash equilibrium of every subgame, called a subgame-perfect equilibrium. In a nutshell, what is optimal at each point in time is a NE for the particular subgame (O'Neill 1999; Powell 1990). Rational players remain on the equilibrium path identified via reiterated rollback induction.

On the next page is a real-world example. Immediately prior to the outbreak of World War I, France and Germany were competitively mobilizing their troops (Avenhaus 2008; McCain 2010). Their strategies and payoffs are presented both in a simultaneous game (Table 4.1) and in a game tree (in Figure 4.2). In the sequential game, France

Table 4.1 Troop mobilization

		Germany	
		Diplomacy (C)	Mobilize (D)
France	Diplomacy (C)	2, 2	0, 3
	Mobilize (D)	3, 0	1, 1

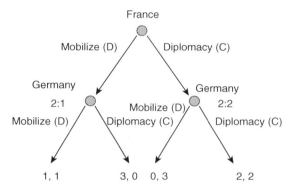

Figure 4.2 Troop mobilization

mobilized its troops, thinking that even if it did not do so, Germany would. The same reasoning process is applied to the German decision to mobilize, opting out of conciliatory diplomacy.

In calculating its best choice in a sequential game tree, France needs to anticipate where its initial decision might ultimately lead. Germany will get a higher payoff by troop mobilization than inaction at node 2. By taking the future German decision into account, France has to choose "mobilize"; as the subgame moves to the left branch, the game ends with punishment payoff 1 for each. In this game, the subgame-perfect equilibrium is "mobilize," resulting in the punishment payoff of war (McCain 2010). Unfortunately, "diplomacy" was not on the equilibrium path.

In the game described above, even if the French had not mobilized, Germany would have chosen to do so, given the benefit of a temptation payoff 3. To avoid a sucker payoff 0, in turn, the French mobilized their troops at the initial node. Whoever goes first, they will go down to the branch of mobilization (D), and the second player also always selects D regardless of what the first player does. Thus there is no first-mover advantage in a PD game. In such games as the Battle of the Sexes and Chicken, however, by moving first, a player earns a higher payoff than by going second. Even if the player moving first chooses D, the second player has a higher payoff by selecting C. These points are illustrated by Figures 4.3 and 4.4, converted from Tables 3.2 and 3.5.

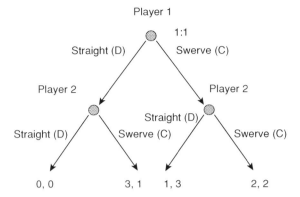

Figure 4.3 Game of Chicken

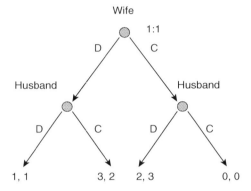

Figure 4.4 Battle of the Sexes

Equilibrium refinement

A game tree can help distinguish an equilibrium worthy of our attention from an unreasonable and not credible scenario (Harsanyi and Selten 1988). Table 4.2 shows a game matrix that describes actors' strategies in Colonial Struggle. The indigenous populations have two strategies, "rebel" or "not rebel." The colonial power's choice is either "retaliate" or "acquiesce."

Table 4.2 Colonial Struggle

		Colonial power	
		Acquiesce	Retaliate
Inhabitants	Not rebel	0, 4	0, 4
	Rebel	2, 2	−4, −4

In the matrix, if the colonized subject does not rebel, a colonial power earns a payoff 4. If colonies rebel, it is better for the colonial administration to acquiesce, giving the inhabitants more autonomy and power (payoff 2 each). If the colonialists retaliate with military action, both parties incur a loss of −4.

Two pure-strategy NEs exist in Table 4.2 for a simultaneous game. If a rebellion starts, the best response of the colonialist is to acquiesce. The best response of the colonized is to rebel if the colonialists acquiesce. On the other hand, if the colonialists are going to play "retaliate," it is better not to rebel. These two NEs in the matrix are not equal, however, since an equilibrium strategy of "retaliate" is supported only by a particular choice of "not rebel." In other words, retaliation is the best reply for colonizers, but only if a rebellion does not arise.

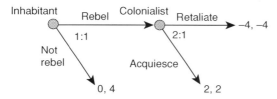

Figure 4.5 Colonial Struggle

In the tree diagram in Figure 4.5, retaliation is an equilibrium choice only in the counterfactual circumstance of no rebellion. Any claim by the colonial power that they will retaliate is not a credible threat. By the time the decision node is reached (about whether to retaliate or acquiesce), it proves irrational for the colonialists to choose "retaliate." Once a rebellion starts, it is better for the colonialist to acquiesce for a higher payoff at node 2. The strategy set of "rebel" and "acquiesce" is the subgame-perfect solution for a single play of this game. The other NE in the matrix ("not rebel," "retaliate") is not on the equilibrium path in a tree diagram. This pair can therefore be eliminated by backward induction.

When no particular strategy looks more plausible than all others, the problem becomes selecting the best one by ruling out other outcomes. One equilibrium is made more convincing than another by the effects of equilibrium refinements, which provide reasonable grounds for excluding some of the multiple NEs and focusing on others (Powell 1990). The subgame-perfect equilibrium identified in Figure 4.5 supports the refinement of NE, with a more demanding standard for solution.

In the deterrence game just discussed, we have discovered that "retaliate" is not a credible threat because it is in their best interest for the colonizers not to retaliate if the inhabitants actually choose to rebel. Given that "retaliate" is a threat colonialists would prefer not to carry out (should rebellion occur), is there any rationale to consider the strategy "retaliate"? Perhaps the mere threat of retaliation induces the rebellion to

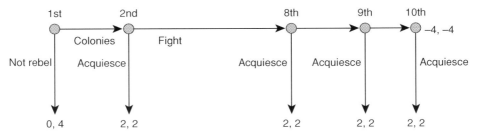

Figure 4.6 Colonial Struggle in a repeated game

be subdued, ensuring that the colonial power does not actually follow through on this threat. This might explain, in part, why the European colonial powers kept their empires so long in Africa and Asia.

A repeated game: Colonial Struggle

Now let us assume that a colonial power is anticipating a series of rebellions in ten different colonies. We have to examine the repetition of a single-event game tree over ten iterations. Each game is determined separately from and independently of the previous games. Once a rebellion starts in the first town, the colonialists have to decide either to acquiesce or to fight. If a rebellious group agitates the second town later, the colonialists have the same choice again. If no region starts to rebel, the colonial power earns payoff 4 times ten in all. In the event that the rebellion has already spread and the colonial power acquiesces in every incident, they earn payoff 2 each time. If we consider only a single game, "acquiesce" is always better than "retaliate." However, the colonial power might decide to fight a few games to deter the later entry of rebellion even though fighting with all of them is not feasible. Though it takes losses by at least retaliating against the first few rebellions, it creates a reputation as a retaliator with deterrence effects in the remaining colonies.

In the game tree in Figure 4.6, we can check first what will happen in the tenth game and move back to the previous games with the logic of backward induction. When the rebellion enters the tenth town, there is no need to fight since there is no one left to deter after this; it is the last play for the colonialist. The colonial power acquiesces. A threat to retaliate in the last game is not credible. The same reasoning is applied to the ninth game, inviting another rebellion. Continuing this way, every time a new rebellion emerges in the eighth and seventh game and so on, colonialists always acquiesce. The rollback tree proves that not fighting all the way down to the first game is a subgame-perfect equilibrium. Fighting as a means to discourage future rebellion is not regarded as the best response strategy in this game.

As history shows, some colonial powers (e.g., France) did not give up their colonies easily until the cost from fighting became unbearable. Once the purpose of threat is gone, the deterrence value becomes zero, with only a commitment being left to motivate fulfillment (Schelling 1960). In the case of failure of deterrence, it basically becomes a war of attrition. In contrast to France, other European colonizers (e.g., Britain) were engaged in undoing the commitment, thus removing the need to make a decision about fulfilling the threat involved in the second stage of the game when the rebellion starts.

By extending the above case to the prospect for an eternal war on terrorism, what if there is no last game from which backward induction starts? If there is not a last game – from which any benefit of a reputation for deterrence is gained – then does the subgame-perfect equilibrium tell us that retaliation is required against every terrorist group which emerges on the horizon? Once it starts, the war on terrorism may never end as long as the last terrorist remains.

In negotiating of a peace accord in Northern Ireland, the British government chose to deal with the Irish Republican Army (IRA) despite the appearance of its acquiescing to the terrorist organization. If a state has limited resources while facing multiple challenges, it might appease in one arena for conserving sufficient resources to deter others. This differential response creates a separating equilibrium, "appeasement" and "deterrence" (Treisman 2004). An appeasement equilibrium might arise when the stakes of conflict are low along with high costs of fighting.

Strategic moves

Strategic moves are designed to elicit certain behavior from the other side by changing the future course of events. A move can be added to incur an actual gain in payoff numbers by influencing others' acts. They are commonplace, sometimes implicit and other times more explicit. As players do not need to be passive, game specifications can be manipulated to produce a more advantageous outcome. What do many governments intend to achieve when they announce that "we will not negotiate with terrorists"? If a government declares "no more bailouts," could that stop big bankers from engagement in reckless lending and investment practice? Would the Chinese government pay serious attention to a US threat of trade sanctions contingent upon the former's refusal to correct its undervalued currency designed for trade advantage?

Strategic moves are basically actions taken to reorder the rules of later play to improve the existing payoff. In the situations above, extra moves (such as the declaration of one's intentions prior to the occurrence of a future event) are made to gain advantage by altering an opponent's action that otherwise would not occur. The payoffs are affected by creating or removing future moves as well as changing the order of moves. The choices

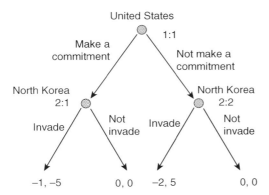

Figure 4.7 Defense of an ally

available to players can be modified to obtain a strategic advantage by inviting new players or strategic delegation of decision-making power to another source of authority or a mechanism beyond one's control (e.g., disapproval of a negotiated outcome by constituents or a system of automatic retaliation against an adversary's military attacks).

A larger game emerges with the addition of new subgames formed by a strategic move that creates different incentives or forces new actions. A higher subgame value can originate from effectively rearranging the existing rules regarding how a game is played. An actor ceases or reverses actions because the costs imposed by others will outweigh the gains of the original actions.

A strategic move entails some notion of commitment, whether it is real or fake. A declaration (e.g., announcement or plan) attains strategic influence if the audience interprets the act as altering payoffs. Figure 4.7 shows a historical example that demonstrates how a strategic move could have changed the course of history, preventing approximately two million deaths. In his January 1950 speech, the US secretary of state Dean Acheson omitted the Korean peninsula as part of the all-important US "defense perimeter." That was seen by North Korea and its backer, the Soviet Union, as a signal that the US government would not defend South Korea in the event of communist attack.

In Figure 4.7, a game tree shows different payoffs for each player with and without a US commitment to intervention. In the absence of the left branch descending from node 1, what North Korea has to compare is two payoffs, one from "not invade" and the other from "invade." If we consider only the right branch of the game tree descending from node 1, a subgame-perfect equilibrium path is "no commitment to intervene" and "invade." Given the higher payoff of invasion, it is obvious which strategy Pyongyang would choose. On the contrary, the announcement of the inclusion of South Korea in the defense perimeter in the Asia-Pacific could have prevented North Korean invasion, given its negative payoff −5 that is produced by the path of "commitment to intervene" and "invade." By making a commitment to the defense of South Korea, the United States moved prior to the North's action, producing a deterrent effect. The US action effectively conveys a selective subtraction of "invade" from North Korea's equilibrium strategies in the game tree.

Commitment

In general, commitment is employed to seize the first-mover advantage when one exists. Such a move usually entails being committed to a strategy that would not have been on an equilibrium path in the original game. In the above case, the incorporation of South Korea into the US defense plan could have produced an unconditional first-mover advantage. If the intention to intervene had been known prior to the game, the other actor could have taken the appropriate action. This commitment could have been made even irreversible and observable by forming a defense alliance. If the North Korean leadership believes its credibility, the move in effect reorders the game, altering the equilibrium outcome.

In order to have its desired effect, a commitment to take unconditional future acts should be regarded as credible (Hovi 1998). The credibility issue arises from a lack of incentive to act when the time comes. Strategic moves are not cost-free, often involving a course of action that a player does not want to fulfill. For instance, such a commitment, constituted by the formation of the NATO alliance and the presence of US troops in Cold War Europe, could have been accomplished only through grave mutual harm in the event of aggression.

Because a costly strategic move (e.g., automatic involvement in an ally's war) is not considered in the player's best interests, it has to be communicated credibly and ex-ante without leaving any doubt that it is binding and irreversible. In the above case, North Korea did not know of the US intention to intervene militarily, in that South Korea was not part of the announced US defense plan in 1950. In fact, the communists were struck by the surprise of an unexpected American move. An unobservable costly strategic move is always dominated, as illustrated by an unannounced plan of protecting an ally unknown to others.

Hostage negotiation

A commitment not to negotiate with terrorists has been popularly adopted by many governments. It is, however, a different matter whether terrorists take its credibility seriously. If a hostage is taken, should a government continue to insist on its never-negotiate policy under any circumstances? Does the commitment carry a strategic value such as a deterrence effect?

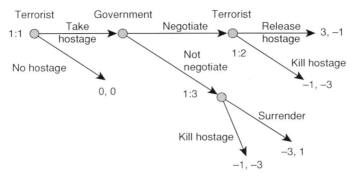

Figure 4.8 Negotiation with terrorists

The credibility of a strategic move can be checked by reasoning backward. In the rollback decision tree in Figure 4.8, not negotiating with terrorists presents two outcomes: terrorists take no hostages or kill them if they are taken. The best outcome for the government is nonoccurrence of hostage-taking and no negotiation. If hostages are taken (the upper branch from node 1), however, the payoff of negotiating −1 is higher for the government than letting the terrorists kill the hostages (payoff −3), assuming that the government cares about its citizens' lives (and it is feasible to accommodate the terrorist demand). As the best response strategy, negotiation is a subgame-perfect equilibrium.

The government commitment is derived from a blind, general principle statement; the target is not a specific group. It is unclear by whom the commitment is taken seriously. In the game tree in Figure 4.8, the motivation of the terrorists is assumed to be that killing a hostage does not provide a higher payoff than their goals being met (e.g., release of political prisoners). The game tree can be readapted to other types of terrorists with different motivations. Despite its staunch opposition to its bitter adversaries, the Israeli government has occasionally been engaged in the exchange of Hamas and Hezbollah prisoners for Israeli soldiers kept as hostages.

When decisions are made in sequence, freedom of choice sometimes produces a suboptimal outcome. One country may make an initial commitment, for example, to paying back a loan borrowed from another country unconditionally. Yet later when faced with economic hardships, it becomes a more popular move to rescind the obligation, as seen in Argentina during the 2014 debt crisis. The player has natural incentives to take advantage of the decisions reached by others in early stages (e.g., not paying the loan back). In a sequential PD game, the other player's earlier move (e.g., lending money) offers an advantage of seizing the second-mover advantage. An earlier commitment can be reneged upon later, creating a time-inconsistency problem.

When an actor's incentives change over time, their credibility becomes inherently questionable. Players in the early stages then want to shy away from decisions that create vulnerability to opportunism, with inferior results for everyone (e.g., not lending any money in the first place). In these circumstances, some freedom of choice can be given up before the game moves to the stage allowing reneging. The potential opportunist might voluntarily accept some sort of constraint that would block an opportunistic act at the later stage. A choice at stage 2 (i.e., an opportunity to cheat for a higher payoff) can be irrevocably relinquished at stage 1 (e.g., holding an agreement to an enforceable action). How could this be practically achieved? In the event of default, that has remained a core of difficulties in international debt talks, recently involving Greece. In injecting additional bailout money in July 2015, Eurozone creditors sequestered €50 billion worth of Greek public assets in a special Luxembourg privatization fund as collateral, since they doubted both the will and the capacity of Athens to pay back the loan and wanted ironclad guarantees.

A binding contract or legislation is often required to diminish or remove one's own freedom of future action if it becomes optimal to eliminate uncertainties for the other player to act. No credibility is attached to cheap talks that do not entail any cost. For instance, repeated bank bailouts by European and American governments despite public outcry are, in a large part, ascribed to cheap talks. Even though government officials or politicians may speak out loudly about no more bailouts, in the absence of legislation to prohibit it, the banks would think this unlikely. Once big financial institutions have accumulated huge losses after their engagement in attractive but risky loans, the government will once again rescue the banks with the excuse of preventing economic recession.

A player's best interest could be better served by changing his/her future payoffs in such a way that they have no choice but to bind themselves to things to be done at a later stage. The passage of legislation credibly removes the government's temptation to renege on its own policy (i.e., not rescuing banks from irresponsible investment) or to condone transgressions. It is often context specific to develop a device or mechanism for automatic implementation of the response. Negotiating ways to enhance credibility is up to local specifics (Dixit and Skeath 2004). A credibility device in international negotiation includes the establishment of an institution to monitor a treaty's implementation as well as sanctions and reward incentives.

Conditional response

Not every commitment is anchored to an unconditional move. The fulfillment of a commitment may be based on a conditional response. At the first stage, one player may declare that their future action is contingent upon the other player's completed action.

An example is the failed Israeli–Palestinian peace accord built into a step-by-step implementation of their agreement. While a conditional response guarantees an irrevocable fulfillment of the agreed actions, it can be left vulnerable to political opportunism. The 1995 Oslo peace accord contains too much latitude in accomplishing each side's obligations, for instance, compared with the 1978 peace accord between Egypt and Israel. The successive Israeli governments after Prime Minister Yitzhak Rabin's assassination reneged on the scheduled return of land to Palestinians. The phased implementation stipulated in the accord was used as a bargaining chip rather than a fixed schedule. To a significant degree, this contributed to gradual unraveling of a Palestinian commitment to their borders from extremist groups who launched attacks against Israelis.

Threats and promises

A negative threat or a positive promise is a strategic move intended to alter the other's action in the desired direction. It is intended to produce a conditional first-mover advantage in changing the beliefs and behavior of an adversary.

Promises

Through a promise, a player is committed to an action that rewards an opponent if she accedes. The opponent's payoff can be improved, being contingent upon her action. For instance, the United States declared the removal of economic sanctions and improvement in other aspects of its relations with Burma once its military regime released democratic movement leaders. Japan has been trying to weaken a ban on whaling at international whaling commission meetings by buying votes of landlocked countries with a promise of economic assistance. If successful, the promise has to be paid off by actual gifts or bribes. Since inducement often entails tangible cost, the amount of reward is kept to the minimum but large enough to have a desired effect.

Threats

By its response rule, threats punish others who fail to cooperate. As diplomacy of coercion, threats are intended to either deter an opponent's certain move or compel actions favorable to the party issuing the threat. The threat of punishment for noncompliance works differently between compellence and deterrence. Ordinarily, deterrence is intended to convince an adversary not to take an action challenging the status quo by manipulating the opponent's payoffs (O'Neill 1999; Powell 1999). It is intended to deter a rival's actions opposed to preserving the status quo. In successful deterrence, an opponent's expected utility of inaction outweighs the utility from challenge. The target of threat has to believe that gains from pursuing an action are offset by the imposed costs.

The status quo can be altered by compelling a rival's actions (Hovi 1998). A compellent threat comprises an action that hurts the opponent who does not accede. It is intended to alter the status quo by convincing a rival to make concessions or suffer the consequences. By its compellent move, country A may impose a cost on country B which has been committed to action Z. The compellent move succeeds if the imposed cost is greater than the gains from B's action Z. In a successful compellence, an opponent's expected utility for altering the course of action exceeds the expected utility of staying with the current one.

Compellent threat in bargaining

When each player acts tough, seeking one's preferred equilibrium in a set of all feasible, Pareto improving outcomes, threats may be adopted for inducing involuntary cooperation. Bargaining strength originates in the ability to alter that status quo unilaterally. Player A is able to establish a credible threat point if the imposition of penalties against noncooperation brings about improvement in A's utility, combined with a substantial setback for player B, relative to the status quo. At the onset of negotiations, perhaps, country A was to impose sanctions against country B unless B agreed to support A's most-preferred cooperative equilibrium. The involuntary cooperation nonetheless can generate welfare gains for both actors. B agrees to cooperate despite a setback if the utilities of cooperation are higher relative to the initial noncooperative status quo. Successful threats may account for an essential preference change (Bolt and Houba 2002).

Table 4.3 United States–China trade

		China Open	China Closed
United States	Open	7, 5	4, 8
United States	Closed	5, 2	3, 1

In its trade with the United States, China does not need any strategic moves, in that it has the best payoff in the existing equilibrium (see Table 4.3). It is the United States that wants to change the status quo and improve its payoffs by adopting a threat against China. The question is "will China cooperate?" The United States knows how the second stage will work by using rollback reasoning. This threat aims at an open market in China; the United States attempts to get its best outcome.

In a simultaneous-move game (presented in Table 4.3), a dominant strategy for China is "closed" combined with an open American market. However, faced with the US threat, can China still stick with its dominant strategy? In the two-stage game

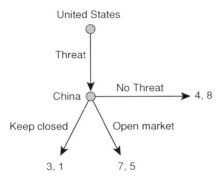

Figure 4.9 Credibility of the US threat in a trade dispute

in Figure 4.9, the United States moves first with the threat, then at the second stage China has a choice of keeping its market closed or cooperating by opening its market. If China opens its market, then the US threat has worked; its payoff improves to 7 and China has payoff 5, which is lower than the previous equilibrium. At the branch descending from node 2, if the United States carries out its threat after China refuses to cooperate, the US payoff is 3 with the Chinese 1. China has a higher payoff by cooperating than facing a closed US market.

If threat works, it does not have to be carried out. The threat, when deployed credibly, results in a change in China's action. However, China knows that the United States will not carry out its threat even if it is ignored. The post-threat payoff for the United States, 3, is lower than payoff 4 obtained when the Chinese market is closed while the United States is still open. The credibility of the threat is problematic. If China puts it to the test, the Unites States faces the temptation to refrain from fulfilling a threat that would cause mutual harm. The US threat of trade sanctions against China is not credible since the American government does not want the fallout.

In this case, bargaining power hinges, to a great extent, on the credibility of threats. The application of strategic moves entails ways to make a credible commitment and develop credibility devices. Being committed to "a firm final offer leaves the other party the last chance to avoid a mutually disastrous breakdown" (Chevalier-Roignant and Trigeorgis 2011, 30). However, a mere verbal insistence on firmness is not likely to be credible. In the above case, a credible threat could have been made by enacting a law that mandates the threatened action in response to Chinese noncooperation. Limiting one's freedom to give in by deliberately restricting one's options turns weakness into strength by forcing others to make concessions (Schelling 1960). In games of bargaining, greater freedom of action may plainly indicate readiness to concede to the other's demands. Tying negotiators' hands with strong mandates or instructions, while narrowing room for maneuverability, strengthens the ability to take a firm stance.

On its own part, China took its own strategic actions to defeat or disable the US attempts to use the threat. A threat can be eroded in small steps when a single game is broken into smaller ones. By salami tactics, a threat can become disproportionate, being cut up in multiple iterated games. As the best response to compellent threats, salami tactics delay their implementation. In repelling an American demand to adjust its currency valuation to a market mechanism, the Chinese adopted salami tactics. The Chinese acceded in principle but stalled in practice, pleading for necessary delays with the claim that its domestic financial market was not mature enough to cope with the upheavals of an international currency market. Simultaneously, the Chinese government took small steps in letting its currency value rise slowly and gradually. The creation of smaller games in a sequence allowed its currency value to rise incrementally on its own terms rather than being decided by market forces as desired by the United States. In spite of agreeing to the principle, the Chinese government took its own approach, undoing the American threat slice by slice. No matter how unsatisfactory to the US government and business, each extra small step has not created enough of a reason to pull out the big guns (e.g., heavy tariffs or trade sanctions).[1]

Short comments on strategic moves

In order to produce an optimal outcome, strategic moves have to rest on intersubjective interpretations such as the potential attacker's beliefs about the defender's likely response. The assessment may hinge on whether the expected costs exceed the expected gain. The accuracy of perceptions about the other's values and fears (e.g., expected punishment, or fruits of victory) is critical to the success of compellence and deterrence attempts. Threats and promises are both costly if they actually occur, so they might be left implicit. However, strategic moves have no teeth once it is known that their implementation is not in the player's best interests. Therefore, an incredible threat or promise is not a subgame-perfect equilibrium. A lot of intellectual skills and intuitions are involved in discovering or developing devices for credibility in a particular context.

Remember, too, that strategic interactions are a two-way street. Then what about proactively encountering a strategic move that seems likely? If a threat is looming, one may gain by searching for a corresponding action in advance, turning the threat into a less effective or less credible one. It is often more prudent to force the other player to make a promise. Given the role of communication in strategic interactions, credible deniability immunizes a player against an adversary's commitments and threats. Being unable to ascertain your opponent's strategic move is totally different from remaining ignorant. In the end, it remains an art to decipher how a given strategic setting opens or closes the possibility of the means (for instance, communication of threats, etc.) for realizing an actor's preferences.

Incomplete information

A decision-making environment for individual negotiators is fraught with uncertainty if players are unsure of what action their counterpart is taking. How a player should act becomes difficult in the absence of information about who or what the opponents actually are (i.e., their character, rationality, the set of strategies and preferences). What American negotiators said about their first encounter with North Koreans in 1993 is telling. "None of the US delegates in the front row had ever met a North Korean before. Robert Gallucci, the chief negotiator for the United States, was struck by the grim faces of the North Koreans... This negotiation was the first critical test in the most serious nuclear crisis the world had experienced since the superpower confrontation over Soviet missiles in Cuba some three decades earlier" (Wit et al. 2004, xiii).

When the payoff function for each player is not fixed at the outset, it contributes to an inability to cut through information sets in search for subgame-perfection. Insufficient information leads to the determination of the game's outcome by chance (Powell 1990). A player's choice becomes a chance move with known probabilities about the other player's type and payoff. The probabilistic analysis inherent in a Bayesian game spells out every information set that belongs to a particular type of player (e.g., hostile or friendly). The actions of each player type are identified in their strategy space. This framework, adopted by John C. Harsanyi, has served as a primary tool for modeling a Bayesian game which assigns probabilities to every node in a game tree (Harsanyi 1967).

When subgames do not contain complete information sets, an imagined player "Nature" represents a chance move. Thus "Nature" can become a new player in an incomplete information game. In a Bayesian game, a complete plan of actions exhibits every contingency attached to each player type. In determining payoffs for players, Nature randomly assigns a probability distribution to player types (O'Neill 1999).

United States–North Korea in 1994

When the United States faces North Korea, whose actual types and payoffs are unknown, Nature generates a player type space. In Figure 4.10, for instance, a set of all possible player types for North Korea comprises hardliners and moderates. The former's probability is p, which falls between 0 and 1. Then the latter's probability becomes 1–p. The probability distribution between the two North Korean player types determines the chance of the United States engaging with each type.

The game tree in Figure 4.10 features the situation faced by the United States in June 1994. The Clinton administration was demanding North Korean acceptance of full, thorough inspection of their nuclear facilities by the International Atomic Energy Agency prior to reaching an agreement. As the government in Pyongyang rejected the

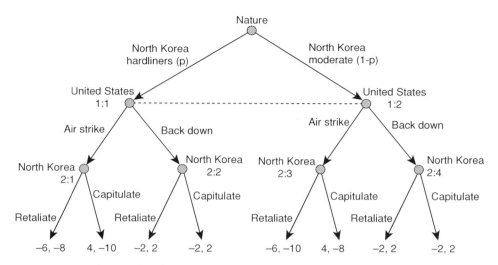

Figure 4.10 US threat with unknown North Korean types

demand, the US government threatened to strike the North's nuclear facilities. In return North Koreans made a counterthreat of retaliation instead of backing down. The White House National Security Council had to make a decision on whether to go ahead with the threatened air strikes or not. North Koreans had two choices, capitulation or challenge. The difficulty was that nobody, perhaps even including North Koreans, knew what the actual North Korean response might be in the event of the escalated crisis. For North Korean moderates, the payoff for backing down is higher than for challenging, but the preference order is reverse for the hardliners. Then the US payoff hinges on the probability of each North Korean faction winning their contest.

The game tree in Figure 4.10 represents the main features of an incomplete information game: the US payoffs are affected by the probability distribution between the two North Korean types. What is most important at the outset of the US decision is to compare the expected payoffs of air strikes and of backing down. If the United States decides to back down after making threat, North Koreans do not need to do anything. Their player types do not really matter in determining the US payoff −2. In contrast, the outcome is quite complex and unknown if the United States indeed moves to air-strike the North's facilities. The US payoff will differ according to which type of a player (a hardline or moderate North Korean faction) shapes the ultimate decision. This payoff quantification in Figure 4.10 is rough guesswork but the conclusions would not rely on the exact numbers; other numbers can substitute the above ones as long as the relative ranking of the outcomes remains identical.

In Figure 4.10, the game starts with an outside force (Nature) determining the North player type. The left branch of Nature's choice represents a hardliner North Korean type.

This leads to node 1:1 where the United States has to decide whether to go ahead with an air strike or not. Along the right branch of nature's choice, North Koreans are moderate. This leads to the lower node 1:2 where the United States has the same choice as the left branch.

A distinctive aspect of this game tree is that the United States does not know from which branch it makes a decision. To represent the incomplete information, the two US nodes are enclosed in the information set. The United States takes the same action at both nodes within the set. This decision has to be made in light of the probabilities that the game might be located at the one node or the other.

The left path in each subgame descending from nodes 2:1 and 2:3 indicates the North's retaliation. On the right path, North Korea backs down. Uncertain is an actual North Korean payoff. If the United States moves along the right branch descending from node 1:2 (occupied by the moderates), North Koreans will back down in response to the US action. The capitulation path has a higher payoff −8 than retaliation payoff −10 for a moderate North Korean type. As the North Korean moderates capitulate, thus, the US payoff becomes 4. On the other hand, the hardliner North Korean player type (descending from 1:1) will react differently to an American air strike. As the two paths separated from 2:1 show, retaliation has a higher payoff −8 than capitulation −10. Being encountered with the hardliner North Korean type, the US payoff becomes −6.

In the calculation of the expected utility for US air strikes, payoff −6 needs to be weighted by its probability of being in the left branch departing from node 1. On the other hand, US payoff 4 has to be weighted by playing in the right branch (i.e., identified with North Korean moderates). The air strike in the left branch will yield −6p. If the game is actually moving along the right branch (with probability 1−p), the expected US payoff from the attack is 4(1−p). The average payoff of US air strikes is thus −6p+4(1−p), which can be simplified to 4 − 10p. This payoff needs to be compared with the US backdown payoff −2. The US air strike has a higher payoff than backing down if 4 − 10p is greater than −2. It is formally represented as follows: 4−10p>−2, 6>10p, 6/10>p. This means that only if the probability of playing with North Korean hardliners is smaller than 6/10, the United States finds an air strike to be an acceptable risk.

Signaling and screening

In the above case, the higher is the value of p (i.e., the increased chance of playing with a hardliner type), the less the United States is inclined to air-strike North Korea. It is then advantageous for the North to make their adversary believe that they will turn out to be a hardliner player, responding to the attack militarily. In fact, the North Korean hawkish reaction caused panic in South Korea with the anticipation of an impending war (e.g., nose-dive of stock prices and depletion of food and other basic necessities in supermarkets, and the withdrawal of family members of American diplomats and troops from South Korea, etc.). Eventually the crisis was diffused by the intervention of former US president Jimmy Carter as a mediator. However, an uncontrolled escalatory spiral could have easily provoked another major war in the peninsula with the complete collapse of negotiation, even though the true intentions of both parties might have not been thus.

This incident raises the question, "is there a strategic advantage of information revelation by North Korea about its player type?" If player A knows that player B will infer her information from A's actions, then A attempts to think of B's possible interpretation and acts accordingly. By manipulating what B knows about A's abilities and preferences, A can have an effect on the game's equilibrium outcome. Information asymmetries naturally bestow an opportunity for the manipulation of beliefs in one's opponents using signaling messages.

In general, signaling contains clues by which one actor reveals their intentions to another. If asymmetric information creates difficulties in producing a mutually desirable equilibrium, selected information can be revealed truthfully through credible signaling (Banks 2013). In this situation, signaling is intended to help the other party identify the actor's true type. For instance, the release of Nelson Mandela in 2000 signaled the white South African government's seriousness about negotiation. Another well-known example is the visit of Egyptian President Anwar Sadat to Jerusalem in 1977 that signified his irrevocable commitment to peaceful settlement with Israel. True signals may involve an action that would not be desirable if the circumstances were inappropriate.

In instances when many players do the same thing (e.g., "cheap talk" in escalation), it creates a "pooling" equilibrium where observing an action reveals nothing about the true actor type. It might be considered optimal, by many actors, to respond to an adversary's threat with a counterthreat. Since everyone does the same thing, it does not remove uncertainty about the rival's "type" (e.g., more or less aggressive). The less informed player can use screening, which is a counterstrategy of signaling.

Below is a great example of how to elicit information or filter truth from falsehood. The "Judgment of Solomon" reveals a way to determine who is speaking the truth between the two women claiming to be a child's true mother. Once the verdict was announced – to cut the boy in two, giving each woman half of the body – his true mother pleaded with the king to give the other woman the live child while the liar happily welcomed the verdict. By forcing both women to reveal their true feelings and instincts, Solomon could instantly detect the baby's real mother. In this biblical incident, an equilibrium strategy for the true mother is to protect her child, while the liar's equilibrium was revealed by the exposition of jealousy but not true love for the child. As a less-informed player, King Solomon paid attention to what a better-informed player would do. In general, words alone do not suffice to convey credible information; actions often speak louder than words. In conclusion, signaling and screening games are played in changing beliefs of players.

Conclusion

In this chapter, an optimal strategy for the best outcome has been identified by a sequence of moves. In particular, "backward induction" provides a tool for identifying the best course of action by analyzing decision paths in a game tree. The later players may have an ability to condition their moves based on information about the other player's previous choices. Each move is shaped by the structure and rules of the underlying game. While plays are made within the system, the game can be modified by players.

One of the key aspects of a strategic move lies in restricting one's own choices in the way its employment serves the player's best interest. The existence of a predetermined order permits one player to prepare the right moves in strategic interactions. In a nutshell, each player's moves can be assessed in terms of their strategic effect with a time difference. In the next chapter, the logic of sequential games is applied to bargaining games where the players alternate their offers.

Note

1 Salami tactics could bring about the eventual possession of the entire piece by taking something bit by bit.

5 Bargaining games

> A man has free choice to the extent that he is rational.
>
> Thomas Aquinas

BARGAINING focuses on a possible division of gains from joint action through cooperation between two or more parties. Gains may include a peace dividend from the cessation of violent conflict, new revenue from joint ventures or partnerships, allocation of water in a shared river stream, etc. In bargaining games, a gain from cooperation is often called a surplus.[1] In spite of their common interest in the division of available gains, negotiators often differ over the precise partition, given a desire to attain as large a share of the "pie" as possible. The partition of a surplus constitutes bargaining activity in many negotiations. In this chapter, the principles of bargaining theory are derived from a game theory methodology. Bargaining theories help agents assess the relative value of different offers presented to them and also determine the relative value of their offers to be made to the other during negotiation.

In a two-person bargaining situation, for example, two individuals "have the opportunity to collaborate for mutual benefit in more than one way" whereas each individual has the desire to maximize her gain in bargaining, in solving the joint efficiency problem, bargainers have to search for a mutually beneficial but unique contract that determines "the amount of satisfaction each individual should expect to get from the situation" (Nash 1950, 155). In so doing, we ask such questions as how knowledge about the division, enforceable through a binding agreement, can lead to a reasonable share of the available gain. In this context, we are not so concerned about what people have to do to achieve those payoffs, in contrast with strategic settings where players have to act independently without being able to prearrange each other's actual behavior and its outcome. As will be seen in the section immediately following, this chapter departs from the previous ones, in which deviation from a Pareto optimal solution is derived from a situation in which individual incentives play a prominent role with diverging interests.

In this chapter, bargaining problems are constituted by both a payoff distribution and strategy coordination. In particular, the "rules of a bargaining game" have implications for whether and when an agreement can be reached and, if it can, what the likely division is. In a "take-it-or-leave-it" game, for instance, when one actor makes a demand for a share, the other has the sole choice of either its acceptance or rejection. In contrast, actors can make alternating offers throughout a sequential game. The chapter also examines how a player can improve the likelihood of striking an optimal agreement more quickly so as to minimize a costly delay. What factors are involved, for instance, in the division of values created in a contract between a developing country and a multinational corporation with different economic assets and technological abilities? What would be the conditions for parties to reach a negotiated settlement on the division of disputed territories rather than engaging in armed conflict?

Bargaining as a game

A bargaining solution may be interpreted as selecting a unique outcome in a set of all feasible payoffs. In classical bargaining theory, each participant is supposed to reach an agreement on a deal that satisfies such conditions as individual utility maximization as well as being Pareto efficient or group rational (i.e., at least one party becomes better off without any cost to the other). In choosing between possible agreements, two or more players have to sufficiently narrow down a "bargaining set" (Nash 1950), but they may still not have a single optimal strategy agreeable to all. Many deals can be individually rational with multiple Nash equilibrium solutions. For instance, if two friends divide $100 received for helping an elderly person, there are numerous possible divisions, all of which can produce gain to each player, as long as the share for any player is more than $0. The existence of multiple equilibria with varying payoffs for each player compels the players to negotiate on which equilibrium to target. The payoff distribution directly involves an equilibrium-selection problem.

A theoretical analysis of bargaining has been developed through cooperative game theory that sheds light on a general characterization of the equilibrium division between players (Carmichael 2005; Chatterjee 2014; Muthoo 1999). In a nutshell, cooperative game theory sheds light on joint efficiency in payoff distribution, by asking how value should be divided, rather than specifically featuring the process of decision-making (Kibris 2010). In a cooperative game, players are permitted to directly communicate and, most important, "negotiate before the game is played about what to do in the game. It is standard to assume that these negotiations culminate in the signing of a binding agreement [on a joint plan of action]. Under these conditions... the precise strategies available in the game will not matter very much. What matters most is the preference structure of the game, since it is this structure that determines what contracts are feasible" (Binmore 1996, xiii). It is contrasted with noncooperative game theory, covered in the previous three chapters, which examined what strategies rational players are expected to choose; with a lack of collaboration, the players' (independent) actions explain the terms of the agreement or any failure to strike one. In a noncooperative game, the emergence of any agreement has to be self-enforcing. As cooperative game theory asks how value is to be divided, its premise focuses on a particular strategy to be developed to exclude jointly inefficient or inferior outcomes (i.e., dominated payoffs). Even though the particular joint strategy may, or may not, produce enforceable contracts, it is still worth treating the bargaining outcome as the same solution attained by an impartial arbitrator (Heap and Varoufakis 2004). This is, of course, based on the proposition that no one is expected to get into a binding agreement unless it is supposed to be fair and increasing value to oneself.

Nash solution

The bargaining solution over the partition proposed by John Nash (1950, 1953) describes the principles of cooperative bargaining with a fairly simple formula that picks out a unique pair of utilities for a maximization problem. Nash's bargaining solution (serving as the origin of formal bargaining theory) is a concept unrelated to a Nash equilibrium (covered in Chapter 3) except that both concepts originate from the same person. In the division of the pie, Nash's bargaining theory identifies a method to determine "the amount of satisfaction each individual should expect to get" or "how much it should be worth to each of these individuals" (Nash 1950, 155). According to Nash (1950), a classical bargaining problem is illustrated both by a set of all feasible payoff outcomes for each of the parties and by the disagreement point. For the bargaining outcome to be individually rational, each bargainer's utility should be better off than what s/he is able to obtain upon the breakdown of negotiations. It is called the *disagreement* (or threat) *point* – the default payoff for each of the parties in the event of the failure to reach a mutually acceptable division. Thus a set of all feasible payoffs should encompass at least one point that all the players favor over the disagreement point (Muthoo 1999).

Suppose Italian and French companies decided to collaborate to develop a package product that could increase their profit through a joint venture. Individually, the Italian company makes a $2 profit per unit of soap and towel sold together; the French company has $4 profit per bottle of exotic perfume on its own. They can increase their combined profit to $12 by selling a joint package of their products; the extra $6 profit per set is a newly created profit through the joint venture; now they have to negotiate over how their joint profit will be split up.

First, the bargaining solution has to define a set of possible utility pairs obtainable through agreement with the elimination of irrelevant alternatives (i.e., the division not to be used). The solution has to give each player at least her disagreement utility. In considering individual rationality, the utility pair selected for the solution should not be inferior to the disagreement point for any bargainer (Muthoo 2000). The amounts $2 and $4 (the profit they can make alone) are what each company would still get if they chose to walk away from the deal. Once we subtract each company's original profit margin, $6 is available to split. As long as each of their claims to the new surplus does not exceed $6, any combination of shares is a Nash equilibrium. An agreement is justifiable if its result is better than a party can get without a negotiated agreement by acting unilaterally. Theoretically, a feasible set of contracts include such divisions as $5/$1 and $4/$2 as well as a claim to the entire new surplus by one of the players. Any of these sets is a Nash equilibrium, in considering that no one can increase their return by unilaterally switching their strategy.

The perfume company may argue that since their original profit margin of $4 was twice as much as the soap company's $2, their gain should be twice as well; accordingly the new surplus of $6 should be divided as $4 and $2. Should a perfume company's claim to two-thirds of the newly generated surplus be accepted by the other company? Would it be more fair to split the newly created $6 surplus down the middle?

A division rule and bargaining power

By adopting a split-the-difference rule, Nash division suggests an even share of the remaining pie above a disagreement point. In this example, the players divide equally the new surplus of $6 over what each makes on their own. This division is based on the premise that both players have the same bargaining power. It is largely defined by the capacity to obtain a maximum possible share of the joint benefits derived from any agreement. More specifically, its amount is usually decided by a player's inefficient outcome derived from a failure to agree.

In Nash's proposal, a solution for the division of gains relies exclusively on the relative strength of parties' bargaining position. The surplus (above the total of the players' disagreement points) should be divided in the same proportion as their bargaining power. The Nash solution attributes fairness in distributive bargaining to some form of equal treatment, but does not necessarily presuppose absolutely equal amounts if different opportunities, abilities or needs call for departures from equality (Bolton 1991). The surplus benefits can also be allocated proportionally according to the worth of each party's contribution to the cooperative venture.

If the agents have asymmetric bargaining positions, a player's share becomes larger with his/her increasing disagreement point, and the other's decreasing disagreement point. It is often advantageous to enhance one's own disagreement payoff while causing harm to the opponent's. Each player may adopt a minimax strategy in order to change disagreement payoffs by inflicting loss on the opponent as much as possible should they choose to leave the negotiation table (Muthoo 1995b). If threats to exercise an outside option are adopted to manipulate an opponent's disagreement point, then a separate game is constructed to show each player's threat payoff.

If one of the players can easily quit bargaining and take up some "outside option," her best alternative to a negotiated agreement goes up. In the above example, one way for the soap company to exercise its outside option is to set up an improved deal with a different perfume company for a joint venture. If the offer is greater than $3 profit per package (which is available through the existing deal), then the soap company's threat to form an alliance with another company is credible. Faced with this situation, all that the perfume company ought to do is immediately match the outside offer by giving a penny more. If the outside option is smaller than the $3 gain per package for the soap company, then it has no impact on the agreed profit sharing. Bargaining power correlates to the attractiveness of a player's outside option. However, the other negotiator would not be fooled by empty threats or promises that will not be carried out. A gain from cooperation does not exist if all the outside options are more beneficial to each respective player than cooperation.

Shapley value

Allocation becomes complex with the involvement of more than two players. As each player bargains with more than one other player, each subgroup works together to create or capture a certain amount of value through coalition formation (Muthoo 1999; Hart 1985). The payoffs to the players depend on the way a coalition is formed. Imagine the division of $60,000 international aid among three ethnic groups A, B and C in a majority-rule decision with the requirement of only a two-player majority in the division. Suppose the game starts with A offering B the even split of the total amount between the two. Now being left out, C proposes a split of $40,000 and $20,000 in B's favor. Before B takes the offer, now A suggests even split to C, $30,000 per each. Obviously that is an improved deal for C. As this process can continue, every division opens a door for at least one of the players to make a deal that is more attractive than the current one. What type of allocation will provide a reason for a subset of players not to abandon the coalition?

One of the best-known solutions is the Shapley value, which determines an allocation of payoffs to each player in a coalition (Barron 2013; O'Neill 1994). As another cooperative concept, it seeks a unique solution like Nash's bargaining theory. In developing a set of all undominated coalitions, "we must consider the payoff to each player individually rather than the total payoff to the coalition" (McCain 2004, 195). In the axiomatic solution set, no player could become better off by switching to a different coalition structure without making some other player worse off. A player is offered a payoff representing the average of the player's contribution to each coalition that could be formed.

How much of the total pie each player deserves depends on how much value each new member adds to the coalition. The value created by the addition depends on who is already in the coalition. In the above case, only the second player to join increases the value of the coalition. If we add each player to the grand coalition in every possible order, one third of the time, each player becomes a second member to be added. The available money is divided into three equal portions.

Sequential bargaining models

As seen above, pure cooperative bargaining theory sheds light solely on an outcome of division through the simultaneous demands or offers but does not specify a precise timeline of offers and counteroffers; this question requires the methodology of noncooperative games where the solution is found at an equilibrium formed by the agents' strategies. Contrary to Nash's cooperative model, a sequential bargaining model proposes or hypothesizes a specific process in which players make an offer or respond at a given time. Its advantage lies in identifying any existing agreement point and a (sequential) movement for its attainment. The logic provides more explicitness and precision in figuring out costs in the pursuit of preferences (Powell 2002). As we shall see later, the timing of players' choices along with the details of the ordering are critical to determining a bargaining game's outcome.

Ultimatum game

In an Ultimatum game, one player moves first to propose a division of the sum; then the other player is given an option to either consent to or refuse this proposal. The amount is distributed according to the proposal only if the second player agrees to the split. If the second player vetoes the suggested division, neither receives anything. It represents a "take-it-or-leave-it" form that is the simplest sequential-move bargaining game. Since only one proposal is made in this primitive form of bargaining game, reciprocation is not an issue. No matter how arbitrarily the split was made, the only choice for the second player is to decide between something and nothing. Whatever is more than nothing is better. Self-interested responders are expected to take any positive offer whatsoever. A proposer who anticipates this is supposed to make the smallest offer possible (Camerer and Fehr 2004). A model of a take-it-or-leave-it offer has been applied to a choice between bargaining and fighting (e.g., Banks 1990; Fearon 1995; Filson and Werner 2007).

Suppose state S makes an ultimatum offer in a territorial dispute; a rival state R has the choice only of accepting or rejecting it by fighting. How much should S demand?

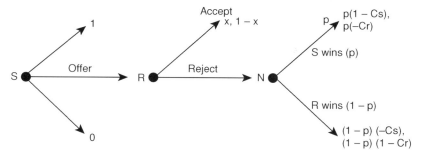

Figure 5.1 An Ultimatum game: a choice between bargaining and fighting

How much is appropriate for R to accept? Before they make a decision, the players need to know the utility attached to the choice between a military contest and bargaining. The terms of the settlement are decided by the probability of winning the fight, its gain and costs.

In Figure 5.1, the range of possible agreements is represented by the interval between 0 and 1. The Ultimatum game starts with S making demand x to change the status quo, leaving 1 − x for R. If the demand x is rejected, then the outcome is determined by the war. "Nature" becomes a third actor to determine the fight's probabilistic outcomes. Here p indicates S's winning probability; thus 1 − p is a probability of S's losing and R's winning. The two players' costs of war are represented by Cs and Cr.

S's expected utility is calculated by adding up both payoffs of winning and losing the fight. Thus S's utility from the fight is p (1 − Cs) + (1 − p)(−Cs). If we calculate the equation, p − pCs − Cs + pCs = p − Cs. In the same manner, R's expected utility is calculated to produce p(−Cr) + (1 − p)(1 − Cr) = 1 − p − Cr. To avoid the fight, the ultimatum offer to R should be at least equal to their disagreement point of the fight. Thus 1 − x has to be the same as 1 − p − Cr; then S's demand should not exceed more than x = p + Cr. In reality, information about the outcome of fighting between potential belligerents is often unknown; without knowing the cost of fighting, a potential attacker does not know what to ask for without provoking war (Powell 2006). In addition, in misperceiving the capabilities of an opponent, a player might mistakenly initiate a fight (Fearon 1995). Information asymmetries provide incentives to misrepresent one's capabilities for obtaining better bargaining outcomes.

Alternating offers

A standard process of alternating offers is modeled as haggling; bargaining interactions between two players are represented by a series of "offers" and "counteroffers" before one of them is acceptable. The utilities are proportional to the values of the object to each party. The possible consequences of persistence in making an extreme proposal that is bound to be rejected by the other are a permanent standoff or costly delayed agreements. If the settlement is considered less valuable with the passage of time, demands represent compensation for the deferred payoff and waiting (associated with opportunity costs). These examples include concessions made after the occurrences of trade wars, labor strikes and boycotts as well as a protracted peace settlement process in a civil war. A bargaining game of alternating offers shows the value lost that could have been easily shared.

Finite-horizon version

The desired properties of a solution for a repeated bargaining game with many offers can be identified by game-theoretic methodology. In modeling the bargaining procedure in a sequential game, a history of offers and counteroffers constitutes a unique equilibrium sequence. A finite number (N) of offers in sequential bargaining was modeled first by Ingolf Stahl (1972). In searching for the subgame-perfect equilibrium (SPE), we can use backward induction, starting from the final offer.

For simplicity, assume N = 2. At t = 2, the game is about to end after player B makes a final take-it-or-leave-it offer. As player A will accept any positive split, B can offer close to nothing. What does this imply for A's initial offer? A knows that if B rejects A's offer at t = 1, B can get almost the entire pie in the next period. Thus, to get his offer accepted, A must offer B most of the pie. In the N = 2 offer sequential bargaining game, the unique subgame-perfect equilibrium produces an immediate split by which B has almost everything. The above game can be extended to increasingly more counteroffers (Bolton 1991; Levin 2002). We can search for a subgame-perfect equilibrium offer for any number of periods.

Diminishing returns with decay

Theoretically speaking, players can reject the present offer for a more favorable division in the next time period. As the surplus value can be divisible in many ways, the two sides may decide to wait for the other to back down before reaching an agreement that is as favorable as possible. With every rejection, however, the prize generally shrinks by a certain proportion. As the delay in reaching agreement in each round has costs, the ultimate payoff depends on how much the initial offer shrinks in the next round once each offer is rejected (Heap and Varoufakis 2004). Costly delayed agreements can be avoided by searching for an equilibrium where an offer is accepted immediately.

Below is a case in which, every time an offer is rejected, the utility of the same pie shrinks by a certain proportion. Two tribal groups called here A and B in a famine-stricken village are dividing $10,000 food aid available to them (represented by s in the calculation below). In the division of the surplus, each player takes turns making alternating offers, with one offer per round in the back-and-forth bargaining. Each makes one offer a day. If it is rejected, the other player makes a counteroffer the next day. The entire game cannot have more than 10 rounds represented by t = 1, 2, 3 ... 10. In fact, $1,000 of the food supply decays at every round when an agreement is not reached. If the two sides do not reach an agreement in ten days, all the food donated has to be discarded. Suppose player A makes an offer to split the total surplus at t = 1; if B rejects it, the total sum available (s) drops by value (d_1) $1,000. When B proposes a counteroffer at t = 2, the remaining surplus to divide is s − d_1 ($10,000–$1,000). In the second round, B has to offer a split of $9,000, the reduced value of food aid left after the first round. If A refuses B's counteroffer, the original total drops by another $1,000 to s − d_1 − d_2 ($10,000–$1,000–$1,000). If this series of an offer-and-counteroffer process continues until, eventually, say, after ten days, it becomes s − d_1 − d_2 − ... − d_{10} = 0. The game is over.

In the solution to a bargaining game where two players split a fixed amount, the rollback equilibrium of a shrinking pie can be searched for, as in other sequential move games. Here the principle of looking ahead and reasoning back decides the equilibrium shares (Powell 2002). So we start our analysis at the end to look for the full strategy behind the equilibrium. Rollback procedures help us find out how much the total value shrinks in a sequence in which costs arise from the elapse of time without a specific contract. If haggling goes on to the bitter end with a refusal at every single step, nothing will be left. If the negotiators use the foresight derived from rollback reasoning, the actual agreement on the distribution of the prize is thus immediate on the very first offer, avoiding costly delays at the later stages.

Therefore complete contingent plans of action suggest what each player would do if the game reached a later stage. If the game has reached the point (where only d_{10} is left), player B has an opportunity to make a final offer that keeps most surplus d_{10} ($1,000) to herself, leaving close to 0 for player A (similar to an Ultimatum game). If A is making an offer at t = 9, d_9($1,000) + d_{10}($1,000) are left. A knows that he has to offer at least d_{10} to B, otherwise B will refuse to accept the offer and take the game to round 10 where B can get that amount. A does not need to offer any more than B's share at t = 10. So in round 9, A offers a split where he keeps d_9 and leaves d_{10} for B. Then in round 8 when d_8($1,000) + d_9($1,000) + d_{10}($1,000) remains, B offers a split where B keeps (d_8 + d_{10}) and gives d_9 to A. In continuing with this logic, the game rolls back to the beginning. If B refuses A's first offer at t = 1, the total available surplus drops by d_1 to $9,000; the reduction by $1,000 is the surplus that could have been awarded to the other player (A), had B not rejected A's offer in the very first round of the game.

In this game, "diminishing returns" are reflected in the surplus value lost with the passage of time. More surplus is destroyed by each player's refusals. If we add up the entire amount that could have gone to the other player in the absence of another player's refusal, it becomes the equilibrium share of this alternating-offer game (Dixit and Skeath 2004; Muthoo 1999). The initial offer by A would give $5,000 ($d_2 + d_4 + d_6 + d_8 + d_{10}$) to B, whereas he keeps $5,000 ($d_1 + d_3 + d_5 + d_7 + d_9$). This offer should be immediately accepted by B. She cannot get more than that amount even if she rejects A's initial offer and moves the game to a later round.

Impatience

Even if a player is free to make a counteroffer in lieu of accepting a particular offer, the future value of the possible benefit to waiting decreases. Moreover, the game may end between now and the next offer. Eagerness to settle may derive from fear that the process will break down due to a sudden emergence of adverse conditions or unmanageable exogenous events. The risk of not receiving a payment may in fact lower the marginal utility derived from the continuous haggling. The longer one holds out, the larger the chance of receiving the prize might be, but the costs are bigger if the other side does not back down. Facing the possibility of such an occurrence may generate incentives for early compromise. Intuitively speaking, "a bird in the hand is worth two in the bush." The more risk-averse a player is, the more anxious she is to minimize the risk of collapse, with a smaller net surplus vis-à-vis her counterparts (Muthoo 2000).

The eagerness to reach an agreement for a smaller share is derived from valuing present benefits higher than distant future ones, subjectively weighting a current advantage over possible future losses. We need to find ways to assess a future value in terms of its current equivalent. A player is considered impatient if she prefers to achieve agreement sooner rather than later by attaching less importance to the future relative to the present. Impatient players, who are more eager to settle, are penalized by receiving a smaller share (Muthoo 1999; Powell 1999). Here a small reward now is valued as equal to a greater gain later. Discounting the future means placing a value on future receipts that is lower than on the present receipt of an equal sum.

The relative degrees of players' impatience determine the partition of the net surplus (Muthoo 1999). If both players value time equally with the same degree of impatience, they split the surplus evenly. If a player can hold out longer (with lower costs for noncooperation), she is more likely to get her preferred outcome in bargaining. If one player is eager to receive essentially any share of the surplus for striking a quick deal, all of the surplus would go to the patient player.

The levels of "impatience" translate into a different cost of waiting. The loss of a proportion of value is called a discount rate. The smaller the waiting cost, the lower a player's discount rate on the terms of the agreement. Those with high discount rates are willing to accept lower value, as they want quicker payoffs without deferring gratification. In negotiations over a debt bailout, for instance, a cash-stricken country has more eagerness to strike a deal, increasing their discount rate (e.g., Greece's willingess to accept all the harsh terms demanded by Eurozone governments in return for immediate financial relief). Given a lower discount rate, on the other hand, international creditors easily dictate their stringent conditions.

If impatience is represented by a rate of return "r," $1 (to be obtained) in the next round is equivalent to $1/(1 + r)$ immediately offered. Here "r" indicates the rate at which a gain shrinks when it is earned now. If r is 0.05, tomorrow's $1 becomes today's $0.95; the discount value (i.e., the current amount of a future value discounted at a predetermined rate) is $1/(1 + 0.05) = 0.95$. The initial offer should be less than when accepted a period later.

The example below shows how patience confers bargaining power. A multinational agricultural firm is selling grain to a poor country with a dire need to feed its population. Since the country cannot pay a full market price for grain, the purchasing price is subsided by a UN agency. The external funding led to $10,000 surplus after covering the payment to producers, storage and transportation costs. The country now has to negotiate with the grain sales firm to divide the surplus value. Here we assume that the two players are in identical situations except for their different impatience rates.

For simplificity, we will use here $1 as a unit of comparison in finding out how the entire sum will be divided. For the company (identified as player A), let us assume that $1 in the next round is considered worth $1/(1 + 0.10)$ now; the country (denoted player B) considers $1 in the immediate future round equivalent to current $1/(1 + 0.20)$. B is willing to accept a smaller amount to get it sooner. Thus the rate of impatience will eventually be converted into unequal equilibrium payoffs in bargaining (Muthoo 1999).

The actual deal can be struck on the first round if one player's initial offer is accepted by the other; the question is figuring out how large that offer should be. If A starts an alternating offer process, a is the amount that A takes, with 1 − a for B. If B makes the first offer, b is what B gets, leaving 1 − b for A. How big should a and b be?

Rollback reasoning works to elucidate an equation that figures out the value of a and b. The equilibrium offer should be the same as the actual deal that goes through on the first round. When A makes the offer, the value of offer for B (i.e., 1 − a) should be greater than or at least equal to the current value of what B will get in the next round. The present value of the next round's b is $b/(1 + 0.20)$; thus 0.83b is what B can get by waiting to make his counteroffer, so 1 − a must be at least 0.83b; thus a = 1 − 0.83b. Otherwise B will reject the offer in favor of what he knows he will get in his turn to make the offer. With an equilibrium share, B cannot get any more even if B rejects A's offer and makes a counteroffer.

If B starts an alternating-offer process, A's share is $1 - b$. By rejecting the offer, A will get a in the next round. The current value of a is $a/(1 + 0.10)$. B knows that she has to offer A at least the equal amount to $0.91a$; that means that $1 - b$ has to be as good as $0.91a$. Thus $b = 1 - 0.91a$. The two equations $a = 1 - 0.83b$ and $b = 1 - 0.91a$ now permit us to solve for a and b.

$$a = 1 - 0.83(1 - 0.91a), \; a - 0.83(0.91)a = 0.17, \; a = 0.71$$
$$b = 1 - 0.91(1 - 0.83b), \; b - 0.91(0.83)b = 0.09, \; b = 0.38$$

Each of these amounts is the payoff for the player who makes the first offer; when A makes the first offer, A receives 0.71 with 0.29 for B. If B makes the first offer, she has 0.38, leaving 0.62 for A. The main difference in the payoffs represents mainly unequal rates of impatience (Dixit and Skeath 2004). As the shares are governed by the relative cost of delay, the more impatient player gets a lot less than the patient one. The proportion of A's shares to B's is almost 2:1. Relatively higher patience bestows greater bargaining power with a larger share of the surplus. In negotiating for the 1978 Camp David Accord, by refusing to make an easy concession on the return of the Sinai, Prime Minister Menachim Begin of Israel was more successful in achieving his objectives than his counterpart President Anwar Sadat of Egypt.

Rubinstein bargaining games

The above discussion can be put in a more systematic context to find an equilibrium in alternating-offer bargaining on infinite horizons. Nash backward induction cannot be applied to the unlimited sequence of alternating offers and counteroffers (as it needs a last stage at which to anchor itself before unfolding backwards). This problem was solved by Ariel Rubinstein's bargaining model with infinite alternating offers in the early 1980s.

Returning to our earlier example (in Chapter 2) about the partition of a fruit pie between two children, here we consider that both want a larger slice, but dislike delay. In addition, one child wants to eat the pie sooner and has a higher discount rate than the other. While the two children come up with many different divisions through infinite rounds of bargaining, a search for a unique partition of the pie of size 1 focuses on a perfect equilibrium. Each child demands an amount corresponding to a perfect equilibrium share in a subgame; the other child accepts any demand which does not exceed that amount.

The haggling cost is directly related to bargaining power. A player's bargaining power grows by being more patient relative to the other negotiator. Future receipts or payments are discounted to have them immediately (Rubinstein 1982). If a discount rate

Table 5.1 Subgame-perfect equilibrium of infinite-horizon games

Time	A's share	B's share
t = i, offer by A	$1 - \partial_B(1 - \partial_A x)$	
t = i+1, offer by B		$1 - \partial_A x$
t = i+2, offer by A	x	

is denoted as r, the present discounted value of the next round's 1 is $\partial = 1/(1+r)$; ∂ ranges between 0 and 1. If a player discounts a future value heavily, ∂ is low with high r. If a player regards future value highly vis-à-vis the current one, ∂ is high with low r.

Bargaining interactions can be captured until an agreement is struck (Fudenberg and Levine 1983; Sutton 1986; Yildiz 2011). Table 5.1 shows offers and counteroffers as well as the history of their sequence in the subgame. Payoffs are denoted by the discounted sum to which a player is entitled at each stage. In Table 5.1, x is a fraction of the pie that A asks for in bargaining round t_{i+2}. In solving this game, we need to know how much x should be by calculating a unique perfect equilibrium partition. No matter where it starts, the structure of this subgame is always the same, besides a rescaling of payoffs, in the way the maximum share which A can attain in any perfect equilibrium of the game does not exceed x. In the table, t = i represents the fact that the subgame can start in any round of the original game. Discount factors for the two players are respectively ∂_A and ∂_B.

A unique solution is produced by A's desire to take as large a share as possible and B's ability to make an attractive counteroffer. When A makes an offer at t = i + 2, A and B receive their respective equilibrium shares, x and (1 − x). In the preceding period t = i + 1, B has to offer A the same value of x that is obtainable at t = i + 2. $\partial_A x$ is the discounted value of x that A can receive in the following round. Any offer less than that will be rejected by A. Then B's share in this round should be at least $1 - \partial_A x$. It is also a minimum share that B accepts in any perfect equilibrium of the game.

Regarding how much A ought to offer B at t = i, B will surely reject any offer that is smaller than $\partial_B(1 - \partial_A x)$ that is a discounted value of $(1 - \partial_A x)$ at t = i + 1. Then A can have at most a share of the pie equivalent to $1 - \partial_B(1 - \partial_A x)$. In fact, this should be the same as x that is A's share in any perfect equilibrium of the game. In equilibrium, a player makes the same offer whenever she has to make an offer. It is mathematically represented by the equation: $x = 1 - \partial_B(1 - \partial_A x)$; $x = (1 - \partial_B)/(1 - \partial_A \partial_B)$.

It is an equilibrium share for A in any subgame for the division of the pie. Because B receives share 1 − x, her payoff is $\partial_B(1 - \partial_A)/(1 - \partial_A \partial_B)$. B accepts A's offer without delay, for it is the same as an amount corresponding to a perfect equilibrium at any stage of the game. The shares received in this solution are uniquely defined, reflecting on Perfect Equilibrium Partition (Baird *et al.* 1994; Powell 1999; Rubinstein 1982; Sutton 1986). No player can make a profitable deviation, in one single period, from this equilibrium strategy by holding out.

The equilibrium partition ultimately depends on the players' relative bargaining powers – as captured by relative differences in discount values (i.e., degrees of impatience) – and not so much on absolute magnitudes. In the above case of pie division, it is intuitively appealing that the more impatient one child is, the smaller share she receives. In a game-theoretic language, A's payoff $(1 - \partial_B)/(1 - \partial_A \partial_B)$ is proportionately enlarged with ∂_A and lessens with larger ∂_B (Muthoo 1995a). The share for a player increases along with her patience level (i.e., a lower discount rate), but decreases with her opponent's growing patience.

Bargaining power is associated with the cost of delays in agreement. In fact, the difference in discount values reflects the relative magnitude of the players' costs of haggling (Heap and Varoufakis 2004). One's bargaining power increases with her smaller costs of haggling and her rival's larger cost. In a dispute over the prices of international commodities, for example, an importer's bargaining power is enhanced by having a larger inventory, which reduces the cost of haggling. On the other hand, the exporter's haggling cost decreases with a larger storage facility, to keep their products for a longer period. The exporter's greater ability to keep haggling lowers the importer's bargaining power. In this case, bargaining power is also increased by unity within each party, financial reserves and reputation for toughness (which contribute to a lower discount rate).

With an identical discount set $\partial_B = \partial_A = \partial$, one player takes $1/(1 + \partial)$, leaving $\partial/1 + \partial$ for the other player. In the event that ∂_A equals ∂_B, the first-mover's advantage becomes the only asymmetry. Whoever goes first has an advantage in considering $1/(1 + \partial) > \partial/(1 + \partial)$ and $0 \leq \partial \leq 1$. However, as ∂ gets closer to 1, this first-mover advantage goes away, since each gets half. If both parties are equally patient, then they are supposed to divide up the net surplus by half. Its basic solution – similarly situated players divide the surplus evenly between themselves (Baird *et al.* 1994; Muthoo 1999).

If discount rates for both players are 0 ($r_A = r_B = 0$), then the players do not incur any costs by haggling. In this scenario, no one is truly bothered by when to settle. The existence of many subgame-perfect equilibria in a continuum allows each player to continuously insist on or demand terms that are most favorable to her. When neither player is concerned about the time required to strike an agreement, then nothing prohibits them from haggling. Since the costs of a waiting game (in the hope of more favorable future conditions) are less than immediate concessions (being impatient with the status quo), the negotiators are not inclined to make a compromise to produce a deal (Meerts 2006).

In such circumstances where deals (wanted by each side) are not available, negotiations wind up in an impasse (or Deadlock) as seen in the protracted negotiation between Turkish and Greek Cyprus and between Armenia and Azerbaijan over new territorial boundaries.

Conclusion

In this chapter, bargaining outcomes have been explained, in particular, using the concept of the Nash equilibrium along with its refinements such as subgame-perfection. To prevent costly delays and inefficient outcomes, players can agree to an equilibrium payoff at the outset. Traditional negotiation models have, to a great extent, been concerned with the efficiency properties of both the process and the outcomes. In general, higher initial demands will not produce a favorable final settlement if they produce increased costs in an extended period of bargaining with a larger discount rate. As examined in this chapter, continuing to stand firm carries greater loss of benefit (1) when the value of a good evolves through time with surplus decay after the rejection of each offer and (2) time has value, creating a disadvantage for a delayed agreement.

Bargaining theories in this chapter assume that each game always looks the same except for the passage of time. This stationary assumption about bargaining suggests that a player does not learn anything during the course of the game, with the same linkages among sequences. In a continuing sequence of bargaining, thus, its beginning is considered identical to the payoff at the later stage. The player is assumed to be in the same position except for his/her alternating roles between making and receiving an offer. As players are interchangeable, the same utility is assigned to each player in the same role. Thus identical payoffs are given to identical players through a unique equilibrium. The notions of a fair division in a bargaining game prescribe the same utility payoffs for players in completely symmetric roles (Heap and Varoufakis 2004; Klamler 2010). Thus the solution does not hinge on the noneconomic properties of bargainers – for example, such broad categories as gender, race and ethnicity.

We have assumed a sequential-move game in which players have perfect information at each move. In reality, however, the assumptions of perfect information would be unrealistic, for instance, if bargainers do not know each other's relative levels of patience (i.e., one another's discount factors). Indeed, perfectly rational decisions for the optimal solution may not be feasible in the event of limited cognitive ability as well as insufficient information. In US–Soviet arms-control talks during the Cold War era, the negotiation was driven by "instinctive calculation, not based on the notion of strategic stability or computer analysis," as both sides pursued a strategy to deploy a weapons system most feared by the other side (Smith 1985, 87). Negotiators had to calculate not only existing but also projected weapons capabilities.

A period of disagreement is often inevitable due to a lack of perfect information as to each other's preferences and equilibrium outcomes. With asymmetric information, bargainers may start with a higher demand and gradually reduce it, whereas the other player waits for a lower demand. In considering that a more patient player gets the higher fraction of the pie, bargainers have more than enough incentives to signal that they are patient even if they are not. Acting unconcerned about time passing, negotiators may not respond with counteroffers right away.

In ordinary experience of daily business, factors other than efficiency (e.g., an emotional reaction to a particular offer) might often be critical in determining an agreement. Formal bargaining models also do not fully incorporate the occurrence of bluffing and posturing. Moreover, a bargaining environment is regarded as deterministic with the ignorance of the effects of changes in external circumstances on bargains. In the construction of convincing models, the analysis of negotiation problems may need to be complemented with psychological insights about how specific beliefs form and their role in decision-making. Equally important, a crucial dimension of our understanding could be missed if we neglect the fact that a set of feasible outcomes might, in fact, be decided by a peculiar political and social context within which bargaining is bound. The remaining part of the book will cover both structural and psychological variables in examining negotiation behavior and process.

Note

1 If the territorial status quo is peacefully modified rather than through the costly use of force, the resources saved from destructive fighting can be considered a gain to be divided through coordinated action. Then each side's claim can be made according to the outcome of fighting that might have occurred. In reality, the exact outcome may not be known prior to the war.

PART II

Negotiation process, behavior and context

6 Negotiation dynamics

> Negotiating in the classic diplomatic sense assumes parties more anxious to agree than to disagree.
>
> Dean Acheson

THE FUNCTION of many international negotiations is to develop an explicit agreement for the allocation of benefits and/or costs. In resolving opposing interests, each side's demands need to be reconciled and transformed through a form of joint decision-making. As we shall see later, the efficiency of negotiation is often hampered by a lack of sufficient information about each other's priorities for effective decision-making. In fact, negotiators may not always find it easy to define even their own best interests and alternatives especially in a setting that entails multiple actors, evolving sets of issues and their linkages. Since many negotiations are neither self-contained nor stand alone, they navigate in the past history of conflict and other contexts of relationships. When the parties encounter uncertainties, negotiation behavior may evolve over time as they interact.

In the remainder of this book, we focus not only on a process internal to the negotiation (i.e., what is happening at the table) but also on its context. As is discussed in this chapter and the one immediately following, a negotiation process is examined by changes in negotiators' activities, their interactions and effects. While Chapter 8 looks at bargaining behavior and mechanisms (e.g., concession-making patterns), Chapter 9 covers the role of "nonrational" factors (i.e., the interference of psychological biases and institutional and political interests) in shaping negotiation process and outcomes. In Chapters 10 and 11, we will look at how the increased number of disputants and issues, as well as the presence of interveners, has a direct bearing on the behavior and strategies of all participants.

In this chapter, negotiation functions are examined in light of the way they are instrumental in reaching a joint decision by overcoming substantial differences. A negotiation process is, in part, presented as segmented into a trend or a series of uninterrupted events, ranging from decisions on coming to talks, putting a serious offer on the table or reaching a closure rather than continuing to haggle. Such activities as information exchange, debate and bartering are involved in developing agreement packages. However, these activities are embedded in an overall mechanism of interactive dynamics of negotiating parties.

Noncooperative nature of negotiation

In the relatively simplified world of game theory, players reason their way toward "settlement" (e.g., the equal division of surplus value) predicated on common knowledge and beliefs (Aumann 1987). In a real-world negotiation, such a premise may not be workable, requiring a refinement. Unfortunately, cooperative game theories do not explain how parties obtain understanding about each other's alternatives and, in particular, how they overcome a stalemate when differences arise.[1] A bargaining theory's axiomatic foundation is shown to be insufficient for dealing even theoretically with situations where impasses set up tensions. Thus good communication needs to be incorporated as an integral part of bargaining (Rapoport 1974).

Below is an example of difficulties in honest communication at a critical juncture in negotiations, the failure of which could have blown up the entire world. Despite their bellicose reactions at the initial stage of the Cuban Missile Crisis in October 1962, both American and Soviet leaders soon realized nuclear exchange was the catastrophe to be averted at all costs. Yet "the problem was that it was practically impossible for them to communicate frankly with one another. Each knew very little about the intentions and motivations of the other side, and tended to assume the worst. Messages took half a day to deliver ... they were couched in the opaque language of superpower diplomacy, which barred the writer from admitting weakness or conceding error" (Dobbs 2008, 114). Indeed proposals were delivered not only through informal official channels but also broadcasting or press release, thus increasing the political stakes in the outcome to each leader at a crucial moment.

The terms of trade would not be easily established without a shared cognitive structure of the referents for a solution as well as developing a common image of the problem (i.e., where their interests overlap or diverge). A mutually acceptable solution arises from shared meanings that are in turn facilitated by the exchange of information. A collective perception of an applicable criterion of fairness or justice is often essential to an enduring settlement. Transparent knowledge about each party's priorities and interests is critical to realizing the potential benefit of bargaining (e.g., identifying common interests in a search for joint gains). One of the main reasons for negotiating in the first place is to develop knowledge about a counterpart's bargaining range as well as how they set their resistance point.

The course of negotiation is shaped by the way each side presents an initial position and reveals priorities via information sharing. Extensive knowledge (about each other's desires and core interests) can be accumulated in a process of prenegotiation and formal bargaining (Dowd and Miller 2011; Gettinger *et al.* 2012). Although facts might be clearly presented if quick settlement is of mutual benefit, caution might be required to have the information readily accessible in the absence of reciprocal moves. Despite shared interest in striking a deal, the actions directed toward that may not be the same. As part of strategies to alter the bargaining set, negotiators attempt to influence the way the other players perceive it.

The range of sensible outcomes is certainly delimited by the alternatives of the various parties and their utility functions. When a player is faced with more than one individually rational and efficient solution, the complete knowledge of the bargaining set does often not produce a clear outcome. If many reasonable solutions are available, negotiation situations become fluid and controlled more by the negotiators themselves. A greater degree of indeterminacy with too many choices creates more difficulty in reaching agreement. The inability to settle on any one of the available solutions noticeably increases the danger of the negotiation's breakdown with a contest of wills. Thus it sometimes becomes a critical task for negotiators to coordinate their expectations and come to closure by searching for an acceptable device or procedure such as splitting the difference and other customary shares. The number of credible outcomes could be minimized by adopting some shared principle (such as reciprocity). Unfortunately, "[t]he specific fairness standards that are salient in a given situation vary widely from one class of negotiations to another" (Young 1991a, 5).

In many negotiations, not all the parties benefit either simultaneously or equally. Whereas negotiations rarely have a win–lose structure, it can be safely assumed that neither do they always produce a win–win outcome (Watkins 1999). Even though value gets created, the other side may claim the lion's portion of it. Putting information about one's vital interests up front prematurely may expose oneself to the vulnerability of exploitation (e.g., one's opponent demanding bigger concessions in exchange for one's own priority goals). It reflects, in fact, a classic dilemma captured in the overarching structure of a conflict that arises in many mixed-motive games.

In negotiation, explicit bargaining takes a form of communicating offers and counteroffers in order to reach an agreement. Negotiators have to decide, at some point, whether to accept current proposals from their counterparts or press for more while continuing to negotiate in the hope of securing better terms. It hinges on one's perception about whether an opponent has made all the concessions they could. They may also need to make a judgment about when to break off talks with the confidence that available deals are no better than no-agreement alternatives (Iklé 1964). So long as a more attractive alternative does not exist, negotiators have to make hard choices, for example, as to whether or not to make a concession below some critical aspiration level.

Decisions on striking a deal need to be interpreted through the lens of a negotiator's reasons for pursuing particular interests and determining their salience (Winkler 2006). In general, however, negotiators are uncertain about each other's priorities, bottom lines and alternatives, requiring the deduction of the other side's preferences from their negotiating position.[2] Given the difficulties in seeking out information, negotiators often rely on assumptions or inferences about what their counterparts are likely to value. The resulting ambiguity may leave a door open for others to manipulate perceptions about a bargaining range by selectively sharing or withholding information. In fact, much of a negotiation process consists of an attempt to alter counterparts' subjective beliefs by convincing them that an offer is preferable to no agreement or to continued bargaining (Dupont and Faure 2002).

One's bargaining power is relative to the other's as a direct function of what alternatives each has. It becomes an important source of power to be able to shape one's counterpart's understanding of one's own end of the bargaining range. Each side may push for a settlement toward the other's resistance point, which is often unknown or subjectively assessed; by demanding the greater share of concessions, players intend to gain more control over the outcome by leading opponents to believe that achieving their objective will have an increased cost. With other conditions being equal, a large number of distributive bargaining situations tend to be settled near the deadline.

Perceived power is important in inducing the opponent to take an action that one wants. The capacity to mold the other side's subjective perceptions may flow from possessing objective resources such as military or economic strengths to be employed to make credible threats. As we have seen in the US negotiations with North Vietnam (1968–73), North Korea through the Six-Party Talks (2003–07), and Panama (a much smaller power) over control of the canal (1964–77), conventional measures of power are, however, effective only to the extent that they shape an opponent's expectations. In the absence of tangible resources or if they are ineffective, a bargaining advantage can be garnered by having (access to) superior information that sways an opponent's desired goals.

Negotiating dynamics

Negotiators face uncertainties about an opponent's preferences and goals during the preparatory stages, and ambiguities may persist throughout subsequent interactions (involving initial communication, persuasion and commitment stages). Playing a "language game" is involved in changing a counterpart's beliefs, in that negotiators rely on each other's words at the negotiating table (Ulbert and Risse 2005). Instead of making concessions, a bargainer may bring her opponent's views into line with her own through persuasion and argument.[3] An essential orientation in negotiation is, in part, to induce the other side to accept terms advantageous to oneself while evoking the principles of fairness and relying on the "facts" selectively in framing choices.

In claiming value, strategic moves could be taken to advance one's gain at the expense of one's opponent. Negotiators may announce a course of action that they would follow should an agreement not be reached. Particular types of action could be linked to precise terms that an adversary must accept in order to avoid undesirable consequences. Threats, warnings, ultimatums and delays as well as promises could be adopted to induce an opponent's concessions. The power of a threat hinges, in effect, on a prior communication of the player's willingness to stick to a Pareto inferior outcome. The level of demand can be chosen according to the threat's credibility. In such incident as a tacit nuclear threat by the United States against the Soviets during the 1973 Middle Eastern crisis, its credibility reckoned on "the perception that [it] will be carried out, though not necessarily with certainty but with high enough probability" to make the adversary's noncooperative payoff worse than cooperation (Brams 1994, 141).

In tacit bargaining, demands are communicated less with words than with actions aimed at modifying the other's evaluation of costs borne by not accepting one's own terms (Winkler 2006). Yet coercive actions may hinder compromises and produce an upward escalatory spiral with reciprocal intensification of hostilities. Escalation in demand can lead to several years of stalemate when each side attempts to achieve their objectives outside negotiation. By heavily bombing North Vietnam's industrial and military facilities at various stages of the Vietnam War, the US government attempted to extract key concessions without much success. Whereas a controlled escalation during negotiation is aimed at a gain at the expense of the other, ill-conceived threats can trigger counterescalation, intensifying or widening the conflict (O'Neill 1991). In circumstances where threats create greater uncertainty, the process of searching for a fair solution is destabilized by the purposeful distortion of one's expectations. Backing up a threat further erodes stability, bringing more entrenchment with more defensiveness; it reduces any inclination to accept the other, decreasing communicative ability with highly negative emotions.

A negotiation schedule can be manipulated through blocking progress or setting deadlines. Even though holding back is seen as less intensely hostile than threats or escalations, it is nonetheless adopted as part of tactics to increase costs to an opponent. In considering the discounted value of a future profit, a delay delivers a costly signal, amounting to a failure of settlement. Given the inefficiency and unattractiveness of a protracted agreement process, the cost of delay needs to be compared with how much can be gained through an improved deal at a later period. The elapse of time lowers the current demand's ultimate value unless waiting costs are not compensated for by obtaining a higher payoff. If an impasse incurs a higher cost only to one party, the other player expects a better outcome by waiting longer. It does not matter when the issue is solved if time works only to one's advantage. Blocking is a device for an actor who is bound to negotiate but is not constrained by time pressure.

An ultimatum prevents time allowing negotiating parties to continue to try to squeeze more concessions out of each other. As it forces a trade to occur now or never, an ultimatum is a type of threat, namely, to terminate the bargaining unless a certain last offer is accepted. A threat to end a negotiation serves as a potent weapon to speed up the negotiation process by spurring counterparts and/or pressing even one's own constituents to make hard choices (O'Neill 1991). Although external circumstances may drive action-forcing events by tying negotiators' hands, the ripeness of the process pretty much depends on the state of mind of the parties (Watkins 1999). The decision about setting deadlines calls for careful scrutiny in that premature attempts to drive for a quick closure could simply backfire, setting off breakdown or undercutting credibility.

Process models

In representing changes necessary to produce an agreement, types of activities can be grouped to describe a movement from initiation to settlement. As a negotiation's temporal component, a phase is composed of a coherent period of activities that center on a particular subgoal or milestone in accomplishing a joint solution. Despite differences in the number of phases, various process models characterize negotiation as parsed into an unfolding series of sequentially ordered activities (Gulliver 1979; Holmes 1992). By analyzing the components of negotiations at a more aggregate level, we get the whole picture of how a negotiation moves along with alterations in its focus. The shifts in interaction indicate where phase boundaries are placed. The emergence of an agenda would lead to exploring a range of solutions for the dispute, which helps to narrow the differences (Lister and Lee 2013). This process can coincide with such activities as identifying debatable issues, decomposing and aggregating relevant information as well as explicit bargaining based on different proposals.

In an evolutionary process model, the sequential ordering of goal-oriented activities is critical to outcomes (Borch and Mérida 2013). In a teleological explanation, each phase causes its successor. Thus settlement is the end product of progression through a fixed series of different phases. Negotiation advances point by point to reconcile the divergent positions. While phases are assumed to merge from one to the next without abrupt transitions in a sequential order model, it is nonetheless important to bear in mind that unsuccessful negotiations may be stalled and cycle between phases without advancing toward later ones in the sequence. The process can be inhibited by an impasse at any stage of negotiation.

Despite their generalizability across studies, fixed-phase models are too global to capture the true progression of any given negotiation. Indeed, exact steps and stages do not always exist in a negotiation process (Carrell and Heavrin 2008). A movement in many negotiations is likely to occur in surges with fragmented time rather than an even flow (Watkins 1999). In a variety of actual contexts, a sequence of phases is specific to each negotiation; the lengths and order of each phase (e.g., a continuing series of offers) differ according to how a particular negotiation is shaped by process dynamics. For example, hostage and other types of less-structured negotiations have unexpected transitions from one stage to another; many hostage negotiations develop into a less orderly process, as communication channels become less reliable with the involvement of multiple and incoherent activities (Cristal 2003). In hostage negotiation, an introduction phase quickly proceeds to episodes dominated by demands, and, if settled, concludes with agreement or ends in abrupt violence. The range of the dispute is revealed in the process where demands are raised, met, or refused. The perpetrator displays a commitment to demands with a threat to unilaterally terminate the interdependence of the negotiating relationship. Impasses and suicide threats are quite common in the demand phase. Assuming that the threat is not acted out, the hostage holders may ultimately be induced to search for terms, for instance, on surrender, in a concluding phase. In the absence of a past engagement, institutionalizing a working relationship beyond ascertaining participants becomes an even more daunting task.[4]

In a crisis negotiation, phase boundaries are often arbitrary. Most importantly, stages partially overlap or shade into one another rather than representing exact or rigid boundaries. In this kind of situation, it is more helpful analytically to identify events serving as breaking an impasse or bringing about other dramatic changes (Donohue 2004). When parties have no choice but to start talks immediately with a sudden eruption of a potentially disastrous conflict, the unfolding episodes do not allow an orderly pattern of negotiating structure (Weingart and Olekalns 2004). In the Cuban Missile Crisis, Khrushchev made an early decision to withdraw Soviet missiles, but a series of looming crises interfered in a shift to an end game. While both sides were negotiating conditions for Soviet missile withdrawal, top decision-makers were caught off guard by such incidents as the shooting down of a U-2 spy plane over eastern Cuba, another U-2 going astray over Soviet air space and a Soviet nuclear submarine being forced to the surface by US Navy depth charges. The crisis only came to a climax because of a combination of moves including the transfer of Soviet nuclear warheads closer to Cuban missile sites and the finalization of plans for an all-out invasion of the island by the US Joint Chiefs of Staff. In this type of situation, qualitative differences between phases can be better described as precipitation, turning point, impasses or settlement (Druckman 2013). As a watershed, a turning point either breaks a stalemate or leads to a debacle (such as a war).

In contrast with a phase model, a negotiation process has also been described as a movement from the discovery of a framework of broad objectives and principles to the development of detailed points of agreement (Zartman and Berman 1982). In the Sudanese peace negotiation that started in May 1992, it took more than five years to adopt the Declaration of Principles (DOP) as a basis for negotiations owing to difficulties even to agree to a common agenda. Whereas the DOP embodied all the conflict's contentious and divisive questions, including self-determination and national unity, it did not easily translate into the elimination of gaps between positions on a permanent constitution, the relationship between religion and state, security and military and other long-standing issues (Khadiagala 2007). To move beyond their mutually contradictory positions on each issue, the DOP was eventually condensed into a single text that became the basis of negotiation. The challenge to negotiating on a more comprehensive text was overcome by focusing paragraph by paragraph instead of on every detail. This process produced the June 2002 Machakos Protocol which covered secularization, national identity, future relations between the North and South, and a transition period prior to decisions on succession or staying with a federal structure. In the new rounds of talks, then, the parties discussed wealth and power-sharing, the southern boundaries and the status of disputed territorial jurisdictions. Through three more accords, arrangements were made on the withdrawal of government forces from the south and the creation of joint integrated units alongside separate northern and southern military forces. In a nutshell, the Machakos Protocol and the DOP remained as the frames of references for the negotiations until the Comprehensive Peace Agreement was signed in January 2005.

In the deduction of details from an agreed framework, a mutually acceptable method of reasoning is required for the generation of specific terms (Iklé 1964, 215). In fact, the emergence of sharp differences in negotiating on details could make a comprehensive formula invalid, resulting in a search for a completely new one (Hopmann 1996). A comprehensive proposal on nuclear weapons testing (discussed among the United Kingdom, the United States, and the Soviet Union between 1959 and 1963) backtracked due to a failure to agree on details on verification measures, especially the number of annual on-site inspections for the verification of underground tests. It forced a search for a new framework acceptable to all, i.e., test ban limited to the atmosphere, outer space and underwater but not extended to underground sites. Nailing down details can be protracted or fail with arguments over the methods of deduction that favor different sides.[5] In their negotiation with the United States over opening its domestic rice market during the 1980s, Japan conceded in principle, but made only a little compromise on substance. The Japanese government depended on "vague, ambiguous, noncommittal language in framing proposals" despite its acceptance of the partial or minimum access formula (Blaker 1999, 34).

When a basic principle is not readily translatable to specific details or is not readily acceptable to negotiators, they may establish a bargaining range and struggle to settle the differences.[6] Intense bargaining is inevitable in negotiation over dividing a limited resource pool (e.g., the allocation of water or division of territories between two countries). In the initial stage, deep and irreconcilable cleavage between the parties may surface. This period could be longer in a more adversarial relationship where a hard-hitting critique is used to discredit the other's claim. This initial stage is followed by a phase of reconnoitering the range by trial and error; the sides seek out promising areas of agreement, while still holding firm and pressing for the other side's capitulation. The clear signs of tacit agreement might emerge after extensive interaction, tactical maneuvers and jockeying for position. At the final stage, a decision-reaching crisis might be precipitated. If successful, the negotiation ends with the announcement of a formal agreement. In protracted bargaining, the whole process can alternate between exploring and narrowing the range of differences. A convergence process is often not linear when previous concessions are retracted, increasing divergence in positions.

Negotiation behavior and interaction

Unique insights into how interaction changes over time can be gained by paying attention not only to primary elements of negotiation but also to their relationships. In fact, communication in negotiation can be examined by frequencies and sequences of particular behavior as well as events in phases. The analysis of frequencies in talks about what negotiators care about, for instance, provides insight into their goals and approaches to realizing them. Unified periods of coherent activity (such as an uninterrupted series of offers) can be studied by information and influence strategies. Differences in negotiating dynamics can thus be conceptualized by a trend in the continuity (or discontinuity) of behavior (e.g., a significant increase in the number of proposals). In distributive bargaining, the number of proposals and offers may peak immediately before the deadline.

Each negotiation process can be characterized by different patterns of cooperation or conflict over the object of discussion (Craver 2012). At least in theory, negotiators may regard the decision to cooperate or compete as a choice between opposite poles of behavior (Neale and Fragale 2006). As separate dimensions of behavior, cooperative and competitive orientations are generally considered distinct categories of negotiation activities, for instance, manifested by reciprocal concessions and relationship building vs. arguments and threats respectively. Though information sharing is necessary to avoid settling for suboptimal solutions, high aspirations may foster competition. In the success or failure of negotiation, it becomes crucial to manage the latent tension between the desire to cooperate and inclinations to compete.

In considering the wide variation from predominantly conflict-driven to cooperative orientations in the underlying negotiation process, there is no one "best" strategy universally applicable. The cultivation of appropriate strategies on the distributive–integrative spectrum is subject to where particular negotiations are heading. If concerns with distribution prompt the questions of claiming value, taking positions might be more frequently observed in augmenting self-interest.

In negotiations over a fixed asset such as territory, an expanded supply of the "goods" is not feasible to satisfy an increased demand or claim. Territorial claims fall into "either a hard zero-sum situation, a soft zero-sum situation, or a gray-zone situation, depending on each party's attitude or degree of determination to pay whatever price is required to reach its goal" (Assyd 2001, 48). In the case of the Palestinian conflict with Israel, a hard attitude has been developed, because the claimed territories are considered their communal home or possessions critical to their very survival. The stake in a territorial division is easily multiplied or enlarged with the maintenance of an "us vs. them" mentality. In this situation, a negotiation is locked into a persistently competitive pattern with difficulties in adopting a solution such as a 50/50 split in resolving differences.

In general, mixed-motive negotiations are marked by the display of both cooperative and competitive behaviors. Owing to the blend of shared, conflicting and complementary interests, negotiators face a situation of simultaneously cooperating for the creation of a joint value and competing for its larger share. In striking an optimal balance between cooperation and competition, the supply of benefits available for exchange needs to become as large as possible before ensuring a fair or acceptable share for each side. Whereas trust is enhanced by integrative reciprocity, a shared sense of fairness emerges from a high level of distributive reciprocity.

When a negotiation progresses with the alternation of integrative and distributive orientations, different patterns of a strategic sequence need to be harmonized across stages.[7] While a positional argument can be more frequent in a distributive bargaining stage, an integrative stage may reflect the reevaluation of each other's desires and interests (Weingart and Olekalns 2004). In a mixed-motive negotiation, distributive strategies are likely to be used off and on throughout the whole process. Competitive playing declines to increase a total pie but ascends in frequency at a distributive bargaining stage. Once an attempt at exploiting the other proves unproductive, the number of collaborative acts rises again for problem-solving, exhibiting a continually dialectical interaction of softness and firmness.

Sequential vs. simultaneous negotiation

Differences in multiple issues can be discussed and settled simultaneously or successively, depending on the agenda structure and packaging strategies. Whereas agreements on some agenda items may precede others incrementally, the scope of negotiation is expanded by bundling multiple bargaining issues as a single negotiating package (Khadiagala 2007). All the issues might be discussed simultaneously to minimize the chances of limited agreement. Fixed-pie orientations are more effectively overcome by considering each other's preferences and goals simultaneously (Princen 1992). Indeed, a balanced package is more easily forged when there is an abundance of more "tradable" issues. A creative trade of priorities on different issues enhances the satisfaction of complementary interests.

Therefore, tradeoffs allow the creation of common values or objectives for mutual benefit. In the process of producing a comprehensive package for settlement, simultaneous negotiations of multiple issues permit the exchange of low-cost concessions on matters that carry dissimilar significance to each side. It characterizes the multiparty negotiation that brought peace to Northern Ireland (1995–2007). In the negotiation, a framework of an agreeable final deal was forged, as different positions moved closer to one another on multiple issues (including power-sharing, the acceptance of Northern Ireland's status within the United Kingdom, release of Irish Republican Army prisoners, etc.).

An overall package could also be produced by refining options on each major issue, while gauging the relative intensity of interest. Here a comprehensive pact emerges from proceeding point by point to narrow differences on each agenda item (e.g., from security arrangements to economic cooperation). Individual issues are discussed separately as part of a sequential negotiation process that continues until the emergence of the total package. A settlement on each issue can be kept isolated in a step-by-step approach, but approval of the final package is contingent upon the acceptance of individual settlements on all the issues.

The sequential treatment of issues permits an impasse in one area to be overcome by moving on to underlying concerns of other matters. The utilization of a tentative agreement on a particular issue serves as an incentive to break deadlocks on other issues. Progression from one issue to another was a cornerstone in the talks between the governments and leftist armed groups to end civil wars in El Salvador and Guatemala in the early 1990s. In developing a peace accord in El Salvador, the whole negotiation proceeded from the agreement on the agenda in April 1990 and ended with agreement on the implementation plan in January 1992. Although the discussion of the armed forces began in Mexico in June 1990, the parties could not come to an agreement on demilitarization and immunity for the military. However, momentum was built after the emergence of the first substantive agreement on human rights. Human rights monitoring contributed to confidence building while negotiations on other issues continued (Burgerman 2000). Eventually, a sequential negotiation on each of the remaining issues produced baskets of separate agreements. The demobilization and disarmament of the Farabundo Martí National Liberation Front (FMLN) was the last item on the agenda, because they needed a political agreement prior to it. As the final commitment came with the conclusion of negotiations on all other issues, every agreement became part of the total package of the peace accord.

Process complexities

If negotiations proceeded neatly from initial stage to conclusion in a linear flow, there would be far less need to study the process. However, a sequence of stages is often largely fuzzy, lacking well-articulated patterns over time (Dupont and Faure 2002). The succession of events (e.g., exchange of proposals) may overlap or backtrack in a haphazard manner (e.g., the US–North Korean or the Iranian nuclear negotiation). At the same time, short bursts of substantial movement may proceed from a long period of inaction. Thus nothing is straightforward or predictable in negotiation with the involvement of disjuncture and thresholds.

The time truly devoted to substantive deal-making is often a lot shorter than the passage of time between an initial meeting and eventual closure. In facilitating settlement, some clusters of moves weigh heavily in the outcomes. The negotiations on ending the Vietnam War were subject to various lengthy delays before the Paris Peace Accord was signed on January 28, 1973. The Paris Peace Talks can be characterized as covert bilateral preparatory talks, formal meetings, walkouts from negotiations, and return to the table after intense military engagement. The representatives of the United States and North Vietnam held their first formal discussion in Paris on May 13, 1968, and kept meeting intermittently until January 25, 1973. However, the formal negotiation was intertwined with secret talks between Henry Kissinger and Le Duc Tho of the Vietnamese Politburo (Asselin 2002). In fact, compromise (needed for the agreement) was struck in secret talks outside formal negotiations.

As exemplified by the US–Iranian and US–North Korean nuclear talks over the past decade, international negotiation can be composed of multiple-stage events alternating with entrapment and stalemate. The core dynamics in multiple rounds of negotiations prove to be elusive to characterize (Dupont and Faure 2002). In spite of similar underlying structures, negotiations can occur in diverse contexts (e.g., a changed political atmosphere). When the scope and flexibility of communication evolve over time, the chances of a successful outcome are enhanced if a positive atmosphere is created outside the negotiation room (e.g., softened economic sanctions). On the other hand, talks can stumble owing to negative political changes such as the election of a hardline leadership or escalation of unplanned violence.

Agreements may not be uniform in structure and content. Negotiations can produce either an outline of a settlement or a comprehensive and detailed blueprint. A two-phase timetable for the Israeli–Palestinian peace process (based on the principles of exchanging land for peace) was drawn up in a round of secret talks in Oslo in 1993. The

Israeli–Palestinian Declaration of Principles (DOP), also known as the Oslo Accord, provided a framework for the implementation of the initial stages of the peace process. A series of step-by-step measures were originally foreseen to forge a partnership and form a bond while setting up a timetable for the final status negotiation. The accord stipulated an immediate Israeli withdrawal from the Gaza Strip, Jericho and part of the West Bank with the establishment of Palestinian self-rule during a five-year interim period that was supposed to end no later than May 1999. In return, the Palestinians made their principal compromises such as recognizing Israel's right to exist and renouncing the use of terrorism. The DOP was complemented by the Interim Agreement on the West Bank and Gaza Strip (popularly called Oslo II) of September 28, 1995, which was far-reaching in terms of the amount of territory to be ceded and broadening Palestinian self-government in the West Bank. Under Oslo II, the West Bank was to be divided into three areas: the transfer of the major Palestinian towns to full Palestinian autonomy with the exception of East Jerusalem and parts of Hebron; Palestinian villages transferred to the Palestinian authority but under the purview of Israeli defense and security control; and the remainder of the West Bank left with Israeli exclusive authority. The two main Oslo accords were supported by supplementary agreements such as the Gaza and Jericho Agreement (May 4, 1994) and the Hebron Accord (January 17, 1997), which were replete with practical details concerning implementation on the ground.

Meanwhile, the Israeli–Palestinian negotiations on the permanent status arrangements concentrated on the more fundamental issues of Jerusalem, territorial divisions, compensation for Palestinian refugees and the establishment of a Palestinian state. Yet these highly contested topics were not seriously touched upon at the early stages of the peace process. The emotion-laden issues were left for a later, undefined stage of the peace process. Notwithstanding the prominence of these issues in public discourse, little progress was made in achieving the ultimate goal owing to a breakdown of the Israeli–Palestinian dialogue that resulted from the changed political climate after the assassination of Prime Minister Yitzhak Rabin of Israel, one of the architects of the Oslo Accords. Such agreements as the Wye River Memorandum (reached after intensive negotiations on October 15–23, 1998) simply covered further Israeli withdrawal in return for tougher Palestinian security measures (Swisher 2004). The unfortunate collapse of the whole process in early 2001 was relegated to the failure of the Oslo accords to spell out a substantively envisioned outcome, being limited to setting up an interim process. Despite the fact that its negotiation schedule was timed to end in May 1999, many delays became unavoidable due to Israeli hesitancy to abandon their grip on the occupied land as well as sporadic eruptions of violence by Palestinian radicals against the Israelis. While the Israeli government questioned the sincerity of the Palestinian authority to curb violence, suspicions arose, on the Palestinian side, from the expansion of Israeli settlements in the West Bank.

External dynamics

The process of negotiation is not solely determined by its own inherent logic. Negotiation is not independent of what is happening off the table. Peace processes may be suspended, sometimes for a substantial period, and have to withstand pressures from outside (such as eruptions of violence). The changing nature of external events might put new constraints on the options with a direct impact on bargaining power (Guelke 2003). In ending civil wars, for example, force and negotiation cannot be treated as indistinct phenomena, in that uncertainty or a shift in the balance on battlefields often reduces incentives for rapid settlement. In instances such as the attempt to end the second civil war in Sudan since the early 1990s, "the talks became a hostage to battlefield fortunes" (Khadiagala 2007, 242). When being encouraged by military victories, the government was not willing or inclined to make concessions on substantive positions. On the other hand, the failure of talks often resulted in a further escalation of fighting with more civilian casualities and humanitarian disasters.

Given its advantages on the battlefield, in 1992–93, the Sudanese government refused to budge on key issues of an Islamic state and self-determination with an emphasis on national unity. As power discrepancy in ground warfare was identified as an obstacle to more serious negotiation, external arms and finance as well as diplomatic support were furnished to boost the Sudan's People's Liberation Movement/Army (SPLM/A). By the summer of 1997, the power disparity was leveled out to allow the resistance movement to claim its military gains, prompting the government of Omar Ahmad Al-Bashir back to the negotiating table in July 1997. The efforts to overcome disagreement on secularism and self-determination in fall 2000 failed largely due to Khartoum's military gains in the south. The negotiations foundered again in June 2001 on different expectations raised by the leaders. The Khartoum government wanted a ceasefire to seal its military gains while the southern opposition leadership emphasized the progress in talks on self-determination and secularization (Khadiagala 2007, 237). The escalation of fighting in the oil-producing Upper Nile region coincided with talks on wealth sharing in August 2002. Even though the government temporarily walked away from the peace negotiation after the south's occupation of a key strategic town, the first comprehensive ceasefire agreement was eventually introduced to stabilize the remainder of the negotiation, which successfully produced the 2005 accord.

Frameworks of negotiation

A negotiation can be pictured as an integral whole composed of different components that constitute a structural and procedural framework (Druckman 2011). A bargaining process unfolds within different parameters and constraints. The parameters of a negotiation can be set by the previous agreement through their issue linkages. The procedural framework may restrict the flexibility of a process in which parties interact (e.g., bilateral negotiation vs. multilateral talks). Procedural mechanisms (e.g., determining the participants' credentials and intervals in proposal making, etc.) affect the way negotiators arrive at an agreement. Obviously social interaction in a simple dyad differs from third-party assistance through mediation (e.g., the US role in producing the Israeli–Egyptian peace accord in 1978) or coalition-building in a multiparty setting (e.g., global climate negotiations).

Prior to the talks, a question is likely to linger over whether the negotiation framework could lend support for delivering an outcome close to being satisfactory or just from one's own perspectives (Albin 2001). In Israeli–Palestinian negotiations (1973–81), discussion about such critical issues as territorial boundaries was left for the later period, permitting the continuing expansion of Israeli settlement while the issues were not settled. During the El Salvadoran negotiations' early stage, the representatives of leftist forces wanted to have more comprehensive agendas while the government insisted on talks having limited scope with a restrictive focus (excluding military involvement in mass murder and other gross human rights violations). In ending a decade of Sudan's civil war, such topics as independence vs. political autonomy of the south were added to the agenda at the later negotiation stage due to the government's stiff resistance. By adding issues, negotiations can change the bargaining range of a possible agreement (Sebenius 1983). A myriad of issues in a negotiation radiate from social, economic well-being, security and other fundamental concerns people care about. The relative importance of different issues can be established by identifying basic needs and core interests that do not rapidly change.

A greater capacity to exert control over negotiating procedures confers bargaining power, helping to shape discussion about substantive questions. Sometimes talks can rapidly be bogged down on procedural matters. In the South African negotiation prior to the establishment of black majority rule, the white National Party (NP) government and the African National Congress (ANC) were at loggerheads over the rules and procedures for the democratic transition. The main stake was a transition from the Interim Constitution to the South African Final Constitution. As the ANC anticipated an electoral majority, they wanted to discuss the final constitution after a popular election. The NP wanted the decision to be made via proportional representation at the multiparty Congress for a Democratic South Africa (CODESA) before the ANC's electoral strength determined the outcome (du Toit 2003). The disagreement on the substance of these rules in the constitutional negotiation caused a breakdown in the talks until momentum was revived by a compromise in mid 1992.

Negotiators operate under a given set of rules of conduct to obtain certainty of the result (Meerts 2011). Procedural rules are set to define the playing field of the negotiation (banning procedures and behavior that involve manipulation of the discussion or sabotage). Ground rules can be designed to create a climate for collaboration and problem-solving in drawing up a comprehensive agreement. One of the ground rules in Northern Ireland's multiparty peace talks (1996–97) promoted a protocol such as "disagree but do not be disagreeable," permitting opposing perspectives to surface on their constitutional status within the United Kingdom; the negotiation's procedure was also based on the principle that nothing would become final until everything was agreed.[8]

Decision-making procedures, norms or institutions are normally established prior to a launch of large-scale multilateral negotiations on a global trade or environment conducted over the long term; procedures for communication and rules concerning voting and other methods of decision-making are instrumental in determining who shapes the agenda and how the process for making a proposal is structured. In general, the unanimous rule has the appearance of legitimacy of a collective decision. As further discussed in the later chapter on multilateral negotiation, the procedure and format of a negotiation can prejudice the conduct of the talks and the terms of the outcome. For example, the US government moved discussion about intellectual property rights from World Intellectual Property Organization (WIPO) to the General Agreement on Tariffs and Trade (GATT), where they could control agenda-setting and discussion more easily with sheer bargaining power.

Arguments over representation are not uncommon when one side does not recognize the other's legitimacy.[9] A lack of clarity over just who the legitimate parties are often causes a delay in the initiation of negotiation as well as clouding the negotiating atmosphere. The questions over the identity and attributes of the participants (e.g., North Vietnam vs. its proxy in the south) generated acrimony at the beginning of the Paris peace talks. In a civil war setting, the number of multiple insurgent factions creates complications in reaching an agreement and drawing a commitment (as exemplified by the seventeen factions involved in the Burundi peace negotiation during the late 1990s). The lower rank of the government representation was a particular source of fury for the opposing party at the initial stage of negotiations to end the Ugandan civil war in 1986.[10] Even though they did not attend the official negotiations, multiple sectors in El Salvadoran society (including women's organizations and small business owners as well as political parties) provided an input in the development of negotiating positions of FNLM.

Negotiations' legitimacy is enhanced by providing the representation of all parties concerned at the bargaining table. The acceptability of the process is essential to producing an eventual agreement and its implementation. If Northern Ireland negotiation had been left to the two largest political parties, the Social Democratic and Labour Party (SDLP) and the Ulster Unionist Party (UUP), agreement could have been reached relatively quickly. The two main political parties shared a broad agreement on a number of core issues through a series of bilateral meetings for most of the 1990s. However, the talks became more complicated due to the participation of nine other political parties as well as both the British and Irish governments; those on the political extremes in particular dragged out the talks by expressing their disillusionment with the process.

Though extraneous to substantive negotiation, the determination of venue or meeting space suitable for participants, time, and other logistical elements has implications for negotiating parties' psychological mood and assertiveness. The parties' attempt at control over physical arrangements generates arguments over even the shape of tables, round or rectangular, as well as the locations of delegation seats. During the peace negotiation in Paris, the South Vietnamese government was angered by the arrangement of the seats of the south's insurgent delegation, which gave an appearance of their separation from the north. During the acrimonious period of the first and second rounds of the Six-Party Talks in Beijing (2003–04), the seating arrangements especially for the US and North Korean delegations (next to each other) represented the Chinese host's intention to facilitate private interaction between the two main antagonists. As participants prefer a neutral site for arms-control and other delicate interstate talks, Geneva has emerged as a focal point providing an official meeting place away from home territories.

Preconditions might be required for the initiation of a negotiation. Prior to the resumption of substantive all-party talks in June 1996, the Irish government confirmed that it was prepared to remove its territorial claim on Northern Ireland in the event of an overall settlement. In fact, the 1985 Anglo-Irish Agreement served as a turning point by establishing the "principle of consent" that affirmed majority support required for any change in the constitutional status of Northern Ireland (Mitchell 2003). As an essential condition for joining the negotiation table, each party had to be committed to abiding by the ceasefire. However, the collapse of the Irish Republican Army (IRA) ceasefire led to a temporary expulsion of Sinn Fein, the party politically affiliated to the terrorist organization. The thorny issue of paramilitary demobilization and arms decommissioning also created a hurdle. It was taken temporarily out of the contentious political arena and was treated in a parallel negotiation.

Conclusion

This chapter has examined general dynamics and factors that shape the way negotiations progress. As discussed earlier, negotiation is generally featured as a form of joint decision-making aimed at resolving opposing interests manifested in incompatible preferences. In reaching an agreement, each party may want to embody as much of their own initial position as possible. After the parties verbalize contradictory demands, movement toward agreement can be achieved either by concessions being made or with new alternative solutions, based on mutually agreeable principles.

The strengths of agreements differ, depending on the substance and procedure adopted in negotiation. The process may simply end with agreeing on where the divergence occurs. If some core issues are difficult to resolve, a provisional agreement may be reached, waiting for an opportune moment to produce a more comprehensive agreement. Negotiation should be considered more than being confined to a mere process. In the absence of supranational authority, compliance with an international agreement is not enforceable.

Notes

1 Here "cooperative" means information sharing about each other's reservation and resistance points, facilitiated by an assumption that honest communication produces mutually beneficial outcomes. In its absence, defection (e.g., lying about one's true, unyielding interests) by one party forces the other into receiving a sucker payoff. Thus trust is an essential condition for a cooperative game, overcoming a Prisoner's Dilemma situation.
2 In the renewed talks after the fiasco of the summer 2000 Camp David negotiation, the Palestinian delegation ended up pondering what is true Israeli limit despite their counterpart's insistence on reaching "red lines." Palestinians felt that "the Israeli side was acting as if it were bargaining in a flea market ... [pressing] to wait just a little longer; perhaps Israel would budge more" (Sher 2006, 123).
3 In a hostage negotiation, for instance, upon the establishment of rapport with the captors, a peaceful outcome is likely to hinge on the government negotiator's ability to convince hostage-takers to see their weak alternatives without generating feelings of a threat. It can be combined with the explanation about the reasons for the non-negotiability of the captor's main demand (e.g., changes in laws) while displaying a willingness to consider some other demands.
4 A hostage negotiation is difficult to manage due to an abyss-like gap in the positions derived from totally conflicting belief systems and values of opposing sides. Such dramatic stakes as human life at risk increase the level of stress along with media broadcasting, public opinion, emotional appeals by hostage families and other external interference. Trust is hard to establish during a negotiation process. These characteristics open up possibilities for a wide range of outcomes (Faure 2003).
5 In the case of Israeli–Palestinian negotiations, despite an overarching principle of "land for peace," challenges to resolving differences in core issues arose, in part, from the unacceptability of each side's principal claims to the other. In drawing borders during the 2000 Camp David negotiation, Israeli negotiators adopted "the principle of maximum Israeli citizens and minimum Palestinians ... [while] the borders should also be reasonable, simple and not complicated lines" (Sher 2006, 100–101). On the other hand, Palestinians did not want to leave Palestinian villages under Israeli sovereign control (even though they were willing to accept a land swap). These conflicting claims created difficulties in understanding each other's sensitivities to territorial division. As for refugees, the Palestinian claim for the right of return was difficult for the Israelis to accept although "a limited number of refuges [could be allowed] into Israel on the basis of humanitarian considerations or family reunification" (*ibid.*, 101).

6 The emergence of mutually acceptable principles often becomes difficult with the involvement of political, religious, symbolic and historical factors. In the final status negotiations, Israelis preferred narrowing differences in specific arrangements for the future status of Jerusalem, security mechanisms, land swaps and annexation as well as refugee returns prior to discussion about principles. On the other hand, during the 2000 Camp David negotiations, Palestinians refused the identification of possible areas for compromise or tradeoff while seeking an initial Israeli acknowledgment of the principles of UN Security Council Resolution 242 on inadmissibility of the acquisition of territory by war and UN General Assembly Resolution 194 on return of refugees to their homes. During the summit, Yasser Arafat was "asking for Barak's recognition, in principle, of the right of return first before discussing practical details" (Swisher 2004, 261). The issue was framed differently in each side's mind: security (for the Israelis) vs. injustice (for Palestinians).

7 The US–Soviet arms-control negotiation was full of "the reciprocation of concession, tough, intermedate, [and] moderate bargaining stance" (Bunn 1992, 11–12).

8 This rule was also adopted during SALT I. According to one of the participants, each side accepted, from the beginning, an understanding that nothing would be considered agreed prior to agreeing to all (Smith 1985).

9 In general, it is politically very difficult to officially acknowledge hostage takers as a legitimate counterpart in negotiations. Most governments are concerned about the appearance of bestowing legitimacy on "terrorists" as a consequence of the negotiation itself. In addition, no government wants to jeopardize its reputation or the principle of not negotiating under threat. But there is a moral legitimacy based on the attempt to save lives. Interacting with hostage takers – either directly or indirectly, through an intermediary – is inevitable. At the same time, generally, concessions are not made in public or officially because of legitimate concerns (Faure 2003).

10 In a negotiation held under the auspices of President Daniel arap Moi of Kenya to end the Ugandan civil war in 1985, "questions of standing and identity of representatives lingered throughout the talks ... [and] set the tone for defining the level of trust between the parties." The opposition wrangled over the absence of the government head as a sign of a lack of seriousness (Khadiagala 2007, 27).

7 Negotiation process and activities

Unless both sides win, no agreement can be permanent.

Jimmy Carter, 2002

As progress may not necessarily be linear, the potential for negotiations evolves along vastly different trajectories. Nonetheless, the participants should have an overall, even if vague, notion of how the process is likely to proceed. The whole sequence of negotiations can be envisaged as a developmental process of testing the ground, agenda formulation, proposal making, bargaining and closure. In illuminating the main characteristics of different negotiation stages, this chapter looks at specific negotiating activities that encompass proposal exchange, issue redefinition and conceptualization, exploration of an overall structure of the deal, and a search for implementing details.

The nature of the dispute is initially defined through issue clarification at the agenda phase.[1] Once having voiced a commitment to key issues, each side has to turn their attention to narrowing the differences before any prospect for settlement emerges. This transition serves as a preliminary to final bargaining. More specifically, these preliminaries constitute a search for a viable range of alternative settlements through a serious study of trading possibilities, and honing a bargaining formula. Jostling for position may precede the eventual ironing out of differences. The points of difference may be narrowed by concession-making. Thus a shared sense of the approximate range of possible terms is essential to deal structuring and detailed bargaining. As vividly illustrated, for instance, in Greek debt talks with Eurozone countries and the US–Iranian nuclear deal-making attempt in 2015, the whole process does not stop at the conclusion of an agreement, spilling over into implementation, demanding either associated negotiation or renegotiation for new or improved terms.

Prenegotiation stage

As part of prenegotiation dynamics, each side measures the other's capabilities and desires. Then the first step is a decision as to whether or not to negotiate at all. In general, each party should feel compelled to see the need for negotiation; it can be created by various events and other circumstances. The example of Panama's negotiation with the United States below demonstrates how a weaker party can take advantage of a catalytic event to force a much stronger party to see the need to redress their grievances. The January 1964 riots, precipitated by a confrontation over the Panamanian flag flown alongside an American one, reflected decades of local frustration derived from a lack of control in the Canal Zone. As a tactic of crisis exploitation, the Panamanian president Roberto Chiari allowed the violent protest to run its own course by refusing to call out the National Guard. It raised serious questions about United States' capability of securing the canal against the agitated public. In fact, the riots displayed Panama's ability to disrupt American control over the canal, making its maintenance costly. In transforming the incident into a catalyst for negotiation, Panama internationalized the canal issue by calling an emergency meeting at the Organization of American States (OAS) and had even broken diplomatic relations with the United States until the latter agreed to renegotiate the old treaty (Habeeb 1988).

The negotiability of the main differences requires an understanding of each adversary's goals as well as expectations about desirable outcomes. In the above case, one Panamanian goal was to abrogate the 1903 treaty that gave the United States perpetual control of the Canal Zone. On the other hand, President Lyndon Johnson was willing to talk about the Panamanian grievances but only within the limit of the 1903 treaty. Despite its initial resistance, the US government eventually agreed to accept talks on adjustments to the canal treaty. The parties' differing goals and their existing relationships shape not only the prospect for achieving agreement but also the paths to settlement. Exploratory talks can reveal the motivations and incentives for negotiation.

In order to create a serious commitment, a minimally acceptable agreement should exist. There is no incentive for cooperation in the absence of any improvement from the value to be obtained without negotiation. Parties need to figure out whether their interests are in direct opposition or complementary. Initial jockeying may entail both promises and threats (Pillar 1983). Even though it was rejected by North Vietnam, in 1965, the Johnson administration offered $1 billion in aid in return for the North's ending hostilities in South Vietnam. In fact, the offer was made along with threats of further bombing of vital North Vietnamese facilities upon its rejection.

The decision to negotiate is not always straightforward when preferences over the best time to do so are incompatible. In the effort to end the civil war in El Salvador, it took several years for the two sides to sit down for serious negotiation after its initial announcement of talks. Each side's calculation hinged whether they could win the war or should negotiate instead. Whereas neither side knew what types of settlement might be feasible, none of them was willing to concede to the other's demands that were not attainable through their proven strength on a battleground. As the battlefield situation was unsettled and fluctuating, the initial negotiation drifted due to changes in each side's calculations. In the early 1980s, rebels preferred to pursue outright victory as the government was in political disarray. As the FMLN was a superior military force, its hardline leadership was reluctant to support negotiations. Then the government's increased military strength (with the doubled US military aid) reversed the power dynamics, resulting in the government's decreased interest in negotiated settlement. The initial talks in 1984 immediately broke down due to the hardening attitude of the Salvadoran military following the FMLN's loss of military advantage. A climate in which serious negotiation was possible was created only after the government position shifted; this shift was sparked by more intense public pressure in favor of ending the war, and this public pressure was, in turn, built by increasing civilian causalities linked to government-sponsored paramilitary attacks.

In an unofficial initial phase, negotiating positions emerge from the preliminary determination of the degree of the other side's cooperation. It is well illustrated by the five years of clandestine contact between the white South African government's security agency and the ANC before the release of Nelson Mandela in 1990. Despite a reluctant engagement, each party should have some belief in the possibility of obtaining their goals without coercive means. Informal secret talks assist the partisans with figuring out whether their interests are potentially overlapping and compatible. Trust or friendship is not necessary for negotiations to begin. Negotiations in Sudan, Angola, Burundi, El Salvador, Guatemala and elsewhere have shown that merely agreeing to negotiation does not commit parties to end hostilities nor to specific settlement terms.

The process of informal, exploratory dialogue is aimed at assessing the level of each other's commitment to formal talks and willingness to enter into the interaction. Prior to formal sessions, negotiators explore potential agenda items and ground rules as well as the determination of venue or space suitable for participants, meeting time, and other logistics. The agenda is an essential part of defining the objectives of negotiation. The exploration of an arena for debate in actual negotiation generally coincides with the presentation of each other's positions as well as identifying issue characteristics.[2]

Opening negotiations and setting the tone

The initial activities in a negotiation cycle feature the making of proposals and the updating of knowledge about the other's preferences and priorities. Each party's interests are identified through discussion about the items placed on the agenda. As each side begins to make demands, specific needs, interests and concerns surface. The opening positions generally begin from a point where each party endeavors to maximize their own payoff. As an opening gambit, an initial offer and counteroffer signal which priority is highest for each party. One side's proposals are likely to generate questions for clarification, and often criticism from the other side that the proposal violates its preferences. At this stage, "exaggerated offers cloak real preferences so that one negotiator would not have unfair advantage by knowing what the other really wants" (Raiffa 1982, 103). Strength in one's perceived bargaining power affects the determination of where one sets a goal (e.g., near the minimum acceptable reservation value or the maximum out of the negotiation). High-powered parties are more likely to compare an offer against their aspiration level. A low-power recipient of the other's first offer would be most concerned with how far it is distant from their reservation value.

Psychological manipulation can be set up by a kind of game to control an opponent's perceptions and expectations. Whereas displaying emotional reactions to proposals is as diverse as disappointment, enthusiasm, and indifference, negotiator styles might be shaped by a unique set of personality, cultural or normative values as well as perceptions of the negotiator's power (Van Kleef *et al.* 2006). In addition, the initial patterns of interactions are likely to be set by the relationship between the negotiators embedded in the previous history of the process to date as well as the way in which an offer was delivered. As seen in the initial stages of the SALT I negotiation, held in Helsinki between November and December 1969, more constructive encounters focus on generating a range of options and then selecting from among them.

The initial stage sets the overall tone for the remainder of the negotiation in which proposals and counterproposals continue to be advanced, back and forth, until the emergence of at least a tentative understanding. As a more concrete agenda surfaces, a demand is made, and a response is provided in the next sequence. When one party advances a proposal, the other party may agree, disagree or push forward another item for the agenda. An exploration of the range of the dispute entails clarifying, elaborating and reiterating initial demands. The initiation stage is thus marked by specifying priorities and emphasizing points of difference.

In adversarial bargaining, each party guards against compromise, staking out an unalterable position with an assertion about the nonnegotiability of key issues. In particular, "holding doggedly to an extreme opening position" indicates little interest in producing agreement. It is well illustrated by "the Reagan administration's unwillingness to [back down] from... requiring the Soviet Union to reduce existing intermediate-range missiles in return for potential American equivalents" (Jensen 1988, 71). Incompatible relationships set in, if each party seeks only their own best interests at the expense of the other. Overstating claims in competition for a favorable outcome, in turn, creates an atmosphere of low levels of trust. When each party grudgingly retreats after digging into a position and arguing for it, mutual concessions come slowly and reluctantly.

In mistrust, the slow release or limited disclosure of information is intended to gain the upper hand over adversaries or as a defense against attack. It is difficult to discuss divisive issues as well as real concerns and wants when true positions are not revealed. Sticking with rigid, inflexible positions produces a stalemate with little prospect of meeting the needs of all parties. While information regarding one's own preferences and true intentions is held back, negotiation might be used to gather information about an adversary for unilateral gains.

Once offers are rejected, a new round of negotiations may resume with revised proposals in light of new information. In its first session of bilateral talks with the United States over the canal in July 1964, Panama's demands encompassed the acknowledgment of its sovereignty over the Canal Zone, participation in its administration, increased economic benefits and a fixed date for the termination of the 1903 treaty. In contrast, the United States insisted on its continued role in running the canal as well as ensuring its security. Since Panama's refusal to back down created an initial stalemate, in September 1965, the United States accepted the need for a new treaty with a pledge to abrogate the 1903 treaty for the first time. Even though the United States acceded to Panama's participation in running and administering the canal along with recognizing Panama's sovereignty over the zone, it insisted on retaining the canal's defense (Habeeb 1988). Despite the agreements on these key points to guide future negotiation, it had taken a decade to produce an accord that ended the sole control of the canal that had been exercised by the United States since 1903.

Sources of deadlock

The standard minuet of negotiations proceeds by "proposal, rejection, counterproposal, rejection, argument, concession, argument, concession, and so forth" (Fisher et al. 1997, 128). In a contest of wills, each party demonstrates more stubbornness in an attempt to eventually prevail. In a nonlinear process of negotiation, setbacks might be accompanied by a long hiatus. In a deadlock, parties dig into entrenched positions and are unwilling to listen reasonably to the other, with an insistence that each's proposal is final and the best that will be offered. In an atmosphere of stalemate, each party makes excessive demands while treating an opponent's concessions as inconsequential (de Dreu 2010). Reasons for standoff include (1) imbalance between what one wants to achieve and what the other is willing to concede to and (2) strategic stalling for bigger gains.

The protracted Panama negotiation could have ended in June 1967 with the draft agreements that covered the abolition of the 1903 treaty, the joint administration of the canal, increased toll revenue for Panama, a joint United States–Panama defense of the canal, and the rights to build and operate the new canal. In these draft treaties, *de jure* recognition of Panama's sovereignty was exchanged for *de facto* US control. The offer was well within Panama's acceptance range, but an October 1968 coup by Omar Torrijos brought negotiation back to square one with retraction of Panama's earlier positions.

The previous commitment broke down due to strategic stalling for bigger gains. The new military coup leader pushed a new reservation point toward an American one. As the Torrijos government formally announced the earlier draft unacceptable, President Richard Nixon regressed from the Johnson period by rejecting a treaty with a termination date, something critical in the 1967 draft treaty. In addition, a new American position reversed back to the earlier insistence on unilateral control over the canal's operation and defense (Habeeb 1988). Indeed, these two nonnegotiable demands were not a dramatic change from the 1903 treaty except for the provision of slightly better financial terms. This shift back to the original position represented the Nixon administration's hardening attitudes by not even recognizing Panama's symbolic sovereignty.

A breakdown of talks is inevitable when each party's positions are too far apart to present a prospect for meeting even a minimum level of demand to continue negotiation. The initial stalemate in the Salvadoran peace talks between November 1984 and August 1987 was attributed to the government's demand for the unilateral disarmament of FMLN insurgents without referring to the opposition's core concerns such as a new constitution and reform of the military and police engaged in gross human rights violations (Roett and Smyth 1988). The mutually acceptable bargaining range decreases through intractable conflict where one's demand is anchored in the values held most dear by the opponents.

The appearance of a war of attrition is evident in the continuing manifestation of incompatibilities between each other's demands. In the failed Cyprus negotiations, it proved difficult to develop an agreement on a federal constitution that simultaneously embodied "unity" for the Greek Cypriots and "separation" for the Turkish Cypriots. At the very foundations of the negotiation process lies the formula of an independent, federal, bicommunal and bizonal republic. From the perspective of the Turkish Cypriots (accounting for less than 20 percent of the island population), a federation is more or less an equivalent of legal representation of a limited partnership. The Turkish community desires a guarantee of the sovereignty of each constituent unit, whereas the Greek Cypriots are attempting to preserve the integrity of the federal state (Richarte 2005, 208).

Managing negotiating dynamics and procedures

With the exhaustion of all the productive ideas and persisting intransigence, extricating the parties from a deadlocked negotiation turns out to be a daunting task. In moving out of a stalemate, both substantive and procedural interests of the parties need to converge. The differences in opposing demands will not be narrowed if neither party is willing to concede unilaterally and stands firm with positional statements. In order to induce the other to concede, one side may adopt persuasive arguments or pressure tactics such as the employment of threats. Alternatively, the parties may decide to be engaged in a collaborative search for a mutually acceptable solution.

After the motivation, will and stamina of negotiators to resume talks have evaporated, what can be done in the face of such an impasse? Bargaining strategies, styles and attitudes can be adjusted in the middle of negotiations. The negotiation process is not mechanical, since each party's expectations change through mutual interaction. Exchanging information through new proposals reveals the nature and extent of both differences and possibilities open to settlement. A composite proposal could be devised by selecting ideas from a previously failed formula once the negotiation's course has run into a stumbling block. The 1995 Dayton talks on ending the war in Bosnia-Herzegovina backtracked on the 1992 failure of the intensive Vance–Owen and Owen–Stoltenberg proposals, and reformulated old ideas, with fresh input from the opposing sides, in a newly incarnated package.

In a situation where neither is willing to trust the other's proposal, a complex bargaining problem can be divided into smaller, divisible parts for separate settlement (Schelling 1960). Discussion about less complicated or more agreeable issues will help to nurture an atmosphere of accomplishment in a continuing sequence of negotiations. As neither side's proposals were negotiable, in May 1970 during SALT I, negotiators informally concurred in taking a less comprehensive method, avoiding the larger struggle of trying to attain a complete package all at once. In parallel, the Soviet leadership made a secret move toward President Nixon through back-channel communication between Nixon's confidant Kissinger and Soviet ambassador Anatoly Dobrynin, breaking an impasse by abandoning simultaneous negotiations on the combined offensive–defensive package procedure. The United States agreed to a separate negotiation on the Anti-Ballistic Missile (ABM) Treaty. As a condition, the Soviets had to halt new construction of ICBM silos during the continued negotiation on offensive arms limitation (Smith 1985). This new procedural move to break an impasse led to the development of a preliminary framework on ABMs with a later focus on offensive weapons. In the end, the entire arrangement was organized in such a way as to link the defensive and offensive systems.

Partitioning issues helps limit the scope of contention. A search for a partial agreement becomes easier by dividing a problem into smaller, separate components. For example, Washington's proposed monitoring procedures were not acceptable to the Soviets during the negotiation on halting the tests of nuclear weapons in the early 1960s. The talks were limited to prohibiting the explosions in the atmosphere, outer space and underwater. As the negotiation bogged down in a search for mutually agreeable verification mechanisms, the original package was disaggregated to identify those parts that did not demand on-site inspections (considered necessary by Washington for detecting underground nuclear tests) (Hopmann 1996). The partial test ban treaty signed by the United States, the UK, and the Soviet Union in 1963 was eventually extended to a complete ban on testing in 1996, as initially desired, once the Cold War was over.

When a reward is explored to create positive perceptions, a promise might be decomposed into a series of small steps. Successfully inducing someone to make a small early commitment (from which it is difficult to back away) is often leveraged eventually into more substantial mutual gains. If trust is difficult to build, the danger is a possibility of losing a commitment to producing even a smaller but simpler accomplishment. In moving out of frozen positions in a stalemate, a bargainer may adopt a strategy of incremental concession, starting from lowest priority issues. In breaking a stalemate in the Panama Canal negotiation in 1972, the United States agreed to drop the perpetuity clause. Momentum was eventually produced by agreeing to the need for a new treaty with a fixed term. Yet, the United States did not yield on maintaining control over the canal and its defense for a prolonged period (Habeeb 1988).

Establishing some measure of compatibility may require redefining each other's goals and objectives. The foundation of an agreement can be built, in part, by rearranging or recharacterizing the issues, while avoiding being bogged down in the minuscule details. Irreversible barriers to backsliding can be set up by getting an initial agreement on basic principles or a framework for detailed bargaining (even on ambiguous terms). In propelling the process forward, the 1974 Kissinger–Tack formula formalized the US acceptance of ending its jurisdiction in any part of Panama, and a just and equitable share in benefits for Panama in return for retaining the US ability to use land and water areas necessary to operate and maintain the canal as well as rights to protect vital installations. This principle permitted the final round of the talks in 1977 to concentrate on details on the termination date of the new treaty and the matter of access to and defense of the canal.

Framing and reframing

While substantive objections should not be confused with sensitivities about word choices, carefully crafted statements may contain the recognition of the value in each other's perspectives. Rephrasing a proposed provision can serve as a basis for overcoming an impasse by reframing the terms. When a deadlock was created by an American demand for adequate guarantees in the defense of the Panama Canal for the indefinite future, it was overcome by an arrangement for the United States to ensure the canal's defense against external threats, with Panama tasked with its internal security. It was, in reality, a face-saving device for Panama, since the provision *de facto* allowed the United States to keep the permanent rights to defend the canal.

In a high-stakes battle (charged with emotions, touching on one side's deep values and principles), concession-making is perceived as humiliating or damaging to that party's reputation.³ The issue of the requirement of Israeli approval for the movement of Palestinian police officers between different security zones emerged as a major stumbling block near the conclusion of negotiations at Taba talks in 2000. The replacement of "approval" with "confirmation" was necessary to ease the feelings of the Palestinian side, which felt the initial wording was offensive to their sense of "sovereignty." In Israeli–Palestinian negotiations, creative drafting was required by sensitivity about language choices on other issues as well, for instance, "a (Palestinian) state with limited arms" vs. "defensive arms."

Persuasive tactics

A search for a satisfactory outcome involves persuading others to modify their expectations and requirements (Grobe 2010). The main route to persuasion is appealing to logic or emotion or both in connecting the other side to the central content of the message. In particular, persuasive communication is aimed at appealing to listeners "by joining an idea or an image with an emotion or feeling" (Carrell and Heavrin 2008, 118). At the defining moment of the Cuban Missile Crisis, the president's brother Robert Kennedy became "the best channel for direct, informal communications between the Kremlin and White House." In his delivery of John Kennedy's proposal of guarantees against an invasion of Cuba in return for dismantling the Soviet missile bases, Robert Kennedy "addressed the Soviet ambassador as a fellow human being trying to save the world from nuclear destruction. He began by describing the [Soviet] shoot-down of the U-2 and the firing on low level US Navy jets as an extremely serious turn in events." Instead of delivering an ultimatum or using threats, he "was simply laying out the facts." According to Dobrynin, Robert Kennedy was "very upset with little of his normal combativeness," "persistently [returning] to one theme: time is of the essence and we shouldn't miss the chance" (Dobbs 2008, 308).

Procedural innovation: limiting conflict and uncertainty

Informal deadlock-breaking rules and procedures could be inserted when the process encounters intransigence. When negotiation becomes a hostage to the most reluctant group in multiparty negotiations, an attempt at full consensus produces deadlocks or least-objectionable agreements. In contrast with the requirement for unanimity, "sufficient consensus" allows an agreement predicated on give-and-take at least between the major players. A "sufficient-consensus" rule permitted proposals to be enacted with the joint support of both National Party (NP) and African National Congress (ANC) regardless of objections from smaller groups after the near collapse of South Africa's negotiation over transition to black-majority rule in 1992.

Deadlocks in formal bargaining can be averted by an informal option-generation session (in a noncommittal setting). The entire brainstorming session takes place off the record to avoid attribution. In the above mentioned South African case, the planning committee's informal subcommittee devised preemptive strategies with the anticipation of logjams through daily meetings. In addition, formal proceedings were also smoothed out by informal bilateral summits such as Bosberade (i.e., a meeting in an isolated retreat to break a political gridlock). The "bush summit" allowed close working relationships to be built among negotiators in overcoming a major standoff about South Africa's new constitution. The utilization of private sessions played a pivotal role in hammering out major differences.

Options for settlement can be more creatively searched by other types of procedural innovativeness. A less formal process away from the table might complement preapproved formal statements read out at the negotiating table. During the US–Soviet negotiations leading to the SALT I Accord, informal meetings enabled negotiators to present options, rather than positions, by making hypothetical proposals as well as exchanging questions. After proposing three different approaches to limiting ABMs, the United States noticed, based on their comments about proposals, that the Soviets clearly desired to limit the ABM Treaty to local systems in such places as Moscow and Washington (Smith 1985). As the negotiation later unfolded, this initial exchange of information helped the American side develop a better understanding of how their different proposals would be perceived and what to demand in return for satisfying Soviet concerns.

Informal consultation behind the scenes creates a climate for a free exchange of ideas. In spite of a series of criticisms of each other's official positions during a tough period of the 1994 Geneva negotiation over North Korea's denuclearization, a creative process such as private tea meetings helped the US delegation garner key concessions from their counterparts. Informal meetings between the two chief negotiators, away from public view, before each formal session, were arranged to gauge a deeper level of understanding beneath the other side's official positions. The breakthrough was achieved by US negotiators' willingness to engage North Koreans at a more personal level, managing their psychological and social relationships.

Change in the negotiation climate

Serving as a psychological buffer, robust relationships help ease tension in the times of rough struggle (Watkins 1999). Although the war had been waged outside the El Salvadoran negotiations, negotiators maintained a mutually respectful, cordial relationship. General Mauricio Vargas's fellow government team members even teased him about divorcing his wife and marrying one of the FMLN leaders, referring to the general's fondness for his counterparts at the table (Messing 2000). In Guatemala, with the progress in the negotiation to end the civil war, the government ceased to be engaged in its ideological and political attacks on Unidad Revolucionaria Nacional Guatemalteca (URNG) as a "defeated force" or "subversive terrorists." In November 1995, the newly elected president even valued the insurgent group's "patriotic motives" unlike the previous government (Jonas 2000). The respect for the URNG as a negotiating partner was a key element in the eventually successful negotiation. The vastly improved bilateral relations helped, in turn, decrease international pressure on the government, actually boosting its negotiation position.

Control of the political environment

Unless negotiation is carried out in complete confidentiality, the players are subject to immediate external pressure. Public scrutiny of the negotiation process generates concerns about how an outcome will be received and accepted.[4] When a shift in a long-held public stance is seen as a capitulation by a wider audience, it would be difficult to entertain fresh proposals along with thoughts about possible concessions. Transparency can therefore sacrifice flexibility, weakening the hope of an agreement (Albin 2001). The resistance of constituents and powerful audience groups creates obstacles to taking bold positions in negotiation. A negotiation process is affected by each party's ability to control the surrounding political environment.

The negative spillover effects of political events can be controlled by restrictions on the flow of information associated with negotiation. Secret high-level talks could be introduced in the event of deadlocks in official meetings. A tight lid was put on information coming out of talks during the 1978 Camp David negotiation between Egypt and Israel. In Guatemala, after general elections in November 1995, the newly elected president held direct, secret meetings with the URNG in different venues sponsored by various governments and the Vatican. In the Salvadoran peace negotiation, the failure in a continuing series of talks on demilitarization and military immunity in August 1990 led the UN secretary-general to announce that all future negotiations would be conducted in secret.

Meaningless official talks may camouflage actual negotiations carried out in complete privacy. The Oslo peace process was kept under wraps until the breakthrough was announced in August 1993, whereas formal talks were going on in public at the same time in Washington without carrying much significance. The complete surprise with the revelation of the Oslo peace accord permitted negotiators to benefit from the enthusiasm among the public, but thereafter negotiations failed to mobilize a broad public consensus. Even though covert talks were held in Sweden between Israelis and Palestinians in June 2000, prior to the Camp David meeting, the efforts to locate common ground were undermined by the leakage of information about such events to the news media.[5]

Setting deadlines

In order to build momentum, negotiators may employ a wide range of techniques, including setting up action-forcing events such as deadlines tied to a particular calendar date. As seen in the production of a peace accord in Northern Ireland and South Africa, setting deadlines may endow negotiators with a clear mandate to develop an overall strategy. As part of specific targets set within a particular chronological sequence, the election date of 26 April 1994 in South Africa put pressure on the negotiators to conclude settlement. In reaching the 1992 Salvadoran peace accord, the two sides had to rush to complete their negotiations before the departure of the UN Secretary General Javier Perez de Cuellar, whose support was pivotal to any successful outcome. Deadlines are also adopted as a mechanism to exert control over the negotiation by imposing time costs on a counterpart through unilateral action, such as the US Christmas bombing in North Vietnam near the agreement's conclusion in January 1973.

As a jointly recognized ultimatum, a deadline can convert a proposal into a final offer. The failure to meet the deadline can "turn an alternative to a negotiated settlement into reality" (du Toit 2003, 66). In Israeli–Palestinian negotiations, negotiators had to race with time in the midst of escalating violence that eventually destroyed the process. Negotiators were desperately seeking to salvage the entire peace effort immediately prior to Israel's election, being overshadowed by a widely forecasted overwhelming victory for hardliner Ariel Sharon over the incumbent, Prime Minister Ehud Barak of the Labor Party. Their last meetings at the Egyptian resort of Taba, on January 21–27, 2001, more effectively tested new parameters with Israeli offers that were improved from the terms presented during the Camp David negotiation six months earlier. After a week of off-and-on negotiations, Israel's negotiator Shlomo Ben-Ami announced "[w]e are closer than ever to the possibility of striking a final deal." Echoing this sentiment, Saeb Erekat, the Palestinian chief negotiator, uttered, "My heart aches because I know we were so close. We need six more weeks to conclude the drafting of the agreement" (Carter 2009, 60). However, tragically, political time had run out too quickly.

Wise counselor

In the negotiations over the Limited Test Ban Treaty of 1963, British prime minister Harold Macmillan's intermediary role was seen as "crucial to bridging the gulf between the United States and the Soviet Union," bringing back some of the momentum lost after deadlock over the number of on-site inspections (Hampson 1995, 70). Being informed that "it's not science but politics that holds back the President," Macmillan reminded Kennedy of the Soviet acceptance of three annual inspections while mentioning the reduced Western demand from twenty to seven. In his letter to the US president, Macmillan wrote: "[even] to the layman ... it would be almost inconceivable that the gulf could not be bridged ... the Test Ban is the most important step that we can take toward unraveling this frightful tangle of fear and suspicions in East–West relations" (Horne 1989, 506–507). In his brokering role, the British prime minister coaxed both Kennedy and Khrushchev into not breaking off while making suggestions of alternative possibilities for Kennedy (Hampson 1995).[6] In spite of its close alliance with the United States, Britain, as the third nuclear power, played an intermediary role in informal talks between the United States and the Soviet Union.

Outside intervention

Negotiators are not the only players engaged in the management of conflict. Various types of orchestrated action can be taken by interveners at or away from the negotiating table. Third parties seek to affect the outcomes of disputes either at the invitation of the opposing sides or by unilateral action (Jeong 2009). In breaking a deadlock, outside parties might be called upon to mediate or exert pressure on either or both parties who have put a stumbling block in the way of progress.

Outside intervention may control existing or potential sources of dynamics that might poison the attempt to reach agreement. During the Salvadoran negotiation, the April 27, 1991, agreement in Mexico produced a commitment to creating a truth commission to investigate human rights violations and forming an independent civil police force as well as constitutional reforms. These commitments were reluctantly accepted by the right-wing legislature only after the exertion of highly visible pressure from the US government and the international community. Then the Salvadoran government asserted the FMLN's demobilization prior to any further progress in talks while rejecting the language that called for a purge of human rights abusers (Burgerman 2000; Messing 2000). The FMLN was not in the mood to discuss its demobilization based only on vague promises of the security sector transformation that was its core demand. As the negotiation was faltering, UN Secretary General Perez de Cuellar took an active role in reviving the stalled talks on the armed forces. His invitation of both President Alfredo Cristiani and the FMLN General Commander Francisco Jovel to New York generated enough pressure to break a three-month impasse. The meeting produced not only compromise on substantive issues blocking the talks but also created a foundation for further negotiations, with the establishment of the National Commission for the Consolidation of the Peace (COPAZ). COPAZ was instituted to oversee the reform of the armed forces and other changes envisioned in all the political agreements reached up to that point.

In addition to UN mediation, pressure from the US Congress played a substantial role in overcoming difficulties arising from the resistance of the Salvadoran military and right-wing political establishment against constitutional and armed forces reforms. The threat of cutting funding was quite effective in weakening the Salvadoran elite's opposition, since the government heavily relied upon American military and financial aid to keep afloat (Karl 1992). Both the attitudes and positions of the negotiating parties were also swayed by a neutral outside perspective and valuable financial support for the negotiation coming from an amalgam of parties called the Group of Friends, including Mexico, Venezuela, Costa Rica and Spain.

Midcourse corrections

When a stalled negotiation is resumed, initially nonnegotiable agendas can be seriously discussed (e.g., Salvadoran, the US–Panamanian and US–Soviet arms-control negotiations). As expectations diverge from the initial assessment of negotiability of issues, further positioning is accompanied by the new judgment about the basis of the other party's bargaining position. After the reassessment of the objectives and interests, entrapment can be overcome by having a realistic perception of the other party (e.g., the US government's reversal of an initial mantra "not one centrifuge spins" that proved to be a nonstarter for Iranians during the early period of nuclear talks).

An adjustment process involves changes at least in one party's values. The deadlock continued for three and a half years in the Paris peace talks until Washington had to drop its initially uncompromising demand for withdrawal of all northern troops from South Vietnam. In return, Hanoi retreated from its refusal of a provisional South Vietnamese government headed by its incumbent leader Nguyen Van Thieu (Asselin 2002). In order to end the war, the United States was willing to make bigger concessions than originally expected.

Concessions are considered a necessary evil to create an exit from a deadlocked situation once each party becomes eager to settle. The convergence of expectations can be facilitated by (1) the discovery of shared interests and compatibility of preferences, and (2) the possibility of gain as an incentive to avoid impasse. In the Iranian nuclear negotiation, a breakthrough arose from a shift in focus from the number and type of centrifuge machines to the "breakout time" (i.e., the amount of time for amassing singular bomb-grade material in a race for a nuclear weapon). This helped formulate an option to permit Iran to keep at least some of its centrifuges running while severely constraining uranium-enrichment far below a typical threshold for weapons-grade material. Equally important, a momentum was built by the offer of a small reward and its further promise. An interim deal known as the Joint Plan of Action (JPOA), introduced in November 2013, obliged Iran to put "meaningful limits" on its nuclear fuel program in return for some sanctions relief (e.g., access to some of its hard currency held abroad). This targeted sanctions relief was reversible, being renewed every six months. Its extension served as a reminder of a continuing commitment to seeking a negotiated settlement. Given the program's tenuous nature, it created urgency, setting a sort of deadline. After JPOA terms were extended twice and expired on June 30, 2015, the deadline was prolonged further through July 7, then to the 10th, and once again to the 13th, prior to a final agreement (called the Joint Comprehensive Plan of Action) reached on July 14, 2015.

If one or both sides have high aspirations and are resistant to conceding, it may not be possible to resolve the conflict unless a new bargaining method is found to reconcile the two parties' interests. If the parties accede to some middle ground by a more easily perceived or self-evident principle or method, splitting their differences on each issue might yield equal utility to all negotiating parties. Yet premature compromises are often unsatisfactory to the parties which have to reduce their aspirations in order to reach an agreement, leaving a potential for the issue to resurface at a later time. Given that it is mutually rewarding and is producing a higher joint benefit, integrative agreements based on collaborative efforts tend to be more stable.

Most importantly, the real difficulty may no longer lie in making concessions but in defining types of concessions the parties are ready to make. In the failed talks on Cyprus in the early 2000s, Turkish Cypriot insistence on territorial separation was incompatible with Greek Cypriot demand for the rights of refugees to return to their homes and freedom of movement (Guelke 2003).[7] As the Turkish Cypriots insisted that their safety depended on being autonomous and separate, their concept of "security" did not leave room for compromise with the way "autonomy" is understood by the Greek Cypriots. It is not at all clear for both communities to be able to concede on "security" or "autonomy" as conceived by each side. Even in the division of land, a struggle often concentrates not on the amount of land but on its quality and type. For instance, the collapse of the Syrian–Israeli negotiation over the Golan Heights in 1999–2000 is attributed to not a simple matter of the percentage of the occupied territory to be returned but a question of who would keep a narrow, small corridor strategically valuable with access to a water reservoir.

In a successful example of the Iranian nuclear negotiation between October 2013 and July 2015, the most significant tradeoff was a decade or so of restrictions. The initial US desire to curtail Iran's nuclear program for decades was met by Iran's demand for the indefinite expansion of its nuclear program within a few years. In the end, Iran's enrichment activities would remain at a very low level for the first fifteen years with the promise of their full-scale resumption thereafter. Tehran agreed to roll back the infrastructure of uranium enrichment, along with the acceptance of intrusive inspections, in exchange for the Western recognition of its renewed nuclear rights without limits upon the expiration of the agreed deal in 2030.

Different types of concessions may create a sense of balance and imbalance between benefits and concessions. In the above-mentioned nuclear agreement, what mattered most to Tehran was the legitimization of its nuclear program and its symbolism epitomized by forcing major international powers to respect Iran as an equal sovereign state. If we add its loss of a symbolic, ideological status (championing the Arab cause), Egypt made more concessions than Israel in the Camp David negotiation (Albin 2001). In the Good Friday Agreement at the end of the Northern Ireland peace talks (in April 1998), the concessions made by the mostly Loyalist (i.e., Unionist) Protestant community and the mostly Republican (i.e., Nationalist) Catholic community differed in nature. In conflict over the same territory's political future (with opposing visions for national identity), the main difference between Loyalists and Republicans was whether Northern Ireland ought to stay part of the UK or be united with the Republic of Ireland to the south. In the end, mostly symbolic concessions were made by the Republican side with the passive acknowledgement of the constitutional status of Northern Ireland. Thus the Republicans accepted the status of Northern Ireland by removing the possibility of joining the Irish Republic in the absence of majority Protestant support. On the other hand, the concessions made by the Unionists represented a more specific, vital program of governance to address Republican grievances that had to be carried out more promptly (Aughey 2005). These included the release of several hundred IRA prisoners and power-sharing with the assignment of two cabinet posts in the new executive power to Sinn Fein as well as joint North/South institutions. In contrast with 96 percent support among Catholics in Northern Ireland, only 52 percent of Protestants voted to approve the agreement in the 1998 national referendum. The wide disparity reflects how each community saw some of the sections, particularly the prisoner release and the decommissioning of paramilitary weapons.

Fair division scheme

In the absence of a mutually acceptable standard, a contest of wills may be avoided by adhering to a procedure to involve some notion of fairness – reciprocity, an even split of the differences or some other customary division rules that entail common expectations. Being seen in the example of one child's dividing a cake into two pieces with the other's selection (in Chapter 2), divide-and-choose procedures are applicable to a situation where a similar valuation of the resources is made by all sides. As an integral part of the Law of the Sea Treaty (1982), a parallel system was devised to give mining companies in industrialized countries a right to divide a proposed mining site into two parts with the International Seabed Authority's ability to choose which of the two parts to keep for itself. In addition to a "divide-and-choose" scheme, auction mechanisms were also adopted in reaching an agreement to guarantee a "fair chance" to affect the outcome (Sebenius 1984).

In the June 2002 Sudanese negotiation, the Machakos Protocol produced a provision that allows sharia to remain in the north, but the south to be governed by a secular administration. Both parties abandoned previously nonnegotiable items such as Khartoum's desire to Islamize southern Sudan and the SPLA's determination to secularize the entire country (Khadiagala 2007, 241). In a January 2004 agreement, the differences over wealth sharing were resolved by a 50/50 split of oil revenue between the north and south.[8]

Issue linkage

The substance of issues and their priority ranking are factored into a range of possible solutions. Mutual gains can be identified if each party cares about different issues. If one issue matters more to one party than the other, the latter can yield on that issue for a tradeoff. Bargaining on disparate issues through linkage could open up possibilities for mutually acceptable arrangements with integrative tactics. In negotiations between the Unionists and Republicans in Northern Ireland, for instance, the formation of a power-sharing executive was linked to the decommissioning of paramilitary weapons. Eliciting gains may utilize either exploiting common interests or uncovering differences for the exploration of mutual benefit with tradeoffs. Issue linkage helps avoid a situation where early concessions by one party eliminate the other's incentives for reciprocation (Princen 1992). Settlement on easier issues should be utilized to create joint gains with more difficult issues.

In the absence of issue linkages, each party would support a solution in its own beneficial arena without accepting negative payoffs in others. By a linkage, one party obtains a highly preferred outcome on one issue while the other has their favorite outcome on another. Each side's zone of possible agreement can be expanded by various types of issue linkages. In the Iranian nuclear negotiation, a gradual lifting of economic sanctions and the arms embargo has been tied to Tehran's entitlement to a very limited amount of uranium stockpiles for medical and other peaceful purposes as well as a significantly reduced number of uranium-enriching centrifuges for fifteen years. In a tradeoff on sanctions, more upfront, quick relief for the energy and financial industries was offset by a longer trade ban on ballistic missiles (to be lifted after a maximum of eight years) and conventional weapons (for five years). In a "horsetrading" strategy, attaining more important concessions can be exchanged for giving up something less valuable to oneself but more crucial to the other. Each party gets what they want when each's high-priority issues are low-priority for the other. As a negotiation tool, a linkage is designed to produce a Pareto superior decision where the linkage's expected value is more than an individual actor's original endowments (Tollison and Willett 1979).

Tradeoffs among multidimensional issues in the formulation of package deals can utilize an offer strategy known as logrolling based on exchangeable concessions. The satisfaction of one's demand is contingent upon meeting her counterpart's interests in other areas where he has a high priority. In tradeoffs among different values on multiple issues, the first party gives in a little on one issue, but the second party does the same on another one in reciprocation. Thus tradeoffs on different issues permit the simultaneous consideration of underlying interests and ways to meet them (Lewicki *et al.* 2007). In contrast with reciprocal tradeoffs, circular logrolling is created by tradeoffs in which each group makes an offer to another with a concession on one issue but receives a concession from yet another group on a different issue. Ideally, the concessions should be more appreciated by the recipient than by the giver (Thompson 2001). Circular tradeoffs demand more vigilance, in that the reciprocity involves the cooperation of more than two parties.

The existence of complementary goals creates easy conditions for this formulation. Building blocks for tradeoffs can be based on the expectation of the return offer on an item of similar weight and somewhat comparable magnitude. If the structure of issue metrics consists of lower or higher priorities on different issue areas among the parties, low-priority matters can be used as bargaining chips in exchange for gains in high-priority areas. Transitive values on issues permit all the negotiators to get what they desire most at little or less cost than required in the absence of trading. Each actor pursues an option ranked highest according to their own preference schedule. In order to attain concessions on higher-priority issues to itself, each side is willing to give in on low-priority issues in return. The linkage of the underlying preferences demands information about issues which are of higher and lower priority to each side.

Delinkage

Difficult issues can be decoupled or unbundled by reprioritizing different interests. Through delinkage, certain issues can be excluded to avoid derailment. Palestinian issues during the 1978 Camp David negotiation became a major hurdle to reaching an agreement due to the intransigence of then Israeli prime minister Begin. The negotiation was ultimately saved by unbundling Palestinian autonomy from the Sinai. While a separate accord was needed to cover the determination of the West Bank's and Gaza's future status, it did not obligate Israel to give up anything, simply referring to a vague promise of separate, follow-up negotiations in the future.

Bridging

When compromise or expanding the pie is not feasible, a bridging solution satisfies different interests typically by reformulating the issue(s) on the basis of meeting their underlying objectives. Even though neither party has its initial demands met through a tradeoff, a new option is devised in such a way as to satisfy the most important concerns beneath separate proposals. The positions of all sides are considered at the initial phase of a search for a bridging solution. If different sets of high-priority interests are not reconciled to generate a mutually acceptable alternative, the search for a solution begins anew after some demands are dropped. Successful bridging, as in logrolling, has to fulfill key interests of all sides through the creation of a new alternative (Thompson 2001).

As the British decolonized Cyprus in 1958, the Greek Cypriots desired reunification of the whole island with Greece while the Turkish Cypriots proposed partition, insisting that their safety depended on being separate and aligned with Turkey. The first choice of each of the two communities was incompatible and had to be abandoned. Since neither unification with Greece nor the partition of Cyprus turned out to be an acceptable solution, independence, as a third way, became the "least evil" for the respective communities involved (Richarte 2005). Even though independence was never pursued by any of the parties, there was no other way out of the violence. The Turkish Cypriots were ensured that majority rule would not be imposed with the establishment of three distinctive administrations, one Turkish Cypriot, the other Greek Cypriot, and another of mixed nationality for a total population of only half a million.

Compensation and cost-cutting

When one party's gains come at the expense of the other, compensation for losses can be made through repayment in unrelated areas or substitution that carries a roughly equivalent value (e.g., land swap). The conceding party is repaid in some unrelated benefit or acquires something, via the redistribution of other gains or costs. In attaining one's objectives, thus, a payoff needs to be made to accommodate an adversary's interests via a form of offset by other types of benefit that were originally outside the bounds of the negotiation (Lewicki *et al.* 2007).

In devising adequate compensation for concessions, it is important to know something about the interests, values and aspirations underlying the sacrificing party's overt position. The valuation of the compensation can be appropriately determined by information about the degree of loss absorbed by the conceding party. The item's worth to the other party could be counterbalanced through compensatory payoffs. The repayment requires knowledge about not only the costs posed to the conceding party but also methods for mitigating or eliminating these. In US–Soviet arms-control negotiations, finding potential tradeoffs was not easy due to different strategic force structures and ongoing weapons programs between the two superpowers (Haslam and Osborne 1987). Yet each side's concession was still contingent upon what was expected in return. The strategic arms negotiations were made complicated, in part, by Moscow's insistence on an adequate compensation for the US forward-based systems (i.e., American missiles and other delivery vehicles located abroad and capable of directly striking Soviet territory). The Soviet proposals between August 1970 and July 1973 included keeping higher ceilings on numbers of missile launchers in return for allowing the United States to retain its forward-based system in Europe and the Far East.

An offer can be improved by minimizing another's sacrifice or loss from making concessions. In such instances as easing the economic burden of pollution control through technology transfer, cost-cutting measures are taken to minimize loss to those who comply with the other party's expectations. Whereas one party acquires the desired object, the other's costs can be lessened or eliminated in lieu of compensation. In meeting the first party's demand, the second party suffers less through cost-cutting even though it may not deal with the precise costs (Thompson 2001). If the object's value is sacred or infinite, no compensation or cost-cutting would be feasible. Indeed, some stakes escape a creative reformulation due to their indivisibility. As problems resist more finely graded divisions or compromise, an outcome could depend on the determination of which issues are negotiable or deal-breakers.

Despite an attractive formula, it may prove intractable in detail. In Israeli–Palestinian negotiations, territorial concessions on the West Bank were relatively easier to discuss vis-à-vis control over Jerusalem, which contains less tangible and more symbolic value. Handling the zero-sum aspects of politically salient negotiations on such issues as the "Jerusalem Problem" goes beyond positive-sum creativity that helps meet everyone's essential needs through the exploration of an ingenious device for joint gains. The trade-off of intangible goals (e.g., identity and security) needs to be based on respect for historical meanings or intrinsic values held by each party. A specific notion of a creative formula might derive from manipulating the notions of justice or restructuring perceptions of the stakes to remove the zero-sum nature of the outcome.

The last stage of negotiation

The psychological cost of concessions emanates from the sacrifice of original aspirations. The parties may become emotional, after intense bargaining, with difficulties in managing their aspiration levels. The end stage may face unexpected hurdles due to attempts to extract last-minute concessions. Although financial compensation had played only a minor role in the early years of the negotiations, it increasingly became a crucial issue to the Panamanians, all the more so in light of their large concession on the canal defense issue. With an agreement in sight, Panama felt the time was ripe to push for a large financial reward by making last-minute extreme demands. In a response to an American offer of a $50 million lump sum, Panamanian leader Torrijos demanded a $1 billion lump sum plus a $300 million annuity for the life of the new treaty. The great disparity in positions provoked a last-minute crisis that was eventually resolved by President Carter's warning letter about the failure of Senate ratification caused by the excessive demand. Refusing further concessions, though, Carter offered an increase in Panama's share of the canal's toll revenues, amounting to $40–50 million a year (Habeeb 1988).

As an actual gain is likely to be lower than one's most desired value, a win–lose dimension may reappear at the last stage of negotiation. In order to make up the shortfall in aspirations, each party often seeks extra gains and generally ends up exchanging some smaller concessions that help in finalizing the settlement. Last-minute concessions can be squeezed out with "salami" tactics (seeking "one slice" more). The methods of closing a deal could also involve splitting the difference and asking an opponent to choose among alternatives (Lewicki *et al.* 2007). A deadline may be set up to press the other party to agree quickly with exploding offers. In ending the Panama Canal negotiation in 1977, the United States sweetened the final package with a promise of $295 million in loans and guarantees over the following five years and $50 million in military assistance in the following ten years.

A long negotiation process may bring about modifications in relationships as well as a shift in the core issues. The Camp David Accord between Israel and Egypt had to wait several months to formulate details on a formal treaty (finally concluded in March 1979). Each side adopted less amicable negotiating styles, stiffening the other side's position. In general, constituents' concerns are seldom put in concrete terms at the beginning of negotiations, because positions and interests tend to get constructed in the evolution of interactions (Watkins 1999). In the Panama negotiation, with the politicization of the canal issue in the 1976 American presidential election, the input of such domestic actors as the US Senate became more critical in formulating the terms of final agreements. In trade negotiations, industries, labor unions and other groups may attempt to provide last-minute input to prevent effects that are adverse to their own interests. Prior to a ratification process, the United States extracted further concessions on behalf of its car industries in reaching a free-trade agreement with South Korea in 2012. French farmers and other vociferous groups have often used violent protests to express opposition to provisions on the elimination of agricultural subsidies presented during global trade negotiations.

When the final stages are conducted with great speed under time pressure, the provisions might be vague, demanding interpretation and reinterpretation. In the Salvadoran negotiations, the loose ends of an implementation agreement had to be tightened up before signing Chapultepec Peace accords on January 16, 1992, in Mexico City. With a heavy focus on military matters, the final agreement still lacked concrete provisions for human rights, judicial and police reforms, land distribution and other socioeconomic issues. While laying out a basic principle, these provisions left the implementation details for later decisions (Albin 2001; Messing 2000). The socioeconomic reforms in particular were in an especially obscure manner as stipulated in the following sentence: "The Government of El Salvador shall seek to strengthen existing social welfare programmes designed to alleviate extreme poverty" (Goverment of El Salvador and Frente Farabundo Martí para la Liberación Nacional 1991). Phrasing the agreement in a broad manner curtailed a path toward more effectively carrying out social welfare programs and land redistribution provisions.

In the case of the 1998 Belfast Agreement, in order to prevent refusals to sign, few details were provided, with a simple referrence to "exclusively peaceful and democratic means." The spirit of "constructive ambiguity" was applied to allow deliberate vagueness on methods or dates for prisoner release and paramilitary decommissioning with side letters of promise and (vague) guarantees. The general description was necessary to producing a more inclusive agreement on each of the core contentious issues, forming a significant foundation on which to build trust for future interaction, but the vagueness created inherent difficulties for later implementation.

If it is not so easy to seek a detailed, as well as comprehensive, blueprint, ambiguity and uncertainty in an outline of a settlement are often facts of life even after bridging major differences. In bringing a settlement to Northern Ireland's sectarian conflict, Unionist supporters had to argue that it made the Union safe for the future; on the other hand, Nationalists had to be able to stress a dynamic toward Irish unity by presenting any deal as transitional (Aughey 2005). The expectations of each party need to be put in obscure language to manage other contentious issues (e.g., decommissioning of armed groups) so that both sides can claim victory. Rather than risking the collapse of the entire process, certain statements may be left untouched, leaving some questions unasked.

As contentious issues may simply be deferred to smooth the way for an agreement, a sense of disillusionment may arise from these unresolved issues at the postagreement implementation stage. The less detailed the terms of the settlement, the greater challenge is posed. If a hurried conclusion of any kind of complex agreement results in indeterminateness, parts of the terms and clauses have to be reinterpreted or altered with the renegotiation of some details. A continuing negotiation is necessary to produce a series of new agreements that put specific terms on the original settlement to avoid a dispute over its interpretation. As the deal proved difficult to implement, the 1998 Belfast Agreement had to be amended in the 2006 St Andrew's Agreement which specified timetables and procedures to discuss power-sharing, policing and finance.

Negotiation procedures and objectives certainly have an impact on types of agreements. A framework agreement provides overall guidance for a step-by-step approach to developing details. An interim treaty may precede a comprehensive agreement (as in the US–Soviet arms-control negotiation). In addition, agreement can be negotiated to specify implementation methods and key deadlines along with provisions on timing for review or revision as well as monitoring. The ABM treaty has an unlimited duration and a built-in dispute-resolution system. The Standing Consultative Commission (SCC) was instituted, as an ongoing, bilateral US–Soviet review panel, to execute the treaty's provisions. The SCC is a forum for discussion of alleged treaty violations and their possible resolution through private communication of differences with a minimal risk of embarrassment (Fisher *et al.* 1997).

Legitimation and sustainability

Subjective assessments of an outcome are often tied to the fairness of the process employed to resolve a dispute. In fact, procedural justice increases not only the opportunity for integrative bargaining but also the favorability and acceptance of agreements (Hollander-Blumoff and Tyler 2008). At the same time, a true litmus test lies in garnering constituent support for endorsing the outcome. Northern Ireland's Good Friday Agreement of 1998 included a special provision for the endorsement of the settlement through a simultaneous but separate referendum in both the Republic of Ireland and Northern Ireland. Political considerations can be made to postpone signing an agreement until external circumstances are changing. Jordan's King Hussein did not announce his agreement with Israel to avoid a backlash from key constituents or political opponents until the Israeli–Palestinian peace accord emerged in 1993. A ratification process of SALT II Treaty at the US Congress was abandoned with anticipation of difficulties in getting approval after heightened tensions following the Soviet invasion of Afghanistan in December 1979. The negotiated outcome was not legally binding but remained politically effective, being partially observed.

As international "commitments are not enforceable anywhere," in fact, they become "statements of intention to do or refrain from doing something. The very fact of a nation's being willing to make such statements can be as important as their contents. The aims of a negotiation like SALT are not limited to agreeing on specific terms" (Smith 1985, 464). Likewise, a nuclear accord with Iran only buys "time to try to restructure the relationship" while diminishing the prospect for Tehran's development of nuclear weapons (*New York Times*, July 15, 2015). Its current significance lies in preventing a steady slide toward war with Iran's acceleration of uranium-enrichment capabilities, but its ultimate success relies heavily on a search for a forward-looking outcome that avoids the old conflict's resurgence in a new, perhaps even more intense, form by broadening opportunities for cooperation. In fact, a negotiated agreement is not a panacea for providing an answer or solution for all the difficulties, but should be able to furnish a mechanism to prevent or resolve a future conflict.

Despite an agreement's own political value, it may not be considered successful until everything is implemented (Albin 2001). The postagreement phase is often dominated, with waning urgency, by dragging commitments to compliance (Jeong 2005).

Its prospect is plagued by inadequate incentives to live up to fulfilling promises or taking costly actions, especially if the agreement's soundness or attractiveness fades away.[9] The distribution of benefits or burdens may no longer look reasonable in changing circumstances. The original solutions may turn out to be obsolete and antiquated over the years, demanding another round of talks. To rebuild confidence, the foundations beneath the initial formula may have to be explicated with the incorporation of different sets of concerns. The process could develop more flexibility into the provisions to preserve sustainability over time with the emergence of new conditions. In Northern Ireland, postagreement power-sharing had to adjust to the electoral defeat of the moderate parties representing the two opposing communities.

With the passage of time, the essence of a negotiated settlement may be chipped away by various challenges. First of all, the issues may have evaded a more conclusive resolution, being obscured by a provisional or partial settlement. In an agreement on principles or procedures, the questions may linger not only on clarity and specificity of the rules but also on their fairness. After an arrangement has been made, one's original provisions could be met with new challenges. In a substantively comprehensive agreement, most significantly, the nature of a problem, its possible remedies and effects can still be evolving (e.g., transborder air pollution or depleting fish stocks to the extinction level). The implementability of an agreement is supported by the evaluation, monitoring and dispute-resolution mechanisms. In the case of the historic Iranian nuclear deal, the prospect for successful implementation will be seriously eroded by charges of any real or perceived failures of compliance despite the existence of a dispute-settlement panel. While a complaint against Iranian cheating opens a door for the reimposition of sanctions through a "snapback" mechanism, Iran preserves the right to simply walk away from the agreement. Beyond just the negotiated agreement itself, thus, the post-negotiation political climate, as such, could dramatically shape the eventual outcome of the settlement as vividly demonstrated by the 1994 genocide in Rwanda, the collapse of the 1993 Oslo Peace Accord and the abandonment of the 1994 US–North Korean Framework Agreement.

Therefore, the process of implementation can be profoundly affected by how a particular political settlement turns out and survives uncontrolled, destructive external events as well as resistance from its domestic opponents. Owing to the imbalance of power between the parties, the Palestine Liberation Organization (PLO) was in too weak a position to secure a more legitimate outcome which in turn caused dwindling support among ordinary Palestinians. As Israeli representative Benjamin Netanyahu obstructed the 1993 Oslo Accords by setting new conditions, it only deepened a sense of injustice in many segments of the Palestinian society, contributing to growing support for the Islamic resistance movement Hamas (Albin 2001). Progress in Israel–PLO negotiations, as well as fulfillment of the interim agreements, was difficult to achieve in the midst of a series of Palestinian suicide bombings and heavy Israeli military retaliations. The complete collapse of the Oslo process (designed to negotiate permanent peace) is, to a great extent, ascribed to the mismanagement of a postnegotiation process to sort out many details on Israeli troop withdrawals and expansion of the Palestinian authority in the West Bank. Embittered battles could have been circumvented by putting confidence-building measures in place as well as keeping the lines of communication open.

Conclusion

This chapter has shed light on changes involved in a transition of negotiation from one stage to another. Prenegotiation generally sets broad boundaries of the agenda, helping to determine what is excluded from the table as well as identifying the participants. Formal negotiation is marked by bargaining along with the exchange of proposals. The way a joint solution emerges is affected by strategies of presenting a position and repackaging proposals. The overall procedures are characterized by various activities involved at a particular negotiation point.

As reviewed in this chapter, a negotiation process can be defined not as the isolated activity of a single party, but rather by its interactive nature. The shift in relationships influences progression toward settling differences. As a negotiation starts, unfolds and ends, a set of related functions and challenges is involved in the movement. The system of interaction is constituted by recurring behavioral and communication patterns (e.g., cooperation vs. competition). In addition, external events may shape both the substance and process of talks. As we shall see more clearly in later chapters, challenges entail diverse psychological, organizational decision-making processes. In the next chapter, we will examine the bargaining process and its strategies more closely.

Notes

1 The agenda-setting strategies entail the consideration of the order and linkages of issues as well as decisions on issues to be excluded.
2 Differences in agenda priorities are inevitable when each party wants to talk about their priority concerns first. As opposed to Israeli preferences, in a prepatory meeting for the 2000 Camp David negotiation, the Palestinian delegation put a higher priority on discussion about permanent borders over security arrangements which include the installation of military stations inside the newly created Palestinian state border and the Israeli use of its air space.
3 Reframing serves as a face-saving mechanism that justifies the concessions that have to be made once the original hardline position is given up.
4 Public pressure serves not only as a constraint on concessions but also as a force pushing for agreement. External events brought about fluctuations in public interest in the Test Ban Treaty. Following the shooting-down of an American U-2 spy plane in Soviet air space and the

subsequent cancellation of a US–Soviet summit, support for the moratorium on nuclear testing declined from almost 80 percent in November 1959 to a mere 27 percent in June 1961. In the aftermath of the Cuban Missile Crisis, unqualified support for a test ban went up to 51 percent by July 1963, eventually climbing to 81 percent with the signing of the treaty (Hampson 1995, 72).

5 The negotiation was conducted by two people trusted by their leaders on each side. The Swedish prime minister's official residence in Harpsund served as a venue; the extreme northern latitude was an ideal location for nonstop negotiations. The talks were leaked to an Israeli journalist one day after their commencement by a high-ranking Palestinian official who was excluded from the two-member delegtiation. It produced "a fire storm of controversy," with the criticism of "selling out" in the Palestinian press while "other Palestinian negotiators in the front channel felt blindsided" (Swisher 2004, 208). No more secrecy was left as every move came under intense domestic scrutiny. Both sides agreed to bring the Swedish channel back to the Middle East with one last meeting held in mid June prior to the Camp David summit.

6 The British ambassador to Washington, David Ormsby-Gore, also advised a strategy of answering Khrushchev's conciliatory letter, which was sent first, but to ignore his rude and harsh second letter that stresses that there was no point in going over old arguments on inspection (Hampson 1995).

7 Around 165,000 Greeks in Northern Cyprus lost their homes and properties during the 1974 Turkish military invasion with the capture of a third of the island, resulting in partition between north and south. Meanwhile, roughly 45,000 Turkish Cypriots left the south for the north.

8 "The fairness of a 50/50 split depends on the comparative fairness of the two numbers being used as anchors" (Bazerman and Neale 1992, 121).

9 On this matter, a negotiated settlement needs to be justified by solutions to the problem rather than the process (Borch and Mérida 2013).

8 Bargaining behavior

> We cannot negotiate with people who say what's mine is mine and what's yours is negotiable.
>
> John F. Kennedy, July 25, 1961

IF ANY deal is struck, settling on a precise point in a bargaining range is necessary. In real-world bargaining situations, a single determinate solution is not easily found due to incomplete information or misinformation. Even after the discovery of a range of possible settlements, the outcome – in terms of the partition of the benefits or costs to be shared – is still indeterminate. In this chapter, bargaining is described as a search for a range of feasible settlement options and selection of an outcome that sticks out from the rest. It is contrasted with static bargaining theory, which concentrates mostly on the initial conditions and outcome rather than the procedures in use. The chapter examines bargaining actions as part of an adaptive process with an incremental logic. Modification in one negotiator's behavior triggers a change in the perceptions of their counterpart that, in turn, is likely to reset the former's bargaining position. Its evolutionary dynamics can be examined to narrow the gap between a cooperative game setting and actual bargaining behavior.

Through an interactive process, two or more bargainers are engaged in seeking an agreeable focal point in a situation where possible outcomes are mutually beneficial but the order of their preferences is negatively correlated. For instance, whereas two countries could be better off with a new trade agreement, prospects for different relative gains would generate discord on sectors to be open to the other side's industries. When universal mechanisms for allocation of benefits are not established or accepted, for instance, in the division of land or irrigation water in a shared river, the difficulty lies in how to single out one among multiple prominent alternatives (Brochmann and Hensel 2011). Different settlement points have advantages for each side, generating competition over selection. It is essentially the challenge faced in the Battle of the Sexes where agreeing to one point is mutually better off, yet differing interests generate discoordination of activities.

Therefore, a bargaining problem falls in the familiar territory of a negotiation dilemma: how players in conflict arrive at an agreement that serves their mutual interest while individuals have incentives to hold out for a more favorable settlement (Filzmoser and Vetschera 2008). As seen in Chapter 7, this process can be costly, often opening a road to protracted acrimonious relationships. The outcome ultimately hinges upon what is bargained about and the degree of incompatibility in the structure of preferences. It also depends on how the negotiators feel about the consequences of disagreement as well as the attitude toward taking the risks of costly delays and uncertain outcomes, searching for a better deal in lieu of the immediate acceptance of a less favorable but certain deal.

The most significant premise of this chapter is that bargaining does not exist without the exchange of offers that is likely to involve "give and take" in the classical problem of exchange. An outcome is produced by a series of sufficient moves from each party's initial position. In producing the terms of the agreements in the Cold War arms-control talks, for instance, differences were steadily narrowed over time through various sets of concessions. Expectations are gradually modified by each party's bargaining behavior in a reactive but calculated process of adjustment to the other's previous concessions (Borch and Mérida 2013). From a behavioral bargaining perspective, negotiation is thus regarded as activities toward convergence over time with a sequence of offers and counteroffers conveyed in order to strike an agreement. More specifically, tactical considerations entail opening stance, concession patterns and final offers along with such questions as whether it is more effective to concede early or late.

Outcome indeterminacy

In order to avoid either individual or joint losses, an agreement ought not to be reached outside a bargaining zone that spreads between the reservation values (i.e., each participant's walk-away point on the opposite end). An agreement is worse off below this "rock-bottom lowest offer" (also known as a resistance point). On the other hand, a bargainer's target point is essentially set by the maximum one gets out of negotiations. Thus a negotiator's offer is represented by a point in the set of feasible outcomes, between the aspiration and resistance values.

If we imagine that two friends divide a surplus dollar bill, there will be numerous solutions somewhere between 1 and 99 cents. In a situation where each competes for more and wants to settle near the other's resistance point, one's maximum aspiration point (i.e., 99 cents in the above case) encroaches the other's reservation value (1 cent).

A rational player is predicted to seek maximum possible benefits, but each bargainer's persistence in making an extreme proposal is bound to be resisted by the other if the latter's payoff falls near her reservation level. To be realistic, thus, an aspiration level has to be anchored to the assessment of what seems attainable given one's own and other's past experience.

In general, concessions are likely to reflect the evaluation of each other's series of moves as manifested in the Israeli–Palestinian negotiation over land annexations and swaps that resembled bazaar-style bargaining. During the July 2000 Camp David negotiation, different Palestinian delegation members suggested 3 to 7.5 percent Israeli annexation of the West Bank in a response to an Israeli delegation member's offer of 11 percent (Sher 2006). In the December 2000 talks, Palestinians expressed willingness to consider Israel's appropriation of up to 2 to 4 percent. However, the Israelis wanted to annex 8 percent of the occupied territory. Later a compromise figure of 4 to 6 percent emerged.

In the US–Soviet negotiations during the Cold War period, a conversion process was also used, for instance, to settle differences in numerical limits on nuclear missiles. In seeking a breakthrough on the average number of cruise missiles to be permitted on any American aircraft in SALT II negotiations, the US figure was lowered from thirty to twenty-eight, whereas the Soviet offer had to come up from twenty-five to twenty-seven (Talbott 1979). Prior to reaching the Partial Test Ban Treaty (PTBT) in 1963, an attempt was made to reach an agreement on the annual number of onsite inspections. The US position shifted from the initial insistence on twenty on-site inspections a year to between eight and ten in December 1962. In the event that Moscow had shown flexibility, the Kennedy administration was willing to accept even six in June 1963. In the end, the Soviet refusal to offer more than three led to a decision to abandon a comprehensive nuclear test ban treaty that could have expanded the scope of the agreement. In this type of negotiation, true limits are indicated by how much each side concedes and in what sequence (or in what manner).

In bargaining, each party has to decide a minimum and maximum claim level (i.e, a resistance and target point) to be made in a shared utility zone while exploring their partner's levels. When interests are diametrically opposed, the set of all payoff combinations from various possible settlements can be arrayed along a continuum. In Figure 8.1, the contract zone is a unidimensional continuum represented by a diagonal between the two bargainers' extreme-most desires on the opposite ends, being indicated by the two points (x_m, y_d) and (x_d, y_m).

In Figure 8.1, concession toward compromise in single-issue negotiation is made in a linear dimension of positional bargaining. Thus taking positions along a single continuum is central to a bargaining approach seeking distributive gains (Hopmann 1996). Negotiators have to develop some idea about the other's target and reservation

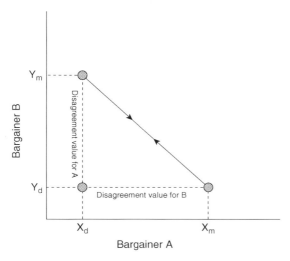

Figure 8.1 A unidimensional contract zone

points through concession-making along the linear bargaining range. In an effort to obtain the best deal possible, each party maneuvers to shift the zone of agreement toward the other's reservation value in their favor. It becomes especially fierce when one's target point ends up at the other's resistance point, and vice versa. An increased payoff to one party along the bargaining continuum decreases the payoff to the other; one's gain becomes the other's loss. If one party makes small concessions, the other bargainer (still wanting a settlement) may have to concede up to their minimum expectancy.

A unidimensional model opens the possibility of having an infinite number of settlement points as appear in the solid diagonal line unless there is a finite set of discrete points. When the French company, Compagnie Nouvelle, sold the United States their holdings in Panama (comprising 30,000 acres of land, buildings, railroad, machinery etc.) in 1904, multiple years of extended haggling preceded the eventual settlement of the amount the United States would pay for the French holding. The French had initially asked for $140 million, while the Americans had offered $20 million. Each side eased gradually to $100 million and $30 million respectively. It eventually ended up $40 million, close to the American position, after a series of events that reduced the incentives for French haggling (Raiffa 1982).

Negotiating on a single continuum ignores the prospect of redefining or expanding bargaining space because it focuses on purely distributive aspects of gains and losses. The quantities alone do not reveal what both bargainers might gain or lose simultaneously. However, even simple deals can be transformed into more complex ones with the inclusion of other issues (such as payment types and time) leading to the chance of a more integrative outcome. Bargaining space can be opened up by partitioning a single issue into multiple dimensions or by the simultaneous consideration of divisive issues. Doing this creates a process that incorporates all sorts of opportunities of trade-offs and side payments to yield joint gains. In settling their territorial disputes, Saudi Arabia and Qatar also used fractioning to turn a seemingly intractable issue of drawing their boundaries on desert sand into a complex set of exchanges. They encompassed differential divisions of various parts of the disputed territory and revenue sharing from oil exploration. In producing their 1994 framework agreement, both American and North Korean negotiators were engaged in swapping concessions on different dimensions of the latter's denuclearization instead of attempting to seek gains toward one another's security point (i.e., the minimum value to be obtained, in the absence of an agreement, regardless of whatever the opponent may do) on a single dimension. More specifically, the timing of special international inspections and the removal of the spent fuel from North Korea's existing nuclear facilities were tied to the percentage of light water reactor constructions arranged by the US government.

As another example, the finalization of the Iranian nuclear accord is full of mutual concessions on multiple dimensions: a two-thirds reduction in the number of centrifuges was combined with uranium-enriching capacity far below the 90 percent typical threshold for weapons-grade material as well as cutting down the current stockpile of low-enriched uranium by 98 percent. The initial US demand for full accounting of Iran's past nuclear activities had to be sidelined by a more important priority of monitoring its future program. The notification of twenty-four days for Iran to comply with an International Atomic Energy Agency request, as well as the introduction of a dispute-settlement process for Iranian objections to some visits, also represented a compromise between the US position on "anytime, anywhere" inspections vs. Tehran's insistence on no inspections of military facilities. The final stumbling block was the difference between the Iranian demand for immediate lifting of the arms embargo and the US insistence on its permanent placement. In the end, a sequential lifting of the ban was made contingent upon Iran's compliance with the accord's principal requirements and the IAEA's certification of the nuclear program's peaceful purpose.

Representing bargaining space geometrically underlines that bargainers' interests are at least partially overlapping, not diametrically opposed. In depicting bargaining space geometrically, Figure 8.2 shows that all the bargaining sets fall in a two-dimensional contract zone. Each feasible outcome is identified as a point in the bargaining set that belongs to the entire quadrant bounded by the axes (that falls on x_d and y_d respectively) and the curved line. Payoff combinations in the Cartesian coordinate plane are associated with joint utility allocations from all possible agreements; the utility of any settlement to Bargainer A is represented by the x-coordinate, with the utility to

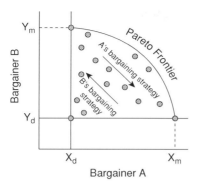

Figure 8.2 Geometric representation of bargaining space

Bargainer B as the y-coordinate. Thus the offers (for the feasible outcome sets) correspond to the points (x_i, y_i) (a list of interchangeable preferences).

In Figure 8.2, a minimum payoff from bargaining is set at the disagreement point (d); whichever way they agree, each bargainer gets at least the minimum acceptable as long as they settle on and above their disagreement point (x_d and y_d); the region toward the curve delineates all the possible agreements that are individually rational to both parties. An agreement is not supposed to leave a bargainer worse off than a noncooperative situation of no negotiation (x_d and y_d).

The outer boundary curve of all the utility combinations is the Pareto optimal, social welfare frontier for the negotiators. Once the settlement under consideration reaches this frontier, one party's payoff cannot be improved without making the other party worse off. A point inside the social welfare frontier curve is less efficient than (i.e., dominated by) any point to its northeast. Efficiency can be improved by moving northeast. While joint utilities increase with any movement in a northeasterly direction through a collaborative process, the mutually beneficial settlement points bear differential payoffs for the players; distributive gains in the northeasterly moves thus generate conflicting interests that stem from the variable attractiveness to each party of the possible settlement points within the contract zone (Princen 1992).

As seen in Figure 8.2, any point on the upper left or lower right along or parallel to the curve is still efficient, but not equitable to one party. In our earlier example, both US and North Korean negotiators could agree, after some tussle, to North Korea being supplied with light water reactors in return for commiting to abandoning existing facilities that were suspected of being able to produce nuclear weapons materials. However, much of their remaining time during the negotiation was spent haggling over such issues as whether a special international inspection of the latter's past nuclear activities should be conducted with 70% or 80% of delivery of the parts to be put in newly built light water reactors (which do not produce weapons-graded plutonium).

Upon reaching the frontier, the specific distributive value of an agreement at any point along the continuum diverges for each party. In fact, Pareto optimal division does not guarantee a fair share despite the possibility of mutual improvement (Hopmann 1996). By its definition, it is optimal for one player to get everything, for example, points (x_d, y_m) and (x_m, y_d). The disappearance of possibility for mutual improvement puts one party's goal in a direct conflict with the other. The allocation of the values at stake along that frontier engenders distributive bargaining because joint gains are no longer feasible. Intensive distributive bargaining along the Pareto optimal frontier may end up with gains for one party at the other's expense. Thus bargaining on the Pareto optimal frontier generates a distributive question even in an otherwise integrative bargaining structure.

The size of a contract zone (i.e., space for bargaining) directly affects the scope of haggling over the choice of an exact point by both players. A large contract zone means there exist many mutually profitable outcomes from which to select. It is created by smaller disagreement points x_d and y_d. When the x_d and y_d get closer to 0, this movement generates a greater number of settlement points acceptable to both sides. It may take longer to reach an agreement with a bigger contract zone that contains many equilibrium points (Young 1975). The larger the area (encircled by x_d, y_d and the curve), the more choices are available to settle. Of course, this has implications that one benefits more than the other, depending on which settlement point both agree to. Thus, the struggle to seek favorable terms tends to be more intense. The greater the contract zone, the more important role each party's bargaining capacity plays in determining a settlement point.

If we regard the possibility of a rational solution to the bargaining problem as a determinate like arbitration (whose outcome, for instance, is represented by a Nash solution), "a unique rational solution in a cooperative game can be forged," as revealed in Chapter 5, by dividing the difference, 50/50, in an equal bargaining power relationship. In Figure 8.3, a fair, equitable outcome (on the Pareto optimal frontier) is identified by a point of intersection between the frontier and a 45-degree diagonal displaying an even split of the gain above the bargainers' disagreement points. A fair division in a cooperative game is based on the assumption of honest and free discussion needed for a joint rational action plan along with the enforceability of an agreement. If negotiators are rational, by design, they will choose the Nash solution. Then "what is [left] to negotiate about" (Bartos 1974, 53)? If everybody's payoffs are known to each other, the size of concessions can be determined by principles of rationality; there is no need for strategic manipulations such as control over an agenda. What remains is to ascertain the rules for a fair solution along with uncovering each other's true interests.

At the same time, we may also consider the situation in which negotiators are not rational to start with, but experienced negotiators would surely strive to be rational

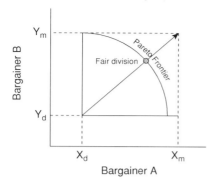

Figure 8.3 A fair solution on a Pareto optimal frontier

because doing so – they know – brings in a higher payoff than otherwise (Bartos 1974). Even though the participants may have had only obscure ideas about each other's payoff at the beginning, with each move the amount of uncertainty should become sufficiently small for a feasible settlement, as they would be able to learn everybody's true interests toward the end of the session.

Does the above description mirror real-life negotiations? Negotiators may not be content to stick with a single determinate solution stipulated by game-theoretical rules of efficient and "fair" division (which could have been applied in arbitration). In spite of the prescribed rules, each negotiator would still attempt to go after a bigger share, as one bargainer overvalues what has been ceded whereas the other minimizes her own gain. Perhaps, real-world bargaining might be more similar to a noncooperative game with incomplete information. The solution of the classic divide-the-dollar problem offers many deals that are more than fallback; it is individually rational to split a dollar anywhere between 1 cent and 99 cents inclusive. Suppose that each bargainer insists on a larger share and is committed to one of their favorable points, what might justify this demand?

Even though fairness includes some form of equal treatment, it may not absolutely amount to awards of the same value or distribution. Indeed it is by and large not a plain matter of an equal share division. First of all, reciprocity would be difficult to practice in the absence of either comparable power or prior understanding of a distinct outcome as fair and desirable.[1] Departures from numerical equality could also be compelled by different needs, abilities or opportunities (Pruitt 1981). A disproportionate sharing of oil revenue or of water resources may be justified by equity principles; perhaps, rewards could be divided in proportion to different levels of contributions. Thus a stable outcome hinges notably on the principle and method of formulating the division process.

In real life, many different arguments might be adopted, with little agreement that "fairness" should be the means of coordinating expectations (Müller 2004; Pillutla and Murnighan 2003). When people are "rarely asked to justify inequality," fairness becomes irrelevant (Bartos 1974, 54). Rather, difficulties in establishing criteria for equal payoffs are likely to invite the application of vague principles of fairness, leaving the door open for a more favorable division for one party than is deserved by the merit of their claim (Bartos 1974). Moreover, negotiators who are not at all interested in fairness may threaten to refuse to agree at all besides what they demand. In the above case of a dollar division, assuming that one person demands, for example, 80 cents, in a take-or-leave-it offer, should the other person accept it, knowing that no one will get anything in the event of no agreement? While a 50/50 split could be suggested as a fair solution, 20 cents is still a gain that should prompt a rational player to accept the inequitable deal.

In the absence of recurrent bargaining relationships, all potential exchange situations are embedded in the reward structure of Prisoner's Dilemma (Pruitt 1981). When competition for relative gains takes place in the absence of complete knowledge as to the other party's utility zone, misinformation about intended moves and preferences could help each side to achieve a better outcome for itself. Whereas a fair division demands truthful communication about one's valuation (e.g., minimum demand or reservation prices), bargainer interaction can be shaped by manipulating information about payoffs, choices and other expectations, leaving plenty of incentives for exploitation and also the possibility of being exploited (Putnam 2010). When the parties are unlikely to abstain from knowingly making false statements, a cooperative bargaining outcome would be difficult to predict under Nash bargaining rules (i.e., "a solution independent of an irrelevant alternative," for instance, derived from cheating). Incomplete information about preferences makes finding each other's utility functions difficult.

Models of concession-making

This chapter assumes that a negotiator's behavior is guided by their beliefs about the future, especially related to an opponent's degree of willingness to make concessions. If we understand negotiation activities in the context of a sequence of offers and counteroffers, the conversion of differences is supposed to arise from a series of concession exchanges. Then the question is when (and under what circumstances) negotiators are likely to make concessions and to what effect (i.e., the consequent outcome). At which stages of negotiation are higher concession rates and less competitive strategies more visible or prevalent? The exchange process (involving the timing of particular demands and concessionary offers) can indeed be modeled using theories that capture the evolution of bargaining. Bargaining positions are likely to evolve as information is gained through the interpretation of the other party's concessionary behavior (Pruitt 1981).

In an interactive bargaining process, offers usually command a response: either an acceptance, a counteroffer or an outright rejection. In the sense that it is subject to change, usually altering over time, an offer is in general tentative. After the presentation of the opening positions, the subsequent negotiation focuses on how to bridge the discrepancy between the two. Initial offers are likely to be put forth without accurate and reliable (or verifiable) information about the other side's utilities. Estimates about opponents' utilities based on reasonable guesses go through a trial-and-error adjustment process. It is, in essence, a fluid, evolutionary process: a bargainer frequently modifies offers, conceding in increments or more drastically in light of new information.

In an exchange process, offers provide a central communication function, revealing information about what bargainers claim for themselves and what they are willing to give to the opponent (Coddington 2013). Indeed, an offer serves as a mode of communicating one's motives and priorities through modifications of demands in the course of bargaining; what continues to be demanded is contrasted with what has been dropped (Pruitt 1981). In the modified proposal, those elements retained prove to be more salient than those left out. Conveying intentions to opponents is designed to bring about alteration in their moves and aspirations (Bacharach and Lawler 1981). Therefore, an offer is made not merely to inform but, more importantly, to persuade. An essential aspect of bargaining is, then, the way negotiators attempt to shape each other's positions and behaviors in a continuing series of offers.

Concession dynamics and behavior

In general, concession-making has something to do with how each party sets and adjusts their positions in a bargaining range. Bargaining behavior can be observed by the magnitude and rate of concessions as well as by initial offers. The first offer is mostly affected by a bargainer's aspiration level and the opponent's reservation value. *Concession magnitude* is measured by the discrepancy between an *initial* and a final offer. A bargainer's *concession rate* is the speed at which a bargainer concedes.

In order to maximize their own return in an agreement, bargainers have a strong incentive to manipulate their initial offer, rate and size of concessions (Raiffa 1982). The main strategies are shaped by considerations such as (1) where to start; (2) how to set concession rates; and (3) how far to concede. These questions are related not only to the total amount of eventual concessions but also to their timing and sequence. Modifications in the rate, size and timing of concessions generally indicate changing perceptions of what is obtainable as well as revealing subjective utilities.

The patterns of concession-making evolve from different combinations of an initial offer (high vs. low), concession rates (slow or fast) and size (big or small) as well as timing (beginning vs. end). A few large concessions can be made over a certain bargaining period for a breakthrough (Tutzauer 1992). One party may concede everything on the second offer, and then hold firm if the other bargainer does not budge and demands further concessions. On the other hand, a flurry of relatively larger concessions may come toward the end of the negotiation (followed by a termination offer), perhaps as a final desperate act to save the negotiation, after few concessionary moves. Another pattern could emerge by presenting meager concessions in higher frequency over an elongated period as a response to the other's salami tactics.

To a great extent, the rate of concessions is swayed by interplay among aspiration levels, resistance points and initial offers. A relatively lower initial offer combined with a higher resistance point pushes bargainers more quickly closer to their limit on concessions. Higher aspiration and resistance points may result in a larger initial demand with slow concession-making (Pruitt 1981). As bargaining progresses, a realistic level of aspiration emerges from the accumulation of successive bids; however, a readjusted aspiration level has to stay above a resistance point. The rate of concessionary offers becomes successively smaller when a bargainer's offer is rapidly approaching the resistance point.

A final agreement is likely to reflect the determinants of a concession rate as well as an initial demand level. In order to move the range of indeterminacy to a more favorable point, for instance, a bargainer may open the negotiation with a large *initial demand*, but then yield little. For example, Bosnians during the 1995 Dayton negotiation adopted a strategy of starting high and conceding slowly in order to elicit more concessions from the Serbs (Holbrooke 1999). If both bargainers have high aspirations and resist a concessionary movement with an attempt to lower the other's expectations, it increases the chances for deadlock (as seen in the failure to reach settlement between Armenia and Azerbaijan over Nagorno-Karabakh and many other intractable negotiations). On the other hand, an agreement is more rapidly produced by faster concessions combined with moderate initial demands (Pruitt 1981). Below we will examine a specific justification, the logic behind setting a starting point for an offer and adjusting concession rates.

Opening stances

Tactical decisions on the manipulation of opening bids and initial concessions hinge on whether to risk protracted bargaining or seek an early settlement with lower bargaining costs. The costs of making exaggerated offers encompass the possibility of reducing an opponent's incentives to make serious offers. On the other hand, an offer, made below one's high expectations, may be more readily acceptable to settlement by the other, although it will be less satisfactory to oneself. If a reasonable and cooperative opening stance is construed by one's negotiating partners as a sign of weakness, however, it may raise their level of expectations with increased demand from them, causing eventual difficulties for reciprocal exchange. Once a resistance point is detected, an opponent is less likely to make an offer more than their limit (Pruitt 1981). Therefore, initial demands, as a sort of smoke screen, are typically put considerably above reservation values.

In general, an opening proposal does not start at a resistance point. Opening proposals may even be placed at the far end of the issue with the anticipation of the eventual settlement halfway between the opposing opening bids. Beginning high with an exaggerated demand level allows space for conceding further at a later point while protecting the reservation value; an opponent's counterconcessions can be elicited by the principle of reciprocity. Yet a maximalist bargaining position sends an opponent a wrong impression (i.e., "a settlement is out of reach"), even though the opening bid is put forth only as a starting point. Most importantly, the negotiation may break down as a result of underestimating an adversary's limit and presenting an unacceptably high initial demand.

As the initial offer often sets the perceptions of later bargaining, thus, it needs to be carefully considered in the context of later moves. In arms-control negotiations with the Soviets, American officials faced a difficult dilemma. It is summed up as follows: "[i]f our position is close to what we want as an outcome, the Soviets will start negotiating from there and we are likely to end up being pressed to accept an unsatisfactory outcome." On the other hand, if "our position is padded with a great deal of room for negotiation, the Soviets may not negotiate seriously" (Sloss 1986, 5). When a tough opening offer leads (inevitably) to a later retreat, it creates an image of appearing "weak" to the American public and Congress that has to ratify an eventual agreement. On the other hand, opening with a soft offer and holding firm runs the risk of being seen as uncompromising.

An extreme starting position is most likely to force the negotiator eventually to make large concessions, if she has to avoid a risk of a complete breakdown. The eventual concession (to be made to keep the negotiation going) ends up becoming a signal of willingness to take a less favorable deal to an opponent. Then the opponent will feel less inclined to reciprocate the concession, sensing the other's weaker bargaining position. In the arms-control negotiation, in fact, the Soviets often adopted stonewalling tactics in reaction to the American opening with maximum bargaining stance. A more moderate initial offer may be advocated to achieve a mutually satisfactory agreement (Cross 1996). Being neither too firm nor too soft within the range of feasible settlements leaves room for flexibility. In reality, negotiators are often both reciprocating and exploiting an opponent's concessions (Bartos 1974).

A bargainer's initial demand has to consider two factors: the bargaining cost of achieving a specific outcome and concession value extracted from an opponent. Even if the chances of an improved final settlement may be increased by a higher initial demand, it can easily be offset by a greater cost that is incurred from the extended time in reaching an agreement. A later settlement is less valuable if costs of waiting are too high. The deferred payoff may not be compensated or may not come at all (e.g., the United States negotiating with North Koreans after the latter's possession of nuclear weapons and their increasing stockpiles along with their development of long-range missiles). Thus, the total costs (related to time needed to achieve the gain) have to be factored into setting the most achievable of desirable outcomes (made possible by the other side's concession). More precisely, one's own cumulative costs arising from the length of time required to agree upon a more desirable contract have to be sufficiently compensated by all the concessions expected to be made by the other player over time.

Patterns of concession rates and frequency

One may make concessions more readily early, and resist serious retreat in the remaining negotiations. One of the patterns of offers in the division of a reward is well elaborated in an exponential decay model that evolved out of a classic experiment by Harold Kelley, Linda Beckman and Claude Fischer (1967). A bargainer's concession rate, in the absence of knowledge about each other's resistance points, is proportional to her current offer. A fast concession rate is exhibited at the outset of bargaining when an offer remains high. Then concessions considerably slow down with approximation to a reservation value. Thus an exponential decay model is characterized by a relatively high starting offer, rapid initial concessions and a shift to slower concessions with an approach to a terminal resistance point (Filzmoser and Vetschera 2008).

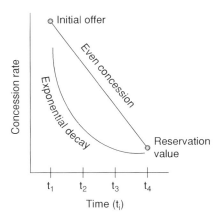

Figure 8.4 Concession rates and patterns: exponential decay model

Figure 8.4 shows that a concession rate drops with progression in time, corresponding to a bargainer's decreasing offers. In this figure, offers are plotted as a function of time (t_i); the slope of the curve denotes a bargainer's concession rate. The steeper the slope (for instance, between t_1 and t_2), the faster a bargainer concedes. The concession curve increasingly flattens out with a continuing drop in the concession rate (e.g., between t_3 and t_4), coinciding with the approach to a resistance point.

There is by no means unanimous consensus as to whether a quick compromise is a good bargaining strategy. Some avoid such behavior, believing that making concessions too readily would only raise an adversary's aspiration level. In contrast with the above model, meaningful concessions may come with a significant passage of time if little momentum would be created by an inconsequential retreat from one's earlier position. In reaching the 1974 Vladivostok Accord, the bulk of concessions were made during the final phase of the negotiation (Jensen 1988, 70). An end spurt might be prompted when bargaining approaches a deadline or when its cost surpasses any prospective gain. A negotiated settlement to end the Vietnam War (1973) came after the loss of more lives and more destruction through intensified warfare. In their protracted trade negotiations during the 1980s, the US threat of a costly trade war was met by Japanese resistance against serious early concessions. In this case, a strong party, believing in its leverage and having more bargaining power, held on to the initial position until the later stage of negotiation while the other party was willing to be engaged in a war of attrition with undue delays in concessions.

Despite its costs, two parties may hold out for the prize in question for some time. On the other hand, a demand for a higher level of sharing from a joint gain is likely to wane when the expense of settlement rises due to protracted bargaining. This is especially the case when the cost of continued bargaining becomes prohibitive, even taking into account the gain to be obtained by an adversary's later concession. A concession rate can thus be linked to costs arising from a delayed contract; increased time pressure produces heightened bargainer restlessness with its mediating effect in the level of aspiration (Craver 2012). The elapse of time enhances a desire for coordination to settle differences especially if it involves the deteriorating value of a desired object or opportunity lost for other pursuits. In this case, high pressure motivates faster concessions and reduced demands (Pruitt 1981). Very high time pressure by one party induces the acceptance of the other party's offer near the limit. The two sides' different patience levels led to more American concessions, with the passage of time, in the agreement to end the Vietnam War.

Diverse forces drive the interactive process of making offers. Forces in favor of concession-making should obviously be stronger than any resistance force that deters it. In particular, the strength of the force resisting concession must be weakened prior to lowering an offer. If demands are not likely to be met simultaneously, offers can be embedded with positional commitments and such manipulative moves as threats that have an impact on the settlement point (e.g., hostage takers warning of killing their victims). What really brings about changes in payoff matrices is, however, only credible threats or the ability to deter the success of "threats."

A change of offer can also be ascribed to exogenous factors (such as economic hardship or a constituent pressure to end a costly conflict) as well as a lack of alternative opportunities directly related to payoff improvement. In addition, external intervention (e.g., sanctions) may result in the disappearance of the gains from winning a protracted struggle; the cessation of economic and military assistance by South Africa in 1979 led to the white minority government's unilateral concession in negotiation over the transition of power to the black majority in Zimbabwe. Appropriate incentives for agreement and the desire to compromise can help avoid the collapse of talks, which could carry a high risk of conflict. The negotiator's own demand can be lessened to the point where accepting a greater risk is worse than acquiescing to the other side's current offer.

The interaction between exogenous and endogenous dynamics of concession-making was displayed in negotiating the Limited Test Ban Treaty between 1958 and 1963. The earlier willingness to make concessions produced considerable momentum and progress. Consequently, "expectations and hopes were raised among both domestic and foreign publics on the prospects of reaching agreement. Leaders in the United States and the Soviet Union may not have been very serious about agreement on a test ban except on their own terms. But they became in effect victims of their own earlier performance, creating an environment in which some kind of agreement" was inevitable (Jensen 1988, 66).

Self- and other-oriented forces

The communication of offers is better represented by vector models that show partially overlapping interests of bargainers. In depicting a solution to bargaining problems, a vector (linked to changing offers) indicates the direction and speed with which an offer moves (i.e., changes) from one point of the feasible outcome set to another at particular time. The strength of force for a movement in the vector field is denoted by the length of the line that links one offer to another. The length shows the magnitude of changes between offers. The arrowhead of the line points in the direction of the movement of change (see Figure 8.5).

The components of a vector represent bargaining forces, self- and other-oriented (i.e., quantity of a claim to oneself and an offer to an opponent respectively), that propel change. Thus offers are modified by change in both self- and other-directed components. The combination of these two forces determines how a bargainer's offers will change over time. A vector field is quite effective in modeling a bargainer's behaviors (by depicting movements from bargainers' previous offers to new ones). In Figure 8.5, the vectors represent gains for both bargainers, but they also show that one bargainer gains more than the other, depending on the direction in which a vector's arrowhead points. The vector movement shows that a bargainer (whose payoff is represented on

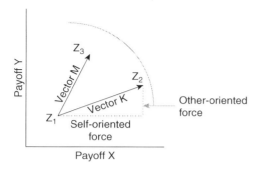

Figure 8.5 Self- and other-directed forces

the x axis in Figure 8.5) seeks more for herself with a larger self-oriented force on vector k (linking z_1 to z_2); on the other hand, a stronger other-oriented force on vector m (displaying a movement from z_1 to z_3) drives more significant gain for the other bargainer.

The interactive nature of bargaining

The bargaining scenario would be crude if a concession rate were chosen and set after an initial offer and determination of the resistance point, regardless of what the opponent does. In fact, it is often the case that concessions mirror those of others. The responses of one bargainer have an impact on another bargainer's behavior. In depicting how a bargainer concedes, an offer model has to be interactive, as well as dynamic, by incorporating the opponent's behavior. Positions may change when affected by the influence of concessions by each party.

One of the interaction patterns is reciprocating and matching each other's offers through concession returned with similar weight or the same magnitude. In this case, concession-making serves as a sign of goodwill and trust. On other occasions, concessions might be taken as evidence of weakness, prompting a further demand; the other side's expectations may be raised with the information communicated by the concession. As opposed to moving toward settlement in concert with the other, an adversary may hold firm, waiting for further concessions prior to reciprocation. Further concessions that are not reciprocated indicate that the negotiator's bargaining position is weak, and there is not much room left to maneuver.

When costs for negotiation differ, the bargainers may be responsive to each other, but with a mismatching degree of responsiveness in a concession rate and magnitude. The advantaged bargainer concedes more slowly, not matching the concessionary movement of the disadvantaged (Pruitt 1981). The lower a party's opportunity cost for non-cooperation, the longer it is able to hold out for a better deal (as India did in its negotiation with Bangladesh over the allocation of water in the Ganges). If concessions are not considered in their best interests by both parties (worse than a guaranteed share of the status quo) despite time elapsing, this establishes conditions for a stalemate.

When one party starts with a higher initial demand and concedes little, a sudden larger concession may not draw an immediate reciprocation. Moscow did not reciprocate the Carter administration's concessions on a ceiling of Soviet heavy missiles even though the upper limit of their missiles in newer American proposals, during a six-month period in 1977, gradually increased from 150 to 190, 220, 250 and eventually to 308. The Soviet Union did not display concessionary behavior on the number of missiles, but in the two months after US acquiescence to 308 heavy Soviet missiles it became more conciliatory on other issues with higher concession rates.

Interactive bargaining models

In the earlier exponential decay model, presented by Kelley *et al.*, only a bargainer's own previous offer matters to setting a current concession rate, regardless of the opponent's demand level. By adapting Lewis F. Richardson's action–reaction system to bargaining settings, Otomar J. Bartos (1974) captures the interactive nature of bargaining (see also Hopmann and Smith 1977). Changes in a bargainer's offers are tied to not only his own but also to the other's earlier offers by some linkage. Thus, an opponent's concession-making behavior as well as one's previous offer patterns sets a bargainer's responsiveness.

The interactive character of offers and concessions can be represented by iterative dynamics of bargaining behavior. One bargainer's offer stimulates the other bargainer's response, which subsequently becomes the source of a new offer by the original one. The new input engenders the respondent's output, which then turns into yet another input for the initiator in continuing bargaining dynamics that eventually ends either with an agreement or impasse. In this series of encounters, new information concerning the other's intentions and the value of outcomes brings about a positional change. As a system output is attributed to an input, this function permits a bargainer to develop an idea about what will come out of this repeated iteration. The dynamic system is designed to show either a settlement point or the last offer made in the deadlock after a series of the feedback process. The weakness in this model lies in difficulties in explaining sudden surges in a movement toward (or away from) agreement, deviating from a steadier flow.

If one makes an offer, the other has to provide a response; the question is how we can find a pattern in the relationship (i.e., what types of response might be generated by a particular type of input; this process then repeats itself, moving on to the next stage). In Frank Tutzauer's work (1986), bargaining systems were analyzed using chaos theory (which examines the role of deterministic systems in producing random behavior). In this model, the extent to which one bargainer can become tough in a bargaining system is measured by the other bargainer's capitulation and resistance parameters. A capitulation parameter is indicated by a willingness to accept a smaller share, while a resistance parameter is tied to recalcitrance (i.e., a demand for a larger share). A high resistance parameter of one bargainer lessens the room for the other to take a tougher position if an agreement is to be produced. A favorable settlement for the tougher bargainer is available only if the other bargainer has a higher capitulation parameter. On the other hand, when every party has a higher resistance parameter (e.g., the current state of Israeli–Palestinian negotiations; the territorial dispute in the South China Sea involving China, Vietnam and the Philippines; ethnic conflict between Azerbaijan and Armenia), it is likely to end up with a deadlock. A permanent standoff is inevitable in a situation in which each refuses to retreat from an extreme proposal, which is bound to be rejected by the other.

It is not unusual to observe sudden breakthroughs or discontinuity in progress toward settlement. Some models attempt to explain this aspect of bargaining dynamics. One way to study concession-making action is to examine not so much changes in the offers per se but more the shifts in their movements and patterns. Suppose two bargainers become gradually argumentative and start to offend each other after making steady progress; then bargaining suddenly turns into outright recalcitrance. Conversely, a muddling-through, incoherent process may shift, bringing about an endeavor to discover joint gains from logrolling through a fresh insight (Tutzauer 1986). Such changes in the approach to bargaining may generate different patterns of offers.

Catastrophe theory explains this kind of abrupt discontinuous change in a system. Continuous, even if small, changes in independent variables could have a cumulative effect in prompting catastrophic turns or disjunctures in behavior (Oliva *et al.* 1981). For instance, a shift in the level of bargainer tolerance may come from a gradual increase in bargaining intensity driven by a strong desire for one's own demands to be met, an unwillingness to compromise, emotional involvement, and concerns about equity (Borch and Mérida 2013; Taylor and Thomas 2008). If one party becomes less tolerant of the differences, the other should be able to be more accommodating. However, there is a limit on this. Then, if one party's demand becomes too excessive, the other's tolerance level reaches its limit. The rising intensities in these opposing tendencies (crossing each other) will eventually throw the negotiation system into collapse; and the whole process will become unable to seek a negotiated settlement. It can be illustrated by the disastrous outcome of the 2000 Camp David meeting that wiped out any positive momentum left in the Israeli–Palestinian negotiation; rising intensities were derived from each party's emotional attachment to several core issues, in particular, the division of Jerusalem, along with Arafat's powerful desire to achieve his demands and the Israeli Prime Minister Barak's strong resistance against compromise.

As opposed to the intractable negotiation seen above, a collaborative turn was exhibited toward the end of the negotiation on the second Strategic Arms Control (SALT II) in 1979. Originally, Americans focused on Soviet heavyweight, multiple warhead missiles called SS-18s, while the Soviets were mostly concerned about American deployment of the Air-Launched Cruise Missile (ALCM) on strategic bombers. By linking the two issues later, however, the negotiators could satisfy the different priorities of each other's military establishment. The Soviet military had a strong desire to curb the deployment of American ALCMs, but their priority was higher on keeping its own SS-18 missiles; the Pentagon was more eager to modernize its aging bomber fleet by deploying ALCMs than restricting the threat from SS-18 (Hopmann 1996). These different priorities opened the possibility of tradeoffs between the two issues. In the end, both sides agreed to limits on increases in their own offensive capabilities instead of working against the other side's desire to keep their favored weaponry systems. Thus, while Moscow retained their SS-18s but with restrictions on improvement, Americans accepted restrictions to a specific number of ALCMs on each bomber in return for counting each bomber as only one delivery vehicle (i.e., agreeing to the reduced missile numbers instead of bombers). Only after a serious struggle did the negotiators discover their own military establishment's priorities and come up with the tradeoffs.

Conclusion

In this chapter, bargaining has been characterized as a selection of one agreement point, devoid of arbitration or adjudication, from all the payoff possibilities. Negotiation analysis cannot be completed without an understanding of concessional patterns and timing. In spite of much past research on interactive and dynamic models of offers and concessions, gaps in our understanding inevitably exist owing to the discrepancy between a variety of real-life processes and baseline analysis (i.e., a reference point for conducting an analysis without much differentiation). Even though we might have been successful in constructing the simplest bargaining models consistent with known facts and such assumptions as individual utility maximization and equal bargaining skills, etc., the problem of selection in the "bargaining set" with large numbers of Nash equilibria still remains paramount. What we have done is an attempt to nail down a predictable outcome set that falls within the rough boundaries confined by bargaining space.

In seeking to predict a bargaining outcome, researchers are likely to have only fuzzy information on many matters of detail. Even the bargainers themselves may not credibly be acquainted with all the detailed structure of the bargaining procedure to recapitulate the "twists and turns" of their negotiation. Any further advancement with theoretical extensions and modifications of the current research should come with the discovery of more about a set of forces that motivate bargainers to change their offers.

It is difficult to cultivate theoretical insights without being fully conscious of psychological, structural, and contextual conditions that materially bear upon the outcome. Beyond behavioral patterns connected to bargaining dynamics (e.g., modifying a bargainer's choices), we need to turn our attention to the varied political, psychological and other facets of a bargaining situation that sway negotiation payoffs in one way or another. In the end, however, "creativity, experience and sound intuition are at least as important to successful negotiation as any amount of analysis" (Young 1991a, 2).

Note

1 Non-reciprocity can be allowed in special circumstances. For instance, European powers grant preferential treatment to former colonial territories in their trading arrangements. The developing world's demands rooted in the perceived immorality of postcolonial economic relations were, however, not well received in multilateral global trade negotiations.

9 Psychological and institutional context

> Sometimes when you stand face to face with someone, you cannot see his face.
> Mikhail Gorbachev (in the aftermath of his summit with Ronald Reagan)

THE NEGOTIATION process and bargaining models presented in earlier chapters provide a guide in narrowing down the predicted outcome, but they are in themselves incomplete. In game-theoretical models, actors have stable and well-defined preferences based on utility calculations in striving to maximize their gains and minimize their losses. In formal models (presented in Chapter 5), a "bargaining set" for a given problem is intricately deduced from the value of a negotiator's alternating offer. As negotiators interact through different stages (seen in Chapters 6 and 7), their preferences have to be adjusted to a new understanding of their counterpart's interests and priorities. In Chapter 8, we saw how bargaining actions reset mutual expectations through a series of adaptations to each other's offers. When bargaining is understood in the traditional utility formation (e.g., payoff maximization), its process is largely considered separate from psychological or institutional decision-making process. However, a negotiator's choices tend to be subject to a decision-maker's bias and are also shaped by institutional and political constraints.

This chapter starts from the premise that understanding a real-world negotiation process and its effect on outcomes has to go beyond the examination of negotiator interactions based on their preferences and utility functions. The chapter discusses the interference of negotiators' perceptions and attributes as well as system influences on a negotiation process and its consequences. It will begin with motivational and cognitive models that explain the role of perception and emotions in decision-making. Recognizing that international negotiation is likely to be propelled by decisions involving larger groups, in the second half of the chapter, I will also incorporate institutional decision-making procedures and the interference of concerns of subgroups on each side in our analysis. In general, government decision-making is entangled with organizational rivalry and bureaucratic politics. The growing number of subactors makes issues that were originally invisible or less visible gain new prominence since parochial interests now have to be satisfied in an external negotiation. With the intervention of more subactors, intraparty (and crossparty) coalition-building plays a crucial role in shaping the final outcome of negotiation. Due to all these complications, hence, flexibility or inflexibility in bargaining positions might stem from events off the table (such as constituency pressure, the emergence of a new leadership through election cycles and changes in public opinion).

Sociopsychological process

The process of assimilating information is essential to the interpretation of an adversary's strategies and one's decisions on appropriate responses. Making optimal decisions hinges on a negotiator's ability to make an accurate appraisal of given information about the other party's expected value of agreement and its alternatives. Therefore, inferences about opponent preferences make a difference to the quality of outcomes. In making judgments about the remarks and behavior of other people, negotiators are often overloaded or bombarded with various impressions of their counterpart's choices. This raises such questions as: how do we know that we pay proper attention to the right cues? How accurate are our judgments, especially when objective information is not attainable?

Encountering the same objective circumstances, two negotiators could still develop a different understanding about their experiences. Rather than seeking out and weighing all the relevant information objectively, negotiators might make prejudgments about the other side's wishes.[1] Most significantly, "making judgments is often clouded by a tendency of attending to only a subset of available information" with the consequences of underweighting unattended information (Bazerman and Chugh 2006, 13). In spite of access to complete information, people may not process all the incoming messages relevant to key decisions. It is not uncommon that, despite a shared zone of interest, bargainers may fail to reach a mutually beneficial. Incomplete information processing would restrict the ability of negotiators to comprehend various choices with consequent difficulties in picturing all the possibilities presented. Selective perceptions block new information by a bias in cognitive framing.

In judging the content of an event or situation, despite the same or shared information, people easily draw totally different conclusions by seeing it from their own vantage point (Carrell and Heavrin 2008). According to a study by Gerben van Kleef and Carsten de Dreu (2002), negotiators tend to make assumptions about their counterpart's preferences and then ask only questions phrased to affirm what they have presumed. Throughout negotiation, people may search for corroborative evidence to hold up their implicit theories of understanding the world. More precisely, confirmatory information searches seek out knowledge that would validate preexisting beliefs, screening out data that would disqualify better understanding. Consequently, a confirmatory evidence bias has direct ramifications for assessing a counterpart's intentions, goals, motives and behavior. As seen in the example below, information processing has implications in the appraisal of a counterpart's objectives and strategies.

In response to Nikita Khrushchev's classic ultimatum on the Western position on Berlin in November 1958, hardliners in Washington quickly adopted the interpretation that the event was a contest of wills, testing American credibility and resolve. Given Moscow's "deliberate and calculated act," they advocated confronting the Soviets on the ground militarily. In contrast, Secretary of State John Foster Dulles read the Soviet call as an urgent plea for negotiations. Dulles interpreted Khrushchev's statement as "the recognition of Soviet problems in the eastern bloc" as well as a reflection of his irascible character. As time was on the American side (with a growing gap in prosperity between western and eastern Europe), he felt no need to push the Soviets further into a corner by military stonewalling in response to Khrushchev's demand for the "neutralization of the city with a new special status" or "leave West Berlin in six months." In defusing the "deadline crisis," Dulles's strategy was to entangle Moscow in a web of negotiations, watering down their demands prior to the emergence of a solution acceptable to the United States. While the hardliners feared negotiation would only encourage the Soviets to press further, Dulles chose negotiation as a means to tie Moscow's hands, believing it would turn to an American advantage once it started (Moermond and Snyder 1988).

In general, cognitive rigidity generates tendencies to turn a complex problem into a simpler one by depending on mental shortcuts. This psychological mechanism generates inaccurate perceptions by not carefully utilizing every detail. In these instances, biased information searches cause erroneous conclusions, which fail to capitalize on the full integrative potential. Systematically flawed inferences diminish the capacity to attain optimal agreements. Negative views of others increase the likelihood of holding a high self-evaluation, with a consequent tendency to view one's own offers as fairer even when those of an opponent are objectively more reasonable (Dewulf *et al.* 2009). The other's concessions tend to be attributed to external circumstances even in the event that they are derived from their benevolent intentions. Thus perceptual rigidity could contribute to a reduction in concessionary activities with a high proportion of impasse outcomes.

Constraints in cognitive capacity are amplified by a situational need for a quick closure on decision-making (Pinfari 2011). Indeed, time pressure, both real and perceived, contributes to dependence on more limited information-processing strategies. Owing to cognitive illusions, political elites may overestimate their perceived control over external events, by relying on unrealistic optimism (Swift and Moore 2012). An unwarranted level of confidence is often produced by optimistic judgments about deservedly grave consequences. During the Cuban Missile Crisis, for instance, the US Joint Chiefs of Staff argued that Moscow would not do anything even in the case of American air strikes on Soviet missile bases and an ultimate attack on the island. In reality, however, when "Khrushchev believed that a US invasion of Cuba was imminent," "he was prepared to authorize the use of tactical nuclear weapons against American troops" (Dobbs 2008, 34). In fact, Soviet commander Issa Pliyev "had dispersed nuclear warheads from central storage to their launch sites" with Moscow's endorsement (Allison and Zelikow 1999, 351).

The elimination of uncertainty is expedited by a disposition to an early closure in the consideration of multiple factors involved in a particular event. A rush to reduce the uncertainty leads, in turn, to making judgments without collecting complete information. Thus cognitive impatience produces a tendency to make quick judgments on the basis of incomplete evidence or opinions formed with insufficient information. In addition, such dispositional forces as impatience undermine the motivation to process information that is needed to entertain multiple interpretations or conflicting opinions (Kruglanski and Sheveland 2012). Negotiators with a great desire for closure are more prone to falling prey to the decision biases, owing to an inability to process information more systematically. When external pressure strains information processing by draining cognitive energy, negotiators take less time to propose counteroffers and make less persuasive arguments (Harinck and de Dreu 2004).

Sources of cognitive bias

A variety of human biases and shortcomings interferes with the ability to think creatively. The failure to access relevant knowledge is linked to the simplification of decision-making by overdependence on general heuristics, a rule of thumb, so to speak, which helps remove uncertainties in our understanding of a given situation. A negotiator's cognitive frame generates category-based information that is in turn adopted in assessing her partner's behavior and motives. An established search pattern is maintained through an individual's cognitive schema (which structures information by way of organized relations between attributes). A set of potential options is often evaluated by paying attention only to their particular attributes, eliminating alternatives that do not fit in familiar patterns of thinking. In particular, the events quickly and easily retrieved in memory could become a reference point. Opposition to negotiation with an enemy has frequently been justified with a reference to appeasement by Britain and France to Nazi Germany in the Munich agreement prior to World War II. One of the most illustrative examples is US senator Henry Jackson's attack on President Carter and SALT II agreement. "By going to Vienna to sign SALT II with Leonid Brezhnev, said Jackson, Carter would be following in the footsteps of [British prime minister] Neville

Chamberlain's ignominious journey to Munich in 1938" (Talbott 1979, 5). Overdependence on a preestablished mental shortcut often contributes to a misapplied association of similarities in different events. It results in a misjudgment of the likely co-occurrence of different events by overweighing or exaggerating certain characteristics.

The cognitive process of assimilating information is influenced not only by existing expectations but also by memory stores. Invalid correlations between events might be established even though they are a mere consequence of being presented at the same time. What is the most accessible in our memories does not always turn out to be the most effective in problem-solving. Faced with uncertain outcomes, disconfirming evidence does not weigh much in reevaluating one's own judgments, especially when a negotiator's confidence is anchored to their initial estimates (Kahneman 2003). In addition, not all the cues from past experiences are likely to be called up due to a general confirmation bias. The availability heuristic often makes us impervious to new insights and ideas by basing our judgments on information or experience coming immediately into our mind. The potential risk or danger of a particular course of action (e.g., unwarranted searches for signs of terrorist attacks) can be exaggerated, regardless of circumstantial differences, by a memory of a hazardous outcome of a similar event in the past (Neale and Bazerman 1991). If some information or memory of events (e.g., the 9/11 al-Qaeda attacks) is presented in a colorful or emotionally vivid manner, decision-makers are prone to overestimating their salience to the current situation.

Human judgment and perceptions are often tinged with a tendency to ignore what we are reluctant to accept, hampering an ability to think creatively. The negative transfer of previous experience could have a harmful effect in new problem-solving situations by restricting a negotiator's ability to develop appropriate strategies. A vividly disappointing experience in a previous negotiation can lead to switching to a different strategy in the next encounter (Jervis 1976, 229–30). For instance, Palestinians thought that they made too many concessions in negotiating the 1993 Oslo Accord, and adopted a tougher bargaining position in later talks with Israelis over the division of Jerusalem and other issues (Ma'oz et al. 2002). Conversely, policy-makers are less likely to pay attention to qualitative differenes in similar situations after successful negotiation and fail to readapt their previous strategies to a new setting (Kahneman 2003). In trade negotiations with Japan over the automobile sector in the late 1980s and early 1990s, the US strategy was modeled on its success in setting numerical goals in the semi-conductor sector in 1986. The Japanese government was increasingly jittery about their semiconductor agreement, which had set up the first quantitative target, and did not want to see its repetition elsewhere. They feared that concessions on such measures as using rigorous numerical indicators in cars and car parts would also be replicated in every agreement under negotiation. Thus Japan resisted a similar settlement that adopted detailed quantitative measures intended to easily monitor market openness.

As seen above, a variety of shortcomings in cognitive heuristics (or procedures) pervade human judgment. Negotiators often hold a different kind of mistaken beliefs about counterparts' choices and behaviors. Rigidity in thoughts and opinions is caused by a heavy reliance on heuristic strategies. Such heuristics as an attribution error and a fixed-pie bias are involved in simplifying a negotiator's social world (Jönsson 2012; Neale and Fragale 2006). Even when a counterpart's preferences are shaped by situational factors, those forces are often ignored while attempting to understand their motives; consequently the behavior of others could be falsely attributed to their personalities or dispositions. A target's particular attributes might be overemphasized when negotiators infer unobservable dispositions or interests from observable acts. The shooting-down of a U-2 during the Cuban crisis in 1961, for instance, was attributed to the Soviet leadership's hostility by the American side, even though it was not ordered by Khrushchev but by a local commander. In an intense conflict setting, it is not unusual for blame to be placed on leaders for the actions of their followers by assuming an adversary's direct hand behind an uncontrolled event. A fundamental attribution error leads to underweighting social situations in explaining others' behaviors that are negatively perceived.

In a competitive setting, heuristic errors are more likely to be manifested in such notions as a mythical fixed pie. In coping with ambivalence about an opponent's preferences and the reasons behind them, negotiators may regard their counterpart's priorities as the same as their own. When the other party is assumed to have identically weighted issue preferences, negotiation is framed in a competition for the same object. Thus the mythical fixed pie of negotiations instigates a fight over dividing a limited object. The erroneous assumption of a fixed-pie bias may eventually expedite a "split-down-the-middle" compromise in spite of opportunities for mutually beneficial tradeoffs (Neale and Fragale 2006).

The rationality of choices may be eroded when the world is seen through the partisan lens of one's own interests; opponents are seen as being the sole beneficiary of their own offers with little benefit to one's own side. Hence, it develops a tendency to minimize the significance of the concessions made by a counterpart. At the same time, one's own concessions are presented as constituting far-reaching manifestations of goodwill, not sufficiently appreciated by the other. In the aftermath of the Oslo Peace Accord, most Israelis did not see a major ideological concession in the PLO recognition of the Israeli state, though it was a big shift from the Palestinian denial of Israel's legitimacy since 1948. Instead, it was attributed to the Palestinians having no choice but to admit the existence of Israel (which was backed by formidable military power). Similarly, Israel's transfer of parts of the West Bank to the Palestinians was not taken by the latter as a major compromise, due to continued occupation of most of their territory as well as a lack of Israel's legitimate legal right to control the whole occupied land from the start (Albin 2001).

Competitive psychological dynamics

The desire to simplify a complex negotiation problem creates a difficulty in finding the most effective balance between cooperation and competition when personal preferences for choosing one type of interaction over another heavily reflect an individual's dispositional orientations. In reaction to the inherently competitive nature of a negotiation process, even the most accommodating people find it difficult to always keep a cooperative attitude toward their counterpart. Hence negotiation dynamics themselves produce an obstacle to finding shared interests once discussions move on. When the other party encounters conflicting needs on the table, its statements undergo a competitive filter.

If individuals assume that they face direct competition upon their entrance into negotiations, one negotiator's gain is seen primarily as the other's loss without the possibility of integrative agreements (McGinn 2006). A win–lose zero-sum assumption leads to a belief that an offer from a counterpart should be treated with great suspicion, as the negotiator receiving the offer reasons that the offerer's gain must be a loss for the recipient. As a consequence, negotiators are likely to come to value a particular proposal less once it is presented by an opponent. By succumbing to reactive devaluation, the likability of a particular proposal or idea is weakened merely by the fact that it is put forth by a counterpart (Neale and Fragale 2006). In this situation, revision of a negotiator's preferences is less directly linked to its objective merit.

Conversely, one may become skeptical of one's own proposals simply because an adversary is beginning to accept them. This is especially so when one is ambivalent about the merit of their proposals. If an adversary does not look so serious, "cheap" concessions are easy to make (given the possibility that they are not likely to go forward). Once agreement is within reach, concessions suddenly appear to be more costly, prompting the temptation to retract. In disarmament negotiations, "the United States [occasionally] reacted to a high level of Soviet concessions by retracting its own previous positions" (Jensen 1988, 64). Reflecting the logic of Cold War politics, the United States had sometimes made concessions only on the assumption that the Soviets would fail to reciprocate.

Competitive actors also suffer from fallible judgment, through nonrational escalation of conflict, as well illustrated in a dollar auction game where winners typically pay more than the item is actually worth in competitive bidding (i.e., the winner's curse). As individual bidding escalates above the actual value of a dollar, staying out of the auction is a better strategy, but each competitor fails to consider the mutual effects of each other's decisions, making themselves worse off. In order to recover at least part of the sunk costs, the goal turns into winning rather than minimizing expected losses

(Young 1991a, 15). The best solution for escape from the escalated commitment is to walk away from the uncontrolled competition by acknowledging and accepting unrecoverable sunk costs (Thompson 2001). Yet it becomes hard to carry out accurate calculations of the other's staying power with a failure to focus on information about each other's goals and the rules of the game. Indeed, the patterns of escalatory behavior are often ascribed to cognitive fallacies that fuel a competitive bidding game to win at any cost. The total collapse of the Oslo peace process in early 2001 resulted in an escalating spiral of Palestinian suicide bombings and Israeli retaliation as an alternative to negotiation.

On another note, competitive perceptions are intensified by negotiators' salient group identities. As illustrated by the stalemate in negotiations between Greek and Turkish Cypriots and between Armenia and Azerbaijan, the mere perception of the negotiation as an instance of competitive rivalry is sufficient to reduce the parties' concession behavior, consequently leading to a deadlock. An identity-based interaction has a great potential for impairing the negotiation process with its deteriorating outcome (Trötschel et al. 2010).[2] While it does increase cohesion within a group, in-group identification may induce more competition with an outer group (Brown 2001). High interethnic competition produces an increase in conformity pressure within one's own group. Negative views about an out-group can be magnified by a tendency to develop uniform views in intragroup decision.

Conformity pressure within a group

By suppressing dissenting opinions through groupthink, according to Irving Janis (1982), decisions tend to be based more on expediency than on wisdom. "Groupthink" is characterized by conformity as a pattern of ineffective, faulty group decision-making derived from excessive cohesiveness. Undue pressure exerted on dissidents to conform to the group's agenda can be ascribed to the eagerness of cohesive groups to instill uniformity of opinion and purpose in conflict with outer groups. Especially in some small groups, striving for unanimity promotes the exaggeration of favorable consequences, while downplaying adverse outcomes. In fact, conformity pressures explain the American military decision-making in escalating the Vitenam War. As a formal group, the Joint Chiefs of Staff of the US Department of Defense provided unanimous support for escalation even though some members individually doubted its potential for success. Despite the anticipation of a disastrous outcome, they continued to recommend incremental escalation, shunning an alternative approach. Lacking confidence in a path to success, they "could find refuge in their collective identity" as a formal group (Allison and Zelikow 1999, 285). Decision-making can be improved by restructuring a committee as well as different rules, personalities and relative power relations. In the successful deliberation of responses during the Cuban Missile Crisis, Kennedy's top advisors were teamed up into two different working groups to cultivate the opposing options of blockade and airstrike.

Anchoring and adjustment: endowment effects

Once a reference point is established as an anchor, its value is adjusted up or down as deemed appropriate. As seen in Chapter 8, a beginning position serves as a reference point from which the perceptions of possible goals can be adjusted. Thus, an initial offer guides subsequent moves by affecting a negotiator's goal setting. A particular anchor may come from a previous contract, one's publicly announced position or an adversary's initial offer (Curşeu and Schruijer 2008). For example, North Korea's positions in the Six-Party Talks over their nuclear program in 2005 were anchored to their reference to the 1994 Framework Agreement; the US position was anchored to publicly announced goals (i.e., improvement from the framework agreement with the goal of rolling back previous concessions made to North Korea).

When negotiation involves issues of uncertain or ambiguous value, the selection of an anchor value relies on estimating unknown objects. Even though a reference point might have been chosen arbitrarily, it becomes salient to value estimates, shaping beliefs about the attainability or acceptability of outcomes (Gimpel 2007). Anchoring a negotiation with high early demands generally represents an attempt to draw concessionary behavior from an opponent. In response to an unacceptable anchor, a counterpart may reanchor the process, if necessary, by threatening to walk away from further talks instead of acknowledging an intolerable proposal as an initial bargaining point (Bazerman and Neale 1992).

An emotional attachment to the initial offer creates an endowment effect. Initial goals could have crucial effects in setting expectations for future performance. As the designated starting point, an anchor is used to assess whether a later offer or settlement option is a gain or a loss. In spite of a positive bargaining range, negotiators may remain committed to initial offers, failing to adjust their reference points, due to the endowment effect (Kristensen and Gärling 2000). As it is often a question of whether the glass is half-full or half-empty, a positive frame for one negotiator becomes a negative one for another (Kotzian 2007).

In order to defuse the explosive crisis created by the 1990 Iraqi invasion and annexation of Kuwait, the Arab League made a packaged offer to Saddam Hussein through several negotiations. The package proposal included the Iraqi control of the Ramilla oilfields in their ongoing border dispute with Kuwait, possession of Bubiyan Island closely abutting the Iraqi shoreline, and renegotiation or elimination of a $14 billion debt with

Kuwait in return for the withdrawal of Iraqi troops. Hussein's flat rejection of the generous offer is attributed to his framing the offer as loss from the referent of a new status quo (i.e., the possession of all of Kuwait and its resources after the invasion). However, concessions from the Arab League's proposal could have been positively framed if he had seen the proposal as a gain by having a referent of what he would win just for a few weeks of military and political maneuvers (Bazerman and Neale 1992).

As seen above, where to anchor may even lead to opposing interpretations of the same proposal. A modest gain relative to the previous status quo may be treated as a loss when measuring against the publicly announced goals. Negotiation framed in terms of fairness enhances the durability of the agreement, but it all depends on where a referent point is anchored – for instance, the previous division, the other side's initial offer or one's own estimate of an opponent's reservation points (Korobkin and Guthrie 2004). A negotiation guided by explicitly formulated principles (e.g., the polluter-pays principle for an environmental cleanup) becomes a pointer in similar situations if it is instituted as a precedent.

Risk-taking vs. adverse behavior

Various studies indicate that attitudes toward risk are driven by the evaluation of potential gains and losses. Negotiation is full of risky choices, as parties are not fully certain about the effects of a particular decision. For instance, in the absence of knowledge about each other's disagreement points and payoffs, a negotiator may not be sure whether negotiations will end with a settlement or with break-off. Faced with risky choices, it would be important to properly assess the known probability of the occurrence of a certain event. Given their partially unknown nature, the outcomes are often referred to as prospects. Prospect theory assumes that in selecting a decision option an individual reaction to a loss is more sensitive than a response to a gain (Kahneman and Tversky 1979). Typical individuals tend, for instance, to take $500 for certain rather than accepting an equal chance at winning $1,000 or nothing. Faced with the loss of $1,000 however, the same person would typically choose an even chance at gaining it back over a sure guarantee of $500 (with a loss of $500). Despite the same amount of $500 assured in both cases, experimental studies show different preferences, depending on whether an individual faces gain or loss. Individuals are risk-averse with the anticipation of assured gains, but are willing to accept more risk in a domain of losses (Barberis 2012; Charness *et al.* 2013). In anticipation of loss, people are more likely to prefer a gamble to taking a certain outcome. The orientation of negotiators toward risk acceptance or avoidance has implications for negotiating behavior in resolving differences. With expected losses, other conditions being equal, many people do not seriously consider maximizing expected payoffs as predicted by standard utility theory (Levy 2000).

Negotiators may conversely be driven to select adventurous approaches in the hopes of reversing or minimizing the loss.

Expected gains in value-creation settings generate a greater desire to avoid taking risks (which arises from tactics of making excessive claims). In light of the perceived certainty of gain (e.g., the African National Congress prior to the conclusion of their negotiation with South Africa's white government in 1993), negotiators feel less comfortable with risking a potential agreement by demanding more and being less concessionary (or holding out for future concessions with consequences of stalemate, etc.). This can also explain North Korean bargaining behavior in 1994 framework agreement; they capitulated to most of US demands once they were assured of gaining the light water reactor that was their long-held goal.

Emotional interference

Emotions may become an inevitable part of a high-stakes negotiation, for instance, by bringing into play defensiveness, mistrust and doubt. As the Cuban Missile Crisis dramatically moved into the public phase, "the immediate reactions of the two leaders [were] shock, wounded pride, grim determination, and barely repressed fear" (Dobbs 2008, 35):

> both men were awed, frightened, and sobered by their power to blow up the world … [they] understood such a war would be far more terrible than anything mankind had known before. Having witnessed war themselves, they also understood that a commander in chief could not always control his armies.
>
> (*ibid.*, 324)

Khrushchev's "responses to the crisis reflected his shifting moods, which were in turn shaped by the signals he received from Washington, official and unofficial" (*ibid.*, 199). Negotiation under serious threat is imperiled by circumstances of surprise. As the conflict headed toward mutually feared outcomes, in the end, "Khrushchev's anger was tempered with caution. To reduce the risk of a confrontation with American warships, he ordered the return of most of the Soviet vessels that had not reached Cuban waters" (*ibid.*, 43).

Negotiation reality tends to be distorted by emotional involvement in the interpretation of the other's intentions and attitudes. The evaluative process of emotions is engaged in putting a meaning on our personal experience and social surroundings, as is well illustrated by Iraqi confidence prior to the First Gulf War which was provoked by its occupation of Kuwait in 1991. After observing the usual calm manner of the US Secretary of State James Baker's statement, Saddam Hussein's half-brother confidently declared that Americans were not "angry" and even "cowardly." This report led to Hussein's misjudgement about American intentions of attacking and failure to retreat from Kuwait (Neale and Bazerman 1991).

Emotional information shapes one's thinking and actions, influencing interactions (Fromm 2008). In fact, negotiators need to adjust their own behavior to a counterpart's affective state, which indicates beliefs and intentions. An emotional reaction to each other's bargaining positions and attitudes conveys information about a negotiator's expectations as well as feelings. Emotion in a negotiating setting is experienced at multiple points of the encounter, often associated with early offers, concessions and other tactical moves, including the adjustment of an aspiration point.

Focal actors' ability or inability to attain their goals generates highly affective states, especially at the evaluative stage (Winter 2012). Positive emotion with less display of negative feelings (such as agitation, anger, resentment) is more likely to be observed when a negotiator regards the process as fair (Barry *et al.* 2004). Negative emotions come from strong perceptions about being thwarted from attaining one's main goals along with anger about the other party's refusal to accept what is deemed reasonable and legitimate.

Emotions have effects in the interpretation of the other's proposal and behavior in various ways. Rapid and automatic feelings could cut off cognitive deliberations through an affective response to data (Bazerman and Chugh 2006). Negative emotions erode analytical ability, increasing the chances of identifying bargaining as a competitive and distributive occasion. For example, a negative affective state engenders cognitive simplification processes, diminishing the disputant's ability to think creatively, with difficulties in complex thinking needed to formulate integrative solutions, for instance, through logrolling (Martinovski 2010).

Information processing can be hindered by undesirable effects of emotions (e.g., anxiety, anger and other negative affective states) which increase misunderstanding and mistrust. Beneath basic human psychological needs lie feelings of being worthy and acceptance of different views and interests. A high degree of acceptance enhances the chances of producing good outcomes by inspiring actions to work out our differences. Excessive stress, arising from difficult interactions, creates an intense physiological reaction that motivates the individual to either fight back or to withdraw from the situation. When that threshold level is reached, the ability to process proposals or requests is often limited. As a result, trying to negotiate under these circumstances remains a futile activity.

The above point is well illustrated by emotional reactions (resentment and anger) added to a bargainer's repertoire of behavior in the failure of the Israeli–Palestinian permanent status negotiations in 2000. Israeli negotiators expressed irritation with what they regarded as the Palestinian leadership's emotional charges and demand for the

Israeli acceptance of the right of return in principle. At one point during the 2000 Camp David meeting, Israeli foreign minister Shlomo Ben Ami screamed at a Palestinian delegation member that they did not deserve to have a state. Emotion may be strategically used as "a tactical gambit" in an attempt at exposing an adversary's vulnerability and controlling their confidence level along with attacks on their competence (Barry *et al.* 2004). The cold emotions of contempt displayed by a rival can detonate anger, dampening perceptual abilities to attend to and process information, consequently lowering the participants' incentives to make concessions. In the above negotiation, as a matter of fact, Palestinians never put their own proposals or suggestions on the table, only rejecting the Israeli offers.

When settling differences involves one's own standing in the outside world, a negotiator can get quite emotional with anxiety and perceptions of insecurity. As have often happened to Israel–Palestinian negotiations, attacks on one's own values pose threats to identity, instigating an emotionally contagious communication process. One negotiator's emotional states mimic or resonate another's at a bargaining table in the absence of the ability to deal with each other's reactions effectively. While anger may prompt the other to search for a solution, wounded pride or spite generally produces feelings of unfairness and rejection of offers that are objectively considered favorable (Thompson *et al.* 2004).

The accumulation of negative emotions leads to the disappearance of trust with little expectation of reciprocity and the questioning of motivations or truthfulness of the opponent. A sequence of retaliatory impulses and behaviors (provoked by anger) may bring about an unexpected or intentional standoff as well as a loss of interest in negotiation itself. Aggressive bargaining tactics hamper the atmosphere of future negotiation by damaging relationships, while ignoring substance by distorting one another's messages. A negative conflict spirals out of control when each side reciprocates the negative affect of the other without ever discussing substantive matters. Negative emotions may trigger an attack–defense cycle with an attempt to force one's own way. This push–pull process is the hallmark of difficult negotiation episodes with a negative emotional spiral; complaints and angry statements prevail in the negotiating atmosphere alongside more extreme demands and charging the adversary with not bargaining in good faith.

Adversarial bargaining styles are characterized by an attempt to put the other down with accusation and intimidation; meaningful substantive discussion is not possible in the mere justification of abusive relationships. Blaming the other side for something they are not responsible for can be intended to evade discussion about core issues. Prior to the Tibetan delegation's visit to Beijing in 2008, the Chinese accused the Dalai Lama of inciting a riot in Tibet as a means of hijacking the agenda for Tibetan self-determination in their homeland. Showing contempt, for instance, by calling the Dalai Lama a "wolf," "jackal," "beast," etc. in public, was designed to show superiority over the other, challenging the legitimacy of the other as a person who deserves respect.

The nature of emotional communication can be employed positively rather than negatively in negotiation. Even in a contentious negotiation, positive feelings present an opportunity to attain a desirable result (through an integrative process) (Kopelman *et al.* 2006). The display of empathy or show of respect contributes to an improved environment for collaborative problem-solving by promoting a positive relationship between negotiators (Caruso 2015). In summer 1994, North Koreans were very grateful for the US delegation's visit to their embassy in Geneva to show sympathy right after the death of their leader at the beginning stage of a difficult negotiation. The North Korean principal negotiator, Kang Suk Ju, even hinted to his counterpart, Robert Gallucci, about forthcoming concessions (Wit *et al.* 2004). A "positive mood" (for instance, created by costless symbolic gestures such as the above-mentioned visit and President Clinton's condolence message to North Korean people) helps facilitate the creation of value. The quality of one's response is enhanced by the capacity to screen differences in a counterpart's feelings and emotions, as well as one's own (Butt and Choi 2006). The US negotiators in Geneva meticulously monitored subtle emotional cues to gain insight into their opponent's priorities and opportunities for logrolling. Positive emotion such as empathy increases the ability to understand the other's perspectives and their role in negotiation.

Emotional functions are often considered a negative factor in stressful crisis situations, which diminish cognitive capabilities, escalating the conflict. In a hostage taking situation, reduction in heightened levels of emotional arousal by hostage takers is essential to fostering their cognitive processing of alternative options (Wells *et al.* 2013). A process of "neutralizing" emotions for rational discussion entails active listening, paraphrasing, pauses and open-ended questions, looking beneath their statements for concerns not clearly articulated. The awareness of emotions and motivations, surging through an opponent's heart, is essential to affecting what is going on in their heads. Wisdom is seldom discovered without balancing reason and emotion (Fisher *et al.* 1997).

Personality and individual idiosyncrasies

Even though a negotiation strategy needs to be adapted to the specific situational context, undoubtedly, heterogeneous personalities cannot be ignored in understanding another negotiator's perceptions and behaviors. As a crucial variable of a negotiator background, individual traits with varied characters and emotions interplay with a given situation, affecting negotiation processes and outcomes (Dimotakis *et al.* 2012). Differences in high vs. low self-esteem are, for instance, considered a factor in setting the bargainer's desire to secure an outcome near either aspirations or reservations. High self-esteem might encourage more willingness to take risks toward a goal of attaining aspirations, not being merely satisfied with beating a reservation level. The effects of personality can be manifested by the combination of different personal dispositions. More self-centered personal traits with high self-esteem could contribute to a less accommodating bargaining stance.

Personalities matter to negotiation because it is conducted by humans whose temperament can interfere in judgments about themselves, others and situations as well as affective states. Egocentrism produces a propensity to consider one's own offers as more generous than others. Discussion is hindered if a self-centered, temperamental negotiator is easily aroused to anger (*ibid.*). The less constrained a negotiator's decision-making role is (e.g., Sadat during the 1978 Camp David negotiation), the more salient the imprint of personality on a negotiation process and outcome. The mesh of the predispositions of the opponents determines how sensitive each will be to the other's behavior (Findlay and Thagard 2011). The summer 2000 Camp David negotiation between Israel and Palestine was, in part, hampered by the incompatible personalities of Israeli prime minister Barak (known for being self-centered and high in self-esteem, and having full confidence in himself) vs. Palestinian head Yasser Arafat (impatient and operating with an abysmal, micro-management style) (Dajani 2005).[3]

Personality variation can help explain a negotiator's predispositions (holding particular orientations or tendencies) toward forming their motives and behavior as well as expectations of particular goals and relations with the other side (Elfenbein 2013). Aside from a shift in bargaining power and public opinion, a personality difference between analytical, methodical Yitzhak Rabin and temperamental Ehud Barak played a role in how they approached their negotiations with the Palestinians. Despite his views of Arafat as "a leader of murders, conniving and ruthless," pragmatism enabled Rabin to put aside his suspicion, and he was willing to collaborate to develop the rules of engagement in controlling attacks of Palestinian militants in Israel (Sher 2006, 3). On the other hand, Barak was seen as determined "but arrogant and aggressive, resolute on dictating the rules of the game, which is why Arafat rejected his proposals" (*ibid.*, 120).[4] Quite often the Israeli prime minister presented his proposal or nonnegotiable condition as "take it or leave it" (Klieman 2005, 117).

Personality features are quite diverse given multiple dimensions of personal variations and social attitudes. People of a highly authoritarian orientation tend to view a mixed-motive game as a setting in which to prove their own forcefulness and ability to outdo their rival (Hermann and Kogan 1977). Cooperation is more likely to be exhibited by a nonauthoritarian and intellectually sophisticated negotiator (Bartos 1974). The less authoritarian a leader is (e.g., former Soviet leader Mikhail Gorbachev), the more willing he is to understand his opponent's stance. Highly anxious people are geared toward less risk-taking, being motivated by a desire to avoid unwelcome outcomes, but are likely to be more cautious, trying to make fewer concessions with the expectation of the worst (Hermann and Kogan 1977). Being mistrustful of others, highly suspicious people (e.g., Stalin) are more likely to suspect motives of any person, making them less cooperative with an attempt to look for ways to beat others.

The combined personality characteristics of key decision-makers could create difficult situations by magnifying individual psychological fallacies. The pair of personality characteristics matters, for instance a mutually suspicious dyad is expected to be less cooperative than dyads composed of empathetic persons. When negotiators develop an empathetic orientation, they are more likely to seek a joint outcome with a mutually accommodating bargaining stance. A major breakthrough in September 2003 Sudanese talks was in part attributed to the chemistry between the south's opposition leader John Garang and Sudan's Vice President Ali Osman Taha. Their personal relationships, quickly built over a three-month period of talks, helped resolve the differences over wealth sharing, enabling them to sign an agreement in January 2004.

A decision about a particular strategy could be attributed to personal behavioral orientations as well as situational forces (Galinsky et al. 2011). Other conditions being equal, such personality traits as agreeableness and quarrelsomeness contribute to dispositional attribution of cooperative vs. competitive behavior. Along with a psychological need for harmony, an amicable personality is more likely to develop empathy, as opposed to being temperamental and stubborn, in support of seeking joint outcomes. A compromising personal style advances "an equal split" or other fair rules of thumb, whereas an aggressive style supports more competitive heuristics, such as "winner takes all." A pair of conciliatory individuals is more likely to exhibit lower levels of demand and make more accommodating offers, trusting their opponents (Dimotakis et al. 2012). In the absence of information about their counterparts in upcoming negotiations, accommodators perceive their encounters to be more cooperative than competitive.

Beyond purely rational calculation, social value orientations (on the opposing dimensions of cooperation and competition) can be implicated in setting individuals' approaches to their goals (relative versus absolute gains continuum). By viewing the world as essentially competitive, some individuals are motivated to maximize their own benefit with no regard for others or to attain a relative gain under virtually all conditions. Others may seek to guarantee their interests by maximizing a joint benefit that can be shared with their counterparts. These opposing personal orientations were revealed by the different positions toward the Soviet Union over seeking relative vs. absolute gains within the Carter administration (1977–81). Along with the opening of diplomatic relations with China, Carter's advisor Zbigniew Brzezinski wanted to utilize the SALT negotiations to "punish" Soviet behavior in the Horn of Africa. This adversarial bargaining tactic created rigidity, putting up roadblocks in the search for solutions to such complex issues as nuclear security. In contrast, the Secretary of State Cyrus Vance assessed that US security would not be guaranteed by fueling a competitive encounter given the likely Soviet retaliation (Hopmann 1995). His basic outlook hinged on understanding that, in superpower relations, one's partner's behavior depends on one's own level of cooperativeness.

When the interaction pattern is characterized by uncertainty and confusion, intolerance of ambiguity is likely to elicit competitive strategies. Tolerating ambiguity, cognitively complex decision-makers are more willing to seek cooperative strategies for lessening unwarranted risk (Hermann and Kogan 1977). They have an understanding that cooperation will be a better policy in the long run since tit-for-tat reciprocity produces retaliation against cheating or other uncooperative behavior. Gorbachev regarded a positive overall relationship between the United States and the Soviet Union as essential to keep open a flexible range of options in the arms-control negotiations. He pursued a joint search for "empathetic understanding" with Western leaders instead of continuing a strategy of minimizing maximum losses through playing competitively. By seeking mutual cooperation, Gorbachev turned the Prisoner's Dilemma exercise into Stag Hunt. He was convinced that the overall security relations between the two superpowers would be transformed by overcoming mutual suspicion and fear of exploitation. In fact, his policy echoed Anatol Rapoport's thesis on a peaceful resolution of conflicts between opposing belief systems through a process of cultivating understanding in the pursuit of mutual gains (Rapoport 1974).

Institutional and political context of negotiation

Apart from intellectual, psychological and emotional aspects of individual decision-making, a complex layer of political and organizational processes shapes a course of negotiation; it might be easier conceptually to see negotiation behavior in a uniform manner, but intraparty decision-making is quite often not a monolithic enterprise. Thus, negotiations have to proceed at the domestic level as well as at the international level, when their outcome creates losers and winners within a country. As a matter of fact, negotiators act as "a bridge between internal decision-making and external negotiating" (Watkins 1999, 262). During the canal sovereignty negotiation, American negotiators had to reconcile an emotionally charged Panamanian demand with US Congress, Department of Defense, and other domestic parties (Raiffa 1982). A negotiator's external credibility is grounded in presenting a uniform position with the reconciliation of the divergent demands of fractious internal factions. When each side contains groups of people whose interests and values sharply differ, many seemingly bilateral negotiations encompass a component of multigroup bargaining at an intraparty level. As former US secretary of state James Baker aptly put it, "[h]ow you worked the other side in developing the solution to the first problem had ramifications far beyond that single issue" (1995, 134). A unified position has to be created out of internal divisions with the aggregation of all different interests and concerns. The shape of the "external" proposal presented to the other side emerges from the internal dynamics of hammering out a negotiating proposal (Fisher *et al.* 1997).

In internal negotiation, different standpoints of individuals and groups are brought together to yield a collective selection of decisions and actions. As collective goals are often interpreted from personal and organizational perspectives, players perceive different faces of an issue and diverge markedly in their favored actions. Issues are framed differently for individuals not only by their characters and attitudes but also by their unique experiences and responsibilities. The participants bring their reputation and power of persuasion for pervasiveness of their positions. Personal stances on the agenda at hand are likely to reflect the obligations of loyalty to a group and commitments to institutional projects. Preferences may be formed by parochial priorities such as the expansion of organizational missions as well as personal beliefs. In the end, the order of preferences among options will be determined by which faction's priorities prevail over others'.

Domestic political consequences of choices may reflect informal coalitions formed in bargaining games among powerful politicians, interest groups and bureaucrats. In US arms-control negotiation with the Soviets, the political poles were represented by "the interdependence" and "peace-through-strength" schools. As opposed to the latter camp, the interdependence school saw arms-control negotiations as an "expanding-sum" game, being convinced that arms control could make the pie larger by improving relations, saving defense expenditure and reducing the risk of nuclear war. Opposing cooperation with the Soviets, the "peace-through-strength" faction advocated unilateral military buildup. The strength of each camp shifted, as "participants switched from one to the other or fell somewhere in between" according to the circumstances (Bunn 1992, 10).

Positional bargaining is often fashioned to allay the concerns of the factional divide. In fact, internal structural constraints create difficulties for altering position and reduce the boundaries of outcome parameters. A principal US objective for the SALT II negotiations was set, under the mandate from Congress, for identical numerical limits of strategic nuclear delivery vehicles on each side (Talbott 1979). Given the mandate, the executive branch pursued its preferred mix of ICBMs, SLBMs and long-range heavy bombers under a scheme that allowed each delivery vehicle to count as one unit. Faced with the constraints of limited mandates and other restrictions, negotiators have to practice their trade creatively and restructure the context by shaping internal and external perceptions.

Delay, stalemate or less-than-optimal agreement is often ascribed to greater initial demands and more rigid commitments that result from the interworking of diverse forces within each party. According to Kissinger, difficulties in completing SALT II between 1975 and 1977 were attributed to discord inside the Ford administration. As their side is not all of one mind, negotiators have to juggle between hard and soft (or between tough and flexible) approaches to negotiations. While enough flexibility must be mustered to smooth out a rigid internal position, the appearance of sufficient toughness is aimed to extract concessions through painful bilateral negotiations. In order to satisfy key constituents, negotiators may attempt to appeal to different audience groups by negotiating from the middle ground, avoiding bold positions. Internal coordination may have to involve reframing the issues and solve micro-negotiation conflicts. During the SALT I period, "the plenary record was filled with tens of thousands of words" in an attempt to persuade authorities back home of the irreconcilability of positions favored by both sides and their reconsideration for progress (Smith 1985, 122).

Negotiators operate with or against decision-making imperatives in navigating their way through the constraints of the organizational politics. In coordinating an internal process, a principal negotiator may provide input in the formulation of the main agenda. In negotiation with North Korea, in 1994, one of the main tasks by the chief US negotiator Robert Gallucci was to build consensus on priorities on issues which had different degrees of significance to the representatives of multiple agencies (Wit *et al.* 2004). Faced with diverse representations of internal interests, an external negotiator may have to act like an internal mediator engaged in managing tensions as well as an internal coalition-builder. Preparing constituents for unfolding realities is necessary to modulate their aspirations. In the event that incompatible interests block the narrowing of internal differences in forming a negotiating position, an external negotiator may even become a partisan coalition-builder (Watkins 1999).

As each external negotiator goes back to their principals for new instructions, the internal arrangement of each country creates a mirror image in the other, producing back-and-forth communication, from external to internal, then to external, etc. (Raiffa 2002). Because the representatives in interparty negotiation are not generally endowed with complete authorization to carry it out, the outcome has to be acceptable to superiors and constituents at home. To conclude a negotiation successfully, a negotiator should be aware of internal dynamics of not only one's own side but also the opponent's. In finalizing the 1994 Framework Agreement, North Korean negotiators accepted the difficulties in its ratification at the US Congress, but they wondered whether the outcome would be respected if a Republican president were to be elected in the future. Negotiators have to perform a difficult dance to meet the other side's concerns while remaining sensitive to the needs, interests and perceptions of important key subactors on the other side. Internal dissension on the other side is not necessarily beneficial. Synchronizing the external negotiation with internal ones should involve "[looking] *within* the other side for opportunities to build cross-cutting coalitions" (Watkins 1999, 261).

Of course, what negotiators can do is limited in the event of heightened tensions off the table.

Organizational (decision-making) context

The complexity of the negotiating process derives, in part, from the fact that governments are not monolithic, but comprise many players, each with their own interests (Allison 1971). In the formation of a national position, competing interests and disagreements have to be ironed out within a complex organizational process. Complications are created by a multilayered decision-making structure, including bureaucratic coordination, legislative approval, etc. In developing an American stance on arms-control or other foreign policies, for instance, tentative alternative approaches tend to be developed in consultation with government agencies and Congress prior to a presidential decision. It generally evolves out of a pulling and hauling game among internal players who have colliding aims, advocating either soft- or hardline positions in a shifting political context.

Bureaucratic as well as political factions often attempt to control government policies and expand their influence with different perspectives on negotiating with foreign adversaries. Bureaucratic maneuvering aims to support proposals that strengthen the agency's organizational imperatives with an opposition to those that diminish its sphere of operation. Organizational interests bring a different light to views about a particular policy. In his "organizational model," Graham T. Allison (1971) observed that each conglomerate of organizations has its own goals and programs. Each player picks the issue on which they can operate with a reasonable probability of success, but single players do not have sufficient power to guarantee satisfactory outcomes to themselves when there is power-sharing among separate institutions. In interagency disputes, factionalism extends down to various bureaucracies beyond the highest turf battle. Organizational decision-making reflects compromise in bargaining for resources, roles and missions. It is pertinently presented by a "bureaucratic politics model" that captures various overlapping and hierarchically arranged bargaining games (Borch and Mérida 2013). When parties on one side lack a unified voice, there will be a struggle to grind out positions.

The dynamics of a transition from internal bargaining to external negotiation was a key part of US nuclear arms-control talks with the Soviets during the Cold War period. It is elegantly described by Henry Kissinger: prior to the materialization of a bargaining position, "numbers of nuclear weapons are strained, first through our bureaucracy, and then through theirs. What starts out as an American bureaucratic compromise goes over to their side, where all their sharpshooters get a crack at it" (quoted in Bunn 1992, 112). Thus any arms negotiation between the two powers was a complex undertaking involving differing factions within the American and Soviet bureaucracies (Kissinger 1979). In a similar manner, Secretary of State Schultz had a sequence of dealings, beginning with President Reagan, the US military, the Soviet government and only then the Pentagon civilians (including Defense Secretary Caspar Weinberger). In overwhelming potential domestic arms-control opponents, Schultz had to begin with getting allies onboard, creating momentum before public disclosure of the deal (Lax and Sebenius 1991). According to a veteran arms-control negotiator's observation, prenegotiation involving the US executive branch, members of Congress and US allies typically "took more time and effort than the negotiations with the Soviets" (Bunn 1992, 7).

The necessity of several layers of negotiation affects not only the process but also the outcome. Bureaucratic-institutional interests often meddle in or veto part or all of the substantive agreements forged at a negotiating table as well as shaping an agenda-setting stage (as seen in the US–Soviet Geneva Arms talks during the 1970s and 1980s). Moscow's wait-and-see attitude and slow concessionary rate at the beginning of SALT I was, in part, "related to the desire to minimize policy differences internally (bureaucratic struggles)" (Jensen 1988, 29). In Kissinger's negotiation over SALT I, early on, opposition from the Joint Chiefs of Staff and hawkish factions in the US Senate closed down any discussion about controlling Multiple Independently Targetable Reentry Vehicles (featured by each missile with ability to hit multiple targets).[5] During the talks on the Intermediate-Range Nuclear Forces Treaty in 1982, Pentagon opposition killed the tentative agreement between the United States and Soviet negotiators had hatched during their memorable "walk in the woods" (designed as part of informal meetings to break a deadlock) down the mountain in the outskirts of Geneva on July 16, 1982. The remarkable deal cemented by Paul Nitze permitted American numerical advantage in total INF warheads over the Soviets in the European theater. Yet despite superiority in the overall force level strength, he was not able to convince Pentagon hardliners to concede on Pershing II ballistic missiles with a quick strike time (Bunn 1992). Bureaucratic and political meddling can be counterbalanced if the leaders show personal commitment, as shown by the direct intervention of Khrushchev and Kennedy at the last stage of negotiating the partial nuclear test ban treaty in summer 1963. They threw the weight of their authority behind the treaty's successful conclusion, undercutting domestic opposition within each side. Kennedy's personal management of the negotiations from the White House was designed to minimize complications from domestic hurdles. The bureaucratic balance was eventually tipped by a shift in the Senate in favor of the treaty.

It may be costly or difficult for leaders to make concessions when this creates a challenge to forging an intraparty consensus among powerful bureaucracies and interest groups. During the initial stalemate stage, Salvadoran government concessions to the FNLM were difficult to make even though it was essential for the negotiation to take off. Despite President José Durante's willingness to concede, he had to face stiff resistance from the armed forces and a powerful economic oligarchy on top of pressure from hardliners within the Reagan administration. Only after a clear legislative election victory in March 1985 was Durante's political hand strengthened against more conservative domestic opponents (Roett and Smyth 1988).

Two-level games: internal negotiation

According to two-level game theory put forward by Robert Putnam (1988), international diplomacy is closely linked to internal bargaining on each side. Negotiating with an external party has to incorporate distinct needs and values of subunits that surface from intraparty bargaining (Lax and Sebenius 1991; Odell 2012). If subplayers, as guardians of their own interests, are able to block unfavorable deals or contracts that fall under the reservation level on an issue dear to them, "the composite agreement has to incorporate the specification of minimum levels of achievement on separate issues" (Keeney and Raiffa 1991, 139). Thus reservation levels are forced upon not only the overall composite agreement but also individual issues. Insistence on reservation levels on individual issues by subplayers could, of course, produce a collective loss if the entire deal were abandoned. International negotiations are conducted with the goal of avoiding any agreement that will severely upset equitable balance among the internal preferences. The domestic political calculus of political leaders has to focus on balancing different desires. Deep polarization within a negotiating party is likely to produce a more protracted process for negotiation.

In mobilizing support, leaders are compelled to respond to the needs of domestic constituencies either by granting internal concessions or by building coalitions across sectors. In this context, with the requirement for social and political support, issue linkage serves as a negotiating device, offering compensation to the losers. If an internal procedure for dividing joint gains is used, a potential loser can be persuaded to give up demanding reservation levels on individual issues. Internal side payments as well as compensation to opposing factions can be made in managing domestic differences with effects on the external bargain (Mayer 1992; Odell and Tingley 2013). In placating the military's opposition to strategic arms-control and earning votes of many hawks in Congress, the White House bestowed substantial funding for the research and development of new weapon systems. In fact, "the B-1 bomber, MX missile, cruise missile and Trident submarine all owe some of their initial budgetary push to the Nixon administration's campaign to sell the SALT I agreements" (Bunn 1992, 127).

Coalition-building across the lines

This topic can be best illustrated by intriguing examples below. In negotiation over the sales of grain to the Soviet Union in the mid 1970s, the apparently agricultural issue swiftly enlarged the circle of concerned parties, ranging from the maritime industry and unions to typical foreign policy actors, beyond farmers with spatial and temporal considerations. Diverse participants were drawn into a struggle either to foil or profit from the deal (Porter 1984). In the end, an unusual coalition built between American farmers and the Soviet Union served as powerful force behind the 1975 US–Soviet Grain Agreement. The alliance between American farmers and the Soviet Union was forged naturally by the combination of an exceptionally poor Soviet grain harvest but a very good American one. The voice of American farmers' associations and their political allies significantly weakened the attempts of political interest groups to link the grain sale to Soviet cooperation in Africa or the Middle East or improvement in human rights.

Mounting pressure in the upcoming farm state primaries ultimately produced the Ford administration's promise to avoid playing the agricultural embargo card with Moscow. The administration was forced to relinquish its key demands and agreed to a long-term arrangement in the absence of any visible concessions in oil prices and other high foreign policy agendas. In the whole negotiation process, who controls the negotiation became a delicate dance of who (e.g., American farm interest groups) is supposed (not) to speak with Moscow. Beyond official protocols and rules, further entanglements were informal arrangements about who represents whom on which matters and at which point. As the administration carefully worked to send the right signals about the process in an effort not to trigger the farmers' rage, the Department of Agriculture was granted a far more visible status in negotiations and their deliberations as well as public announcements (Porter 1984).

Acting in concert as seen above, a natural alliance could be formed against an opposing one, cutting across different group lines (Lax and Sebenius 1991; Odell 2010). Domestic actors in two countries may find common cause, displaying internal divisions. In North American Free Trade Negotiation Agreement (NAFTA) auto talks, Mexicans obtained significant concessions from the United States due to their commonality of interest with the Big Three in Detroit. In a similar manner, the Brazilians were able to ignore the Reagan administration's threat under Super 301, since IBM and other American multilateral corporations offered assurance that they did not support the threat.

Public commitments

Through commitment tactics negotiators may bind themselves to some strategically chosen bargaining positions with public postures (for instance, the Argentine military junta's announcement that it would not retreat from its military occupation of the Falkland Islands in their confrontation with Britain in 1982). It is generally a move calculated to arouse a public view that forces one to make few concessions. A position tied to public statements diminishes the decision-maker's scope for flexibility. Yet the deployment of such commitment tactics can wind up in a stalemate, especially if demands made by the two governments are incompatible with each other (in such cases as the US public stance of accepting nothing but completely verifiable, nonreversible North Korean nuclear programs). The creation of a position causes difficulties in making concessions by stirring up public excitement. Once a position is declared to be final by commitment, it is difficult to reverse it without a loss of one's reputation.

As one party goes public with its demand, the other sees disadvantage in not doing so (Leventoglu and Tarar 2005). Then stalemate is created by the simultaneous use of commitment tactics. Even worse, an escalation of commitments by both parties could mean even a breakdown of the negotiation, leading to war (as seen in the Falklands War). To avoid costly delays or war, at least one government would need to back down and rescind its commitment to reach an agreement, but pulling back from their initial demands is often prevented by the large cost of reneging on public commitments (Powell 2006). Stalemate can be averted by forging an agreement on secrecy. Keeping final outcomes secret makes it possible to avoid comparison with initial demands. Likewise, the outcome could also be concealed by hiding or omitting information about offers (Schelling 1960).

Conclusion

It is important to think carefully about the reality of international negotiation, that is, its "irrational" aspects (e.g., emotional, psychological interference in one's judgment and prevalence of parochial subgroup interests in forming a collective bargaining position). While a simplified assumption might aid our ability to grasp the situation more easily and quickly, it is too costly to ignore the fact that our choices can be distorted by misperceptions, attribution errors and other types of heuristic bias (e.g., overconfidence in one's own ability or an unrealistic unitary actor assumption in the other side's decision-making) despite all the good intentions of producing a rational decision. In the collective decision-making of larger entities, a decision derives from a compromise among subplayers without any coherent design whatsoever. In fact, the complex patterns of cognition and organizational imperatives are involved in the development of national policies at the higher decision-making level. Thus "[t]he effects of shared beliefs and of policy conflict" need to be incorporated into "the negotiation analytic model of bargaining" (Borch and Mérida 2013, 106).

Making commitments in the external negotiation has to be considered in the context created by the inner workings of individual, group and political actors. What is negotiable or nonnegotiable can be determined by intraparty decision-making process and structure. Negotiators should be aware of the need for the management of structural boundaries and informal political processes, as well as the interference of unconscious or irrational elements in decision-making. Some of the themes, for example, decision-making and coalition-building, in this chapter will be picked up again in the following chapters on mediation and multilateral negotiation, respectively.

Notes

1 For example, in his 1999 negotiation with Syrians mediated by the United States, Israeli prime minister Ehud Barak overestimated his counterpart President Assad's willingness to make concessions on the strategic part of the Golan Heights. The initial optimism was based on Assad's readiness to negotiate without demanding a firm Israeli commitment to complete withdrawal from the territory occupied during the 1967 War as well as various manifestations of peace, including a sudden switch to more friendly, conciliatory messages toward Israel through public statements or government banners preparing the population for a possible normalization of relations with Israel. Most importantly, given his assassination, the Israelis felt a sense of Assad's urgency that would induce him to "relent on his firm territorial demand under right conditions" (Swisher 2004, 74). These erroneous assumptions led to the Israeli misperception of the Syrian reservation point; consequently an attempt to reach a peace accord with Syria on Israeli terms proved to be a total waste of precious time and resources that could have been devoted more urgently to the final status negotiation with Palestinians (Daoudy 2007).

2 The role of identity and cognition in negotiation is further revealed by experimental studies of Roderick Swaab *et al.* (2008).

3 "During Camp David II, Barak seems to have exhibited most, if not all, of these forms [diabolical enemy-image; virile self-image; moral self-image; selective inattention; absence of empathy]. Whether he intended to have the above attitude or not... this is how he was perceived... by the very people in the Palestinian camp whose confidence and cooperation became critical for the success of the entire endeavor" (Klieman 2005, 116).

4 Even Barak's advisors tried to help him see his failings to no avail. One of the Israeli delegation members during the 2000 Camp David negotiation mentioned to Barak, "The problem is not the positions... He [Arafat] is supposedly a leader of a people, but in fact he is a person with a deep need for respect, and he feels that you are disrespectful to him. A large part of his ability to become flexible involves this issue of respect" (Sher 2006, 87). In fact, Barak's repeated snubbing of Arafat relates to the former's refusal to speak directly with his counterpart at many critical moments. His puzzling attitude is summed up by such questions as "how at a meal lasting two hours on Sunday, July 17, not once did he turn his head toward the PLO chairman seated next to him" (Klieman 2005, 116).

5 As a matter of fact, "the unresolved battle inside the Nixon administration over nuclear arms control strategy" was paradoxically eased by the unenthusiastic Soviet response to American proposals for controlling multiple nuclear warheads presented at the 1974 Moscow summit. "If the Soviet Union had been more responsive... there would have been greater controversy in Washington over initiatives taken by the President." In the end, according to high-level Nixon administration officials, the negotiations were inhibited by "the combined caution of the Soviet and American military establishments." In fact, "Kissinger left the implication that the military on both sides were demanding too much" (*Washington Post*, July 4, 1974).

PART III

Extensions and variants

10 Mediation

> One of the best ways to persuade others is with your ears – by listening to them.
>
> Dean Rusk

MEDIATION is largely known as an assisted or managed form of negotiation. A negotiating process can be modified or extended by the interference of a third party whose primary interest lies in facilitating an agreement. Intermediary participation is designed to create dynamics necessary to overcome or remove obstacles in the structure of interaction. It would improve efficiency in a situation in which a reluctance to expose preferences produces Pareto inferior solutions. When direct negotiations face stalemate, mediation can be introduced to bring about a settlement that could not otherwise have been achievable – such incidents include peace accords in ending brutal civil wars and other protracted violent conflicts (e.g., Burundi, Sudan, Bosnia-Herzegovina, Northern Ireland, etc. in the mid 1990s and early 2000s) as well as long-simmering interstate conflicts (e.g., the 1978 Camp David Peace Accord between Egypt and Israel; the settlement of territorial disputes between Argentina and Chile in 1984).

A mediator has diverse degrees of interest in the conflict and its outcome, but is, in general, endowed with an ability to shape both the context and substance of negotiation through process control, although a final decision on acceptance or rejection of the outcome is left with disputants. This chapter reviews various roles of mediators in controlling negotiators' interactions and, by doing so, the outcome as well. It examines change in bargaining dynamics through assistance in communication, along with restructuring the agendas and drafting proposals. Our main focus will be on the way changes in the number of parties as well as the control of information flows bring about structural alterations in direct interactions between negotiators. As interference in communication channels forms the core of the mediation dynamics, we will also investigate its impact on strategic games played by both a mediator and disputants.

Intermediary functions

Missed opportunities for agreement might be ascribed to communication links fraught with misunderstanding and misperception. The supply of alternative and additional information would be effective in overcoming cognitive limitations such as discounting an opponent's conciliatory moves, reduction in each disputant's fear, prejudices and stereotypes. By keeping the communication flow balanced and productive, negotiation becomes viable in situations where there would otherwise be an impasse. One of the primary tasks of mediation is to open contact, clarify meanings and identify concerns that each party fails to reveal openly. Intermediary roles can be expanded from setting schedules, organizing the order of offers and counteroffers to drafting settlements and supporting the implementation of an agreement (Vukovic 2014).

The most basic and essential level of intervention (needed to forge an agreement) is based on a communication function. It can be performed by diplomats of small or larger states, internationally or regionally known political figures, envoys of international organizations, a host of religious or other transnational actors, or even a group of individual professionals who do not represent particular interests or organizations (Svensson 2013). These actors have different degrees of effectiveness in influencing a bargaining process with diverse sets of knowledge, skills and capabilities (Bercovitch 2014).

Mediators shape the informational environment faced by primary negotiators. When parties are not ready to formally meet, intermediaries are confined to passive message deliveries. Shuttle diplomacy constitutes the most basic and standard form of supporting communication. In facilitating communications between antagonists who deeply mistrust each other, "good offices" are oriented toward relaying information to the disputants as well as ascertaining facts. The clarification of issues in the transmission and interpretation of proposals is designed to remove communication obstacles created in the absence of direct exchange of information (Fey and Ramsay 2010).

The acquisition of information and exchange between the parties were the intermediary's most basic functions in diffusing the Iranian hostage crisis of 1979–81. While simply sticking to procedural matters, the Algerians screened communications as part of strategies for managing information. In transmitting messages between the United States and Iran, the Algerian delegation reviewed the substance of nearly every communication, taking a hand in the wording. Their insistence on having the final word on what was to be transmitted turned out to have a positive effect on negotiations (Princen 1992). As was illustrated by Algerian assistance, it is ultimately not part of good offices to bargain with each of the primary contestants to steer the direction of the negotiation.

The general parameters for settlement of the Iranian hostage crisis did not result from Algerian intervention. The hostage crisis was ready to be settled in 1980 due to a shift in both sides' expectations, creating conditions for an acceptable agreement. With such external circumstances as the Shah's death and US willingness to transfer his assets to the new Iranian government, a substantial change was not needed in either Iranian or American positions to produce a possible agreement framework. Nonetheless, it was essential to have Algerian engagement in straightening out the details of the complicated final negotiations on the methods to verify the transfer of almost $8 billion to an Iranian government bank account as well as the release of hostages.

In a basic mode of communication, as seen above, an intermediary has a direct stake in neither the outcome nor resources applied to resolving the differences. In general, confinement to communication support produces less risk with a low profile but has diminished expectations about the outcome. In Nigeria's Biafran civil war (1967–70), Adam Curle and two other Quakers conducted shuttle diplomacy but were not able to alter the Nigerian military government's intransigent positions on its treatment of eastern Nigeria's rebellious Ibo ethnic region.

More active roles

By providing a procedural framework (e.g., setting deadlines and prioritizing issues), mediators can shape the way opposing parties interact in a bargaining situation. In the case of deep divisions, subtlety of intermediary suggestions about venue and drafting agendas in arranging negotiation sessions may become a tipping phenomenon. A mediator's capacity can be enlarged to include reasoning and bargaining with disputants on content-related issues in suggesting alternatives or drafting possible solutions to be adopted as a starting point to narrow difference. Agreement becomes more attractive with an insurance scheme or security guarantee to reduce risk. Thus an intermediary can go beyond facilitating communication and setting up a procedural framework. Possible settlements might be forged by proposing substantive solutions along with suggestions of concessions needed for the moderation of extreme demands. Disputants who want to improve an outcome by waiting need to be persuaded that a future outcome would not be better.

In addition, setting a firm deadline has the effect of producing a positive turning point in stalled talks when parties face undesirable consequences, but stalemate persists. Frustrated with the lack of any real progress, in March 1998, George Mitchell, chairman of Northern Ireland's All-Party Talks, set a deadline as a sensitive procedural move to break a deadlock reinforced, in part, by a climate of hostility and fear of uncertainty. When the Vatican injected itself as a mediator in defusing the Argentina–Chile tension over the ownership of the Beagle Channel islands of Picton, Lennox and Neuva in the South Atlantic between May 1979 and December 1980, the papal mediation utilized a deadline as a traditional action-forcing mechanism with a threat of withdrawal after inconclusive negoations. In the absence of tangible resources to bring the process to closure, the Vatican threatened to withdraw, since the two countries still refused to accept the settlement despite the existence of all the necessary conditions. However, it did not work until the very end of the mediation in 1984, when it was clear that reverting to the status quo ante did not look viable. The threat is credible only if the mediator's withdrawal is more costly to the partisans than continued stalemate. When no better terms are available, accusation cannot be made against the mediator of "not doing everything possible to bring about the agreement" (Princen 1992, 57).

In general, an intermediary role evolves with accumulated information that allows an active attempt at pulling different positions closer to each other. Since information gathering naturally occurs due to the exchange of offers and counteroffers, a mediator's influence comes from this pooled information from all the disputants. Once mediators have more knowledge about each party's priorities, they develop an ability to bargain with them. A proposal for integrative bargaining can be forged by a mediator who transforms a perceived zero-sum structure by suggesting tradeoffs as well as different arrangements of issues.

The mediator strengthens the appeal of proposed solutions via the addition and subtraction of benefits. When the mediator has considerable investment in the mediation's outcome, they back up an agreement by putting their own resources on the table. In support of the 1978 Camp David Accord, the US government offered loan guarantees and funding needed not only for Israeli withdrawal from the Sinai but also for the construction of a new airfield on the Israeli side. On top of that, as side payments, Israel received a large quantity of sophisticated weapons systems as well as $3 billion in aid; Egyptians were also given $1.5 billion in financial aid as well as military equipment. The continuing US engagement was substantial to ensure that the deal would not break down.

Different degrees of intermediary influence over the process and outcome (e.g., whether their proposals are to be taken seriously by disputants or not) derive, in part, from third-party relationships with partisans. Noncoercive actors do not take directive approaches of pressing reluctant parties to moderate intransigent positions, mostly being limited to communication. No fear would be generated by the inconsequential power of a neutral mediator (Princen 1992). Small and middle-rank states engage in low-profile strategies of dialogue and communication with only limited ambitions to enhance their prestige and diplomatic status. Since Qatar does not have any serious ability to pose a threat, it has been more acceptable as a mediator than regional powers in easing conflicts in the Arab world without causing fear of interference.

Powerful actors can apply a carrot-and-stick approach to press for concessions, altering the payoffs and motivations (Beardsley 2009). A powerful third party can manipulate payoff structures with an ability to arm-twist as well as to offer side payments. Powerful interveners are capable of pulling off a deal with high-pressure tactics, making the continuing conflict unattractive and maintaining leverage by employing such means as military aid, an economic down payment or better future relations. As seen in Bosnia-Herzegovina, in a high-stakes conflict, powerful mediators have the ability to alter a payoff structure more directly by withholding or preventing an outcome pursued by one of the parties (e.g., NATO bombing to stop genocide by Serb militias).

Managed negotiation through an intermediary

Whereas mediation has few institutionalized patterns and no formal rules or standard procedures, a proposal by intermediaries can help start negotiation and end bargaining. The process of setting the agenda and drafting agreements can be used to exert influence over bargaining outcomes. The discussion could start with a skeleton draft agreement if enough private information has been shared between a mediator and each negotiating party at a prenegotiation stage. The evaluation of proposals and counterproposals by each side propels the process of bargaining and tradeoff until different interests are fully represented and resolved (Mauleon and Vannetelbosch 2013). In brokering agreements, a mediator may talk to each of the parties in turn, trying to persuade them to make concessions. Faced with intransigence, they could be reminded of the consequences of nonsettlement and might be pressed to be flexible. As seen below, in the Camp David negotiation, President Carter set the parameters for determining the satisfactory level of progress during thirteen days of negotiation (which ended on September 17, 1978).

The 1978 Camp David mediation did not adopt formal rules or procedures in discussing various terms and conditions for the return of the Sinai and the status of West Bank and Gaza, which had been occupied by Israelis during the six-day war in 1967. An American mediating team led by President Carter developed a single draft based on the identification of differences in positions. The initial draft went through continued amendment, incorporating the main concerns and criticisms of both Israelis and Egyptians, until the emergence of a draft that could not be further revised without risking the danger of failure. During the entire period, roughly thirty-three drafts were produced prior to the announcement of the Egyptian–Israeli peace accord. Pressure for change in positions was exerted in a series of intense private individual meetings held separately between President Carter and each of the two protagonist state heads, Prime Minister Begin of Israel and President Sadat of Egypt (Quandt 1986).

The involvement of multiple groups increases the importance of process management. In a more structured mediation demanded by the participation of a larger number of parties, procedural rules may focus on the format of discussion. In the mediation between warring factions in the Burundi civil war (1995–2001), five committees were organized to negotiate separate topics ranging from peace and security, to democracy, to reconstruction and transitional institutions, before full discussion at a plenary. The progress of negotiation in each committee was reported to the mediating team's chairman, former Tanzanian president Julius Nyerere. The proposals coming out of the committee negotiation process were further discussed for approval at the plenary session. The collective decision-making process produced different dynamics in intragroup and intergroup relations. Most strikingly, a rapport among a core group of negotiators grew naturally in an intimate committee environment. By working together on separate issues, the committee members (from different warring factions of Hutus and Tutsis) developed a common bond and defended their positions against other participants in plenary discussion (Maundi 2003).

Process assistance

A lengthy focus on procedure might be needed, in hostile and suspicious relationships, to cultivate a willingness to engage in direct dialogue. Discussions on the relatively less divisive procedural matters could create a basis for talks on substantive issues. Too early an attempt to get the deal done could contribute to a blow-up, especially if a bitter endemic feud led to unwillingness to compromise with the creation of a toxic climate for further discussion. As part of procedural tactics, a focus on substantive issues for tough tradeoffs could wait until mediators fostered rudimentary understanding of each other's interests.

At the beginning of Northern Ireland's All-Party Talks in June 1996, former US senator George Mitchell and other co-chairs (i.e., former Finnish prime minister Harri Holkeri, and former Chief of the Canadian Defense Forces General John de Chastelain) solidified their authority and strengthened participants' commitment by steering the discussions to focus almost exclusively on procedure. Instead of generating background information by setting up working groups on individual issues, the talks applied a sufficient consensus requirement to decisions on even somewhat routine procedural matters in an open forum. The politically literate and intelligent handling of the floor by the chairperson helped participants vent their anger at the process rather than each other (Curran and Sebenius 2003). The co-mediators let the participants agree on a negotiation procedure for themselves rather than blindly imposing the Anglo-Irish rules. Time to listen to each other in all-inclusive discussions created ample opportunities for developing a working relationship.

Too early a focus on substance could have inhibited productive interaction with extremist voices dominating the debate, inciting adversaries to further entrench in polarized positions. In fact, more than a year (i.e., from September 1996 to October 1997) was needed to institute a vague agenda, decision rules, and procedural order even after the devotion of three months, from June to August 1996, to discussion about ground rules for the procedures. The lengthy process was attributed to a lack of time constraints imposed on even long-winded and repetitive arguments in plenary meetings. As part of preliminary negotiation over substantive issues, it took five months to develop outline statements for issues (from October 1997 to March 1998). Then, only two weeks were spent on creating options and explicit substantive negotiation. Only at this last stage were the delegates pressed to bridge substantive differences on political arrangements, prisoners, decommissioning, policing, parades and other polarizing issues.

An innovative design is necessary when talks get bogged down. The most divisive and immediate barrier to launching the All-Party Talks was the full decommissioning of weapons by the Irish Republican Army (IRA) as a precondition for its political representative Sinn Fein to enter the talks. The Catholic Republicans bitterly opposed this demand, made by the Unionist parties and British government. As each side's stance on decommissioning was an impediment to further talks, the issue was carefully isolated and decoupled from developing a larger package at the All-Party Talks. The decommissioning issue was eventually transferred from the main negotiation procedures to an International Commission on Decommissioning on Mitchell's proposal in August 1997.

Progress in substantive discussion can often be blocked by the insistence of one of the parties on the exclusion or inclusion of certain agendas. Talks designed to end a civil war in southern Sudan faced major hurdles in January 2003 because of the opposition movement's insistence on the inclusion of jurisdiction over the Nuba Mountains, Abyei and the Southern Blue Nile despite the government's objection. The Kenyan mediators had to remove the gridlock by devising supplementary negotiation for the issue on its own, outside the original framework. The inevitable compromise permitted negotiations to proceed on to such main topics as the cessation of hostilities, power-sharing and distribution of resources (Khadiagala 2007).

Emotional control

Beyond considering the strategic nature of bilateral bargaining games, a mediator has to ensure that compromise and other paths to a rational choice are still relevant by controlling psychological dynamics (i.e., resentment and anger). Controlling "emotional reactions" is indispensable to warding off the destructive exchange of accusations. After emotions ran high in an early meeting of the 1978 Egypt–Israel negotiation, Prime Minister Begin and President Sadat never spoke to each other, spending most of their time individually with the mediator President Carter, leading up to their final agreement, despite their cottages being only about a hundred yards apart (Carter 1982). In the hope of prevailing over fear and distrust, President Carter depended on personal persuasiveness and charisma to manage the psychology of human interaction. He had to press

Begin hard to show flexibility, since the latter was a methodical strategist, hiding his own cards (and not easily conceding). Carter reined in Egyptian president Sadat, who wanted to leave Camp David out of frustration in the middle of peace negotiations (Findlay and Thagard 2011). At the same time, Carter had to generate empathy, becoming sort of an audience, representing transcendent values and world opinion Sadat could appeal to.[1] Pressing for an agreement that would be considered feasible, Carter put himself in the role of "psychotherapist" as well as a messenger who conveyed positions and shared impressions back and forth (Quandt 1986, 5).

Improving efficiency

Mediators are, in general, favored by their ability to produce an improved outcome to disputants. The involvement of an intermediary is supposed to improve each party's payoff (Pareto optimal). Mediation can improve the efficiency of negotiations by changing communication patterns. Concessions are not seen as a reflection of weakness when the suggestions are made by a mediator. Reaching an agreement through indirect talks lessens the audience costs for concessions (e.g. defusing criticism of domestic opponents). Hence intermediary involvement reduces political risks by protecting the image of a conceding party. Third-party intervention relieves a negotiator's sense of personal insecurity that interferes in making concessions.

Changing payoff structures

In moving parties to an agreement, mediation might rely on such strategies as manipulating the agenda, and making proposals, as well as cajoling and flattering. Intermediary bargaining leverage increases with an ability to take action that alters a payoff structure (e.g., rewards or threats of punishment such as withdrawal of support).[2] Strong leverage by mediators and their allies helps more forceful mediation against an obstructive party. In a mediation equipped with coercive tactics such as a threat of sanction, directive approaches involve a push for a particular option (e.g., ending the stalemate in the Kosovo conflict). Some mediators are even willing to add their own resources in expanding a bargaining range.

Reducing indeterminacy in bargaining

Mediation's procedural and informational resources assist in overcoming a specific set of formal constraints to negotiation. By shedding uncertainty or imperfect information in a setting plagued by the existence of competing solutions, a mediator guides the partisans not to miss an opportunity to make a mutually advantageous trade. Once acquainted with each negotiator's preferences, a mediator is likely to know whether certain agreements will advance everyone's interests; thus this knowledge can be used for circumventing delays and impasses that are common in bargaining with two-sided incomplete information.

In clearing away the indeterminacy of the outcome that derives from the availability of multiple solutions, a mediator enables negotiators to end their struggle over a choice among multiple equilibria through a function similar to a decision-making device, as is needed in Battle of the Sexes. In this process, one party might be endowed with a more advantageous outcome than the other. As long as a mediator brings about efficient agreement to both sides by getting rid of the causes of stalemate, the role should be acceptable regardless of different distribution in the eventual share of the gain.

Selection among multiple equilibria

In a situation in which a mutually acceptable point needs to be sought in brokering agreement, a mediator eases the way to agreement at one of the feasible Pareto optimal points in a bargaining range. When the two sides have reasonable but conflicting standards of fairness, a mere suggestion of solutions by an intermediary can be effective due to their detachment from the strategic element inherent in bargainer interactions. Proposals presented by a mediator function as a "focal point" around which bargaining converges (O'Neill 2006).

In the absence of an agreeable point, a mediator can forge one by making suggestions (Schelling 1960). In the Beagle Channel award, the Vatican set the terms that satisfied Chile's sovereignty over the island but permitted Argentine access to the territorial waters along with navigation and economic rights. While retaining ownership of the territory, Chile accepted equal participation in resource exploitation, scientific investigation, and environmental management with Argentina through the establishment of an ocean area designated as the Sea of Peace (Princen 1992).

Once one of the existing equilibria stands out from the rest, a settlement is more easily facilitated by alluding to it as a focal point. It will be embraced and implemented by being made a viable choice that the negotiators mutually expect.[3] Selecting a focal point is not rooted in extraordinary authority or even persuasive skill. In fact, point selection opens up a role for the mediator as an extra-game-theoretical factor in deciding acceptable settlement terms even without any specific knowledge, information, coercive ability, or means to bribe the parties.

In the Cuban Missile Crisis, a search for an endgame became more complicated once Khrushchev made a public demand for the removal of the Jupiter missiles in Turkey. It was apparent to John F. Kennedy that Khrushchev would not simply "back down without getting anything in return" after raising the issue as a public bargaining chip (Dobbs

2008, 291). Even though he "was willing to withdraw the Jupiters within four to five months," he did not want to "make any kind of public commitment." He offered a secret deal through informal channels between his brother and the Soviet ambassador. In the event of Khrushchev's rejection of the proposal, as a fallback plan, Kennedy had made a discreet arrangement for the UN secretary general to "publicly call for the removal of missiles from both Cuba and Turkey" simultaneously (*ibid*., 312). In the worst-case scenario, it would be far easier to heed the UN secretary general U Thant's dramatic last-minute plea for the swap of the missiles in Cuba and Turkey than to accept the Soviet public offer of a Turkey–Cuba trade. In this incident, one of the protagonists secretly installed a mediator as a point selector.

Faced with comparable but competing preferences, a mediation procedure can create a focal point by serving as a randomizing device. A certain outcome becomes more readily acceptable and is likely to prevail once it is chosen among existing equilibria.[4] Thus focal points provide consistency as anchors in negotiation. It is well illustrated by determining the rotational order of postconflict Burundi's presidency. Nelson Mandela's randomizing device effectively ended squabbles among the warring factions in Burundi's post-civil war power-sharing negotiation. At the final stage of settlement talks held in July 2001, he proposed the incumbent Tutsi president Pierre Buyoya as an interim state head with a main Hutu group leader Domitien Ndayizeye as his deputy for the first eighteen months (Maundi 2003). This decision left very little room for continued political struggle, as the choice was unanimously backed by the Organization of African Unity summit as well as the leaders of the Great Lakes region.

Focality becomes a matter of degree when all suggestions do not carry equal influence. The variables determining its strength are typically nonstrategic, ranging from personal prestige to an ability to easily obtain institutional endorsement of a mediator's initiatives. The choice may become more prominent if it is made by respected ex-presidents, international statesmen or celebrated individuals who enter the scene with fanfare. Besides randomization, a mediated negotiation process could be directed toward a new equilibrium if creating a new focal point improves a payoff structure (O'Neill 2006). Some equilibrium agreement might not be obtainable if the negotiation is left to its own dynamics.

Conduit for rationality

Indeterminancy can be resolved by removing the strategic role of information through mediation. In the standard models of bargaining with incomplete information, exchange is naturally inefficient, due to "exploitative and protective incentives to act strategically" (Princen 1992, 34). In compromise agreements, the exchange of concessions is based on different tradeoff values. Once true needs or interests are known to the other side, bigger concessions are demanded as the price for attaining one's own priorities (Harinck and Ellemers 2006). In direct bargaining, thus, negotiators are likely to hesitate to fully exhibit their preferences for the fear of an opponent's demand of greater concessions. This information inefficiency can be effectively overcome by communication via intermediaries.

In uncertainty about some fundamentals (e.g., bargaining range), negotiators are not eager to make concessions promptly. In addition to bearing the direct consequences of accepting a smaller portion of the pie, the concession exposes the weakness of one's bargaining position vis-à-vis the other side. As time passes, however, negotiators may realize that concessions are unavoidable if an agreement is to be produced. Speeding up mutual concessions, assisted by three-way communication, decreases the inefficient delay.

Mediators can supply and filter information in such a way as not to leave an impression of each side's eagerness to make concessions (Princen 1992; Putnam 2010). This allows negotiators to feel free to change their proposals at any point, as they are less concerned about exposing their zone of an agreement to the other party. In mediation, the negotiators face less risk in initiating compromises by taking actions without their opponent's knowledge. Otherwise negotiators would fear that any partial concessionary move would produce pressure to move all the way to the position of the other side.

Negotiators may feel free to confidentially confide to the mediator concerning the agreements they are willing to accept as well as their aspiration point. When the possibility of compromise is concealed, an opponent is not in a position to exploit possible concessions. A mediator is not supposed to reveal partial concessions until each side *fully* concedes (Jarque et al. 2003). Separate acceptance from each side can be secured prior to forging an agreement. It is not necessary to disclose the actual offers of individual negotiators in declaring their compatibility.

Therefore, a compromise proposal might need to be hidden before the gap between divergent positions gets narrower and eventually closes. In the absence of any agreement, thus, the separate conditional acceptance of a proposal to the mediator does not prejudice the negotiator's position (Kydd 2010; Princen 1992). In a nutshell, communicating concessions through a mediator is "safer" in the sense that its private nature does not amount to raising an opponent's expectations and higher demands, unlike direct negotiations.

For mediation to be a preferred strategy, its optimal solution should not be worse than any optimal unmediated equilibrium. A mediation equilibrium (ME) point should yield a higher expected payoff for everyone than an unmediated communication equilibrium. No one gets better or worse off at ME. In the absence of enforcement power, a mediator is able to propose only self-abiding agreements (Bercovitch 2014).

As a substitute for assurance, mediation would never be able to present a lasting way out of the predicament. In fact, trust is not something to be built up permanently by mediation. Most importantly, thus, the actual nature of the mediated solution is better represented by acquiescence to the mediator's personal credibility and a sense of obligation than by new attitudes and perceptions formed by the internalization of the agreement (Hörner et al. 2010). Upon a mediator's departure, in the end, the representative power no longer delivers a guarantee.

Control of communication

Credible communication of the relevant information to the uninformed party is critical to averting the risk of failure of negotiations or of costly delay. Thus it is widely believed that credible reports to the conflicting parties constitute part of a successful mediation. However, it is a suboptimal reporting strategy to unscrupulously expose that one player is weak, even if this may be the case. When an opponent learns that the other side is weak, efficient and equitable mediation plans could face a challenge from a strong party seeking "a high payoff." It is not likely to be optimal to convey to a self-declared hawk that they face a dove (*ibid.*).

As a "scanning device," a mediator can hold back part of the information or selectively reveal it (Princen 1992). Even a passive mediator (i.e., one not actively manipulating each side's payoffs) can have a direct impact on a negotiator's outcome by filtering the communication flow (Rauchhaus 2006). The intermediary pool of knowledge can be used to adjust negotiators' expectations. Offering or denying information can alter the material interests of each party.

Strategic nature of communication

Information sharing between a negotiator and a mediator is an essential aspect of mediated bargaining, in that a mediator controls an element of communication that is normally withheld by negotiators. Indeed, clarifying messages serves to correct and reinterpret perceptions, eventually altering each negotiator's expectations. It becomes important how a mediator extracts private information and credibly communicates it to negotiating parties. If a mediator is not really concerned about the exact settlement, she is more likely to be trusted as an impartial source of information. An unbiased mediator is believed to convey private, conflict-relevant information more credibly.

However, this does not eliminate the possibility that a mediator can be manipulated by one or both of the parties for strategic gains. Three-way communication is subject to the possibility of information manipulation. Knowing that a proposal delivered through a mediator is more trusted, demands can be exaggerated to sway an opponent's choices.

One party may present thorny or minor issues as crucial for extracting concessions or tradeoff while avoiding major concessions on an agenda that is high in the other's hierarchy of priorities. Thus uncertainty arising from this trust gap does not disappear with intermediary intervention (Princen 1992). Indeed, mediation does not necessarily fully remove the strategic nature of bargaining interaction itself. Offers and proposals in mediation can still be made without perfect information, generating doubts about their true values.

Faced with the persistence of the credibility question, the structure of communication still matters in deciding the truthfulness of a negotiator's statement. In fact, negotiators may selectively expose information to be delivered to the other side by the intermediary. Thus a mediator would not be able to clear up the credibility question (which afflicts direct bargaining) especially if a form of cheap talk (i.e., costless verbal claims used in attepts to deceive) becomes a convenient vehicle of communication among players to enhance their equilibrium payoffs. By conveying deceptive information, cheap talk aims to modify the other side's behavior without involving any expense attached to lying.

If a nonbinding dialogue simply becomes "cheap talk" for manipulating the other's understanding of payoffs and expectations, a mediated outcome is not likely to have a truth-telling equilibrium based on the receiver's trust of the sender's information. In contrast with costly commitment (readily observable and relatively easy to predict), how can a mediator discern a genuine demand that does not bear a direct cost or penalty? If it is genuine, how could the mediator convince the opponent to believe it? Thus these questions still remain unsettled in bargaining through mediations.

When disputants have incentives to exaggerate their strength in an attempt to extract an advantageous settlement, a mediator is not likely to know each side's claims accurately. No settlement could be found acceptable to both sides if they overestimate their respective expected gains (Miller and Watson 2013). Therefore, a mediation procedure must be "incentive compatible" for being honest and provide no benefit for sending misleading signals. If out-of-equilibrium signals based on lying do not yield a better payoff, honest communication becomes a Nash equilibrium. It costs little to convey honest signals at equilibrium. In fact, a signaling mechanism hardly involves a cost when signals are released in equilibrium. In the event that honest signaling becomes too costly a mode of information exchange at equilibrium, all involved might be better off simply not negotiating through a mediator (Zollman *et al.* 2013). Truth-telling equilibria would be more easily obtained by interests in common or at least no conflicts of interest. There are no incentives to lie when a message-sender's welfare is perfectly aligned with the receiver's (as in such coordinated games as Stag Hunt) or when the sender is indifferent to the receiver's interests.

In a nutshell, truthfulness can be communicated to a mediator with confidentiality if honest communication is believed to furnish a higher payoff. At the same time, bargaining dynamics in mediation cannot avoid strategic behavior involved in manipulating the other's perception of one's true range. Mediation does not necessarily eliminate a situation of trading on asymmetries in information where one party is not aware of something of relevance to a negotiation under way (Carment and Rowlands 2007). In seeking an asymmetrical advantage in terms of ideas and knowledge that have a direct bearing on the outcome, each party can take steps to mislead an opponent to believe that they have a high-value alternative. Thus a mediator may not be able to alter some of the key features prevalent in a game of incomplete information where a negotiator knows her utilities for the possible agreements but prefers to remain silent, holding private knowledge in a pursuit of individual gains.

Bayesian mediation equilibrium

In interpreting messages, a mediator may privately ask negotiators about their types through a mediation design. Once negotiators reveal their true types, the mediator could make a private suggestion about what to demand. By merely depending on the parties' reports about reservation points and discount factors in determining the allocation of surplus value, the mediator crafts a game in which being honest is not an equilibrium. Each player may present an impression of the irrational type (i.e., not changing an initial demand), and make only insufficient concessions. Each side may claim to be a high-resolve type, aiming to draw concessions by threatening to withdraw from negotiation if their committed points are not accepted (Carment and Rowlands 2007; Myerson 1991).

Mediators may not fully know whether players have exposed their full bargaining range or the exact value placed on agreement, thereby failing to remove the strategic nature of a game between the two players. Each party is ultimately concerned only with the expected payoffs for their true type. While primary negotiators already know how much value a particular deal carries (as well as the costs of the conflict playing itself out even further), they are more likely to take a negotiating position favored by their stronger type, for instance, with an ability to prevail in a military or economic conflict. By claiming to be the probable dominant party, everyone is likely to seek an outcome reserved for victory in the event of a fight. So difficulties lie in more accurately assessing private information in formulating a mediation plan (Goltsman *et al*. 2009; Aoyagi 2005). In this situation, a mediator can create a game mixing the relative weight of the types. Thereby mediated bargaining outcomes may be designed to reflect a Bayesian equilibrium where a player would not be able to make any more concessions.

Principle of intervention: impartiality and neutrality

A neutral mediator is supposed to be disinterested and unprejudiced, not intervening in any situation that has implications for the results of the negotiation (Svensson 2013).

Impartiality means not favoring or harming either side without a linkage to one or all of the parties. An unbiased mediator has no direct stake in the outcome, as exemplified by the Norwegian mediation efforts to end civil wars in Sri Lanka (2002) and Aceh in Indonesia (2005). While impartiality and neutrality may need to be openly professed values, this seems to go against the notion that the involvement of an intermediary in itself affects the material interests of disputants.

At a practical, operating level, a mediator's assumptions and biases as well as her own interests can result in favoring one of the parties. A mediator has different ways to collect information, suggest a solution, structure the offers or manipulate the information flowing between the two negotiators. A mediator's judgment meddles either implicitly or explicitly even in the delivery of contents in a go-between as well as suggestions of a solution as a facilitator. In order to bring an effective end to the stalemate, it may be difficult to maintain an unbiased position on every issue. In a status disequilibrium between a mediator and primary parties, such elements as pressure, threats or rewards can be introduced to cajole or vex disputants in steering the direction of negotiation. This leads to a question about the likely consequences of mediated negotiations attributed to the nature and type of mediator bias.

The relationship between bias and mediator effectiveness demands careful scrutiny especially when one party needs to be counseled to concede to avoid a fight. A biased mediation might be advocated at least for the reason that a disputant is more inclined to accept the need for a concession when it is presented by an ally than by a neutral intermediary (Kydd 2003). Biased mediators more easily extract the necessary concessions from their allies for a settlement if private information indicates that, in its absence, their preferred sides would do poorly. In this case, biased mediators can credibly convince their clients of a concession prerequisite for the agreement.

What if the settlement is only obtainable not by the concessions of a mediator's preferred side but by the other? In that case, could mediators be trusted if they press the disputant for a concession? Biased mediation is likely to fail. Thus it becomes an important matter in whose favor a mediator is biased. The problem with the effectiveness of a biased mediator lies in what happens if a disfavored disputant is unlikely to take their suggestions. In mediating the British and Argentine conflict over the Falkland Islands, the US secretary of state Alexander Hague delivered a message to the Argentine military about the British resolve to take the islands back militarily. Because Hague was seen to be favoring the British, the Argentine military did not put much trust in his words. If Argentina thought that Hague had been on their side, then perhaps they could have taken his advice more seriously.

Biased third parties may not be more easily accepted until they begin to be perceived to play a more balanced role or to improve a payoff through their intervention. The initial mediation efforts by the Intergovernmental Authority on Development (IGAD) in the mid 1990s were largely ineffective in ending Sudan's civil war concentrated in the south of the country. The organization, formed by Sudan's neighboring black African states, was accused of being biased against Khartoum's Islamic government. The government even refused to make concessions that reflected battlefield realities (Lanz and Gasser 2013). In the government's perception, the mediation (sponsored by Uganda, Ethiopia and other IGAD states) was negatively predisposed toward the Bashir government. In the renewed mediation efforts since 2001, however, the IGAD position on Sudan was reformulated more by an interest in ending the conflict than by being motivated to have a desired result. This helped significant progress toward settlement, being aided by the government's loss of control over much of Sudan's south as well as the European and American support of IGAD mediation.

If a mediator is not impartial or neutral, why does a disfavored party accept the mediation role? The most important consideration is whether each party will have a more positive outcome through a mediator intervention. The efficiency of mediation has less to do with a strictly balanced intervention toward the parties than their improved payoff. Thus the acceptance of mediation depends more on the expectations of the parties based on their assessment of both the potential addition and the loss in value by the intermediary. It is not a matter of relative gains vis-à-vis the other, but new gains not obtainable within the dyadic relationship. Partiality cannot be disadvantageous if the intermediary can wield some power over the other side on behalf of the party seemingly in disfavor. For example, realistically, Palestinians have no other means available to altering Israel's positions than accepting the US mediation.

It may often not be clear that the intervening party is indeed, in the first place, exhibiting bias. In addition, negotiators may find it difficult to ascertain the direction of the bias. President Carter's main priority at Camp David in 1978 was producing an outcome acceptable to both sides; he was less concerned about the exact balance of its substantive nature. However, Israeli officials initially complained about an American bias in favor of Egyptian positions on such issues as the future status of the West Bank and Gaza.

If the intervention is seen as too excessively skewed toward serving only one party's interests, the mediator's role becomes dysfunctional and can even be destructive. Trust disappears when all interaction becomes manipulative, serving the intermediary's strategic interests. In this kind of situation, mere presence of nonstrategic intermediaries can keep a negotiation going. This is well represented by the scrupulous commitment of Mitchell and other co-mediators to an evenhanded approach and patient impartiality in producing the 1997 Belfast Agreement. Even though their initial stand on decommissioning was opposed to the Unionist demand in early 1996, they applied the principled criteria of nonviolence to their support for the expulsion of Sinn Fein and others affiliated with violent groups prior to their readmission to the talks. In fact, nonstrategic behavior (such as a neutral proposal) has its own unique merit.

In the end, the mediator's credibility hinges upon the extent to which their statements and ability can actually translate into the delivery of the promised agreement. The more credible the mediator is perceived to be, the more likely it is that the partisans accept their offers. When mediators do not know how credible they might appear, this uncertainty needs to be considered in their decisions on types of their intervention strategies.

Triadic interaction

The structure of a bargain changes with circular deal-making and dynamics of side deals as well as coalition-building with the involvement of an intermediary in reconfiguring a bargain. In three-way bargaining, each party strives to create a favorably unbalanced situation through coalition-building with a mediator (Faure 1989). By getting involved in the initial dyadic relationship, the mediator modifies the structure of the conflict along with changing the payoff structure (Kydd 2010). A powerful mediator is courted by each side that is more eager to win her support than to come to terms with agreement by themselves. In the formulation of details of a formal treaty signed between Israel and Egypt in March 1979, both parties pressed for American support to extract last-minute concessions from their opponent. In the end, the Egyptian acceptance of the Camp David Accord was motivated more by the prospect of improved relations with the United States than with Israel (Quandt 1986). With changes in dynamics and structure of bargaining, thus, an original issue in bilateral negotiation becomes secondary or indirect. Third-party intervention provides not only opportunities but also risks. The third party's coalition-building with an opponent might mean not only missing the benefit of a three-way deal but also receiving a payoff worse than the bilateral deal that was originally possible. In designing an agreement that allots as much as possible to a favorite side, a biased mediator could be less sensitive to costs that are associated with the intermediary function if the expenses are offset by the utility of being able to affect the outcome.

A triadic interaction may elicit a full gamut of complex strategies, ranging from information sharing to persuasion to reward and threat. While rewarding one party for cooperation, a mediator may take measures to create cost either materially or symbolically for the other in order to modify their behavior on and off the table. In strengthening the hands of the mediators, in the late 1990s, neighboring regional states brought sanctions to the governments of Sudan and Burundi (which had uncompromising positions) as forceful, pressing tactics. As part of pressure tactics, a mediator may criticize one of the sides, which is obstructing negotiation. Former Nigerian president Olusegun Obasanjo serving as UN chief mediator, scolded Congo's Tutsi rebel leader Laurent Nkunda for violating a ceasefire during peace talks in the middle of November 2008.

In multiparty situations with changing numbers and identities of parties, in such places as Burundi and Northern Ireland, mediators may serve as tacit coalition-builders. If any result has to be broadly supported with "sufficient consensus," a one-sided victory by one faction over another is thwarted. The rule of sufficient consensus effectively marginalizes the extremes, laying the groundwork for the formation of a centrist coalition on substance. In entering the Northern Ireland peace talks, parties had to subscribe to nonviolence, dialogue and democratic methods. These principles were used as a basis for the inclusion and exclusion in the All-Party Talks. Extremist parties were either kicked out (e.g., the two temporary exclusions of Sinn Fein over continued IRA violence) or walked out voluntarily. The boycott by the uncompromising Democratic Unionist Party (DUP) opened the way for the Ulster Unionist Party (UUP) and other moderate Protestant Unionists to hammer out a crucial political deal with the Catholic Social Democratic and Labour Party (SDLP) in the final days of the talks. Both Britain and Ireland sought to strengthen the hands of moderate leaders in Northern Ireland such as David Trimble and John Hume, the leaders of the UUP and the SDLP respectively. In the end, approval by the two largest parties helped successfully end nearly two years of long negotiations on Good Friday 1998. By framing terrorist violence as signals of last ditch desperation of the extreme fringes in a concerted media campaign, Mitchell and his mediating team couched a message of success, ultimately increasing constituency pressures on hard-line factions (Curran and Sebenius 2003).

In contrast with a consistent format and one mediator's dealing with a constant set of negotiators, multiple groups may interfere in one way or another with different effects. Relationships between an intermediary and disputants can evolve along with changes in the mediator's stance on particular issues and bias as perceived by the disputants. If the intervention of a mediator leads to an obvious loss for one party, the disadvantaged may merely break the triadic relationship (e.g., the Sudanese government's acceptance of Egyptian and Libyan intervention for the purpose of derailing IGAD Peace Initiative in the late 1990s). Contestants may develop intricate links with multiple intermediaries (endowed with competing motives, expertise and networks). In mediation to end civil wars in Burundi, former Tanzanian president Nyerere's mediation was undercut by the secret talks sponsored by Sant'Egidio (an Italian-based Catholic relief organization) from July 1996 to May 1997, which offered an opportunity for manipulation by the Tutsi-led military leadership. The Tutsi-dominated government favored Sant'Egidio, which did not demand change in its uncompromising negotiating position contrary to the regionally sponsored mediation. The Tutsi government sidelined and circumvented the existing process until regional heads of state reaffirmed the Nyerere-led mediation in early September 1997. Competitive mediation initiatives, in parallel, create multiple equilibria, raising different expectations and creating opportunities for the parties to manipulate the nature and scope of negotiations.

Conclusion

A mediation outcome can be assessed in terms of efficiency (Pareto superior to non-mediated settlement with an improved payoff at least for one party, not incurring loss of value to any party). A mediated equilibrium achieved by strategic intervention of an intermediary should be an improvement, compared to nonintervention. Each party may have different discount values, but an agreement forged by a mediator avoids costly delays. Multiple types of intermediary activities (from neutral information gathering to bargaining) are aimed at changing dynamics in bilateral negotiation to bring about efficiency. Overall, strategic interaction between disputants and a mediator has an impact on the process and outcome of mediation, creating conditions under which a mediated solution either emerges or fails. Finally, a mediator's professed impartial procedural standards may translate into not endorsing any particular substantial principles such as justice. Yet the balanced settlement of conflicting claims relies on the need to weigh different interests carefully beyond dependence on internal bargaining criteria alone. In Chapter 11, on multilateral negotiation, we are moving to discussion about a complex array of relationships involving many parties, multiple interests and values.

Notes

1 Carter's role contrasts with President Clinton's outburst during the 2000 Israeli–Palestinian Camp David negotiation. When one of Palestinian delegation members Abu Ala demanded an Israel commitment to negotiating on the basis of the June 4, 1997, line, Clinton discredited him: "Sir, I know you'd like the whole map to be yellow. But that's not possible... This isn't the UN General Assembly... You're obstructing the negotiation." Being humiliated, Ala did not speak again for the remainder of the official summit, being cast into paranoia (Swisher 2004, 275).

2 A stalemate often demands a mediator who is willing and able to proffer a more forceful approach instead of remaining a mere observer. During his mediation aimed at ending the Ugandan civil war in 1985, Kenyan president Daniel arap Moi prevailed on the parties to accept a compromised interim agenda on the composition of power-sharing, disarmament and ceasefire, constitutions and elections. In managing severe disagreement over the issue components, he used a threat to expel all Ugandan exiles [belonging to different warring factions] from Nairobi. He also "threatened to end his efforts if the protagonists did not take the talks seriously" (Khadiagala 2007, 36).

3 During the most critical moment of the US–North Korean negotiation (in June 1994), former president Carter went to Pyongyang as an unofficial mediator and made a public announcement of his agreement with North Korean leader Kim Il-Sung on the conditions for a resumption of negotiations. The announcement, broadcast by CNN worldwide, effectively forced the White

House to accept his proposal on return to the negotiation in exchange for the North's cessation of any existing nuclear activities. Carter created a decisive focal point that favored negotiation over a war.

4. In September 1994, Carter helped avoid the looming US invasion aimed at removing the Haitian military regime headed by General Raoul Cedras. The intervention led to a peaceful exit of the military junta from the country, allowing the elected president Jean-Bertrand Aristide to return to power. The mediated solution diffused a sense of urgency created by the massed US forces poised to enter the country.

11 Multilateral negotiation

> If you want to go quickly, go alone. If you want to go far, go together.
>
> African proverb

RECOGNIZING the necessity for global action in many arenas, multilateral conferences have produced important treaties on rules of free trade, protection of the ozone layer, the Antarctic, preservation of endangered species, management of mineral resources in deep sea beds, nonproliferation of nuclear weapons and so forth. Multiple issues to be resolved by a large number of concerned parties create procedural challenges very different from bilateral negotiations. Decision-making among some 100 to 150 participating governments through a universally inclusive process is not only time-consuming but also proving to be inefficient. The complexity is cut down by deliberations among two or more coalitions based on similar preferences. As will be seen later in this chapter, coalition formation is indispensable for meaningful bargaining in that it permits efforts to maximize a number of tradeoffs on many dispersed issues, interests and positions.

Interactions in multilateral negotiation are shaped by institutional rules and procedures of decision-making. The variations in a negotiation's institutional setting are thus crucial in understanding the effectiveness of strategies used by states and coalitions. The participants are far less able to exert influence on the negotiation process and its exogenous context than in bilateral interactions or with mediation. Negotiators may have to take the institutional and coalitional aspects of bargaining as given. In this chapter, various outcomes of multilateral negotiations are explained by the nature of issues and coalitional dynamics as well as institutional context that shapes the process.

Bargaining structures

Given that many international agreements are not easily coerced, they need to be built upon consensus that emerges from a procedure that allows a participating state to reject any part of the negotiated outcomes unfavorable to them. Indeed, binding legislation through a unanimous decision can be blocked in the absence of a Pareto improving outcome for all. Making such an agreement should be individually rational, providing natural incentives to adhere to it, and thus self-enforcing. As illustrated in a cooperative game, a binding agreement cannot be imposed without ensuring some value to all parties. Then the question is how this value will be divided among the parties, as was a central focus in such negotiations for the 1982 Law of the Sea treaty forged by an agreement on the graduated-royalty scheme in the allocation of benefit from the exploitation of maritime resources in a deep seabed (Sebenius 1984). The representation of coalitional interests is necessary for developing a formula for (roughly) symmetrical outcomes. In fact, the process of reaching a cooperative agreement does not remove strategic interaction among players, raising questions about what strategies are rational in resolving a conflict over differing interests (as in noncooperative game theory).

The intrinsic difficulty in anticipating others' behavior goes up with an increase in the number and heterogeneity of players who have varied approaches to weighing their future value as the issues evolve (Simonelli 2011). In climate control negotiations, a cooperative outcome is more desirable collectively than individually. Even though abatement is optimal from a global cost–benefit standpoint, this does not necessarily guarantee, by any means, that states will agree to supply such a public good. Any effective global agreement for major reductions in emissions carries potential costs from halting activities to be banned and subsidies required for research and production of substitutes for regulated substances.

Moreover, even if a state refuses to join in safeguarding the climate, it is not prohibited from benefits. Positive externalities (i.e., beneficial effects created for all regardless of their contribution) explain difficulties in denying the benefit of pure public goods such as a stable climate to those who do not share the cost. Thus one's own strategic self-interest or free ride pushes actors toward noncooperative behavior, producing a less desirable outcome, characterized as the Tragedy of the Commons (discussed in Chapter 3). This problem is contrasted with multilateral trade negotiations (entailing market-opening contracts). An agreement can alter the status quo by precluding nonparticipants from benefit (e.g., easier access to foreign markets with a mutual grant of lower tariffs within an exclusive club of countries). In a free trade agreement, a strict cost–benefit analysis is made possible by the calculation of the competition from increased imports offset by the opening of foreign markets.

Coalitional bargaining

In coalitional bargaining, individual actors are regarded as members of each category that shares identical interests (e.g., producers of agricultural commodities or an alliance of low income countries in a world trade negotiation). Each coalition, composed of actors with largely compatible interests, strives to promote their shared goals collectively by extracting value from the outsiders. Natural allies are recruited by principal antagonists into their opposing and mutually exclusive blocs. The motive for forming a coalition lies in enlarging one's share that could otherwise not be attained after taking costs into consideration. Actors have a natural incentive to join a coalition that is likely to yield the highest expected gains to them individually. Any coalition member, at least, should not be worse off than on their own. Most significantly, collective bargaining power reflects a coalition's ability to forge unanimity decision-making in favor of their preferences. A stable bargaining outcome arises when each member does not realize extra gains by switching sides or belonging to a different coalition; in addition, any coalition has neither power nor motivation to overwhelm others.

The types of coalitional interactions and their intended results hinge on relative bargaining power. In an asymmetric deadlock, a veto group's alternative is better than any serious agreement.[1] In environmental negotiations, for instance, veto countries simply choose a free ride option, instead of agreeing to share the cost. The current stalemate in climate control negotiation can be explained by asymmetric deadlock derived from veto states' resistance against a commitment to emission control targets and timetables. Besides cost implications, different attitudes toward the likelihood of future events produce divergent, rather than common, interests (Davenport 2006). The potential impact of climate change differs, creating a split among states according to spatial differences (e.g., rising sea levels or extreme weather). Coalitional bargaining in climate change negotiation reflects an opposing position between pro-agreement and veto states on cost sharing and control methods. Despite their vulnerability from a rise in global temperature, China, India and some other large emerging economies have resisted regulations for climate control because they consider fossil fuels to be a vital component of their industrial success (Chasek *et al.* 2010).

Each country has a differently discounted net economic impact (Grundig 2009). States preferring the status quo have lower discount rates of benefits (with less appreciation of the value of emissions control and a higher valuation of costs in controlling their pollution industries). Tragically, a rapid rise in the emission level of a veto coalition (e.g., China and India) lends more bargaining power to those polluters (a higher emission level adopted as a base to be cut in a future negotiation). In global climate negotiation, a higher discount rate means being less patient with the status quo, desiring more urgent steps toward reduction in global emission levels. In producing the Kyoto protocol, these countries even accepted binding emission reduction targets for themselves without the same requirement for the veto states (Kilian and Elgström 2010).

Breaking asymmetric deadlock

A shift in costs and benefits is essential to breaking an asymmetric deadlock. A negotiation's successful outcome depends on the pro-agreement side's ability to lower the payoffs of the anti-agreement coalition. A pro-agreement coalition should have resources to change the other side's calculus of gains or losses, reducing their incentives to walk away. In order to induce Russia's ratification of the Kyoto Protocol, the EU supported Russian entry into the World Trade Organization (WTO) as well as an offer of trade and investment opportunities (McLean and Stone 2012). If the most powerful state, such as the United States, is not in the pro-agreement coalition, fewer resources are available to manipulate preferences of a veto coalition.

Asymmetric deadlock can be broken in majority voting procedures, but only if the veto states accept the outcome. The procedure's weakness is illustrated by the defiance of a veto coalition in the global whaling commission. While a stalemate over the moratorium on commercial whaling was broken by a majority vote, major whaling states such as Japan, Norway and Iceland effectively derailed the collective decision (Gregory and Paleokrassis 2014). Outnumbered by the anti-whaling coalition in support of an existing ban, Japan has been recruiting new members to the whaling commission as part of buying voting power needed to override the existing rule. The veto coalition also adopted a noncooperative strategy with sabotage. While Iceland had already chosen an exit strategy, Japan and Norway, being empowered by their ability to threaten to do so, have openly defied the moratorium under the guise of scientific whaling. Norway's outright violation of the policy includes setting its own commercial quotas for Minke whales in violation of the International Whaling Commission's ban. Japan's large-scale "scientific whaling" has been extended even to Antarctica, killing several thousand whales per year for a meager economic gain. The American government successfully used the threat of a seafood import ban against Peru and Chile to force them to abide by the moratorium (Chasek *et al.* 2010). However, the application of this action against Japan was not adopted due to a likely Japanese retaliation against US seafood exports.

Value-claiming conflict

As seen above, the successful manipulation of veto states' preferences is essential to moving out of an asymmetric deadlock. The acceptance or support for an agreement by less committed states can be contingent upon compensation in other areas (Arriagada and Perrings 2011). One side may want to claim a value by linking its contribution to the creation of collective good to something more valuable to itself. In fact, debt relief, technology transfer or another form of aid is often offered as part of positive redistribution measures for reluctant actors whose costs need to be ameliorated. An actor's decision to walk away depends on whether the pro-agreement coalition has something attractive.

Value-claiming increases the cost of manipulating the reluctant party's preference. The value of the agreement to pro-agreement parties decreases with the newly added costs in meeting financial, technological assistance and other demands of resistant parties. The expected benefits ultimately have to be larger than the expenses for the pro-agreement coalition (Davenport 2006). The cost–benefit equation may shift if value-claiming pushes up the manipulation cost too much. The United States decided to back out of the 1972 UN convention to halt the loss of biodiversity with a shift in its cost–benefit calculation derived from the demand of tropical states for transfer of biotechnology and concession on intellectual property rights.

Negotiating in a "value-claiming stalemate"

The ozone negotiations (1986–92) can be marked mainly by managing differences between pro- and anti-strict control proponents. Owing to the initial asymmetric deadlock, the negotiation was devoted to agreeing to general principles prior to discussion about specific regulatory controls. Eventually a compromise was forged to settle the differences in control mechanisms and timetables. This served as a stepping stone for a more decisive consensus on a commitment to a total ban on ozone-depleting substances. Interestingly, a shift in coalitions was produced by issue packages on the type and quantity of chemicals to be regulated and the timing of a phase-out as well as the support of developing countries for implementation (Davenport 2006).

A comprehensive pact emerged from a gradual expansion of partial, limited agreement. Incremental approaches allowed one negotiation to end with an agreement on an agenda for the next one. The 1985 Vienna Convention for the Protection of the Ozone Layer was limited to cooperation in research, monitoring and information exchange, but produced a set of goals and a policy framework. It contained general statements of problems and a possible solution, but did not identify ozone-depleting substances, nor did it set any legally binding targets or control measures. It left some disagreement latent in an ambiguous context, but was structured in a manner to permit room for future agreement by linking a need for controls to a firmer scientific basis. The 1987 Montreal Protocol accompanied discussion about concrete steps and technical standards consistent with the convention. In light of new scientific assessments, the protocol had to be revised at the March 1989 London Conference on Saving the Ozone Layer with a pledge to eliminate the production of chlorofluorocarbons (CFCs) and other chemicals threatening the ozone shield by the year 2000. The acknowledgment of the need for more comprehensive and stringent controls on a diverse range of chemicals was forged progressively by modifying and enhancing earlier solutions once they were tested and became familiar with continual review and renegotiation (Benedick 1991; Davenport 2006).

After initiating its domestic regulation unilaterally, an urgent US priority was to negotiate with other major producers and consumers, namely, the European Community (EC), Japan and the Soviet Union. Being led by the UK, France and Italy, the EC was open to discussion about some restrictions on production but was reluctant to ban CFCs in aerosols. As the United States was concerned about its own industry's competitiveness, the threat of an import ban of CFC gas by the US Congress put pressure on the negotiation (Hoffmann 2005).

The initial stage of negotiation for the Montreal protocol was set by confrontation between the EC and Toronto groups (composed of Canada, Australia, Austria and the Nordic countries) over the degree of controls and types of measures. The EC was ready to freeze but preferred reductions on a more relaxed schedule. However, being backed by the Toronto group, the United States championed tighter controls with a large-scale reduction in ozone-harming substances. The EC position was soon weakened by internal split and defection. While Belgium, Denmark and the Netherlands favored a stricter regulatory regime on a number of key issues, Germany went even further with a threat to break ranks and unilaterally ban aerosols, creating a crosscutting coalition with the pro-control Toronto Group.

Bargaining impasses were broken by crafting formulas that redefined core issues along with the identification of focal points for solutions such as splitting the difference between competing interests (Benedick 1991). The most contentious issue was noticeably the timing and stringency of reduction. In producing the Montreal protocol, a compromise between the EC's proposed 20% cut and the US preference for 95% cuts in CFC emissions produced the 50% reduction in the production and consumption of the most widely used gas to 1986 levels by 1999. Key differences were bridged by novel proposals in a search for an alternative to control of either production alone or consumption control alone. The need to balance foreign demands and domestic market supplies resulted in a formula of "production-plus-imports-minus-exports" (Hampson 1995).

With the adoption of the principle of common but differentiated responsibilities, underdeveloped countries had been granted a ten-year grace period before taking on the commitment, even permitting a slight increase. Equity and fairness became important principles in addressing the concerns of many developing countries looking for technological and financial aid in finding substitutes for CFCs. Eventually a multilateral fund was created, at the 1989 London Conference, to help developing countries comply by providing assistance in making the conversion to new non-CFC-based technologies.

The agreement became universal with the number of participants growing from only twenty-five states at the first round of the ozone protocol negotiation in 1986 to ninety-six in 1990. Developing countries were given support for technology on substitutes for ozone depleting substances. Nonparticipation was penalized by being excluded from a trade regime for ozone-depleting substances.

As negotiation progressed, there was a reversal of roles between the initial leaders and veto states, as most dramatically featured by the evolution of the EC position from opposing even the discussion of control measures to fully accepting the tight regulation. In 1990, EC states even took a leading role in the first set of negotiations on adjustments and amendments. More dramatic was a complete role reversal between the United States and the EC, manifest in the 1992 Copenhagen meeting. In response to accelerating ozone depletion, the EC proposed control on the second most widely used chemical hydrochlorofluorocarbons (HCFC). This time a veto coalition included the United States as well as India and China (Chasek *et al.* 2010).

Issues are often typified by a compilation of diverse interests of actors and their coalitions. Of course, negotiation does not take place in a vacuum: it is steered by domestic political pressure, technological innovation and changing economic interests. The credibility of the proponents for a ban was enhanced by scientific evidence such as the 1985 discovery of an ozone "hole" above Antarctica, and growing warnings about the occurrence of serious damage to the ozone layer under the weaker control options. In particular, the EC position was softened by new scientific evidence and a changing political atmosphere. Faced with pressure from environmentalists and Parliament, British prime minister John Major hosted a meeting that decided on a shift toward calling for a CFCs phase-out. The US call for the chemicals' complete phase-out is attributed to DuPont's announcement of the cessation of its CFC production by 2000 along with a plan of production of CFC substitutes in 1998. There was little resistance from large producers and other domestic industrial actors. The industry even saw the promise of a new market for CFC substitutes in developing countries with a financial mechanism (for example, funding for a transition to new technologies).

Climate control negotiation

Concerning climate control negotiation, the European Union has been a pusher with the United States being seen as a dragger. In contrast with its initial policy on the ozone gas control, the United States did not have domestic emission standards on global warming gases, being concerned about economic competitiveness. Reflecting on the "economics of climate change mitigation," the American government perceived "the expected costs of the commitments (to developing substitutes and halting harmful activities) outweigh the expected benefits" (Davenport 2006, 190). In addition, a commitment to the transfer of resources and new cleaner technologies to the developing world would entail far more cost than the United States is willing to bear.

Asymmetric deadlock in the 1992 UN Convention on Climate Change (UNFCCC) was created by a strong American opposition to greenhouse gas (GHG) reduction schedules and specific targets. The EC was at the forefront of intitating the negotiations with a commitment to cut its joint CO_2 emission to the 1990 level by 2000. The same commitments were also pledged by Japan and New Zealand. The United States was the only industrialized country opposed to a binding commitment in the 1992 negotiation (Hoffmann 2005). After a struggle mainly between the United States and the EC, the agreement's value was adjusted to win US acquiescence through downward compromises. As a result, there was no reference to any specific actions on reductions such as a mandatory control for meeting specific targets or timetables in the convention (signed by 152 countries at the Rio global environmental summit).

In reaction to US attitudes (not to undertake relatively costly but effective measures to mitigate climate change), many countries became more reluctant to make a commitment. For instance, the governments of Norway, Australia and some other early pro-control states have become opposed to timetables and targets after initially paying more attention to their vulnerability to climate change in a response to domestic pressure (Chasek *et al.* 2010). The change in the US position following the election of President Bill Clinton shifted negotiating the Kyoto Protocol (1997) to value-claiming conflict. The Protocol set guidance for implementing the Convention with a commitment to a reduction of greenhouse gases. As a leader, the EU made proposals, and others offered compromise (*ibid.*). In spite of its acceptance of a timetable and legal commitment to reduction, the Clinton administration attempted to lower the costs to itself through compromises that reduced its overall effectiveness with insistence on flexibility mechanisms and other qualifiers. In the end, the United States and other developed countries made a commitment to 5% reduction in the emissions of six target gases at the 1990 level by 2008–12. Through emissions trading, developing countries were allowed to sell their emission rights to industries in developed countries with income redistribution effects (Farhana 2014).

Since the Kyoto Protocol, global climate control negotiations have unfortunately stalled over how to share the load of greenhouse gas reductions and how to assist low-income countries in meeting their burden through financial and technological transfers. A phased approach from incremental to comprehensive steps was applied to climate change negotiation, modeled on the ozone-negotiation precedent. Although designed to be flexible and evolving, the incremental approach did not produce a desirable effect in the climate negotiation with a shift in bargaining power more toward veto states, whose number has increased since the 1996 Kyoto Protocol.

Even agreements with the lowest common denominator have become difficult due to divergent interests and differences in basic value orientations. It has proven challenging to separate the political from the scientific, unlike in the ozone agreement, as various industry and economic sectors (contributors to the problem) directed heavy criticisms against the Intergovernmental Panel on Climate Change (IPCC) and other scientific institutions that produced data on warming trends and effects (Hoffmann 2005). The sources of global warming are everywhere, with the involvement of every economic sector, in contrast to the emissions of CFC production, which was confined to seventeen companies. Too much focus on higher costs to major industries overshadowed the positive economic benefits of research and development of energy-efficient systems replacing the inefficient use of fossil fuel (Davenport 2006).

Two dimensions of coalitional bargaining

When a conference process works through consensus, conflicting positions are combined to form a common decision through the aggregation of interests at different levels (subgroup, intergroup and at the entire conference forum). In extended negotiations, each party strives to attain its preferred positions. Hence the negotiated outcomes are shaped by both subgroup dynamics and intergroup interactions. More specifically, the process is divided into two stages: intracoalition negotiations on a common position within a group and bargaining between representatives of the coalitions. The overall EU offer during the Kyoto climate control negotiation was the outcome of intracoalition bargaining. As a leader state, Germany accepted deeper emission cuts to allow less-industrialized EU states such as Romania to increase their levels (McLean and Stone 2012).

In contrast with the above example, intracoalition bargaining potentially entails challenges to producing compromises acceptable to their own members as well as the other coalition. If any concession has to be offered to a rival coalition for collective gain, each coalition member tries to exclude their priorities from being sacrificed. At the same time, a coalition member may demand an opposing group's concessions exclusively for their own benefit without any concessionary offer in exchange.

Intercoalition bargaining is recalculated against a backdrop of strategies to hold one's own coalition together as well as splitting rival coalitions. Defending against an outsider's attempt to divide one's own group is essential to increasing credibility for the coalition's position. Gains of a coalition diminish to the extent that the group fails to maintain its unity and fragments. The two-track game has been quite visible in the multiparty negotiations where the two basic processes were played out against the backdrop of unequal power relations (Drahos 2003). Powerful parties traditionally adopt a sequential, divide-and-conquer approach in prevailing over the opposition. The credibility of a weaker coalition's position ultimately hinges on their reaction to a stronger opponent's strategy of isolating and overwhelming them individually.

In multilateral trade negotiations, developing countries are generally endowed with a potent weapon of blocking the entire process by vetoing an agenda or proposal of powerful states. Faced with the superior bargaining power of the United States and the European Union, success of any developing country coalition in attaining concessions lies in the credibility of a threat to block the entire WTO negotiation. The credibility of the coalition's threat is higher when the group is larger, increasing the cost for powerful states to coerce or bribe a large number of opposing countries to abandon their collective position.

In multilateral trade negotiation settings, dominant economic powers typically mix carrots with sticks and other power tactics to create cracks in a unified position of a developing country coalition. It is obviously cheaper to buy individual members out with separate deals on a preferential market access as well as promises of aid packages or financial assistance. In addition, a threat of withdrawal from previous concessions can be made against continued resistance. Heterogeneous economies within a weaker coalition create a greater susceptibility to the dominant coalition's mixed strategies. In trade affairs, a heterogeneity of commercial interests within a coalition increases both the temptation to defect with separate deals and vulnerability to a threat on an issue that is more vital to a particular country than the entire group.

Intracoalition interactions

From an individual country's perspective, it is safer to grab opportunities to gain even partial concessions in return for backing away from some of the coalition's collective demands (especially if it looks clear that the powerful coalition prefers a deadlock to giving in to coalitional demand). In the event the coalition breaks, an individual state is forced to make concessions without attaining anything valuable. In the worst circumstances, a country eventually has to reap only losses once it proves difficult to block the whole negotiation process on its own, bearing all the pressure (Narlikar and Odell 2006). This prospect increases the insecurity of individual coalition members, who are susceptible to abandoning the collective position.

Especially poor countries have difficulty in resisting fragmentation, even though holding firm with the collective coalition is more likely to yield higher gains. For poorer countries, it is harder to wait for the fruit of collective action with enough patience (i.e., a bird in the hand is more valuable than two birds in the bush). If a coalition member knows that others are "starving" and impatient and the others are aware that the country is, too, it sets a perfect condition for mutual defection in Stag Hunt (Narlikar and Odell 2006). If the other defects, cooperation yields nothing. Being imprisoned by this uncertainty of collective action, it is difficult to have trust for others. Then it becomes more rational to switch to a defection strategy, believing that all others will do the same. It is this calculated motive of mistrust that illustrates the failure to cooperate. When self-interest prevails over a group, collective action becomes merely "cheap talk."

Can other coalition members collectively do anything to decrease a member's impulse for defection? They may offer side payments to keep potential defectors onside, perhaps with a bigger share of collective gain for those who are vulnerable to a temptation to defect. If members are successfully persuaded to spurn taking a separate outside offer, the coalition has a greater threat capability to block a consensus on issues vital to them, inducing outsiders to consider concessions more seriously.

Coalitional bargaining strategies

Negotiating gain rests on a coalition strategy as well as the ability to remain united. A coalition can be formed either to resist a rival's demand or to extract concessions from them. Distributive strategies can be employed to pursue offensive interests geared toward an unmistakable demand for alteration in existing policies or practice (Odell 2000). If successful, a strict distributive strategy could gain more, for instance, by taking others' priority issues hostage (Neumayer 2011). Yet it is challenging for poorer states to arrange this tactic in a trade negotiation. A strict distributive strategy may bet on the retreat of an adversary in a final brinkmanship. So long as other parties see the group's demand as worse than an impasse, gains are not likely to come. Adhering to an uncompromising position (as a central principle for claiming value) implies everything or nothing. It is too big a risk for smaller countries when they fear passing up an opportunity for a smaller gain available to them individually.

Even if the coalition realizes the necessity of mixing integrative elements into distributive strategies, greater heterogeneity serves as an obstacle to intracoalitional bargaining, for instance, over concessions to be made to outsiders. If principal beliefs as well as intrinsic interests are critical to the maintenance of coalitions, dislodging even a provisional commitment carries costs. Renegotiating becomes increasingly costly and uncertain to the extent that the internalized value gains psychological prominence and attractiveness as a focal point of group cohesiveness (Narlikar and Odell 2006).

In the 2001 WTO negotiation, the Like Minded Group (LMG) demanded changes in a large number of the existing rules, basically asking for renegotiation of many aspects of previous Uruguay Round agreements touching upon development issues. They also had systemic concerns such as the removal of the Trade-Related Aspects of Intellectual Property Rights (TRIPS) agreement from the WTO. The coalition's extremely ambitious opening position was presented with a threat to block consensus (on priority issues for the United States and the EU) prior to launching a new round unless LMG demands were heeded. The proposals, covering detailed demands, indicated no gain to the developed countries with a rationale predominantly legitimized by the correction of past injustices, and the exceptionality of developing country problems. If fresh concessions had to be made by developing countries at the Doha Round, "it would be tantamount paying two, three or even four times" for what they had paid for in the past rounds (Narlikar and Odell 2006, 126). These rhetorical moves did not offer any exchange of concessions for mutual gain while at the same time they lacked collective fallback positions. In addition, the coalition did not develop strategies about how to fend off pressures from the developed countries with little posturing for actually realizable goals.

In response, the European Union and the United States made concessions that affected larger numbers of smaller subgroups, as part of their mixed strategies, while warning that their continued opposition would result in the withdrawal of their preferences. The coalition's fragmentation was inevitable following the US aid package to Egypt and Pakistan as well as the EU's increase in import quotas on textiles and other products from particular LMG countries (Narlikar and Odell 2006). This prompted the loss of the group's credibility to block consensus. At the end, India stood alone with little gain. This example illustrates that, other things being equal, cohesion formed by shared interest in subissues is more sustainable in fending off an outside group's mixed strategies aimed at splitting the coalition. Sticking to encompassing principles creates more vulnerability to a threat to break a weaker coalition by stronger states offering private deals that are attractive to individual developing countries.

The public health coalition

The November 2001 Ministerial Conference at Doha adopted a declaration concerning the application of the WTO agreement on intellectual property rights to matters of public health. Before the WTO ministerial declaration, populous Brazil, India and all of sub-Saharan Africa built a coalition of sixty states which formed a credible force in the new round of world trade negotiation (Lister and Lee 2013). In spite of its large size, this coalition showed a well-orchestrated response to an attempt of the US government to break up its unity with offers to a subset of the members. Leading coalition members persuaded others not to give up a larger gain by accepting a smaller one. As a split was avoided to keep the coalition's credibility to threaten the conference procedure, the vigorous response bore the fruit of a significant gain for the coalition as a whole, relative to the status quo ante, at the expense of global pharmaceutical firms whose interests were actively guarded by American and Swiss governments.

In weakening the ability of powerful actors, the public health coalition also utilized transnational alliances by working with activists from developing countries, who enhanced the ability of their governmental coalition by instigating the "access to medicines" campaign. The informal groups of activists were supported by a network of public health workers in more than seventy countries. The campaign eventually drew the participation of Oxfam, Médecins Sans Frontières and other notable NGOs, equipped with international networking and analytical resources as well as reputation for serious public policy work. Their careful technical analysis linked to public policy recommendations discredited the pro-patent position of the large pharmaceutical industry (Odell and Sell 2006). A coalition of health activists and organizations mounted a global campaign against the negative effects of patents and trade rules on the availability of medicines. The potentially fragile composition of the actors stayed together, with a willingness to fight everywhere, being united by a single focus on the winnable goal of enhancing access to treatment for AIDS (Drahos 2003). This transnational campaign turned out to be a big asset to developing country negotiators, eventually garnering the support of the World Health Organization, and even some developed countries.

The public health coalition utilized a public campaign which made an emotional appeal with media exposure that was highly effective in arousing mass public concerns about the WTO negotiation. Public understanding was shaped by the mass media portraying intellectual property rights as a source of obstructing the access to treatment of AIDS and other dire health threats with high medicine prices. Thus a credible position was built by reframing intellectual property rights as a public health question. This reference point strengthened by public support helped the coalition's position prevail in extracting the major concession.

Procedural and institutional context

A multilateral negotiation proceeds simultaneously on different issues in separate negotiating groups before the emergence of a consensus decision on a package deal of all agreements. The entire process is thus broken up into committee procedures designed to look into contentious problems and produce satisfactory solutions. Issues negotiated in separate working groups are incorporated into a single negotiating text. The convention text put forward is generally divided between unbracketed language acceptable to all and bracketed language containing alternative formulations favored by different participants. Bridging the different viewpoints in the bracketed texts becomes part of detailed negotiation in producing a compromise package that serves as the basis of a final deal.

The agreements presented to a plenary session are most likely to confirm what has been achieved through subgroup talks open only to a small group.[2] Particular issues are bundled into possible packages following informal conversations among key players. Thus a final outcome is steered by an informal consultation process apart from a formal group meeting. During the ozone negotiation, for example, a group called "Friends of Tolba" met, outside the official conference proceedings, to develop strategies for breaking a stalemate in support of control of CFC gas emission (Hoffmann 2005).

In "pyramidal" negotiation, the early flow of informal discussion between the major powers moves down to new players in a sequential manner. Once a separate deal is struck among those in a position to block the decision-making, the incipient agreement is presented to other parties. The addition is valued by the new adherent's significance among the parties still left out. The new concerns are accommodated to the extent that changes demanded as a condition for joining the evolving accord are feasible. New supporters for an evolving accord are sought not in one step, but gradually. The growing number of adherents worsens the alternatives of the as-yet left-out (Winham 1986). As seen below in world trade negotiations, the sequencing actions in a pyramidal pattern are actually realized at the expense of marginalized parties.

In understanding a conference outcome, we need to pay more attention to activities of agenda-setting and proposal development than plenary voting. Informal coordination between the major powers and the secretariat constitutes a crucial part of the agenda-setting function. In the past rounds of GATT/WTO negotiations, most successful proposals had a tendency to be drafted first in the capitals of powerful countries, notably, Washington and Brussels (with the EU's main headquarters). Then caucuses, convened and orchestrated by major powers, generally carry out the work of further shaping the content of proposals and frameworks to be introduced to formal working group meetings. In forming informal channels of communication, it becomes important to decide who needs to be contacted first, second and so forth, and on what grounds.

Informal discussion in caucuses of the Quad (comprising the United States, the EU, Japan and Canada), the G7 and the OECD is extended later to other caucuses including some less powerful countries. The Green Room caucuses (attended by twenty to thirty-five countries and the most senior members of the secretariat) decided an agenda for most important formal meetings, and discussed a draft for a formal plenary meeting. During the plenary session, consensus generally prevailed in accepting a draft coming out of the Green Room caucuses without any serious amendments (Drahos 2003). Secrecy and exclusivity surrounding Green Room consultations have been a source of major complaints about the GATT/WTO process.

Owing to their exclusion from the key consultation process, weak countries are generally not well informed of major discussions at the informal caucuses. Weak countries have other disadvantages with a lack of adequate attention to their initiatives introduced to relevant negotiating committees for formal action. During the Tokyo and Uruguay Rounds, powerful countries repeatedly blocked the advancement of such initiatives as "special and differential treatment" for developing countries. Disparity in agenda-setting power is magnified by difficulties in amending proposals once the agenda is set and has moved forward. The processes of committees, working groups and other institutional devices have shown a tendency to support the deliberate expansion of powerful countries' platforms with a seal of organizational legitimacy.

Formal and informal constraints for many poor countries include disadvantages associated with difficulties in keeping up with issues as well as inadequate representation. Monitoring progress beyond attending meetings puts a greater burden on small delegations handicapped in their capacity to analyze evolving issues and make proposals. Therefore, coalition representations are needed to identify the interests of weak and poor countries. For instance, the Caribbean Community and Common Market (CARICOM) enabled small Caribbean islands and Belize to raise their voices for their banana and sugar industries in the negotiations of the Coutonou agreement. The voice of Vanuatu, Nauru and small island states, in favor of a strong climate control convention, has drawn more attention as a group (Deitelhoff and Wallbott 2012). In lowering barriers to negotiation, coalitions facilitate the exchange of research and information among members and reduce costs, especially for those who cannot even afford to pay for their presence at a conference (Drahos 2003).

Institutional structure

The course of multilateral negotiations is set or reset with the bargaining among a number of key actors, reflecting the prevailing institutional structures. When the outcome is unsatisfactory, powerful states can move negotiation to another organization to exercise bargaining power. A "hierarchy" of decision-making processes in world trade organizations favors powerful states when it comes to shaping negotiation outcomes, especially in such issues as the intellectual property rights considered important to their industries. After the United States failed to attain its objectives at the World Intellectual Property Organization (WIPO) favoring developing countries, it used an exit strategy and moved discussion about intellectual property to the GATT. In the Uruguay Round, the US government used issue linkage to force negotiation on intellectual property rights despite developing countries' resistance.

The secretariat

In multilateral negotiations, the development of an agreement text acceptable to everyone arises from well-orchestrated efforts. In overcoming a deadlock in the Montreal Protocol negotiation, UNEP Executive Director Mostafa Tolba hosted a series of informal meetings to generate a convergence of views on appropriate control measures out of the political limelight (Benedick 1991). He convened an informal consultative group of the ten delegation heads (representing Canada, Belgium, Denmark, New Zealand, Japan, Norway, the Soviet Union along with the European Community, the United States and the UK) to have subsequent discussions of an unofficial draft in

June 1987. The group thrashed out a text that became the basis of final negotiations in Montreal.

The UNEP executive director was credited with forging cooperation between the United States and the EU on binding CFC emission cuts. Though the USA and the EU dominated the negotiation, Tolba shaped their discussion through agenda-setting and informal meetings. The actual procedures at the Vienna Convention endowed him with a responsibility for initiating a protocol negotiation that comes with agenda-setting power. By structuring the agenda and inventing novel solutions to seemingly intractable problems, he helped negotiations move forward. Despite his efforts to discover some common ground, he was not shy about taking a strong position in favor of stricter regulation. In addition, he was also active in advocating and promoting the participation of developing countries and eventually offered assistance in improving their technical analysis at the ozone negotiation.

Mediating role

The opportunistic use of mediation is solicited to break bargaining impasses between coalitions and move a negotiation along. In enhancing consensus, some countries cut across traditional boundaries, serving as a bridge between opposing camps (Tallberg 2010). This type of bridging was provided, during the negotiation of the Vienna ozone convention, by a Canadian proposal on the transfer of production quotas for meeting important domestic demands of CFCs. Mediation can be conducted by the representatives of less powerful states in the middle position on an issue. A Swiss–Colombian proposal was able to broker a prenegotiation deadlock in the Uruguay Round even though neither was neutral or impartial given their own preferences and stakes in the outcomes. The more traditional honest-broker role was fulfilled by Montreal conference chair Winfried Lang, an Austrian diplomat who was delegated to craft many of the compromises.

Besides those in official functions, mediation can be conducted by different individuals or groups without formal roles and authority. Different actors can intervene at various points, on an ad hoc basis, proposing bridging solutions to outstanding issues. The final-hour stalemate during the Montreal Protocol negotiation was created by the EC demand for special concessions (arising from the need to manage intrabloc political and economic relations). In response to the EC demand to be treated as a single unit, opponents were concerned about reduction in one country to be offset by an increase in another. New Zealand's environment minister Philip Woollaston stepped in to break the impasse, satisfying both sets of positions with a compromise on the treatment of EC members as a single unit for consumption but not production (Benedick 1991; Hampson 1995).

Special interest groups within powerful states

National preferences formed by important economic or political interests within powerful countries affect a process of setting conference agendas as well as state strategic behavior. The large business players in the United States exercised active roles and power in trade negotiations through ad hoc consultation meetings with a trade bureaucracy. Coalition-building in an internal political process determines the tiers of influential groups to be consulted. At the apex of an elaborate consultative structure in US trade negotiations is the Advisory Committee for Trade Policy and Negotiations (ACTPN), created in 1974 to ensure the "adequate" reflection of commercial and economic interests. It was the ACTPN that formulated the critical strategic thinking on a trade-based approach to intellectual property, ushering in its broad code in a sweeping agenda within the GATT during the 1980s (Drahos 2003).

Procedural tactics

The ultimate distribution of an outcome can be shaped by a class of tactics that influence later events. By getting an item in or keeping it out, agenda-setting eventually shapes the value of a gain. Negotiators may stake out untouchables and position bottom lines with a high degree of posturing. Agenda formation naturally entails squabbling over different approaches in issue framing. The United States set the agenda on intellectual property and services opposed by the developing world before the Uruguay Round (1986–94). In an agenda-setting struggle, India, Brazil, Argentina, Tanzania, Peru and other developing countries insisted on the exclusion of a comprehensive code on intellectual property in the GATT discussion, but were not able to block its negotiation. After the agenda was set, developing countries' primary objective was to block advancement in discussion about intellectual property and reduce the issue scope of public service sectors (Singh 2006). Despite these goals, developing countries lost heavily on intellectual property while they did manage to limit their concessions on services. The differential outcome can be attributed to the events after agenda-setting.

In intellectual property, the drastic expansion of the agenda contributed to an increase in developing countries' losses. While their stiff opposition led to the ambiguous language incorporated in macro agenda-setting, developed countries were later able to bring in an expansive agenda without much notice. Developing countries did not have an early warning of specific campaigns to change the agenda in the Group of Negotiations of Goods (GNG) with a failure to gather information about domestic developments in powerful countries. Progressive hardening of the North's position on intellectual property created cracks in the opposition stance, forcing most concessions by developing countries (Singh 2006). This outcome is, in part, related to the discussion of intellectual property as part of general goods in the GNG rather than a separate but parallel track as created for negotiation on services.

Despite their crucial role in blocking the most controversial agendas, larger developing countries provided no real counterweight to the domination of the procedures by the transatlantic duopoly of the United States and the EU (Drahos 2003). Ineffective opposition by core developing countries to the negotiation's expanded mandate, in fact, contributed to some of the excesses of the intellectual property agreement (e.g., the size of the rent transfers from developing to developed countries). The opposition to a comprehensive code on intellectual property simply fell flat at various negotiation stages that reset the course. The leadership of the developing countries failed to mobilize their group to reduce both the size and scope of their concessions. A few developing countries, present in the agenda-setting "green room" process, failed to speak in unison. A lack of coordination among key third world countries contributed to the development of a full-blown agreement on intellectual property at the trade ministers' mid-term review of the Uruguay Round talks in December 1988 in Montreal and April 1989 in Geneva.

From the beginning of the Uruguay Round negotiations, the majority of less developed economies expressed their intentions not to sign the agreements on intellectual properties and services. In forcing less developed countries to assume the obligations of all the Uruguay Round agreements, including their nonpreferred ones, American negotiators introduced new procedural rules in closing the round. The "single undertaking approach" was used as a tactic to insert the intellectual property negotiation outcome as an integral part of the total package binding on all members. At the end of the Uruguay Round, thus, the emergence of the WTO system incorporated an Agreement on Trade-Related Aspects of Intellectual Property Rights (TRIPS) and a General Agreement on Trade in Services (GATS) into a General Agreement on Tariffs and Trade (GATT) and its associated agreements that had been established in the years since 1948. The final act came from GATT director-general Arthur Dunkel, who enclosed the plan in the secretariat's draft Final Act, issued in December 1991.

The single undertaking is widely regarded as the imposition of consensus in favor of the measure sought by powerful countries via a potent form of coercion. Its presentation is the equivalent of a "take-it-or-leave-it" offer through an irrevocable commitment. The consensus was forged by the threat of advanced economies to exit, leaving a worse alternative to veto states through the liberalization of trade exclusively among the powerful with sheer global market power (Steinberg 2002).

In the end, the decision-making outcomes do not turn out to be Pareto improving to developing countries as a whole. Consensus decision does not prohibit powerful states from contracting asymmetrically with outcomes skewed in their favor. However, this general lesson for more careful scrutiny of agenda-setting processes and tactics was not forgotten by many developing country participants in the Doha Round that started in 2001. By using GATT/WTO rules requiring consensus as a source of power, they could force the EU and the United States to pay more attention to some of their primary interests and concerns in agenda-setting. In the end, the negotiation at Doha has become a hostage to "single-undertaking rules" (Rolland 2010). Needless to say, negotiations easily stall or slow at best, waiting for consensus on everything to be agreed by all (Steinberg 2002).

Conclusion

Multilateral bargaining becomes easily protracted, contentious and prone to failure. Bargaining over the distribution of costs and benefits shapes collective outcomes. Each side weighs relative losses or gains and develops different thresholds on concessions. Multilateral negotiation varies with regard to the process of institutional bargaining. Variable properties of an institutional setting may determine the effectiveness of strategies used by states and coalitions. The distribution of bargaining power plays a key role in controlling the process and eventually its outcome. Inequality in transactions (e.g., a distributive outcome of the Uruguay Round) reflects the extent of asymmetry in bargaining power and the nature of an institutional process in favor of the powerful. The multilateral forum does not mitigate inequalities of bargaining power housed in bilateral negotiation even though weaker parties are still better off in a multilateral setting through collective bargaining.

Notes

1 Some parties at the table may have an incentive to forestall settlement instead of accepting its desire (Thompson 2001). In negotiations on a global protection of the world's forests (between 1992 and 2007), for instance, such countries as Malaysia were mostly engaged in talks to prevent the emergence of a legally binding agreement setting a standard in forest management.
2 In general, two kinds of activities take place simultaneously in United Nations and other international proceedings. In the midst of a continuous flow of public debate, frequent communication among delegates is heard only by those involved. Thus it matters who talks to whom, who initiates the interaction and how long it lasts (Alger 2014). In trade negotiations, many informal conversations over time help shape development of packages that serve as the basis of a final deal (Drahos 2003). This informal group process and dialogue are not easily modeled to show some structural payoff matrix, but they uncover much about the cooperation and conflict imbedded in multilateral negotiation.

12 Reflection and synthesis

> It would be naive to think that the problems plaguing mankind today can be solved with means and methods which were applied or seemed to work in the past.
>
> Mikhail Gorbachev, 1988[1]

THROUGHOUT this book, we have examined what it takes to get a mutually acceptable and desirable negotiation outcome. In understanding the effect of a behavior and strategies in negotiator interactions, we have studied what is involved in negotiating. As a negotiated settlement is presumed to be voluntary, an agreement has to favor everyone. In this book, we have also assumed that negotiating behavior is driven by self-interest; an outcome should bring advantage to all sides. In fact, no rational actor is supposed to agree to a proposal that leaves him/her worse off than the status quo ante. In an economic lexicon, a rational bargaining outcome is represented by a Pareto efficient allocation of values, where a further increase in one party's welfare should not be obtained at the sacrifice of the other's. More importantly, being rational in negotiation translates into making the best decisions to realize one's own objectives or maximize one's own interests (Bazerman and Neale 1992). In that sense, our main interest has not been "getting to yes" (Fisher and Ury 1981).

At the heart of negotiation lies a need to resolve a tension between efficiency and distribution in the outcome (Princen 1992). In a bargaining dilemma, negotiators are caught up in a contradiction between their need for joint action and conflict over the terms of the final agreement (Craver 2012). Cooperation is essential in enhancing efficiency for the maximization of mutual gains, while competition is generated by the existence of many possible outcomes, each favoring a different party. Bargainers can reach an agreement in such a way as to improve their joint welfare by enlarging the pie through cooperation. At the same time, the main impetus of bargaining is to maximize individual total gain, thus creating conditions for a dispute over how to "divide the pie." Thus concerns for absolute gain do not alleviate interest in seeking equal or greater share than an opponent.

Given the dubious link between individual gain and collective efficiency, opposing parties instinctively prefer to protect or build a competitive edge than to simultaneously pursue joint interests. Even in integrative bargaining, concessions are not cost-free, in that issues have different tradeoff values; a negotiator is likely to ask for bigger concessions as a price for helping realize the counterpart's priorities. Under these circumstances, when each party's main concern lies in their own payoff, efficiency has to be produced largely as an indirect byproduct of advancing individual gain. In fact, inventing or discovering integrative solutions could often be left to a process of trial and error.

As examined in the earlier chapters, the failure to converge on one particular solution can be ascribed to a challenge in finding a range of solutions due to incomplete information (e.g., uncertainty about each other's priorities, misinterpretation of the other negotiator's values). In other words, such elements of a bargaining game as each party's no-agreement alternative are not readily known or "common knowledge." As part of strategies and tactics, negotiators concentrate their actions on modifying an opponent's perceptions of the "zone of possible agreement" (i.e., the subjective understanding of a reasonable distribution of negotiated outcomes). A deadlock or delay in agreement is often inevitable due to difficulties in choosing one of multiple solutions (i.e., "equilibria," in game-theory parlance) although quickly agreeing to one of Pareto optimal points is more desirable. With multiple criteria, a bargaining problem is relegated to the determination of division through a series of concessionary activities (i.e., who gets how much on the Pareto efficient frontier as examined in Chapter 8). Thus disagreement as to a share in the fruits of cooperation resembles the situation created by Battle of the Sexes. Obtaining an efficient outcome is inherently difficult in noncooperative games, creating conditions for strategic action. Threats, promises and commitments aim at manipulating the other player's perceptions of no-agreement alternatives. Therefore, negotiation outcomes are conditional on variable possible actions. Keeping the above themes in mind, this final chapter reviews and synthesizes various models and theories studied earlier.

Prescriptive and descriptive models

The main concern in negotiation would be how parties should coordinate their actions with each other in pursing their own interests. As presented in Chapter 5, cooperative bargaining models prescriptively present the best way to achieve optimal, fair and stable agreements without delay. In a search for a similar outcome deduced from arbitration, cooperative theories focus on the ultimate distribution of payoffs among the parties along with the characterization of permissible solutions (Yildiz 2011). Sequential bargaining models based on game theory reveal the most efficient strategy compatible with settling conflicting interests by evaluating the relative value of each offer made during different periods of negotiation.[2] As piecemeal learning does not amount to an exhaustive and accurate search for rational strategies (Afionis 2011), the goal of formal modeling is to find a consistent set of concepts to analyze bargaining moves. Its prescriptive value as a basis for acting rationally is fortified by a logical and hypothetical conceptualization of division problems and procedures.

In this prescriptive model, the bargaining situation is idealized by assuming that players are highly rational and anticipate each other to be rational with full knowledge of individual preferences. A player should be able to assess a way of maximizing her own gain with an inference from the other's strategies and payoffs (Chatterjee 2014). In addition, seeking to predict an outcome demands knowledge about the detailed structure of the bargaining procedure in use. The applicability of Rubinstein bargaining models (examined in Chapter 5) hinges on common knowledge about the sequence of offers, with mutually expected rationality involved in offers and acceptance of decisions. The outcome is not assumed to rest on individual differences in analytical resources, cleverness or willpower other than superior "outside options." In the configuration of the game, bargaining components are relatively fixed (e.g., a single unitary actor; without a linkage to another negotiation; with no anticipated repetitions between actors). Even though formal bargaining models may be inadequate to provide a descriptive account of how negotiations actually operate (i.e., individual differences), they serve as analytical tools in comparison to a bargainer's real behavior, which may not be perfectly rational.[3] A rational baseline offers full knowledge about the possible responses of the rational "other." In assessing an actual outcome, at the same time, we need to incorporate irrational behavior (associated with deviation from bargaining theory) into developing our insight. Many well-known incidents suggest the importance of analysis of nonrational factors.

In the mind of John F. Kennedy, during the Cuban Missile Crisis, the main challenge was not difficulty in rational thinking but rather psychological and political challenges, as he himself expressed:

> Geography does not make much difference... what did it matter if you got blown up by a missile based on Cuba or an ICBM flying from the Soviet Union? The real problem... was psychological and political rather than military. To do nothing would be to surrender to blackmail.
>
> (Dobbs 2008, 16)

In a real-world negotiation, the utility function for each player may be neither fixed nor predetermined at the outset. In the above case, Nikita Khrushchev miscalculated the likely American reaction to the installation of Soviet missiles in Cuba. When Khrushchev accepted that Soviet missiles would have to be dismantled in exchange for the United States promising not to invade Cuba, half the solution was quickly found. The real dilemma for Khrushchev was not so much about the inevitability of his retreat but rather the logistics of how to pull out and what kind of concessions he could extract from Washington in return. Kennedy's main irritation was the Soviet "mere [public] mention of the Jupiter missiles in Turkey" even though "[e]veryone knows that the Jupiters were a pile of junk" (*ibid.*, 233). As a matter of fact, Kennedy had already decided, against the advice of hardliners in the executive committee of the National Security Council, not to risk a nuclear war over a few obsolete missiles. Yet "*public perceptions were all important*" (*ibid.*, 135 [emphasis added]). Kennedy had already planned to sweeten the proposed deal with the Turkey offer, but he clearly wanted to keep it confidential. Meanwhile escalation took its own course while the leaders struggled over tactical maneuvers on a Soviet retreat. "The more planes and missiles were placed on alert, the more stressed the system became... [with the possibility of an] unauthorized launch of missiles from underground silos" (*ibid.*, 276). In fact, "the machinery of war quickly acquired its own logic and momentum... the question was no longer whether the leaders wanted war but whether they had the power to prevent it" (*ibid.*, 114).

As we saw above, actors usually enter negotiations without being well informed about the way the other negotiator values all the transactions. Inadequate planning results from negotiator indeterminacy of relative preferences for various options upon their entrance into a negotiation. The rational actor's choice in a world of uncertainty would not produce the predicted consequences precisely without accurate assumptions about various factors that might interfere in decision-making and its implementation. If rules, beliefs, interests and issues are only imperfectly known, it is hardly a business of merely selecting from a predefined set of options that are consistently preferred over the alternatives. Actors have a tendency to gauge only a given moment, without much concern for its long-term prospects, which tends toward irrational results. For sure, individual chronic preferences for some goals over others are likely to be involved in a decision on seeking aspirations or beating reservations, but would also be affected by changes in an assumption about an opponent's goals during a negotiation. Utility calculation changes along with new expectations, perceptions and assessments reflecting the evolving nature of issues, tactics and circumstances (e.g., a public image, the loss of ally support, economic devastation or a decline in morale, etc.). Many actual negotiations are nonstationary, meaning that utilities often change as a function of time with altering preferences.[4] In arms-control negotiation, for instance, the payoff becomes less certain due to the unpredictability of a projected level of nuclear weapons capabilities possessed by each side.[5]

The detailed structure of a bargaining procedure in use is not generally known in predicting a bargaining outcome. The unexpected twists and turns (e.g., deadlocks in

SALT broken by covert back-channel communication between the presidents) do not reveal themselves before negotiation even to its participants. One negotiator may have uncertainty even about the nature of what is known by another as well as a lack of detailed information about their own side's preferences and alternatives.[6] Most importantly, imperfect information serves as a potential barrier to mutually beneficial transactions. Incomplete information does not necessarily hamper game theory analysis, but sacrifices precision by attempting to bend a state of expectation into a form of bargaining behavior under various probabilities of some contingencies (Aumann 1987). When more than single elements reshape behavior, a decision outcome may not simply be ascribed to an expected value assessment. A lack of "common knowledge," such as bargaining rules, between players creates difficulties in equilibrium-oriented game analysis.[7]

The presence of asymmetry of information puts the less well-informed party on guard, precluding an opportunity for an agreement with mutual gains. Negotiators with asymmetric information make subtle probabilistic inferences about the potential value of the transaction under uncertainty. The more difficult the inferential task, the greater are the bargainers' deviations from optimal bargaining behavior. An ordinary equilibrium analysis of expected utility maximization is rendered even less relevant if one player is not strategically sophisticated in spite of the other's inclination to act rationally (Sebenius 2002). The failure to end the decades of civil war in Sri Lanka and Colombia through peaceful settlement is, in fact, attributed to the rejection of various "objectively" reasonable mediator proposals by insurgent groups in the early 2000s (Chernick 2003; Destradi and Vüllers 2012). The challenge of making decisions in a logical, disciplined manner, as assumed, creates difficulties in foreseeing equilibrium outcomes. Even if negotiators intuitively hate loss, they may not always effectively minimize it (Poundstone 1992). If the deviations from fully rational behavior increase the number of plausible solutions along with mulitiplicity of equilibria, formal bargaining models are not very helpful in explaining disagreements or why a Pareto inefficient agreement may be reached in spite of a significant agreement zone. "Using untested cooperative solution concepts to predict bargaining outcomes with a limited amount of information has been likened to strapping wings on your back and jumping off a high building in the hope that you will fly" (Binmore 1996, xvi).

The best possible advice is contingent upon realistic, empirically sound judgment of a counterpart's actual moves. Real-world relevance is enhanced by including only factors perceived by negotiators and systematically breaking down the decision problem under uncertainty (Bazerman *et al.* 2000; O'Neill 1999). People generally have dissimilar sets of individual knowledge and skills, and use different methods to handle complex problems. Negotiators will be left groping in the dark without constructing new understandings about how each sees problems and facilitating knowledge about each other's goals and reasons for their pursuit (Beers *et al.* 2006). The quality of negotiation is enhanced by making each side's beliefs and values explicit. While being consistent with the known facts, consructing noncooperative bargaining games may incorporate the practical details that have a material impact on the outcome at the negotiating table.

In order to further improve the applicability of game theory, it needs to be augmented by knowledge about an actor's personal judgment styles or orientations (e.g., analytical skills, attitudes toward risk or other psychological tendencies such as seeking certainty). The analysis of a negotiator's decision-making focuses specifically on the systematic deviation from optimality.[8] The actual decision processes should reflect realistic estimates of the other side's motives and responses rather than assuming full rationality. In fact, "[t]$_{\pm}$o assume that the opponent's behavior is rational is clearly irrational if there is good evidence to the contrary" (Young 1991a, 16). The best prescription in response to the other's likely behavior, short of fully being rational, is "thinking rationally in a less-than-fully-rational world" (Bazerman and Neale 1991, 111).

Multiple outcomes in the same setting are very likely to be attributed not only to situational forces but also to individual differences that constrain motivation or ability. Negotiating behavior perhaps needs to be examined, bearing in mind the broad range of variations in cognitive ability, emotional intelligence and personality traits. The subjective character of experience as well as an individual economic value often differ widely in the same negotiation (Sharma *et al.* 2013).

Biased perceptions and erroneous inferences restrict the full capitalization of the integrative potential of negotiations. The quality of negotiated agreements hinges on how to overcome a host of decision biases and perceptual errors. Unfortunately, "specific cognitive biases" are not easily overcome "even with [their] being pointed out." The realistic estimates of the other side's motives and responses are assisted by "the prescriptions offered by game theory as well as the descriptions offered by behavioral psychology and everyday observation" (Young 1991a, 16).

Owing to limited cognitive resources and vulnerability to errors, game-theoretic predictions must be built into the possibility of play outside the equilibrium path. In making a move in a sequential game, according to Reinhard Selten (1975), players may select unintended strategies due to "trembling hands" (i.e., a player's mistake causing a deviation from an equilibrium). If one player slips up, consequently taking the game onto a wrong track, is there any reason for the other player even to consider playing a Nash-equilibrium strategy? In fact, an event off the equilibrium paths could be better understood by assuming "people might usually play as if they believe in trembling hands" (Ross 2014).

Experienced negotiators benefit from utilizing game theory's rationalistic approach while employing descriptive analysis to make sense of different perceptions among the parties (Odell 2000). Yet even experience would not completely remove biases such as individual risk preferences. Negotiating experience is context-specific, and learning may be bound to particular situations and not easily be transferable to others despite trials in repeated negotiations. In addition, it may take time for inexperienced negotiators to be able to maximize their value through the studies of bargaining games. In that sense, it is crucial to appropriately evaluate the effects of such biases as overconfidence in their judgment, a "fixed-pie" assumption, the "winner's curse" or the irrational escalation of commitment to their previous position or action. The accurate anticipation of an opponent's decisions and a better response to them is made possible by a more realistic understanding of their thinking processes.

The gap between game-theoretic assumptions and practical decision-making can be narrowed by identifying factors that hamper an individual's attempt to follow a rational course of action. Experiments on ultimatum and offer–counteroffer negotiations, illustrated by behavioral game theory, suggest the failure of people to always maximize expected payoffs as predicted by standard utility theory (Camerer and Fehr 2004; Stephen and Pham 2008). Data of negotiation behavior or practice produced by inductive methodologies indicate that individuals do not intuitively follow the canons of pure "strategic" (i.e., interactive) rationality. In the description of the possible consequences of each choice, prescriptive confidence is enhanced by understanding "subjective distribution of multiple negotiated outcomes" measured against an equilibrium standard (Sebenius 2009). A zone of possible agreement perceived by a negotiator is ultimately conditional distribution deduced from a subjective calculus of probabilities (Binmore 2007; Odell 2000).

Bounded rationality incorporates unavoidable limitations on knowledge and computational ability in understanding an agent's abilities to draw inferences from given information (Simon 1988). The views of decision-makers in the same situation reflect their values, beliefs and stereotypes. As a matter of fact, negotiators are susceptible to various cues that fashion their thoughts in coping with subjective uncertainties inherent in most negotiations. More specifically, the subjective character of a search for a solution creates vulnerability to a host of perceptual errors and other decision biases (Kahneman 2003). A player's dependence on subjective assessment of a counterpart's behavior in light of limited evidence is a barrier to the achievement of optimal negotiation agreements. In this regard, bounded rationality explains deviation from rigorous behavioral assumptions by pointing out a variety of natural ways of simplifying our understanding of the world through selective perception, attribution errors, overconfidence, stereotypes and other heuristic errors. These hardwired cognitive biases need to be discerned in predicting the other side's likely response and countering impediments to a rational course of action (Bazerman and Neale 1991).

In searching for a systematic insight into a negotiation process, descriptive possibilities may be blended into formal analysis, relaxing the stringent assumptions and requirements for sophisticated computational ability in a fixed game (March 1988). Most substantially, an agent's knowledge about strategies and utility functions may have to be learned and tested from experience embedded in a particular social context. The practical usefulness of negotiation analysis comes from accommodating insights from experience. In this regard, knowledge of systematic decision-making biases offers a crucial analytical standing, supplementing economic approaches to more calculable interests such as cost, time and so forth. At the same time, it needs to be noted that, while motivational models seem to emphasize predictable ways of departure from rationality, the tacit or implicit nature of an individual cognitive process is not easily observable, being reduced to limited patterns of behavior to settle uncertainties. Indeed, information-gathering strategies may reflect dissimilar ubiquitous individual knowledge-seeking behavior.

Negotiation styles and culture

Negotiation styles can be interpreted from persistent patterns of strategies and behavior, unique to particular negotiators, over a period of time. The combination of differences and similarities in negotiation styles between negotiators together produces varying bargaining dynamics and outcomes. This point can be well illustrated by the comparison between Salvadoran and Guatemalan peace processes that ended decade-long civil wars in the early and mid 1990s respectively. Despite many similarities in the negotiation process and structure, in El Salvador, everything was fairly transparent but in Guatemala "people [had to] deny in order to affirm" (Jonas 2000, 39). The subtle differences in communication styles required more gradual approaches to advancing an agreement in Guatemala.

In spite of the need to forge shared understanding through mutual interaction, many negotiation settings involve misperceptions of each other's behavior due to difficulty in the synchronization of communication styles. In examining negotiation style differences, interactive communication dynamics can be attributed to actor characteristics with a particular focus on personal/group backgrounds. Each negotiator has a unique ability to interpret various negotiation situations along with particular value orientations as well as idiosyncratic personalities and temperament. One's orientation toward power and beliefs about justice can be manifested in communication and other negotiation styles (Tyler *et al.* 2004).

In some negotiation literature, culture has been pointed out as an important element in conditioning a negotiator's strategies, tactics and behavior through its impact on cognitive processes. It is based on the premise that perceptions and attitudes of negotiators reflect on their personal experience in a social environment surrounding them. Knowledge structures are internalized by their frequent use and predominance in public discourse. As the representation of shared beliefs and the meanings of a life, culture plays a role in shaping a group's attitudes, norms and behaviors (Mühlen 2010). In a negotiation context, preexisting worldviews (good or bad) can have an impact on cognitive representations of what they are negotiating about.

This was well displayed by Germany's staunch refusal to budge on cutting a mountain of Greek debt, reflecting their broad orientation toward predictability and certainty derived from the adherence to rules. As opposed to a soft deal advocated by France and Italy, in the Eurozone debate in July 2015, the German public would prefer an offer of humanitarian aid to forgiving debts in the event of Greek bankruptcy. A tough response from rule-binding Germany was supported by their attitudes to avoid the risk of "[breaking] the convenant that when money is borrowed, it has to be repaid" (*Washington Post*, July 8, 2015). Indeed, the words for "debt" and "guilt" are identical in German (*Schuld*). As a contextual cue of the social interaction, culture touches upon which frame dominates individual thoughts and behaviors. Group norms and values help define what is more or less important by interpreting a context for social interaction (e.g., the need of self-affirmation derived from a threat to self-esteem in emotionally tense negotiations).

Negotiation research especially in communication and psychology sheds light on the role of norms and values (formed by ethnic, gender or professional identity) in shaping negotiators' strategies and patterns.[9] One's value systems and perspectives are reflected in the formation of perceptions about counterparts and in the interpretation of their behavior. Some cultures are less tolerant of ambiguity, view the world as essentially more competitive, put high value on winning and reward their members accordingly (i.e., a "winner-takes-all" practice). Under such conditions, individuals are more motivated to win relative gains. The efforts to understand the universalizability of negotiation behavior need to be juxtaposed against challenges of communication posed in a culturally diverse setting. The theory and practice of negotiation itself represents "a universal (etic) phenomenon," presenting a basis for comparison, but its rhythms are unique to an individual group culture (emic) (Adair and Brett 2005).[10]

Information sharing is linked to culturally unique aspects of negotiation such as high- versus low-context communication (Hall 1976). Low-context communication is characterized by explicit and direct information sharing. Information sharing is implicit and indirect in high-context communication with less significance attached to words and more to its setting and other cues in the environment. Intercultural negotiations potentially pose strategic challenges in a search for information, since meanings are not merely embedded in words or acts (Brett 2000). Cultural meanings are also embedded in various contexts of developing influence tactics. In low-context cultures, persuasion depends on rationality whereas, in high-context cultures, persuasion makes appeals to emotions and affect (with information exchange used as a means for establishing and maintaining a relationship). In general, the patterns of crosscultural communication exhibit that American negotiators tend to adopt analytic statements based on logic and reasoning for persuasion, while Japanese and Taiwanese negotiators are more actively engaged in the reciprocation of indirect information exchange (Carrell and Heavrin 2008).

The nature and context of interaction validate the relevance of culture to a negotiator interaction. For instance, a low-ball offer and haggling are considered normal parts of a bargaining process, or at least not offensive, in many non-Western cultures, but can be easily misinterpreted as tactics of manipulation by those who do not come from the same cultural frame. The collective cultural dispositions could act even on a process of rational-utility calculation when issues carry symbolic values beyond simple economic rationality. Concerns for fairness could be interpreted through cultural lenses of interests and values. Some experimental studies ascribe differences in the valuation of utilities to gender or cultural groupings.

Beyond primary socialization through primordial attributes based on ethnicity and gender, the conceptions of fairness and trust can be formed by transnational "professional cultures" that arise from organizational, technical and training experiences, as well as past contacts. In processes involving numerous parties over the long term, for instance, multilateral negotiations on arms control are prone to diminish the role of national cultures in favor of conference norms established by collective procedures for negotiator conduct. In bilateral relations, too, professionals from opposing countries can form a shared language and understanding. It is well illustrated by the observation of one of the key US participants in arms-control negotiation during the Cold War period:

> A bizarre aspect of SALT was that military men of both sides were talking to each other for many months in a civil and, in time, even friendly fashion... in one way or another in planning and training for nuclear strikes against each other [they] found themselves working and relaxing together in a way unimaginable a few years before. The respect they developed for each other should be something of an asset in the long process that will be required if real improvement in Soviet–American relations is to occur.
>
> (Smith 1985, 38)

In general, it is difficult to aggregate unique elements in many different cultures or evaluate their relative importance, posing challenges in treating culture as an independent variable (Faure 2002; Zartman 1993). The strategic nature of behavioral expressions (e.g., concession behavior) cannot be easily relegated to gender, ethnic, religious disposition or other group character (in considering wider individual differences within each of these groupings). Because of difficulties in evaluating or measuring its relevant determinant in a negotiation process, culture's effects can be considered subtle and certainly less visible as a unique explanatory variable in a complex process, for instance, involving the US–Chinese trade talks or Israeli–Palestinian struggle.[11] In spite of its limits on the number of situations where culture matters (given weak predictability and prescription value), culture serves as an important residual variable especially in a negotiation process, as shown in experimental research on interpersonal or intergroup business negotiations (Ready and Tessema 2011).

An integral framework of negotiation analysis

Analysis of actor differences and various external circumstances suggests that a negotiation process is not deterministic, in that it is not subject to pure utilitarian calculations or prearranged mechanisms of interaction. Therefore, the eventual payoff (i.e., an outcome of a negotiation) is most likely to be deflected by subjective decision-making variables, intraparty competition, and a random or unexpected development of events off the negotiation table. Differences in bargaining behavior can be explained in part by motivational and cognitive models. At the same time, diverse and competing interests are represented in each party's decision-making procedures, creating inconsistent approaches to negotiation. Coalitions in support of or opposed to concessions can either advance or derail the entire package of conflict settlement forged at the negotiation table. In the end, a negotiator's ability to minimize negative effects from the external environment (e.g., the politics of decision-making at both institutional and system levels) needs to be accounted for in a better understanding of causes and conditions for a particular negotiation outcome. Consequently, the combination of multiple factors can interact differently either to create deadlocks, and even to terminate the entire process or, conversely, to overcome each party's intransigence.

Negotiation context and linkages

Key factors not directly involved in activities and movements at the bargaining table can make a difference in the way negotiators develop strategies and interact with each other, ultimately affecting the outcomes. The increase in the number of interfering factors generates more complications in talks at the negotiation table, subsequently creating more challenges to making sound judgments and producing a satisfactory agreement. Some negotiated outcomes cannot be adequately explained without examining a set of surrounding circumstances. The Cold War context allowed Iceland to use a threat of hosting a Soviet military base as a means to extract unilateral British concessions in expanding territorial waters and fishing quotas in the Nordic Sea in the 1950s and 1970s. In endeavoring to gain sovereign control over the canal, Panama was able to increase the political cost for the United States by transforming the canal question into a frame of the "colonized" versus the "colonizer" at the UN and other international fora with the support of strong nonaligned, anti-colonial movements in the 1970s.

External events off the bargaining table may lead to retraction of promises and commitments made in the previous round of negotiation. The near settlement to end the Ugandan civil war collapsed in 1985, not because of a failure to find a satisfactory formula, but because the sudden deterioration in fighting ability of the government forces provided an opportunity for insurgent groups to win the conflict instead of being satisfied with a power-sharing arrangement. The election of new leaders can either provide a momentum for novel initiatives or completely derail the near completion of negotiated settlement, depending on the fresh leadership's perspectives about the accommodation of the other side's needs. Escalating violence waged by opponents of negotiation can either hasten a settlement process (as shown at the final stage of South Africa and Northern Ireland peace negotiations) or can completely burn the last bridge to peace (e.g., Israeli–Palestinian peace negotiations).

It is not unusual to find bilateral talks grounded in a network of other negotiations with the same parties or over the same issues at regional or multilateral settings (Crump 2009). The interparty negotiation process is subject to linkage to other negotiations (as exemplified by the impact of US bargaining positions in the multilateral Uruguay Round on the United States–Japan bilateral trade negotiations in the 1980s). The linked process and systems can explain either psychological or material effects of another discrete negotiation. External events can also provide a context of comparison through the salience of historical similarities and contagious effects. For example, the Salvadoran peace accord served as a watershed event for the Guatemalan negotiation.

An existing negotiation under way might be halted, suspended or advanced by unrelated events through an external issue linkage. It is contrasted with an internal issue linkage, which refers to a bargaining situation within the same policy area. Bargaining postures may be a reflection of a response to a counterpart's behavior outside the negotiation, as observed by the adoption of American soft or hard negotiation tactics toward Moscow with the consideration of the latter's policy in Africa or other global arenas. It is well illustrated by the US decision not to ratify SALT II in response to the 1979 Soviet invasion of Afghanistan.

Negative linkages to external events have harmful effects in a negotiation by raising stakes in unrelated areas (Sebenius 1983; Tollison and Willett 1979). Unless it can be practiced solely in a unilateral manner, linkage is a double-edged sword (which can be negatively applied to one's own side). For instance, a specific linkage of arms control to Moscow's "good behavior" in unrelated fields (e.g., a regional conflict) did not work well unless US leaders were less interested in agreement than the Soviets or possessed superior bargaining power (Bunn 1992). Thus a negotiation process can be obstructed by links to different policy areas. At the same time, negotiations can be initiated, maintained or concluded by utilizing a positive outside event that produces new interactions with a momentum.

Assessing a negotiation outcome

Negotiation outcomes may reflect not only the opportunities open to the bargainers but also their risk orientations, experiences and strategic skills. In synchronizing diverging expectations and avoiding the impression of giving in, customary procedures, precedents and other types of appeals to fairness are still important for reaching an agreement. In economic rationality, the nature of a just and fair outcome derives from an agreement where everyone is better off than without it. Not being concerned about distributive justice or equity, a Pareto efficient solution does not address division problems except that any change in the status quo should bring about increased utility to at least one of the parties without hurting the other party. As examined in Chapter 5, a Nash rational solution in a cooperative game is anchored to one-half of the maximum gains above each party's disagreement point as a fair division (Nash 1950). In fact, a gain from the value of their respective disagreement points provides the logical reason for negotiators to enter into a deal in the first place. In cooperative bargaining theories, fairness is generally attached to each party's relative bargaining power, which determines the extent of gain. Thus, fair division is determined inside the negotiation, in that prevailing power relations are naturally accepted as given, along with individual preferences (Albin 2001).

When each party's bargaining strength is measured by a disagreement value without reference to any external criteria, a negotiation process does not aim to fulfill any other requirements than translation of bargaining power into an actual payoff. What each party gets depends on the weight of bargaining power and associated tactical advantages. In the bilateral Israeli–Palestinian negotiations, the persistent alteration in the status quo has been made mostly by unilateral actions such as the continuing land confiscation and settlement in the occupied territories of the West Bank. Since the Oslo Accords, in fact, the newly created reality on the ground has served as an initial point for any future talks. For instance, until the collapse of the peace process in 2000, most time was devoted to "[r]enegotiation upon renegotiation of interim agreements – only yielding tiny Israeli withdrawals" through unilaterally delaying tactics and minimalist implementation (Swisher 2004, 172). From bargaining theory perspectives, a legitimate question might arise as to why the Israelis should concede, once there was nothing really left for Palestinians to offer after the 1993 Oslo Accords. Then perhaps the Palestinians should have insisted on not deferring the essential settlement and territorial transfer and other "permanent status" issues (to be implemented mostly by Israeli concessions) to the later stage. This question becomes especially pertinent owing to a Palestinian inability to interfere in Israel's measures to bolster its bargaining power over these issues in the interim period (Albin 2001). Once the Israeli government had dragged out the process, Palestinian leader Yasser Arafat's only leverage was to increase the costs to the Israelis with a lack of enthusiasm in controlling suicide bombing and other violent tactics by radicals. Especially given the price of reining in Hamas and other Islamists, he did not find any incentives to stop them without the prospect of a tangible fruit of peace.

Besides the practical difficulties of quantitatively measuring gains, on some occasions, undesirable conditions can be created by adopting a disagreement point as a common unit to evaluate a negotiation's outcome. In the event that sharp power inequalities are accepted as a starting point for negotiation, the process is unlikely to produce any legitimate outcome unless a dominant party cares for the interests of the weaker one.[12] If relative bargaining power becomes the only yardstick for determining the outcome, for instance, in Tibet's quest for self-determination through its negotiation with China, neither nonviolence nor self-immolation will transform the asymmetric relationship. If one party does not have any means or alternative but the acceptance of whatever is offered by the other, this situation turns into a dictator game where a proposer entirely determines all the allocation without the recipient's input. Unless certain requirements are fulfilled (e.g., a disproportionate obligation in the ozone negotiation along with the acceptance of the "polluter-pays" principle), the notion of fairness in bargaining will not fulfill justice by merely depending on a prevailing balance of forces.[13] In such cases as climate change, polluters have more bargaining power when their actions threaten other countries more direly with devastation (e.g., small island states or sub-Saharan African countries). In fact, polluters may even increase the emissions level so that it becomes a new starting point for reduction in the event of any future agreement.[14]

Even with ethical questions at a practical level being put aside, what if North Korea continues to increase its nuclear stockpiles and develop long-range missiles as a means to increase its bargaining power vs. the United States with the goal of removing the latter's economic sanctions that hurt them severely? In the above situations, a mere focus on bargaining power creates more paradoxes and ironies instead of presenting a just solution. The 1995 negotiated solution in Bosnia-Herzegovina was possible only after heavy NATO bombing which altered the ground military balance that in turn rearranged the bargaining strength of each party. Then an international intervention seems to be required to rebalance relative power relations in many other asymmetric ethnic conflicts before a negotiated settlement. This contradiction would not be dissipated by an attempt to establish prevalent perceptions of justice, as long as those with superior power selectively accepted a variety of principles and norms for the tactical purpose of justifying their positions (e.g., the Chinese justification for their territorial claims to oil-rich continental shelves near Vietnam and the Philippines with dubious historical claims and building an artificial island).

Cognitive aspects

Beyond objective, economic measures of performance, it would be worthwhile bringing in psychological perspectives to understanding the subjective aspects of assessing a negotiation outcome. A negotiator's experience of uncertainty does not stop upon the conclusion of the negotiation. Regardless of the specific context, negotiators are generally left with such questions as whether they obtained a good deal (Naquin 2003). The ways negotiators attempt to settle these questions have the consequences for their own satisfaction, with implications for their behavior in subsequent negotiations. Future strategies might hinge, in part, on negotiators' perception of how they performed in past negotiations (Reb 2010). Especially with insufficient information to make objective judgments, a negotiator's satisfaction is likely to be affected by her original expectations about negotiated outcomes. In fact, equivalent outcomes may lead to differing levels of satisfaction, depending on which particular standard of comparison negotiators call upon.

Most significantly, subjective evaluation takes account of cognitive and motivational factors. It may focus not only on the discrepancy (or distance) between the initial goals and final achievement but also on the initial expectation of difficulties in achieving it vs. the actual difficulties (i.e., immediate acceptance of the first offer vs. several rounds of haggling). First of all, a negotiator's satisfaction levels are likely to be controlled by counterfactual thoughts about an outcome generally anchored to their aspiration or reservation level (Neale and Fragale 2006). In intrapersonal comparisons, internal standards of comparison can be based on the initial reference points set somewhere between aspiration and reservation value. In many situations, having an aspiration level as an outcome target, with great optimism and confidence, would surely contribute to less gratified feelings for a negotiated outcome than starting with a reservation level. This phenomenon can be ascribed to a negotiator's different reference points about what could otherwise have happened (Kristensen and Gärling 2000). At the end of the negotiation, the failure to attain an aspiration goal generates second thoughts about how the lower outcome could have been improved. On the other hand, a reservation value adopted as an achievement standard makes any settlement above it look greater.

In addition, specific incidents during the negotiation could also influence the levels of satisfaction. Even though better outcomes were secured by making the first offer, negotiators might still be less satisfied in the event of its immediate acceptance by a counterpart. It generates more desirable counterfactuals than a settlement after a delay (for instance, involving several rounds of exchanging offers). Being plagued by the winner's curse (i.e., paying more than true value), a negotiator may speculate, counterfactually, that what they have received might be less valuable than what they paid for (Galinsky et al. 2002). All in all, properly understanding each other's interests, notions of fairness and perceptions is essential to a satisfactory outcome.

Beyond the absolute value assessed by a negotiator's internal referent, another determinant for satisfaction can be formed by relative performance (Crusius and Mussweiler 2012). An outcome can be compared with that of either a counterpart in the same negotiation or outside negotiators in a similar situation. Interpersonal comparisons within the negotiation could make the relative outcome of an opponent look better than one's own. In the aftermath of the Northern Ireland negotiations, for instance, the Unionists had some second thoughts, feeling that they had made more concessions to Republicans, as their commitments (such as power-sharing) were more specific and had to be immediately implemented (Albin 2001).

In a competitive relationship, each party may consider relative gains more satisfactory and politically palpable (Butt and Choi 2006). In a rivalry relationship, relative gains are more likely to be sought with less concern for their absolute gain. In some experimental studies, most satisfaction was shown by the knowledge that the settlement occurred near or at the opponent's reservation level. Higher relative gains for one party increase their subjective level of satisfaction, but reduce the degree of positive emotions of the other party about the outcome. The higher the discrepancy in relative gains, the more grievances are likely to emerge. Generally speaking, the prospect of an unfair division decreases the incentives to cooperate and produces inefficient outcomes. As concession begets concession, the principle of reciprocity could be embraced as a general "external standard of fairness in substantive negotiations" (Fisher et al. 1997, 119). At the end of successful SALT I negotiation, Soviet foreign minister Andrei Gromyko shared his feelings with Kissinger, "We are satisfied with the manner in which business was conducted on your side, and we tried to reciprocate" (Kissinger 1979, 1242).

Besides comparisons within the same negotiation, an outcome could be evaluated vis-à-vis those of others in similar negotiations (Novemsky and Schweitzer 2004). Satisfaction levels increase with outcomes that are more favorable than those for comparable others (e.g., a purchase of the same type of house at a lower price than neighbors). In initiating a negotiation, a favorable precedent for others engaged in a similar negotiation can provide a barometer for late comers. In a newly initiated negotiation with the Turkish government in 2013, for instance, the Kurds looked at the outcome of the Northern Ireland negotiation to set their goals. In negotiating with their government, the opposition in Guatemala certainly tried to do better than their counterparts in the Salvadoran negotiations that had ended earlier.

Final thoughts: actor vs. situation differences

From an analytical viewpoint, a negotiation's components (e.g., differential payoffs) and surrounding characteristics (e.g., third-party intervention) are relatively fixed and are structurally determined. Even though "the negotiator does not often have the ability to change the structural characteristics of the negotiation (relative power)," individual differences (e.g., personal orientation or skills) might be worth noting (Bazerman and Neale 1991, 110). In this book, we have regarded a negotiator's decision-making as interactive by assuming that each party chooses strategies with anticipation of the counterpart's possible response. Given its very definition, a negotiation outcome is not supposed to be imposed by only one party's will or preferences. At the same time, most often, negotiators have asymmetric control over the outcome, when each has a different degree of ability to influence their counterpart's actions (Bailer 2010). What negotiators can obtain depends on a bargaining structure endowed, in part, with strength in the merit of each party's unilateral actions in the absence of a negotiation. Equally important, strategies matter in many different ways in manipulating an opponent's preferences, choices and actions. In addition, we need to consider nonstrategic elements interfering in actual decisions. These encompass negotiators' unique decision-making styles, organizational imperatives and political support for key decisions, etc.

If the sources and dynamics of power are considered embedded in a negotiation process, power is perceived with great uncertainty about its effects. Given that perceived power is based on a potential for its delivery against the other actor, negotiators are not able to conclude the precise effects of power ex ante. Equally important, a potent source of influence can be cultivated by the ability to control the process. With the process evolving, negotiators have room to recompose and sequence their choices as well as setting up action-forcing events. The structure can also be reshaped by such actions as inviting or precluding external parties and rearranging the agenda by linking and delinking issues to and from other negotiations (Watkins 1999).

Throughout this book, interactive negotiating behavior has been examined by how a negotiator affects her counterparts and the negotiation context. If we have deterministic views about an outcome in international affairs, it would not require much analysis of bargaining problems and process to settle them. The increase in power could derive from the dynamics of the negotiation process itself, not being traced back to actual capacity. The outcomes may not just represent actual power but could also be manipulated by the strategic use of negotiation tactics. The perceptions of power asymmetry affect actors' aspirations. However, power has a limited ability to bend the will of a determined adversary, as seen in the US experience of negotiating with less powerful countries such as Vietnam (early 1970s) and North Korea (since the early 1990s).[15] Here we see a gap between persuasive and virtual power (i.e., a real possibility presented by mighty destructive capabilities) in negotiation.

It is not uncommon to find an apparently weaker party developing a strategic edge in obtaining what they want or increasing their leverage (Panke 2012). For one thing, the weakness might be able to be compensated via borrowing power – more specifically, by way of taking from or making use of external power sources. In the global climate negotiations from 1990 to 1997, the Alliance of Small Island States (AOSIS) took advantage of the support of a broad civil society movement to reconfigure the negotiations in a way that a priori power distribution would not have predicted (Betzold 2010). In fact, "[they] were the first to propose a draft text during the Kyoto Protocol negotiations calling for cuts in carbon dioxide emissions of 20% from 1990 levels by 2005" (United Nations Framework Convention on Climate Change 2014). Prior to NAFTA, the Mexican government orchestrated a well-prepared campaign to successfully fend off the US government's demand to allow multinational oil companies to operate in Mexico freely. Mexico did this by developing alternatives to the free trade pact by announcing its economic development plans without it (Odell 2010). One of the most common strategies is geared toward promoting a competition by involving more actors. As one of the best-known examples, in the early 1980s, the Algerian government obtained a lucrative contract on natural gas supply (including a higher price base) by generating competitive bidding among multiple Western energy companies and their supporting governments in France, Italy, Spain and the United States (Naylor 2000). Besides having another party to negotiate with, one's leverage can be increased by bringing in potentially related issues; extra issues enhance the possibility of adding something new to offer or exchange.

A wide variation in negotiation structures may not permit a "one-size-fits-all" recipe for success (Watkins 1999). In many circumstances, bargainers neither have equal or similar motives, nor the same computational capacity. Different assumptions about the underlying capabilities of negotiators may be able to explain diverse individual responses to the same situation. Identifying a particular negotiation outcome (for example, through logrolling and other forms of value creation by adding and unbundling issues as well as the discovery of tradeoffs) calls for an ability to sense the other party's priorities along with the evaluation of their subjective distributions. In modifying values at stake, some have high-level cognitive sophistication in understanding their counterparts with quick and adaptable learning ability to generate contingent contracts and reframe issues to allow agreement as well as maximizing value on compatible issues.

As reviewed earlier, actual variations in decision outcomes may reflect the effects of exogenous influences as well as individual or group differences. Decision processes and behavior are contingent upon a host of factors. As an antecedent condition, the overall structural context of international relations can set parameters for possible strategies or create diverse constraints. For one thing, conditions for international negotiation, in contrast to its domestic counterpart, are bound by a lack of institutions to enforce an agreement. Indeed, this has crucial effects in decisions on the selection of negotiation strategies.

In addition, a negotiator does not often have the ability to change some structural conditions presented to them. For instance, a negotiator can only adapt to the personal characteristics of the opponent (Bazerman and Neale 1991). More importantly, uncontrollable random human behavior may also trigger an abrupt breakdown. A protracted process and mounting frustration may prompt negotiators to walk away unexpectedly. There is no definite way to theorize the precise moment when this may happen. By casting doubt, even in identical situations, all actors are not likely to behave the same way, for example, in ranking possible actions needed to achieve the most desirable outcome.

If various negotiating situations present little resemblance, how could most critical decisions be examined by a baseline from which to assess a negotiator's performance? In the case of Carter's numerous interventions at different points of the successful 1978 Camp David mediation, outcomes could not be easily ascribed to one particular action. In what ways could Carter's success be compared with Clinton's failure in his 2000 Camp David mediation? Perhaps, variability in the environment might degrade the reliability of individual experience in developing a learnable insight. If Clinton had chosen a different timing for negotiation and had organized the negotiation procedures differently, however, could these changes have made a difference?[16] Decisions on when and how to negotiate, as well as psychological tactics such as creating urgency, could be regarded as an intervening variable between preexisting conditions (e.g., power differentials) and an outcome.

The role of bargaining skills might be illustrated by the simple example below. At the outset, a customer outside several pottery shops has more bargaining power than a merchant by promoting competition. Once the bargaining starts, however, the seller is in a position to deploy effective bargaining skills with expertise on the conditions for the sales (e.g., color, shape, quality and prices). This is contrasted with a larger complex setting where negotiators are not likely to exert much influence over the exogenous elements of the negotiator's context. Nonetheless, an attempt can still be made to even indirectly alter the unfavorable effects of structural parameters, for instance, through sequencing choices.

Even though neither a sudden insight nor a game-changing event may have popped up, "a brief constellation of personalities and events came into alignment" to propel the Iran nuclear accord. Over a period of two years of intense negotiation leading up to July 2015, "each side came to gradually understand what mattered most to the other." Seizing on a sense of now or never, the top diplomats from both the United States and Iran were "driven by the conviction that they could break an ugly 35-year history," putting aside all other issues (namely, Iran's arms trade, support for Hezbollah and Syria's Assad regime, meddling in Iraq and Afghanistan, etc.). In the middle of discouraging standoffs, the Iranian foreign minister Mohammad Javad Zarif was quoted as saying, "[w]e are not going to have another time in history when there is an Obama and a Biden and a Kerry and a Moniz again... there may be no Rouhani, Zarif and Salehi" (*New York Times*, July 15, 2015). In fact, the top US and Iranian energy officials, Ernest J. Moniz and Ali Akbar Salehi, were credited with the insights on "the physics of enrichment." The new opening was created on the heels of the June 2013 election of Hassan Rouhani as Iranian president and the US overtures to initiate the first direct contact at the top level in thirty-four years. What makes a difference in any tough negotiation is the negotiators' ability to seize ripe conditions for a final push and their determination to translate "a mutually enticing opportunity" into concrete agreement.

Skills could be regarded as being embedded in a process whereby actors explore strategies to influence each other's decisions by attempting to discover and evaluate the other's true preferences. An individual negotiator's efforts to affect outcomes can be supported, for instance, by the ability to set and control the agenda as well as by strategies for information collection.[17] A negotiation's fluid, situational characteristics can be amplified with insufficient information (e.g., a lack of common knowledge about a zone of agreement). In this situation, deploying artful tactics would matter more to influence the other with an ability to commit to a particular focal point as a decisive bargaining move. Thus creativity and experience cannot be ignored in successful negotiation even though "proper training reduces bias" (Bazerman and Chugh 2006, 19). Yet in the absence of an evaluative anchor, how could one know to do better? Some sets of intrapersonal negotiator skills and styles (e.g., propsal presentation and trust generating along with a natural demeanor and approachable personality) are considered inherent and unique to an individual, resisting any meaningful generalization.[18]

Universalizable negotiation theory is certainly "not rocket science, but it is not simple [or pure] intuition either" (Shell 2006, xiv). For instance, a prescription offered by bargaining theories helps us develop efficient negotiation strategies and appropriate tactics with the estimate of the relative value of each agent's offers at different points of a negotiation. This insight can be complemented by knowledge about noncooperative, strategic actions as well as about negotiator characteristics and circumstantial differences. The concepts and approaches presented in this book humbly point to the directions for further research to improve our understanding of a more complete negotiation picture.

Notes

1 From Gorbachev's address at the UN General Assembly (*Los Angeles Times*, December 9, 1988, articles.latimes.com/1988-12-09/news/mn-1338_1_class-struggle).

2. We can certainly argue that Israeli–Palestinian negotiation would not have been doomed to failure if both sides had been rational. The two sides produced the Beilin–Abu Mazen Understandings on November 1, 1995, three days before the assassination of Prime Minister Rabin. It bears a striking resemblance to an agreement draft seriously discussed to salvage the peace process in the latter part of 2000 between Israelis and Palestinians despite time differences (Sher 2006). The 1995 Beilin–Abu Mazen Understandings (as well as the 1993 DOP) also indicate that "when both sides want agreement, it can be done directly" (*ibid.*, 115).

3. Even with only very fuzzy information on many detailed matters, a noncooperative bargaining game can be constructed "to be used within the Nash program. In fact, the less we know about the bargaining procedure in use, the easier it becomes to refute the claim that a given cooperative solution concept will necessarily predict its outcome. The aim is always to begin by constructing the *simplest* noncooperative bargaining games consistent with the known facts... if we are entirely ignorant even of those details which materially affect the bargaining outcome, then [of course] we shall be wasting our time altogether in seeking to employ the Nash program" (Binmore 1996, xvii).

4. In a dynamic game, players' knowledge and beliefs can alter as the game progresses (Vidal-Puga 2008).

5. An American proposal on offensive weapons around the 1974 Nixon–Brezhnev summit was aimed to produce an agreement on controlling the process of deploying multiple (nuclear) warheads, known as MIRVs. It contained a ceiling figure for multiple warheads with an American advantage in an exchange for a Soviet superiority in total numbers of missile launchers. The proposal was intended to keep Moscow from adding more multiple warheads to its larger missiles, eventually to surpass the United States. In the absence of the accurate assessment of the numbers of warheads or launchers presented as a tradeoff, it was not feasible to make a judgment on the adequate level of the US demands or the Russian counterdemands for bargaining. The agreement was essentially made difficult by the future uncertainties of volatile MIRV technology.

6. In uncertainty, as in games of chance, even probabilities are not known exactly (e.g., terrorist attacks in a particular location); any judgment by a decision-maker is met with some degree of imprecision. Decision-making under uncertainty entails the unknown likelihood of events. A negotiator may not have any clue with an extreme degree of uncertainty.

7. In general, a game-theoretic analysis relies on the assumption that a "rational agent, when faced by the same information... should hold the same beliefs about how the game will be played by rational agent" (Heap and Varoufakis 2004, 60). Identical computational capabilities are held by equally rational players. The same information set yields the same expectation of what will happen. Thus, drawing different conclusions is ascribed to different information sets. Acquiring information should not be too costly.

8. The US–Soviet Cold War rivalry generated serious questions, even among the highest-ranking policy-makers, as to the logic behind a drive toward nuclear superiority despite an overwhelming overkill capacity possessed by each side. Right after the American–Soviet summit, Kissinger exclaimed, "One of the questions which we have to ask ourselves as a country is what in the name of God is strategic superiority? What is the significance of it, politically, militarily, operationally, at these levels of numbers? What do you do with it?" (*Washington Post*, July 4, 1974).

9. Some experimental studies suggest interesting results in understanding the role of stereotypically male vs. female traits in negotiation performance. Masculine traits associated with the high-powered negotiator contribute to behavior linked to achieving a more one-sided outcome. If negotiator effectiveness is interpreted in the context of achieving more integrative (win–win) negotiated outcomes, it is likely to be facilitated by feminine traits. Most significantly, an ability to carry out mixed-gender negotiations is highly derived from the cognitions and motivations held by negotiators (Kray *et al.* 2004).

10 "For communication in a negotiation to be effective, it must appeal at some level to both the analytical and the emotional side of the listener" (Carrell and Heavrin 2008, 242).
11 Being concerned about saving face, respecting their "value of harmony," some Western negotiators avoided directly demanding the Chinese government observe the international rules applied to other countries on such issues as the piracy of intellectual property and the government's total control of its currency values, to the exclusion of market forces, for export advantages. Obviously strategic interests are not served by oversensitivity to the other's "cultural values," removing public pressure tactics.
12 In this context, conflict transformation is often essential to ripeness for negotiated settlement (Botes 2003; Jeong 2008 and 2009).
13 In describing the dynamics of power asymmetry in negotiations, there are few events more illustrative than the advice the militarily strong Athenians gave to the weaker Melians during the Peloponnesian War. With the powerful force on Melos's doorstep in 416 BC, the Athenians presented an unenviable choice of either submission to surrender or destruction with the refusal to be conquered. "We recommend that you should try to get what it is possible for you to get ... when these matters are discussed by practical people, the standard of justice depends on the equality of power to compel ... in fact the strong do what they have the power to do and the weak accept what they have to accept" (Thucydides 1972, 401–402). In an exchange of views known as the Melian Dialogue, the Athenians simply regarded power and strength as their virtues and entitlement by natural law whereas the Melians insisted on the abstract principles of justice.
14 For example, China has been dramatically increasing its emissions even after it overtook the United States in 2006, and recently reached double the US level.
15 Each party has a different ability to bend the other's will by increasing costs to an unacceptable level. One party may attach a higher degree of significance to winning a struggle than the other. A weaker party's determination to absorb enormous costs helps achieve their goals by creating costly stalemate with a powerful party which cares less about the outcome (e.g., the 1973 Paris Peace accord after the heavy US bombardment of North Vietnam).
16 The answer might be provided by the following comments of one of the participants in the Camp David negotiation. According to Gilead Sher (2006, 70–71), "[w]e were very wary of the danger of an unstructured and unplanned process. In a process [involving] the two sides [where] a third party participates in the role of a mediator, it is expected that the third party, which convenes the summit, would enforce effective management to ensure the summit's success."
17 Some consider negotiation to be "the creation of solutions through the application of human ingenuity" (Borch and Mérida 2013, 102).
18 Individual skill differences can be illustrated by the following example. In portraying his Israeli partner during refugee talks at Taba in late 2000s, a Palestinian negotiator exclaimed, "That Yossi Beilin – his positions, in the end, might as well be Rubinstein's. But the way he talks and listens – you can't help but trust him" (Dajani 2005, 70–71). It was contrasted with a blunt style of ignoring the other's key issues (illustrated by Rubinstein). In the Palestinian perception, Israelis have often been seen as presenting their positions as diktats, not as proposals.

References

Adair, Wendi L. and Jeanne M. Brett. 2005. "The Negotiation Dance: Time, Culture, and Behavioral Sequences in Negotiation." *Organization Science* 16, 1: 33–51.
Adair, Wendi L. and Jeffrey Loewenstein. 2013. "Talking It Through: Communication Sequences in Negotiation." In Mara Olekalns and Wendi L. Adair, eds., *Handbook of Research on Negotiation*, 311–31. Cheltenham, UK: Edward Elgar.
Afionis, Stavros. 2011. "The European Union as a Negotiator in the International Climate Change Regime." *International Environmental Agreements: Politics, Law and Economics* 11, 4: 341–60.
Albin, Cecilia. 2001. *Justice and Fairness in International Negotiation*. Cambridge University Press.
Alger, Chadwick F. 2014. "Interaction and Negotiation in a Committee of the United Nations General Assembly." In *Chadwick F. Alger: Pioneer in the Study of the Political Process and on NGO Participation in the United Nations*, 87–104. New York: Springer International Publishing.
Allison, Graham T. 1971. *Essence of Decision: Explaining the Cuban Missile Crisis*. Boston: Little, Brown.
Allison, Graham T. and Philip Zelikow. 1999. *Essence of Decision: Explaining the Cuban Missile Crisis*. 2nd edn. New York: Longman.
Aoyagi, Masaki. 2005. "Collusion Through Mediated Communication in Repeated Games with Imperfect Private Monitoring." *Economic Theory*, 25, 2: 455–75.
Archetti, Marco. 2011. "A Strategy to Increase Cooperation in the Volunteer's Dilemma: Reducing Vigilance Improves Alarm Calls." *Evolution*, 65, 3: 885–92.
Archetti, Marco and István Scheuring. 2011. "Coexistence of Cooperation and Defection in Public Goods Games." *Evolution*, 65, 4: 1140–48.
Arriagada, Rodrigo and Charles Perrings. 2011. "Paying for International Environmental Public Goods." *Ambio*, 40, 7 (November): 798–806.
Asselin, Pierre. 2002. *A Bitter Peace: Washington, Hanoi, and the Making of the Paris Agreement*. Chapel Hill: University of North Carolina Press.
Assyd, Anatole. 2001. "Territorial Conflicts: Claiming the Land." In I. William Zartman, ed., *Preventive Negotiation: Avoiding Conflict Escalation*, 41–66. Lanham, MD: Rowman & Littlefield.
Aughey, Arthur. 2005. *The Politics of Northern Ireland*. London: Routledge.
Aumann, Robert J. 1987. "Correlated Equilibrium as an Expression of Bayesian Rationality." *Econometrica*, 55: 1–18.
  1995. "Backward Induction and Common Knowledge of Rationality." *Games and Economic Behavior*, 8, 1: 6–19.

Austen-Smith, David. 2009. "Economic Methods in Positive Political Theory." In Robert E. Goodin, ed., *The Oxford Handbook of Political Science*, 810–25. Oxford University Press.

Avenhaus, Rudolf. 2008. "Game Theory as an Approach to Conflict Resolution." In Jacob Bercovitch, Victor Kremenyuk and I. William Zartman, eds., *The SAGE Handbook of Conflict Resolution*, 85–101. London: Sage.

Axelrod, Robert. 1984. *The Evolution of Cooperation*. New York: Basic Books.

Bacharach, Samuel B. and Edward J. Lawler. 1981. "Power and Tactics in Bargaining." *Industrial & Labor Relations Review*, 34, 2 (January): 219–33.

Bailer, Stefanie. 2010. "What Factors Determine Bargaining Power and Success in EU Negotiations?" *Journal of European Public Policy*, 17, 5: 743–57.

Baird, Douglas G., Robert H. Gertner and Randal C. Picker. 1994. *Game Theory and the Law*. Cambridge, MA: Harvard University Press.

Baker, James A. 1995. *The Politics of Diplomacy*. New York: Putnam.

Banks, Jeffrey S. 1990. "Equilibrium Behavior in Crisis Bargaining Games." *American Journal of Political Science*, 34, 3: 599–614.

  2013. *Signalling Games in Political Science*. Abingdon, UK: Taylor & Francis.

Barberis, Nicholas C. 2012. "Thirty Years of Prospect Theory in Economics: A Review and Assessment." Working Paper No. 18621. Cambridge, MA: National Bureau of Economic Research.

Barron, Emmanual N. 2013. *Game Theory: An Introduction*. Hoboken, NJ: John Wiley & Sons.

Barry, Bruce. 2008. "Negotiator Affect: The State of the Art (and the Science)." *Group Decision and Negotiation*, 17, 1 (January 1): 97–105.

Barry, Bruce, Ingrid Smithey Fulmer and Gerben A. Van Kleef. 2004. "I Laughed, I Cried, I Settled: The Role of Emotion in Negotiation." In M. J. Gelfand and J. M. Breet, eds., *The Handbook of Negotiation and Culture*, 71–94. Stanford University Press.

Bartos, Otomar J. 1974. *Process and Outcome of Negotiations*. New York: Columbia University Press.

Bazerman, Max H. 1983. "Negotiator Judgment: A Critical Look at the Rationality Assumption." *American Behavioral Scientist*, 27, 2 (November 1): 211–28.

Bazerman, Max H. and Dolly Chugh. 2006. "Bounded Awareness: Focusing Failures in Negotiation." In Leigh L. Thompson, ed., *Negotiation Theory and Research*, 7–26. New York: Psychosocial Press.

Bazerman, Max, Jared Curhan, Don Moore and Kathleen Valley. 2000. "Negotiation." *Annual Review of Psychology*, 51: 279–314.

Bazerman, Max H. and Margaret A. Neale. 1991. "Negotiator Rationality and Negotiator Cognition." In H. Peyton Young, ed., *Negotiation Analysis*, 109–30. Ann Arbor: University of Michigan Press.

  1992. *Negotiating Rationally*. New York: Free Press.

Bearce, David H., Katharine M. Floros and Heather Elko McKibben. 2009. "The Shadow of the Future and International Bargaining: The Occurrence of Bargaining in a Three-Phase Cooperation Framework." *Journal of Politics*, 71, 2 (April 1): 719–32.

Beardsley, Kyle. 2009. "Intervention Without Leverage: Explaining the Prevalence of Weak Mediators." *International Interactions*, 35, 3 (September): 272–97.

Beers, Pieter J., Henny P. A. Boshuizen, Paul A. Kirschner and Wim H. Gijselaers. 2006. "Common Ground, Complex Problems and Decision Making." *Group Decision and Negotiation*, 15, 6 (November 1): 529–56.

Benedick, Richard Elliot. 1991. *Ozone Diplomacy: New Directions in Safeguarding the Planet*. Cambridge, MA: Harvard University Press.

Bercovitch, Jacob. 2014. *Theory and Practice of International Mediation: Selected Essays*. New York: Routledge.

Bergstrom, Theodore C. 2002. "Evolution of Social Behavior: Individual and Group Selection." *Journal of Economic Perspectives*, 16, 2 (Spring): 67–88.

Betzold, Carola. 2010. "Borrowing Power to Influence International Negotiations: AOSIS in the Climate Change Regime, 1990–1997." *Politics*, 30, 3 (October): 131–48.

Bicchieri, Cristina. 1993. *Rationality and Coordination*. Cambridge University Press.

Bildt, Carl. 1998. *Peace Journey: The Struggle for Peace in Bosnia*. London: Weidenfeld and Nicolson.

Binmore, Ken. 1996. "Introduction." In John F. Nash, ed., *Essays on Game Theory*, ix–xx. Cheltenham, UK: Edward Elgar.

2007. *Does Game Theory Work? The Bargaining Challenge*. Cambridge, MA: MIT Press.

Blaker, Michale, 1999. "Japan Negotiates with the United States on Rice." In Peter Bertoni, Hiroshi Kimura and William I. Zartman, eds., *International Negotiation: Actors, Structure/Process, Values*, 33–62. New York: St. Martins Press.

Bolt, Wilko and Harold Houba. 2002. *Credible Threats in Negotiations: A Game-Theoretic Approach*. New York: Springer.

Bolton, Gary E. 1991. "A Comparative Model of Bargaining: Theory and Evidence." *American Economic Review*, 81, 5: 1096–1136.

Borch, Kristian and Fredesvinda Mérida. 2013. "Dialogue in Foresight: Consensus, Conflict and Negotiation." In Kristian Borch, Sandra Dingli and Michael Søgaard Jørgensen, eds., *Participation and Interaction in Foresight: Dialogue, Dissemination and Visions*, 97–117. Cheltenham, UK: Edward Elgar.

Botes, Johannes. 2003. "Conflict Transformation." *International Journal of Peace Studies*, 8, 2 (Winter): 1–27.

Bowles, Samuel and Herbert Gintis. 2009. "Beyond Enlightened Self-Interest: Social Norms, Other-Regarding Preferences, and Cooperative Behavior." In Simon A. Levin, ed., *Games, Groups, and the Global Good*, 57–78. Berlin: Springer.

Brams, Steven. 1990. *Negotiation Games: Applying Game Theory to Bargaining and Arbitration*. New York: Routledge.

1994. *Theory of Moves*. Cambridge University Press.

2011. *Game Theory and Humanities*. Cambridge, MA: MIT Press.

2014. "Mixed Strategies and the Minimax Theorem." Encyclopedia Britannica, www.britannica.com/EBchecked/topic/224893/game-theory/22617/Mixed-strategies-and-the-minimax-theorem.

Brett, Jeanne M. 2000. "Culture and Negotiation." *International Journal of Psychology*, 35, 2: 97–104.

Brochmann, Marit and Paul R. Hensel. 2011. "The Effectiveness of Negotiations over International River Claims." *International Studies Quarterly*, 55, 3 (September 1): 859–82.

Brown, Rupert. 2001. *Group Processes: Dynamics Within and Between Groups*. Oxford: Blackwell.
Bunn, George. 1992. *Arms Control by Committee: Managing Negotiations with the Russians*. Stanford University Press.
Burgerman, Susan D. 2000. "Building the Peace by Mandating Reform: United Nations-Mediated Human Rights Agreements in El Salvador and Guatemala." *Latin American Perspectives*, 27, 3: 63–87.
Butt, Arif Nazir and Jin Nam Choi. 2006. "The Effects of Cognitive Appraisal and Emotion on Social Motive and Negotiation Behavior: The Critical Role of Agency of Negotiator Emotion." *Human Performance*, 19, 4: 305–25.
Camerer, Colin and Ernst Fehr. 2004. "Measuring Social Norms and Preferences Using Experimental Games: A Guide for Social Scientists." In Joseph Patrick Henrich, ed., *Foundations of Human Sociality: Economic Experiments and Ethnographic Evidence from Fifteen Small-Scale Societies*, 55–95. Oxford University Press.
Carment, David and Dane Rowlands. 2007. "Formal Models of Intervention: A Stocktaking and Analysis of the Implications for Policy." In Rudolf Avenhaus and I. W. Zartman, eds., *Diplomacy Games*, 45–68. New York: Springer.
Carmichael, Fiona. 2005. *A Guide to Game Theory*. Harlow, UK: Financial Times Prentice Hall.
Carrell, Michael R. and Christina Heavrin. 2008. *Negotiating Essentials: Theory, Skills, and Practices*. Upper Saddle River, NJ: Pearson/Prentice Hall.
Carter, Jimmy. 1982. *Keeping Faith: Memoirs of a President*. New York: Bantam Books.
   2009. *We Can Have Peace in The Holy Land: A Plan That Will Work*. New York: Simon & Schuster.
Caruso, David R. 2015. "International Negotiation and Emotional Intelligence." In Mauro Galluccio, ed., *Handbook of International Negotiation*, 181–89. New York: Springer.
Charness, Gary, Uri Gneezy and Alex Imas. 2013. "Experimental Methods: Eliciting Risk Preferences." *Journal of Economic Behavior & Organization*, 87: 43–51.
Chasek, Pamela S., David Leonard Downie and Janet Welsh Brown. 2010. *Global Environmental Politics*. 5th edn. Boulder, CO: Westview.
Chatterjee, Kalyan. 2010. "Non-Cooperative Bargaining Theory." In Marc D. Kilgour and Colin Eden, eds., *Handbook of Group Decision and Negotiation*, 141–49. New York: Springer.
   2014. "Game Theory and the Practice of Bargaining." In Kalyan Chatterjee and William Samuelson, eds., *Game Theory and Business Applications*, 189–206. New York: Springer.
Chernick, Marc. 2003. "Colombia: International Involvement in Protracted Peacemaking." In Chandra Lekha Sriram and Karin Wermester, eds., *From Promise to Practice: Strengthening UN Capacities for the Prevention of Violent Conflict*. Boulder, CO: Lynne Rienner.
Chevalier-Roignant, Benoît and Lenos Trigeorgis. 2011. *Competitive Strategy: Options and Games*. Cambridge, MA: Harvard University Press.
Coddington, Alan. 2013. *Theories of the Bargaining Process*. New York: Routledge.
Colman, Andrew M. 2013. *Game Theory and Its Applications: In the Social and Biological Sciences*. Boston: Psychology Press.

Colman, Andrew M. and Lindsay Browning. 2009. "Evolution of Cooperative Turn-Taking." *Evolutionary Ecology Research*, 11: 949–63.

Craver, Charles B. 2012. *Effective Legal Negotiation and Settlement*. 7th edn. New Providence, NJ: LexisNexis.

Cristal, Moty. 2003. "Negotiating Under the Cross: The Story of the Forty-Day Siege of the Church of Nativity." *International Negotiation*, 8, 3 (September): 549–76.

Cross, John G. 1996. "Negotiation as Adaptive Learning." *International Negotiation*, 1, 1 (January 1): 153–78.

Crump, Larry. 2009. *Linkage Theory and the Global-Multilevel System: Multilateral, Regional and Bilateral Trade Negotiations*. Rochester, NY: Social Science Research Network.

Crusius, Jan and Thomas Mussweiler. 2012. "Social Comparison in Negotiation." In Gary E. Bolton and Rachel T. A. Croson, eds., *The Oxford Handbook of Economic Conflict Resolution*, 120–37. Oxford University Press.

Curran, Daniel F. and James K. Sebenius. 2003. "The Mediator as Coalition-Builder: George Mitchell in Northern Ireland." *International Negotiation*, 8, 1: 111–47.

Curşeu, Petru Lucian and Sandra Schruijer. 2008. "The Effects of Framing on Inter-Group Negotiation." *Group Decision and Negotiation*, 17, 4 (July 1): 347–62.

Da Conceicao-Heldt, Eugenia. 2008. "Assessing the Impact of Issue Linkage in the Common Fisheries Policy." *International Negotiation*, 13, 2: 285–300.

Dajani, Omar. 2005. "Surviving Opportunities: Palestinian Negotiating Patterns in Peace Talks with Israel." In Tamara Cofman Wittes, ed., *How Israelis and Palestinians Negotiate: A Cross-Cultural Analysis of the Oslo Peace Process*, 39–80. Washington, DC: United States Institute of Peace Press.

Daoudy, Marwa. 2008. "A Missed Chance for Peace: Israel and Syria's Negotiations over the Golan Heights." *Journal of International Affairs*, 61, 2 (March 22): 215–20.

Davenport, Deborah Saunders. 2006. *Global Environmental Negotiations and US Interests*. New York: Palgrave Macmillan.

de Bruin, Boudewijn. 2010. *Explaining Games: The Epistemic Programme in Game Theory*. New York: Springer.

de Dreu, Carsten K. W. 2010. "Social Conflict: The Emergence and Consequences of Struggle and Negotiation." In Susan T. Fiske, Daniel T. Gilbert and Gardner Lindzey, eds., *Handbook of Social Psychology*. New York: Wiley.

de Dreu, Carsten K. W., Peter J. D. Carnevale, Ben J. M. Emans and Evert Van De Vliert. 1994. "Effects of Gain–Loss Frames in Negotiation: Loss Aversion, Mismatching, and Frame Adoption." *Organizational Behavior and Human Decision Processes*, 60, 1: 90–107.

Deitelhoff, Nicole and Linda Wallbott. 2012. "Beyond Soft Balancing: Small States and Coalition-Building in the ICC and Climate Negotiations." *Cambridge Review of International Affairs*, 25, 3: 345–66.

Destradi, Sandra and Johannes Vüllers. 2012. *The Consequences of Failed Mediation in Civil Wars: Assessing the Sri Lankan Case*. Rochester, NY: Social Science Research Network, August 13.

Dewulf, Art, Barbara Gray, Linda Putnam, Roy Lewicki, Noelle Aarts, Rene Bouwen and Cees van Woerkum. 2009. "Disentangling Approaches to Framing in Conflict and Negotiation

Research: A Meta-Paradigmatic Perspective." *Human Relations*, 62, 2 (February 1): 155–93.

Dimotakis, Nikolaos, Donald E. Conlon, and Remus Ilies. 2012. "The Mind and Heart (Literally) of the Negotiator: Personality and Contextual Determinants of Experiential Reactions and Economic Outcomes in Negotiation." *Journal of Applied Psychology*, 97, 1: 000–00.

Dixit, Avinash K. and Susan Skeath. 2004. *Games of Strategy*. 2nd edn. New York: W. W. Norton.

Dobbs, Michael. 2008. *One Minute to Midnight: Kennedy, Khrushchev, and Castro on the Brink of Nuclear War*. New York: Alfred A. Knopf.

Donohue, William A. 2004. "Critical Moments as Flow in Negotiation." *Negotiation Journal*, 20, 2: 147–52.

Dowd, E. Thomas and Angela N. Roberts Miller. 2011. "Tacit Knowledge Structures in the Negotiation Process." In Francesco Aquilar and Mauro Galluccio, eds., *Psychological and Political Strategies for Peace Negotiation*, 75–85. New York: Springer.

Drahos, Peter. 2003. "When the Weak Bargain with the Strong: Negotiations in the World Trade Organization." *International Negotiation*, 8, 1: 79–109.

Druckman, Daniel. 2011. "Negotiation and Mediation." In James N. Druckman, Donald P. Green, James H. Kuklinski and Arthur Lupia, eds., *The Cambridge Handbook of Experimental Political Science*, 413–29. New York: Cambridge University Press.

2013. "Social Psychology and International Negotiations: Processes and Influences." In Robert F. Kidd and Michael J. Saks, eds., *Advances in Applied Social Psychology*, 52–82. Boston: Psychology Press.

du Toit, Pierre. 2003. "Rules and Procedures for Negotiated Peacemaking." In John Darby and Roger Mac Ginty, eds., *Contemporary Peacemaking: Conflict, Violence, and Peace Processes*, 65–76. New York: Palgrave.

Dupont, Christophe and Guy Olivier Faure. 2002. "The Negotiation Process." In Viktor Aleksandrovich Kremenyuk, ed., *International Negotiation: Analysis, Approaches, Issues*, 39–63. 2nd edn. San Francisco: Jossey-Bass.

Earnest, David C. 2008. "Coordination in Large Numbers: An Agent-Based Model of International Negotiations." *International Studies Quarterly*, 52, 2: 363–82.

Easley, David and Jon Kleinberg. 2010. *Networks, Crowds, and Markets*. Cambridge University Press.

Edgar, David. 2001. *The Prisoner's Dilemma*. London: Nick Hern Books.

Elfenbein, Hillary Anger. 2013. "Individual Differences in Negotiation." In Mara Olekalns and Wendi L. Adair, eds., *Handbook of Research on Negotiation*, 00–00. Cheltenham, UK: Edward Elgar.

Farhana, Yamin. 2014. "The Use of Joint Implementation to Increase Compliance with the Climate Change Convention." In Jacob Werksman, James Cameron and Peter Roderick, eds., *Improving Compliance with International Environmental Law*, 229–46. New York: Routledge.

Faure, Guy. 1989. "The Mediators as Third Negotiators." In E. Mautner-Markhof, ed., *Process of International Negotiation*, 415–26. Boulder, CO: Westview.

    2002. "International Negotiation: The Cultural Dimension." In Viktor Aleksandrovich Kremenyuk, ed., *International Negotiation: Analysis, Approaches, Issues*, 392–415. 2nd edn. San Francisco: Jossey-Bass.

    2003. "Negotiating with Terrorists: The Hostage Case." *International Negotiation*, 8, 3: 469–94.

Fearon, James D. 1995. "Rationalist Explanations for War." *International Organization*, 49, 3 (Summer): 379–414.

    1997. "Signaling Foreign Policy Interests." *Journal of Conflict Resolution*, 41, 1 (February): 68–91.

    1998. "Bargaining, Enforcement, and International Cooperation." *International Organization*, 52, 2: 269–305.

Fey, Mark and Kristopher W. Ramsay. 2010. "When Is Shuttle Diplomacy Worth the Commute? Information Sharing Through Mediation." *World Politics*, 62, 4: 529–60.

Filson, Darren and Suzanne Werner. 2007. "The Dynamics of Bargaining and War." *International Interactions*, 33, 1 (January): 31–50.

Filzmoser, Michael and Rudolf Vetschera. 2008. "A Classification of Bargaining Steps and Their Impact on Negotiation Outcomes." *Group Decision and Negotiation*, 17, 5 (September 1): 421–43.

Findlay, Scott D. and Paul Thagard. 2011. "Emotional Change in International Negotiation: Analyzing the Camp David Accords Using Cognitive-Affective Maps." *Group Decision and Negotiation*, 23: 1–20.

Fisher, Roger, Andrea Kupfer Schneider, Elizabeth Borgwardt and Brian Ganson. 1997. *Coping with International Conflict: A Systematic Approach to Influence in International Negotiation*. Englewood Cliffs, NJ: Prentice Hall.

Fisher, Roger and William Ury. 1981. *Getting to Yes*. Boston: Houghton-Mifflin.

Fromm, Delee. 2008. "Emotion in Negotiation." In Colleen M. Hanycz, Trevor C. W. Farrow and Frederick H. Zemans, eds., *The Theory and Practice of Representative Negotiation*. Toronto: Emond Montgomery.

Fudenberg, Drew and David Levine. 1983. "Subgame-Perfect Equilibria of Finite- and Infinite-Horizon Games." *Journal of Economic Theory*, 31, 2: 251–68.

Galinsky, A., Debra Gilin and William W. Maddux. 2011. "Using Both Your Head and Your Heart: The Role of Perspective Taking and Empathy in Resolving Social Conflict." In Joseph P. Forgas, Arie W. Kruglanski and Kipling D. Williams, eds., *The Psychology of Social Conflict and Aggression*, 103–18. Boston: Psychology Press.

Galinsky, Adam D., Vanessa L. Seiden, Peter H. Kim and Victoria Husted Medvec. 2002. "The Dissatisfaction of Having Your First Offer Accepted: The Role of Counterfactual Thinking in Negotiations." *Personality and Social Psychology Bulletin*, 28, 2: 271–83.

Gettinger, Johannes, Sabine T. Koeszegi and Mareike Schoop. 2012. "Shall We Dance? The Effect of Information Presentations on Negotiation Processes and Outcomes." *Decision Support Systems*, 53, 1 (April): 161–74.

Gimpel, Henner. 2007. *Preferences in Negotiations: The Attachment Effect*. New York: Springer.

Gintis, Herbert. 2009. *Game Theory Evolving: A Problem-Centered Introduction to Modeling Strategic Interaction*. 2nd edn. Princeton University Press.

Goltsman, Maria, Johannes Hörner, Gregory Pavlov and Francesco Squintani. 2009. "Mediation, Arbitration and Negotiation." *Journal of Economic Theory*, 144, 4: 1397–1420.
Government of El Salvador and Frente Farabundo Martí para la Liberación Nacional. 1991. "Economic and Social Development: Chapultepec Peace Agreement." New York, September 25, https://peaceaccords.nd.edu/provision/economic-and-social-development-chapultepec-peace-agreement.
Gregory, Rose and George Paleokrassis. 2014. "Compliance with International Environmental Obligations: A Case Study of the International Whaling Commission." In Jacob Werksman, James Cameron and Peter Roderick, eds., *Improving Compliance with International Environmental Law*, 147–74. New York: Routledge.
Grobe, Christian. 2010. "The Power of Words: Argumentative Persuasion in International Negotiations." *European Journal of International Relations*, 16, 1: 5–29.
Grundig, Frank. 2009. "Political Strategy and Climate Policy: A Rational Choice Perspective." *Environmental Politics*, 18, 5: 747–64.
Grüne-Yanoff, Till. 2008. "Game Theory." *Internet Encyclopedia of Philosophy*, May 25, www.iep.utm.edu/game-th/.
Grüne-Yanoff, Till and Paul Schweinzer. 2008. "The Roles of Stories in Applying Game Theory." *Journal of Economic Methodology*, 15, 2 (June): 131–46.
Guelke, Adrian. 2003. "Negotiations and Peace Processes." In John Darby and Roger Mac Ginty, eds., *Contemporary Peacemaking*, 53–64. New York: Palgrave.
Gulliver, Phillip H. 1979. *Disputes and Negotiations: A Cross-Cultural Perspective*. New York: Academic Press.
Guthrie, Chris and David F. Sally. 2004. "The Impact of the Impact Bias on Negotiation." *Marquette Law Review*, 87, 4: 817–28.
Habeeb, William Mark. 1988. *Power and Tactics in International Negotiation: How Weak Nations Bargain with Strong Nations*. Baltimore: Johns Hopkins University Press.
Hall, Edward T. 1976. *Beyond Culture*. Garden City, NY: Anchor.
Hampson, Fen Osler. 1995. *Multilateral Negotiations: Lessons from Arms Control, Trade, and the Environment*. Baltimore: Johns Hopkins University Press.
Hardin, Garrett. 1968. "The Tragedy of the Commons." *Science*, 162, 3859: 1243–48.
Harinck, Fieke and Carsten K. W. de Dreu. 2004. "Negotiating Interests or Values and Reaching Integrative Agreements: The Importance of Time Pressure and Temporary Impasses." *European Journal of Social Psychology*, 34, 5: 595–611.
Harinck, Fieke and Naomi Ellemers. 2006. "Hide and Seek: The Effects of Revealing One's Personal Interests in Intra- and Intergroup Negotiations." *European Journal of Social Psychology*, 36, 6: 791–813.
Harsanyi, John C. 1967. "Games with Incomplete Information Played by 'Bayesian' Players, I–III. Part I. The Basic Model." *Management Science*, 14, 3 (November 1): 159–82.
Harsanyi, John C. and R. Selten. 1988. *A General Theory of Equilibrium Selection in Games*. Cambridge, MA: MIT Press.
Hart, Sergiu. 1985. "Axiomatic Approaches to Coalitional Bargaining." In Alvin E. Roth, ed., *Game-Theoretic Models of Bargaining*, 305–20. Cambridge University Press.

Haslam, Jonathan and Theresa Osborne. 1987. *SALT I: The Limitations of Arms Negotiations*. Washington, DC: School of Advanced International Studies. Foreign Policy Institute.

Heap, Shaun Hargreaves and Yanis Varoufakis. 2004. *Game Theory: A Critical Text*. London: Routledge.

Hermann, Margaret G. and Nathan Kogan. 1977. "Personality and Negotiating Behavior." In Daniel Druckman, ed., *Negotiations: Social-Psychological Perspectives*, 247–74. Beverly Hills, CA: Sage.

Hoffmann, Matthew J. 2005. *Ozone Depletion and Climate Change: Constructing a Global Response*. Albany: State University of New York Press.

Holbrooke, Richard C. 1999. *To End a War*. New York: Modern Library.

Hollander-Blumoff, Rebecca and Tom R. Tyler. 2008. "Procedural Justice in Negotiation: Procedural Fairness, Outcome Acceptance, and Integrative Potential." *Law & Social Inquiry*, 33, 2: 473–500.

Holmes, Michael. 1992. "Phase Structures in Negotiation." In Linda Putnam and Michael E. Roloff, eds., *Communication and Negotiation*, 83–105. London: Sage Publications.

Hopmann, P. Terrence. 1996. *The Negotiation Process and the Resolution of International Conflicts*. Columbia: University of South Carolina Press.

　1995. "Two Paradigms of Negotiation: Bargaining and Problem Solving." *Annals of the American Academy of Political and Social Science*, 542 (November 1): 24–47.

Hopmann, P. Terrence and Theresa C. Smith. 1977. "An Application of a Richardson Process Model: Soviet–American Interactions in the Test Ban Negotiations 1962–1963." *Journal of Conflict Resolution*, 21, 4 (December 1): 701–26.

Horne, Alistair. 1989. *Macmillan, 1957–1986*. London: Macmillan.

Hörner, Johannes, Massimo Morelli and Francesco Squintani. 2010. *Mediation and Peace*. Discussion Paper. Cowles Foundation for Research in Economics, Yale University.

Hovi, Jon. 1998. *Games, Threats, and Treaties: Understanding Commitments in International Relations*. London: Pinter.

Iklé, Fred Charles. 1964. *How Nations Negotiate*. New York: Harper & Row.

Janis, Irving L. 1982. *Groupthink: Psychological Studies of Policy Decisions and Fiascoes*. 2nd edn. Boston: Cengage Learning.

Jarque, Xavier, Clara Ponsati and Jozsef Sakovics. 2003. "Mediation: Incomplete Information Bargaining with Filtered Communication." *Journal of Mathematical Economics*, 39, 7: 803–30.

Jensen, Lloyd. 1988. *Bargaining for National Security: The Postwar Disarmament Negotiations*. Columbia: University of South Carolina Press.

Jeong, Ho-Won. 2005. *Peacebuilding in Postconflict Societies: Strategy and Process*. Boulder, CO: Lynne Rienner.

　2008. *Understanding Conflict and Conflict Analysis*. London: Sage.

　2009. *Conflict Management and Resolution*. Abingdon, UK: Routledge.

Jervis, Robert. 1976. *Perception and Misperception in International Politics*. Princeton University Press.

Johnstone, Naomi and Isak Svensson. 2013. "Belligerents and Believers: Exploring Faith-Based Mediation in Internal Armed Conflicts." *Politics, Religion & Ideology*, 14, 4: 557–79.

Jonas, Susanne. 2000. *Of Centaurs and Doves: Guatemala's Peace Process*. Boulder, CO: Westview Press.

Jönsson, Christer. 2012. "Psychological Causes of Incomplete Negotiations." In Guy Olivier Faure, ed., *Unfinished Business: Why International Negotiations Fail*, 167–84. Athens: University of Georgia Press.

Kahn, Herman and Thomas Schelling. 2009. *On Escalation: Metaphors and Scenarios*. New Brunswick, NJ: Transaction.

Kahneman, Daniel. 2003. "Maps of Bounded Rationality: Psychology for Behavioral Economics." *American Economic Review*, 93, 5 (December): 1449–75.

Kahneman, Daniel and Amos Tversky. 1979. "Prospect Theory: An Analysis of Decision Under Risk." *Econometrica*, 47, 2: 263–91.

Karl, Terry Lynn. 1992. "El Salvador's Negotiation Revolution." *Foreign Affairs*, 71, 2: 147–64.

Keeney, Ralph and Howard, Raiffa. 1991. "Structuring and Analyzing Values for Multiple-Issue Negotiations." In H. Reyton Yang, ed., *Negotiation Analysis*, 131–52. Ann Arbor: University of Michigan Press.

Khadiagala, Gilbert M. 2007. *Meddlers or Mediators? African Interveners in Civil Conflicts in Eastern Africa*. Boston: Martinus Nijhoff.

Kibris, Özgür. 2010. "Cooperative Game Theory Approaches to Negotiation." In Marc D. Kilgour and Colin Eden, eds., *Handbook of Group Decision and Negotiation*, 151–66. New York: Springer.

Kierkegaard, Søren. 1843. "Journals IV A 164," www.naturalthinker.net/trl/texts/Kierkegaard, Soren/JournPapers/.

Kilian, Bertil and Ole Elgström. 2010. "Still a Green Leader? The European Union's Role in International Climate Negotiations." *Cooperation and Conflict*, 45, 3 (September 1): 255–73.

Kissinger, Henry. 1979. *White House Years*. New York: Little, Brown and Company.

Klamler, Christian. 2010. "Fair Division." In Marc D. Kilgour and Colin Eden, eds., *Handbook of Group Decision and Negotiation*, 183–202. New York: Springer.

Klieman, Aharon. 2005. "Israeli Negotiation Culture." In Tamara Cofman Wittes, ed., *How Israelis and Palestinians Negotiate: A Cross-Cultural Analysis of the Oslo Peace Process*, 81–132. Washington, DC: US Institute of Peace Press.

Kline, Harvey F. 2007. *Chronicle of a Failure Foretold: The Peace Process of Colombian President Andrés Pastrana*. Tuscaloosa: University of Alabama Press.

Kopelman, Shirli, Leigh Thompson and Ashleigh Shelby Rosette. 2006. "The Three Faces of Eve: Strategic Displays of Positive, Negative, and Neutral Emotions in Negotiations." *Organizational Behavior and Human Decision Processes*, 99, 1: 81–101.

Korobkin, Russell B. and Chris Guthrie. 2004. "Heuristics and Biases at the Bargaining Table." *Marquette Law Review*, 87: 795–808.

Kotzian, Peter. 2007. "Arguing and Bargaining in International Negotiations: On the Application of the Frame-Selection Model and Its Implications." *International Political Science Review*, 28, 1: 79–99.

Kray, Laura J., Jochen Reb, Adam D. Galinsky and Leigh Thompson. 2004. "Stereotype Reactance at the Bargaining Table: The Effect of Stereotype Activation and Power on

Claiming and Creating Value." *Personality and Social Psychology Bulletin*, 30, 4: 399–411.

Kristensen, Henrik and Tommy Gärling. 2000. "Anchor Points, Reference Points, and Counteroffers in Negotiations." *Group Decision and Negotiation*, 9, 6: 493–505.

Kruglanski, Arie W. and Anna Sheveland. 2012. "The Role of Epistemic Motivations in Knowledge Formation." In Shulamith Kreitler, ed., *Cognition and Motivation: Forging an Interdisciplinary Perspective*. Cambridge University Press.

Kuhn, Steven. 2007. "Prisoner's Dilemma." In Edward N. Zalta, ed., *The Stanford Encyclopedia of Philosophy*, Spring, plato.stanford.edu/entries/prisoner-dilemma/.

Kydd, Andrew. 2010. "Rationalist Approaches to Conflict Prevention and Resolution." *Annual Review of Political Science*, 13: 101–21.

 2003. "Which Side Are You On? Bias, Credibility, and Mediation." *American Journal of Political Science*, 47, 4: 597–611.

Lanz, David and Rachel Gasser. 2013. "A Crowded Field: Competition and Coordination in International Peace Mediation." Research Paper. University of Pretoria.

Lax, David A. and James K. Sebenius. 1991. "Thinking Coalitionally." In H. Peyton Young, ed., *Negotiation Analysis*, 153–94. Ann Arbor: University of Michigan Press.

Lepard, Brian D. 2010. *Customary International Law: A New Theory with Practical Applications*. Cambridge University Press.

Levenotoglu, Bahar and Ahmer Tarar. 2005. "Prenegotiation Public Commitment in Domestic and International Bargaining." *American Political Science Review*, 99, 3: 419–33.

Levin, Jonathan. 2002. "Bargaining and Repeated Games." Stanford University, www.stanford.edu/~jdlevin/Econ%20203/RepeatedGames.pdf.

Levy, Jack S. 2000. "Loss Aversion, Framing Effects and International Conflict: Perspectives from Prospect Theory." In Manus I. Midlarsky, ed., *Handbook of War Studies*, 193–221. Ann Arbor: University of Michigan Press.

Lewicki, Roy J., David M. Saunders and John W. Minton. 2007. *Essentials of Negotiation*. 4th edn. Boston: Irwin/McGraw-Hill.

Lewis, Michael. 2003. *Operations Management: Critical Perspectives on Business and Management*. Abingdon, UK: Taylor & Francis.

Lipman, Barton L. 1986. "Cooperation Among Egoists in Prisoners' Dilemma and Chicken Games." *Public Choice*, 51, 3: 315–31.

Lister, Graham and Kelley Lee. 2013. "The Process and Practice of Negotiation." In Ilona Kickbusch, Graham Lister, Michaela Told and Nick Drager, eds., *Global Health Diplomacy*, 73–86. New York: Springer.

Luce, R. Duncan and Howard Raiffa. 1957. *Games and Decisions: Introduction and Critical Survey*. New York: Wiley.

Ma'oz, Ifat, Andrew Ward, Michael Katz and Lee Ross. 2002. "Reactive Devaluation of an 'Israeli' vs. 'Palestinian' Peace Proposal." *Journal of Conflict Resolution*, 46, 4: 515–46.

March, James. 1988. "Bounded Rationality, Ambiguity and the Engineering of Choice." In David Bell, Howard Raiffa and Amos Tversky, eds., *Decision Making: Descriptive, Normative and Prescriptive Interactions*, 33–57. Cambridge University Press.

Martinovski, Bilyana. 2010. "Emotion in Negotiation." In Marc D. Kilgour and Colin Eden, eds., *Handbook of Group Decision and Negotiation*, 65–86. New York: Springer.

REFERENCES

Mauleon, Ana and Vincent Vannetelbosch. 2013. "Relative Concerns and Delays in Bargaining with Private Information." *Games*, 4, 3 (June 27): 329–38.

Maundi, Mohammed Omar. 2003. "Preventing Conflict Escalation in Burundi." In Chandra Lekha Sriram and Karin Wermester, eds., *From Promise to Practice: Strengthening UN Capacities for the Prevention of Violent Conflict*, 327–48. Boulder, CO: Lynne Rienner.

Mayer, Frederick W. 1992. "Managing Domestic Differences in International Negotiations: The Strategic Use of Internal Side-Payments." *International Organization*, 46, 4: 793–818.

McAdams, Richard H. 2008. "Beyond the Prisoners' Dilemma: Coordination, Game Theory, and Law." Working paper, University of Chicago, www.law.uchicago.edu/Lawecon/index.html.

McCain, Roger A. 2004. *Game Theory: A Non-Technical Introduction to the Analysis of Strategy*. Mason, OH: Thomson/South-Western.
  2010. *Game Theory: A Non-Technical Introduction to the Analysis of Strategy*, 2nd edn. Singapore: World Scientific.

McCarty, Nolan M. and Adam Meirowitz. 2007. *Political Game Theory: An Introduction*. New York: Cambridge University Press.

McGinn, Kathleen. 2006. "Relationships and Negotiations in Context." In Leigh L. Thompson, ed., *Negotiation Theory and Research*, 129–44. New York: Psychology Press.

McLean, Elena V. and Randall W. Stone. 2012. "The Kyoto Protocol: Two-Level Bargaining and European Integration." *International Studies Quarterly*, 56, 1 (March 1): 99–113.

Meerts, Paul. 2006. "Entrapment in International Negotiation." In William I. Zartman and Guy Olivier Faure, eds., *Escalation and Negotiation in International Conflicts*, 111–40. Cambridge University Press.
  2011. "Boundaries in Bargaining: A Multidimensional View." *Group Decision and Negotiation*, 20, 2: 155–64.

Messing, Barbara. 2000. "El Salvador." In Melanie C. Greenberg, John H. Barton and Margaret E. McGuinness, eds., *Words Over War: Mediation and Arbitration to Prevent Deadly Conflict*, 161–81. Lanham, MD: Rowman & Littlefield.

Miller, David A. and Joel Watson. 2013. "A Theory of Disagreement in Repeated Games with Bargaining." *Econometrica*, 81, 6: 2303–50.

Mitchell, Christopher. 2003. "Mediation and the Ending of Conflicts." In John Darby and Roger Mac Ginty, eds., *Contemporary Peacemaking*, 77–86. New York: Palgrave.

Moehler, Michael. 2010. "The (Stabilized) Nash Bargaining Solution as a Principle of Distributive Justice." *Utilitas*, 22, 4: 447–73.

Moermond, Kim Ian and Jack L. Snyder. 1994. *The Second Berlin Crisis, 1958–1959*. Washington, DC: Georgetown University Press.

Morrow, James D. 1994. *Game Theory for Political Scientists*. Princeton University Press.
  2000. "The Ongoing Game-Theoretic Revolution." In Manus I. Midlarsky, ed., *Handbook of War Studies II*. Ann Arbor: University of Michigan Press.

Mühlen, Alexander. 2010. *International Negotiations: Confrontation, Competition, Cooperation: With Many Intercultural Facts and Case Studies*. Berlin: Lit Verlag.

Müller, Harald. 2004. "Arguing, Bargaining and All That: Communicative Action, Rationalist Theory and the Logic of Appropriateness in International Relations." *European Journal of International Relations*, 10, 3 (September 1): 395–435.

Murnighan, John Keith. 1991. *The Dynamics of Bargaining Games*. Englewood Cliffs, NJ: Prentice Hall.

Muthoo, Abhinay 1995a. "Bargaining in a Long-Term Relationship with Endogenous Termination." *Journal of Economic Theory*, 66, 2: 590–98.

1995b. "On the Strategic Role of Outside Options in Bilateral Bargaining." *Operations Research*, 43, 2: 292–97.

1999. *Bargaining Theory with Applications*. Cambridge University Press.

2000. "A Non-Technical Introduction to Bargaining Theory." *World Economics*, 1, 2 (June): 145–66.

Myerson, Roger B. 1991. "Analysis of Incentives in Bargaining and Mediation." In H. Peyton Young, ed., *Negotiation Analysis*, 67–86. Ann Arbor: University of Michigan Press.

Naquin, Charles E. 2003. "The Agony of Opportunity in Negotiation: Number of Negotiable Issues, Counterfactual Thinking, and Feelings of Satisfaction." *Organizational Behavior and Human Decision Processes*, 91, 1: 97–107.

Narlikar, Amrita and John S. Odell. 2006. "The Strict Distributive Strategy for a Bargaining Coalition: The Like Minded Group in the World Trade Organization, 1998–2001." In John S. Odell, ed., *Negotiating Trade: Developing Countries in the WTO and NAFTA*, 115–44. Cambridge University Press.

Nash, John F. 1950. "The Bargaining Problem." *Econometrica*, 18, 2 (April 1): 155–62.

1953. "Two-Person Cooperative Games." *Econometrica*, 21, 1 (January 1): 128–40.

Naylor, Phillip Chiviges. 2000. *France and Algeria: A History of Decolonization and Transformation*. Gainesville: University Press of Florida.

Neale, Margaret A. and Alison R. Fragale. 2006. "Social Cognition, Attribution, and Perception in Negotiation." In Leigh Thompson, ed., *Negotiation Theory and Research*, 27–54. New York: Psychology Press.

Neale, Margaret A. and Max H. Bazerman. 1991. *Cognition and Rationality in Negotiation*. New York and Toronto: Free Press.

Neill, Daniel B. 2003. "Cooperation and Coordination in the Turn-Taking Dilemma." In Moshe Tennenholtz, ed., *Proceedings of the 9th Conference on Theoretical Aspects of Rationality and Knowledge*, 231–44. New York: ACM.

Neumayer, Eric. 2011. "Strategic Delaying and Concessions Extraction in Accession Negotiations to the World Trade Organization." Working Paper. London School of Economics.

Novemsky, Nathan and Maurice E. Schweitzer. 2004. "What Makes Negotiators Happy? The Differential Effects of Internal and External Social Comparisons on Negotiator Satisfaction." *Organizational Behavior and Human Decision Processes*, 95, 2: 186–97.

Nowak, Martin A. and Karl Sigmund. 1994. "The Alternating Prisoner's Dilemma." *Journal of Theoretical Biology*, 168: 219–26.

O'Neill, Barry. 1991. "Conflictual Moves in Bargaining: Warnings, Threats, Escalations, and Ultimatums." In H. Peyton Young, ed., *Negotiation Analysis*, 87–108. Ann Arbor: University of Michigan Press.

1994. "Sources in Game Theory for International Relations Specialists." In Michael Intriligator and Urs Luterbacher, eds., *Cooperative Models in International Relations Research*, 9–30. Boston: Kluwer.

1999. *Honor, Symbols, and War*. Ann Arbor: University of Michigan Press.
2006. "What Can a Powerless Mediator Do for Strategic Negotiators?" Paper presented at Chicago American Political Science Association, 2004, revised version.
2007. "Game Models of Peace and War." In Rudolf Avenhaus and I. W. Zartman, eds., *Diplomacy Games*, 24–44. New York: Springer.
Odell, John S. 2000. *Negotiating the World Economy*. Ithaca, NY: Cornell University Press.
2002. "Creating Data on International Negotiation Strategies, Alternatives, and Outcomes." *International Negotiation*, 7: 39–52.
2010. "Negotiating from Weakness in International Trade Relations." *Journal of World Trade*, 44, 3 (June): 545–66.
2012. "Negotiation and Bargaining." In Walter Carlsnaes, Thomas Risse and Beth A. Simmons, eds., *Handbook of International Relations*, 2, 379–400. London: Sage.
Odell, John S. and Susan K. Sell. 2006. "Reframing the Issue: The WTO Coalition on Intellectual Property and Public Health, 2001." In John S. Odell, ed., *Negotiating Trade: Developing Countries in the WTO and NAFTA*. Cambridge University Press.
Odell, John S. and Dustin Tingley. 2013. "Negotiating Agreements in International Relations." In Jane Mansbridge and Cathie Jo Martin, eds., *Negotiating Agreement in Politics*, 144–82. Washington, DC: American Political Science Association.
Olekalns, Mara, Jeanne M. Brett and Laurie R. Weingart. 2003. "Phases, Transitions and Interruptions: Modelling Process in Multi-Party Negotiations." *International Journal of Conflict Management*, 14, 3/4 (December 31): 191–211.
Oliva, Terence A., Michael H. Peters and H. S. K. Murthy. 1981. "A Preliminary Empirical Test of a Cusp Catastrophe Model in the Social Sciences." *Behavioral Science*, 26, 2: 153–62.
Osborne, Martin J. 2004. *An Introduction to Game Theory*. New York: Oxford University Press.
Oye, Kenneth A. 1985. "Explaining Cooperation Under Anarchy: Hypotheses and Strategies." *World Politics*, 38, 1 (October): 1–24.
Pacheco, Jorge M. et al. 2011. "Evolutionary Dynamics of Collective Action." In Fabio Chalub and José Francisco Rodrigues, eds., *The Mathematics of Darwin's Legacy*, 119–38. Basel: Springer.
Panke, Diana. 2012. "Dwarfs in International Negotiations: How Small States Make Their Voices Heard." *Cambridge Review of International Affairs*, 25, 3: 313–28.
Perea, Andrés. 2012. *Epistemic Game Theory: Reasoning and Choice*. Cambridge University Press.
Piburn, Sidney, ed. 1993. *The Dalai Lama, a Policy of Kindness: An Anthology of Writings by and about the Dalai Lama*. Ithaca, NY: Snow Lion Publications.
Pillar, Paul R. 1983. *Negotiating Peace: War Termination as a Bargaining Process*. Princeton University Press.
Pillutla, Madan M. and J. Keith Murnighan. 2003. "Fairness in Bargaining." *Social Justice Research*, 16, 3 (September 1): 241–62.
Pinfari, Marco. 2011. "Time to Agree: Is Time Pressure Good for Peace Negotiations?" *Journal of Conflict Resolution*, 55, 5 (October 1): 683–709.
Porter, Roger B. 1984. *The US–USSR Grain Agreement*. Cambridge University Press.
Poundstone, William. 1992. *Prisoner's Dilemma*. New York: Doubleday.

Powell, Robert 1990. *Nuclear Deterrence Theory: The Search for Credibility*. Cambridge University Press.
   1999. *In the Shadow of Power: States and Strategies in International Politics*. Princeton University Press.
   2002. "Bargaining Theory and International Conflict." *Annual Review of Political Science*, 5, 1: 1–30.
   2006. "War as a Commitment Problem." *International Organization*, 60 (Winter): 169–203.
Princen, Thomas. 1992. *Intermediaries in International Conflict*. Princeton University Press.
Pruitt, Dean G. 1981. *Negotiation Behavior*. New York: Academic Press.
Putnam, Linda L. 2010. "Communication as Changing the Negotiation Game." *Journal of Applied Communication Research*, 38, 4: 325–35.
Putnam, Robert D. 1988. "Diplomacy and Domestic Politics: The Logic of Two-Level Games." *International Organization*, 42, 3 (July 1): 427–60.
Quandt, William B. 1986. *Camp David: Peacemaking and Politics*. Washington, DC: Brookings Institution Press.
Raiffa, Howard. 1982. *The Art and Science of Negotiation*. Cambridge, MA: Harvard University Press.
Raiffa, Howard with John Richardson and David Metcalfe. 2002. *Negotiation Analysis: The Science and Art of Collaborative Decision Making*. Cambridge, MA: Harvard University Press.
Rapoport, Anatol. 1966. *Two-Person Game Theory: The Essential Ideas*. Ann Arbor: University of Michigan Press.
   1974. *Fights, Games, and Debates*. Ann Arbor: University of Michigan Press.
Rapoport, Anatol and Albert M. Chammah. 1965. *Prisoner's Dilemma: A Study in Conflict and Cooperation*. Ann Arbor: University of Michigan Press.
Rasmusen, Eric. 2001. *Games and Information: An Introduction to Game Theory*. Malden, MA: Blackwell.
Rauchhaus, Robert W. 2006. "Asymmetric Information, Mediation, and Conflict Management." *World Politics*, 58, 2: 207–41.
Ready, Kathryn J., and Mussie T. Tessema. 2011. "Perceptions and Strategies in the Negotiation Process: A Cross-Cultural Examination of USA, Vietnam and Malaysia." *International Journal of Business and Globalisation*, 6, 2 (January 1): 198–216.
Reb, Jochen. 2010. "The Influence of Past Negotiations on Negotiation Counterpart Preferences." *Group Decision and Negotiation*, 19, 5 (September 1): 457–77.
Richarte, Marie-Pierre. 2005. "Cyprus." In I. William Zartman and Viktor Aleksandrovich Kremenyuk, eds., *Peace Versus Justice: Negotiating Forward- and Backward-Looking Outcomes*, 201–19. Lanham, MD: Rowman & Littlefield.
Risse, Mathias. 2000. "What Is Rational about Nash Equilibria?" *Synthese*, 124, 3: 361–84.
Roett, Riordan and Frank Smyth. 1988. *Dialogue and Armed Conflict: Negotiating the Civil War in El Salvador*. Washington, DC: Johns Hopkins University Press.
Rolland, Sonia E. 2010. "Redesigning the Negotiation Process at the WTO." *Journal of International Economic Law*, 13, 1 (March 1): 65–110.

Ross, Don. 2014. "Game Theory." In Edward N. Zalta, ed., *The Stanford Encyclopedia of Philosophy* (Winter 2014 edn.), plato.stanford.edu/archives/win2014/entries/game-theory.

Rubinstein, Ariel. 1982. "Perfect Equilibrium in a Bargaining Model." *Econometrica*, 50, 1 (January 1): 97–109.

Savun, Burcu. 2008. "Information, Bias, and Mediation Success." *International Studies Quarterly*, 52, 1 (March): 25–47.

Schelling, Thomas C. 1960. *The Strategy of Conflict*. Cambridge, MA: Harvard University Press.

Sebenius, James K. 1983. "Negotiation Arithmetic: Adding and Subtracting Issues and Parties." *International Organization*, 37, 2: 281–316.

  1984. *Negotiating the Law of the Sea*. Cambridge, MA: Harvard University Press.

  2002. "International Negotiation Analysis." in Viktor Aleksandrovich Kremenyuk, ed., *International Negotiation: Analysis, Approaches, Issues*, 229–55. 2nd edn. San Francisco: Jossey-Bass.

  2009. "Negotiation Analysis: From Games to Inferences to Decisions to Deals." *Negotiation Journal*, 25, 4: 449–65.

Sell, Susan K. 2002. "Trips and the Access to Medicines Campaign." *Wisconsin International Law Journal*, 20: 481–522.

Selten, Reinhard. 1975. "Re-examination of the Perfectness Concept for Equilibrium Points in Extensive Games." *International Journal of Game Theory*, 4: 22–55.

Sharma, Sudeep, William P. Bottom and Hillary Anger Elfenbein. 2013. "On the Role of Personality, Cognitive Ability, and Emotional Intelligence in Predicting Negotiation Outcomes: A Meta-analysis." *Organizational Psychology Review*, 3, 4: 293–336.

Shell, G. Richard. 2006. *Bargaining for Advantage: Negotiation Strategies for Reasonable People*. New York: Penguin.

Sher, Gilead. 2006. *The Israeli–Palestinian Peace Negotiations, 1999–2001*. Oxford: Routledge.

Simon, Herbert. 1988. "Rationality as Process and as Product of Thought." In David Bell and Howard Raiffa, eds., *Decision Making: Descriptive, Normative and Prescriptive Interactions*, 58–77. Cambridge University Press.

Simonelli, Nicole M. 2011. "Bargaining over International Multilateral Agreements: The Duration of Negotiations." *International Interactions*, 37, 2 (June): 147–69.

Singh, J. P. 2006. "The Evolution of National Interests: New Issues and North–South Negotiations During the Uruguay Round." In John S. Odell, ed., *Negotiating Trade: Developing Countries in the WTO and NAFTA*, 41–84. Cambridge University Press.

Skyrms, Brian. 2004. *The Stag Hunt and the Evolution of Social Structure*. Cambridge University Press.

Slantchev, Branislav L. 2003. "The Principle of Convergence in Wartime Negotiations." *American Political Science Review*, 97, 4 (November 1): 621–32.

Sloss, Leon. 1986. "Lessons Learned in Negotiationing with the Soviet Union: Introduction and Findings." In Leon Sloss and Scott M. Davis, eds., *A Game for High Stakes*, 1–20. Cambridge, MA: Ballinger.

Smith, Gerard C. 1985. *Double Talk: The Story of SALT I. Reprint*. Lanham, MD: University Press of America.

Sobel, Jordan H. 2005. "Backward Induction Without Tears?" In Daniel Vanderveken, ed., *Logic, Thought and Action*, 433–61. Dordrecht: Springer.

Stahl, Ingolf. 1972. *Bargaining Theory*. Stockholm: Economic Research Institute.

Steinberg, Richard H. 2002. "In the Shadow of Law or Power? Consensus-Based Bargaining and Outcomes in the GATT/WTO." *International Organization*, 56, 2: 339–74.

Stephen, Andrew T. and Michel Tuan Pham. 2008. "On Feelings as a Heuristic for Making Offers in Ultimatum Negotiations." *Psychological Science*, 19, 10: 1051–58.

Sugden, Robert. 2001. "The Evolutionary Turn in Game Theory." *Journal of Economic Methodology*, 8, 1 (March): 113–30.

Sutton, John. 1986. "Non-Cooperative Bargaining Theory: An Introduction." *Review of Economic Studies*, 53, 5 (October 1): 709–24.

Svensson, Isak. 2013. "Research on Bias in Mediation: Policy Implications." *Penn State Journal of Law & International Affairs*, 2, 1 (April 18): 000–00.

Swaab, Roderick I., Tom Postmes and Russell Spears. 2008. "Identity Formation in Multiparty Negotiations." *British Journal of Social Psychology* (March): 167–87.

Swift, Samuel A. and Don Moore. 2012. "Bluffing, Agonism, and the Role of Overconfidence in Negotiation." In Gary E. Bolton and Rachel T. Croson, eds., *The Oxford Handbook of Economic Conflict Resolution*, 266–78. Oxford University Press.

Swisher, Clayton E. 2004. *The Truth About Camp David: The Untold Story About the Collapse of the Middle East Peace Process*. New York: Nation Books.

Szilagyi, Miklos N. 2003. "An Investigation of N-Person Prisoners' Dilemmas." *Complex Systems*, 14, 2: 155–74.

Talbott, Strobe. 1979. *Endgame: The Inside Story of SALT II*. New York: Harper & Row.

Tallberg, Jonas. 2010. "The Power of the Chair: Formal Leadership in International Cooperation." *International Studies Quarterly*, 54, 1: 241–65.

Taylor, Paul J. and Sally Thomas. 2008. "Linguistic Style Matching and Negotiation Outcome." *Negotiation and Conflict Management Research*, 1, 3 (August 1): 263–81.

Thomas, Lyn C. 2011. *Games, Theory and Applications*. New York: Dover Publications.

Thompson, Leigh. 2001. *The Mind and Heart of the Negotiator*. Englewood Cliffs, NJ: Prentice Hall.

Thompson, Leigh, L. Margaret Neale and Marwan Sinaceur. 2004. "The Evolution of Cognition and Biases in Negotiation Research." In Michele J. Gelfand and Jeanne M. Brett, eds., *The Handbook of Negotiation and Culture*, 7–44. Stanford University Press.

Thucydides. 1972. *History of the Peloponnesian War*. Trans. by Rex Warner. London: Penguin.

Tollison, Robert D. and Thomas D. Willett. 1979. "An Economic Theory of Mutually Advantageous Issue Linkages in International Negotiations." *International Organization* 33, 4: 425–49.

Treisman, Daniel. 2004. "Rational Appeasement." *International Organization*, 58, 2: 345–73.

Trötschel, Roman, Joachim Hüffmeier and David D. Loschelder. 2010. "When Yielding Pieces of the Pie Is Not a Piece of Cake: Identity-Based Intergroup Effects in Negotiations." *Group Processes & Intergroup Relations*, 13, 6 (November 1): 741–63.

Tutzauer, Frank. 1986. "Bargaining as a Dynamical System." *Behavioral Science*, 31, 2: 65–81.

1992. "The Communication of Offers in Dynamic Bargaining." In Michael E. Roloff and Linda L. Putnam, eds., *Communication and Negotiation*, 67–82. London: Sage Publications.

Tversky, Amos and Daniel Kahneman. 1974. "Judgment Under Uncertainty: Heuristics and Biases." *Science*, 185, 4157: 1124–31.

Tyler, Tom R., Steven L. Blader and Jeanne M Brett. 2004. "Justice and Negotiation." In Michele J. Gelfand, ed., *The Handbook of Negotiation and Culture*, 295–312. Stanford University Press.

Ulbert, Cornelia and Thomas Risse. 2005. "Deliberately Changing the Discourse: What Does Make Arguing Effective?" *Acta Politica*, 40, 3: 351–67.

United Nations Framework Convention on Climate Change: Party Groupings. 2014. https://unfccc.int/parties_and_observers/parties/negotiating_groups/items/2714.php (accessed on June 2, 2015).

Underdal, Arild. 2002. "The Outcomes of Negotiation." In Viktor Aleksandrovich Kremenyuk, ed., *International Negotiation: Analysis, Approaches, Issues*, 110–25. 2nd edn. San Francisco: Jossey-Bass.

Van Kleef, Gerben A. and Carsten K. W. de Dreu. 2002. "Social Value Orientation and Impression Formation: A Test of Two Competing Hypotheses About Information Search in Negotiation." *International Journal of Conflict Management*, 13, 1: 59–77.

Van Kleef, Gerben A., Carsten K. W. de Dreu, Davide Pietroni and Antony S. R. Manstead. 2006. "Power and Emotion in Negotiation: Power Moderates the Interpersonal Effects of Anger and Happiness on Concession Making." *European Journal of Social Psychology*, 36, 4: 557–81.

Vance, Cyrus R. 1983. *Hard Choices: Critical Years in America's Foreign Policy*. New York: Simon and Schuster.

Vidal-Puga, Juan J. 2008. "Delay in the Alternating-Offers Model of Bargaining." *International Journal of Game Theory*, 37, 4 (December 1): 457–74.

Vukovic, Siniša. 2014. "International Mediation as a Distinct Form of Conflict Management." *International Journal of Conflict Management*, 25, 1: 61–80.

Wagner, Harrison R. 2000. "Bargaining and War." *American Journal of Political Science*, 44, 3 (July 1): 469–84.

Walton, Richard E. and Robert B. McKersie. 1965. *A Behavioral Theory of Labor Negotiations: An Analysis of a Social Interaction System*. New York: McGraw-Hill.

Watkins, Michael. 1999. "Negotiating in a Complex World." *Negotiation Journal*, 15, 3: 229–44.

Weingart, Laurie R. and Mara Olekalns. 2004. "Communication Processes in Negotiation: Frequencies, Sequences, and Phases." In Michele J. Gelfand and Jeanne M. Brett, eds., *The Handbook of Negotiation and Culture*, 143–57. Stanford University Press.

Wells, Simon, Paul J. Taylor and Ellen Giebels. 2013. "Crisis Negotiation: From Suicide to Terrorism Intervention." In Mara Olekalns and Wendi L. Adair, eds., *Handbook of Research on Negotiation*, 473–98. Cheltenham, UK: Edward Elgar.

Winham, Gil R. 1986. *International Trade and the Tokyo Round Negotiation*. Princeton University Press.

Winkler, Klaus. 2006. *Negotiations with Asymmetrical Distribution of Power: Conclusions from Dispute Resolution in Network Industries*. Heidelberg: Physica-Verlag.

Winter, David G. 2012. "Personality Profiles of Political Elites." In Leonie Huddy, David O. Sears and Jack S. Levy, eds., *The Oxford Handbook of Political Psychology*, 423–58. Oxford University Press.

Wit, Joel S., Daniel Poneman and Robert L. Gallucci. 2004. *Going Critical: The First North Korean Nuclear Crisis*. Washington, DC: Brookings Institution Press.

Wolfe, Robert. 2009. "The WTO Single Undertaking as Negotiating Technique and Constitutive Metaphor." *Journal of International Economic Law*, 12, 4 (December 1): 835–58.

Worden, Lee and Simon A. Levin. 2007. "Evolutionary Escape from the Prisoner's Dilemma." *Journal of Theoretical Biology*, 245, 3: 411–22.

Yildiz, Muhamet. 2011. "Nash Meets Rubinstein in Final-Offer Arbitration." *Economics Letters*, 110, 3: 226–30.

Young, H. Peyton. 1991a. "Negotiation Analysis." In H. Peyton Young, ed., *Negotiation Analysis*, 1–24. Ann Arbor: University of Michigan Press.

Young, Oran. 1975. "Strategic Interaction and Bargaining." In Oran Young, ed., *Bargaining: Formal Theories of Negotiation*. Urbana-Champaign: University of Illinois Press.

Zartman, I. William. 1993. "A Skeptic's View." In G. O. Faure and J. Rubin, eds., *Culture and Negotiation*. Newbury Park, CA: Sage.

Zartman, I. William and Maureen R. Berman. 1982. *The Practical Negotiator*. New Haven: Yale University Press.

Zollman, Kevin, Carl T. Bergstrom and Simon M. Huttegger. 2013. "Between Cheap and Costly Signals: The Evolution of Partially Honest Communication." *Proceedings of the Royal Society B*, 280: 000–00.

Index

Agenda, 12, 112, 114, 122, 126, 128, 179, 184, 192, 203, 204, 206, 211, 232, 234, 235
Agreement, zone of, 10, 11, 155, 173, 242, 257
Algeria, negotiation with, 200–201
Alternative offers, 95–96
Altruism, 26
Anchoring effects, 180–81
Argentine–Chile territorial dispute
 mediated by the Pope, 207
Arms control negotiation, 54, 144, 147, 163, 188, 189, 241, 247

Back-channel negotiation, 57
Backward induction, 22, 70, 73, 74, 88, 96
Bargaining
 distributive, 8, 9, 10, 92, 158
 integrative, 8, 9, 148, 202
 interactive bargaining models of, 168–70
 space, 9, 10, 11, 155, 170
Bargaining behavior
 opening stance, 153, 162–64
Bargaining dynamics
 outcome indeterminacy, 153–60
Bargaining game
 alternating offers, 95–96, 97, 100
 finite horizon, 96
 impatience, 98–100
 infinite horizons, 100
 Nash solution, 91–92
 repeated, 96
Bargaining power
 relative, 11–12, 221, 250
Bargaining problem
 Nash solution, 158
Bargaining range
 aspiration point, 9, 161, 183, 209
 resistance point, 153, 162, 163, 167
Bargaining space
 geometric representation of, 156–57
 negotiation on a single continuum, 155–56
 uni-dimensional contract zone, 154–55

Battle of the Sexes
 collective, 65–66
 strategies, 49–50
Bayesian mediation equilibrium, 212
Beliefs, 11, 27, 52, 65, 80, 83, 88, 108, 110, 160, 174, 177, 180, 183, 189, 229, 241, 244, 245
Best alternative to negotiated settlement, 93
Bias
 sources of, 175–77
Bounded rationality, 244
Brazil, 230, 235
Breaking asymmetric deadlock, 222
Bridging, 143–44, 231
Brinkmanship, 229
Britain
 costs of Cod Wars, 8–9
Bully, game of, 59–60
Burundi civial war (1995–2001)
 mediation of warring factions in, 203

Camp David Peace Accord (1978)
 mediation by Carter, 203
 side payment, 202
Carter, 57, 87, 145, 168, 175, 187, 203, 205, 214, 256, 263
Cheap talk, 87, 211, 229
Chicken, game of
 credible threats in, 47–48
China, 6, 28, 59, 81, 82, 169, 187, 221, 225, 248, 251
Claiming strategies
 defensive, 111
 offensive, 170
Climate control negotiation, 67, 220, 221, 225–27
Coalition bargaining
 intra-coalition interactions, 228–29
 strategies, 229–30
Coalition building
 1975 US–Soviet Grain Agreement, 193–94
 tactics, 194
Cod Wars, 8–9
Coercion, 236

Cognitive bias
  sources of, 175–77
Cognitive process, 176, 245
Collective action game, 60–61
Commitment, 12, 65, 75, 76, 77, 78, 79, 113, 126, 127, 128, 133, 179, 192, 211, 229, 244, 270
Communication
  control of, 210
  strategic nature of, 210–12
Competition, 4, 5, 6, 9, 35, 65, 115, 116, 129, 177, 178, 179, 248, 256
Competitive dynamics, 178–79
Compromise, 59, 98, 114, 121, 138, 140, 166, 169, 177, 191, 209, 231
Concession
  behavior, 10, 161–62, 179
  frequency, 162, 164–66
  magnitude, 161, 167
  rate, 161, 162, 164–66, 167, 168
Concession making
  models of, 160–61
  reciprocal, 167
Conflict settlement, 248
Conformity, 179
Conformity pressure, 179–80
Conversion
  change in offers, self- and other-oriented forces, 166–67
Conversion process
  bargaining zone, 155
  US–Soviet negotiation, 154
Cooperation
  mutual, 28, 42, 50, 51, 53, 188
Cooperative game, 90, 108, 152, 158, 220, 250
Coordination game, 51, 52, 54, 64, 66
Cost-cutting, 144–45
Credibility
  threat, 82
Crisis negotiation, 113
Cuban Missile Crisis
  Kennedy, 134
  Khrushchev, 113
Cyprus
  negotiations between Greek and Turkish Cypriots, 131, 140, 144, 179

Deadlock
  breaking, 138
  sources of, 130–31
Deadlock game, 53
Decision making
  intra-party, 188

Defection, 30, 31, 33, 42, 57, 63, 66, 224, 229
De-linkage, 143
Deterrence, 73, 74, 75
Dictator game, 251
Diminished returns with decay, 96–98
Disagreement point, 91, 92, 95, 157, 250, 251
Discount rate, 98, 100, 101, 102, 221
Discount value, 99, 102
Division rule, 92–93

El Salvador
  ending civil war, 127
  the Farabundo Marti National Liberation Front (FMLN), 117, 128
Emotional effects
  negative, 183–84
  positive, 183, 185
Endowment effects. *See* anchoring
  Arab League Proposal to Saddam Hussein, 181
Equilibrium
  cooperative, 81
  pooling, 87
  subgame perfect, 70, 71, 73, 74, 76, 78, 96
  unstable, 51
Equilibrium refinement, 72–74
Escalation, 47, 87, 111, 118, 120, 179, 195, 241, 244
European Community, 224, 233
Exploitation, 39, 59, 109, 160, 188, 207, 220

Fair division scheme, 141–42
Fairness, 6, 25, 92, 108, 109, 111, 116, 148, 159, 181, 207, 251
Falkland Islands, conflict over
  mediation by the US, 213
First move advantage, 77, 80
Focal point
  randomizing device, 208
Formula, 6, 91, 126, 131, 132, 133, 220, 224, 249
Framing, 111, 114, 181
Free riders, 62

Gains
  absolute, 9
  relative, 152, 160, 214, 246, 253
Game
  asymmetric, 60
  constant-sum, 35, 39
  hybrid, 59
  incomplete information, 84
  sequential, 68–70, 71, 78, 96
  simultaneous, 70, 73

INDEX

Game theory
  application of, 27–28, 243
  expected utility, 25–26, 37, 40
  payoffs, 24, 25, 26, 28, 29, 30, 37, 38, 40, 41, 47, 49, 51, 56, 60, 64, 66
  player, 22, 24, 25, 26, 27, 29, 37, 38, 39, 41, 48, 58, 60, 212
  rationality, assumption of, 26–27
  strategy, 22, 24
Game tree, 69, 70, 72, 74, 76, 78, 84, 86, 88
Guatemala, 117, 136, 245, 253, 263, 269

Hardin, Garret, 61
Hybrid game, 59

Iceland
  tactics in Cod Wars, 9
Information
  incomplete, 84, 152
  private, 203, 210, 212, 213
Information processing
  biased information search, 174
Institutional context
  bureaucratic interests, 191–93
  organizational decision making, 191–93
Intellectual property, 14, 122, 223, 230, 231, 233, 235, 236
Interdependence, 4, 22
Intermediary role, 137, 202
International negotiation, 4, 14, 15, 27, 50, 55, 79, 118, 172, 195
Intra-coalition interactions, 228–29, 256
Iranian hostage crisis
  Algerian shuttle diplomacy, 200–201
Israeli-Palestinian negotiation, 145
Issue linkage, 55, 142–43, 193, 233, 249

Kennedy, John F., 57, 134, 207, 240
Kyoto Protocol, 221, 226

Law of the Sea negotiation, 11
London Conference on Saving the Ozone Layer, 223

Maximin, 35. *See* Minimax
Mediation
  conduit for rationality, 208–10
  facilitation, 200
  functions of, 200–201
  improving efficiency, 206
  process a U.S.-negotiation with NorthVietnam ssistance, 204–205

roles, 201–203
  shuttle diplomacy, 200
Mediator
  bias, 212–15
  impartiality, 212–15
  neutrality, 212–15
  scanning device, 210
  selector of a focal point, 207–208
  triadic interaction, 215–17
Midcourse corrections, 139–41
Minimax
  for zero-sum games, 35
  theorem, 35
  value, 35, 36
Mixed motive games, 109, 186
Montreal Protocol, 223, 233, 234
Morgenstern, Oskar, 35
Multilateral negotiation
  bargaining structure, 219–20
  coalition building, 220–21
  institutional context, 231–32
  procedural tactics, 235–37
  secretariat, 233–34
Mutual cooperation. *See* Cooperation: mutual

Nash equilibrium, 44–45, 52, 58, 60, 61, 66, 70, 92, 211
Nash solution
  bargaining problem, 5
  disagreement point, 91
Negotiation
  behavior, 115–16, 188, 244
  context, 248–50
  cooperation, 3–4
  definition, 4
  emotional interference, 182–85
  essence, 5–6
  interests, 3–4
  labor-management, 14
  linkage, 248–50
  non-cooperative nature of, 108–10
  package deals, 142
  personality, 185–88
  skills, 242–43
  social interactions, 3
  socio-psychological process, 173–75
  style, 245–48
  Sudan, 120
  theory, 257
Negotiation analysis
  descriptive, 239–45, 270, 275
  prescriptive, 239–45, 270, 275

Negotiation behavior, 115–16, 263
Negotiation context
   institutional, 188–91
   organizational decision making, 191–93
   political, 188–91
Negotiation culture
   high context, 246–47
   low context, 246–47
Negotiation dynamics, 110–12
Negotiation framework
   ground rules, 122
   issues, 121
   precondition, 123
   procedures, 121, 122, 147, 150, 234
   venue, 123
Negotiation outcome
   cognitive aspects, 252–53
   justice, 250–52
Negotiation process
   breaking impasses, 11, 113, 117, 133, 138, 139
   last stage of, 145–48
   sequential vs. simultaneous, 116–18
Negotiation process models
   episodic, 113
   phase model, 114
Negotiation situation, 5, 8, 111
Negotiation strategy
   distributive, 7, 8, 9, 10, 12, 13, 14, 229
   dominant, 30–32
   influence, 4, 12, 76, 109, 235
   information, 84
   integrative, 8, 9, 12, 14, 140
   sequential mixture of integrative and distributive strategies, 13
   setting deadline, 137
North Korea, 26, 58, 76, 77, 84, 86, 110, 135, 156, 180, 190, 251, 254
Northern Ireland
   All-Party Talks, 201, 204
   intermediary role, 201–202
Nuclear test ban treaty, 154, 192

Offensive claiming, 134, 170
Offer-counter, 244
Oslo peace accord, 80, 136
Outside Intervention, 138–39
Outside options, 9, 93, 240
Ozone negotiation
   bargaining impasse, 224
   Toronto groups, 224

Package deals, 142
Panama
   Canal negotiations, 11, 130–31, 146
   formula proposal, 133
   negotiation tactics, 145–46
   US defense rights in Canal Zone, 130–31, 133
Panama Canal Treaty, 127
Pareto-optimal frontier
   Fair solution on, 158–59
Pareto-optimality, 32, 55
Perception, 108, 109, 111, 139, 179, 212
Personality
   Arafat, Y., 186
   Barak, E., 186
   Brzezinski, Z., 187
   features, 186
   Gorbachev, M., 186, 188
   Israel–Palestinian negotiation, 186
   psychological fallacies, 187
   Rabin, Y., 186
   Sudanese talks, 2003, 187
   Vance, Cyrus, 188
Persuasion, 134
Political environment, control of, 136
Pre-game communication, 57–58
Prenegotiation, 192, 234
Prisoner's Dilemma
   social dilemma, 32
Probability, 39, 40, 41, 63, 111, 181, 191
problem solving, 8, 12, 116, 122, 176, 185
Procedural innovation, 134–35
Promise, 80, 133, 146, 147
Proposal making, 12, 121, 122, 126
Psychological dynamics, competitive
   non-rational escalation of conflict, 178
   reactive devaluation, 178
   zero-sum assumption, 178
Public commitment, 194–95
Public goods, 17, 62, 220
Public health coalition, 230–31
Punishment
   and defection, 31, 46–47

Rapoport, Anatol, 188
Rate of return, 99
Ratification
   domestic politics, 145, 146, 148
Rationality
   assumptions, 16
Reciprocity, 109, 116, 143, 159, 163, 184, 253

Reframing
  Panama Canal negotiation, 133
Repeated games, 83
Repeated interactions, 74, 83, 244
Reputation, 45, 74, 102, 134, 189, 195, 231
Reservation value, 10, 129, 153, 155, 163, 164, 252
Resistance point, 108, 110
Risk
  averse, 181
  neutral, 181
  taking, 181–82
Rollback equilibrium, 97
Rubenstein bargaining game, 100–103

SALT negotiations. See US–Soviet Geneva Arms Talks
  Kissinger, 132, 133, 189, 192, 253, 269
Schelling, Thomas, xiii, 14, 38, 47, 75, 82, 132, 195, 269, 274
Screening, 86–88
Second-mover advantage, 78
Security level, 37
Sequential vs. simultaneous moves, 116–18
Shapley value, 93–94
Shrinking surplus. See Diminished returns with decay
Shuttle diplomacy
  Biafran civil war, 201
Sidepayment, 55–56
Signaling games, 87, 88
Skills
  bargaining, 170, 256
South Africa
  African National Congress, 121, 128, 134, 139, 182
  exploratory dialogue, 128
Soviet Union, 3, 8, 11, 47, 54, 57, 76, 114, 129, 133, 137, 166, 168, 187, 188, 224, 233, 275
Status quo, 9, 11, 48, 53, 80, 81, 95, 168, 181, 202, 220, 221, 230, 238, 250
Strategic interaction, 4, 21–23, 69, 217, 220
Strategic moves
  credibility, 77, 78, 79, 82, 230
Strategy, game theory
  dominant, 30, 32, 41, 47, 50, 53, 60
  mixed, 39, 41
  pure, 38, 39, 40, 41, 63
  randomization of, 39, 41
Structure of game, 52–53, 60, 61, 66, 67
Subgame perfect equilibrium, 70, 71, 73, 74, 76, 78, 83, 96, 101–103

Sudanese civil war
  mediation by Intergovernmental Authority on Development, 213–14
Surplus, 89, 92, 96, 97, 98, 99, 100, 102, 108

Tactics
  persuasive, 134
Third party roles, 201–203
Threat
  in bargaining, 81–83
Tit-for-tat, 188
Tradeoffs, 142, 177
Tragedy of the Commons, 61–63, 66
Trust, 51, 119, 129, 132, 133, 147, 167, 184, 210, 211, 213, 229
Two-level games
  internal negotiation, 193

US–China trade negotiation
  salami tactics, 83
  strategic action, 81–82
  threat, 81–82
US negotiation with North Korea
  Battle of the Sexes, 55–56
  side payment, 55–56
  threat, 56–57
US negotiation with North Vietnam, 110, 118
US–Panama negotiation
  control in the Canal Zone, 127
  Panamanian goal, 127
US–Soviet Geneva Arms talks, 192
Ultimatum game, 94–95
UN Convention on Climate Change, 225
UN Seabed Negotiation, 11, 141
Uncertainty
  in negotiation, 134–35
  in Prisoner's dilemma game, 33, 41
United Kingdom
  Falkland Islands war, 194, 213
  naval base negotiation with Malta, 11
United States
  Grain sales to the Soviet Union, 193–94
  trade liberalization, 236
Uruguay Round agreements
  Trade-Related Aspects of Intellectual Property Rights (TRIPS) agreement, 229
Utility
  payoffs, 103

Value claiming, 9, 222–23
Value claiming stalemate, 223–25
Value creation, 9, 182

Vance, Cyrus, 187
Vatican. *See* Argentine–Chile territorial dispute
    Beagle Channel award, 207
    mediation of, 201–202
Vienna Convention for the Protection of the Ozone
    Layer, 223
Volunteer's Dilemma, 63–64
Von Neumann, John, 35

War of attrition, 6, 9, 75, 131
Winner's curse, 178, 244, 253
Wise counselor, 137–38
World Trade Organization (WTO) negotiation
    Doha Round, 230
    Green Room caucuses, 232
    Like Minded Group (LMG), 229
    Public Health Coalition, 231

Printed in the United States
By Bookmasters